COURTS, JUSTICE AND EFFICIENCY

This study explores the socio-legal context of economic rationality in the legal and judicial systems. It examines the meaning and relevance of the concept of efficiency for the operation of courts and court systems, seeking to answer questions such as: in what sense can we say that the adjudicative process works efficiently? What are the relevant criteria for the measurement and assessment of court efficiency? Should the courts try to operate efficiently and to what extent is this viable? What is the proper relationship between 'efficiency' and 'justice' considerations in a judicial proceeding?

To answer these questions, a conceptual framework is developed on the basis of empirical studies and surveys carried out mainly in the United States, Western Europe and Latin America. Two basic ideas emerge from it. First, economic rationality has penetrated the legal and judicial systems at all levels and dimensions, from the level of society as a whole to the day-to-day operation of the courts, from the institutional dimension of adjudication to the organisational context of judicial decisions. Far from being an alien value in the judicial process, efficiency has become an inseparable part of the structure of expectations we place on the legal system. Second, economic rationality is not the prevalent value in legal decision-making, as it is subject to all kinds of constraints, local conditions and concrete negotiations with other values and interests.

Courts, Justice and Efficiency

A Socio-Legal Study of Economic Rationality in Adjudication

HÉCTOR FIX-FIERRO

·HART·
PUBLISHING
OXFORD AND PORTLAND, OREGON
2003

Hart Publishing
Oxford and Portland, Oregon

Published in North America (US and Canada) by
Hart Publishing c/o
International Specialized Book Services
5804 NE Hassalo Street
Portland, Oregon
97213-3644
USA

Hart Publishing is a specialist legal publisher based in Oxford, England. To order further copies of this book or to request a list of other publications please write to:

Hart Publishing, Salter's Boatyard, Folly Bridge,
Abingdon Road, Oxford OX1 4LB
Telephone: +44 (0)1865 245533 or Fax: +44 (0)1865 794882
e-mail: mail@hartpub.co.uk
WEBSITE: http//www.hartpub.co.uk

British Library Cataloguing in Publication Data
Data Available
ISBN 1–84113–382–5 (hardback)

Typeset by Hope Services (Abingdon) Ltd.
Printed and bound in Great Britain on acid-free paper by
Biddles Ltd, www.biddles.co.uk

For Jacqueline, Valentina, Markel and Verena

The most striking characteristic of law as it has existed in democratic societies has been its inefficiency. This statement must not be understood in the sense merely that the law of such societies represents a system which is designed to work efficiently, but which unfortunately breaks down in practice as the result of the ineptitude of judges, lawyers, and executive officers of government. By its very nature, law is doomed to be inefficient; its innermost structure and basic machinery produce inefficiency; and particularly in democratic societies it is often made or kept inefficient with painstaking deliberation. Law may be described, indeed, as the science of inefficiency.

William Seagle, *Law: The Science of Inefficiency* (1952)

Efficiency is one of the highest cultural values of modernity. As such a value it cannot enter into explanation of those forms which exist in other than a tautological way. Yet, as such a value, it will frequently play a key role in analysis . . . To be efficient is to be modern . . .

Stewart R. Clegg, *Modern Organizations. Organization Studies in the Postmodern World* (1990)

Foreword

The idea for this study was born almost ten years ago, in the first months of 1993. Volkmar Gessner was on a short trip to Mexico trying to find out, in preparation for an upcoming workshop at the International Institute for the Sociology of Law of Oñati, why there was no visible discussion on judicial reform in Mexico and what could be done to start one. With this goal in mind, we conducted a series of interviews and conversations with scholars, judges and other public officials. Diego Valadés, who was the Attorney General of the Federal District at the time, remarked that there was very little debate on this topic because, among other reasons, there was no model for evaluating the efficiency of justice institutions.

Volkmar told me later that he did not know of any study that attempted to provide a broad overview on what efficiency meant in the context of justice institutions. So we decided that I should give it a try, using as many empirical studies and investigations as one could reasonably find for the development of such a model. As the research progressed, we abandoned the idea of developing a 'model', if by model we mean a more or less simple device to measure and assess institutional performance. Instead, the study presents a conceptual framework that results from the effort to introduce some order in the enormous treasure of empirical studies and materials. It is for the reader to decide if such effort has been successful.

This study confesses a very strong connection to the Oñati International Institute for the Sociology of Law. It was there that the search for the relevant literature started and resulted in a 'tesina' for the Master's programme. Indeed, the overwhelming majority of the books, articles and other materials cited here can be found in the magnificent library and documentation center that the Institute has made available to socio-legal scholars of the whole world. Other materials come from the library of the University of Bremen, Volkmar's personal library, the library of the Law School of the University of Georgia in Athens, and the library of the Instituto de Investigaciones Jurídicas of the National University of Mexico (UNAM). Of course, many friends and colleagues have also made valuable contributions over the years.

The study was presented to, and accepted by, the Department of Legal Science of the University of Bremen, Germany, as a doctoral dissertation in law in July 1998. The dissertation, with the title 'Courts and Efficiency. A General Investigation with Evidence from Three Continents', was first reviewed by professors Volkmar Gessner and Johannes Feest. They were joined in the doctoral colloquium by professors Konstanze Plett and Armin Höland. In the present version, new, relevant research has been incorporated, literature has been updated and other editorial changes have been introduced.

An effort such as this cannot be accomplished without incurring in personal and professional debts. I am most indebted to the Institute (and town) of Oñati for the hospitality I enjoyed there on several occasions. I would like to make special mention of Johannes Feest, who was the scientific director of the IISL during a crucial stay in April–July 1997 and has been a good friend ever since, as well as of Sole Aguirre and Elvira Muñoz for their friendly, valuable help with the literature and other materials. I am also indebted to the Department of Legal Science of the University of Bremen. The fact that a doctoral dissertation written in English by a Mexican scholar has been accepted by a German university is by no means evident, and it bears witness to the openness of the University of Bremen and its commitment to the universal cause of science.

José Luis Soberanes and Diego Valadés have given me all possible signs of support and encouragement, both as friends and in their capacity as directors of the Instituto de Investigaciones Jurídicas de la UNAM. I have also received considerable encouragement and support from other friends and relatives. With some of them I have discussed many of the problems analysed here. I should mention Miguel Bonilla López, José Antonio Caballero, José Ángel Canela, Miguel Carbonell, Hugo Concha, Edgar Corzo, José Ramón Cossío, Alberto Díaz Cayeros, Héctor Fix-Zamudio, Jesús Boanerges Guinto López, Sergio López Ayllón, Jacqueline Martínez, Roberto MacLean, Mario Melgar, Rogelio Pérez Perdomo, José Juan Toharia, Guillermo Zepeda, and my colleagues at the Instituto de la Judicatura Federal.

For the opportunity to publish this study I should express my appreciation to Bill Felstiner for his disinterested support, and particularly to Richard Hart, of Hart Publishing, for a friendliness and openness that greatly surprised me at first. I have also benefitted from the comments and suggestions of two anonymous reviewers. Suzanne Stephens helped me to produce a correct English manuscript. Mrs. Eva Suárez greatly contributed to the solution of every-day problems.

I reserve my deepest feelings of gratitude for Volkmar Gessner and my family. My association of many years with Volkmar goes well beyond scholarly concerns. I have to thank him not only for his friendship, patience and help, but also for his uncompromising scientific rigor. As for my family, I hope that this book will compensate them for some of the sacrifices I could not avoid to inflict upon them.

Mexico City, November 2002.

Contents

1

Introduction: Why Court Efficiency?

'CRISIS' IN THE ADMINISTRATION OF JUSTICE: A RECURRENT TOPIC?

IF WE WERE to believe press reports and opinion polls, but also scientific literature and official documents, the administration of justice—ie, the courts—is in a state of 'crisis' in many parts of the world. A few years ago, Germany's courts were said to be 'on the brink of a heart attack',[1] while Spain's civil justice allegedly belonged to 'another century'.[2] According to an opinion poll conducted in Mexico City in 1996, a vast majority of persons believed that judicial proceedings were extremely slow, very expensive and only moderately fair, while a third or more of respondents regarded judges, including Supreme Court justices, and attorneys, as dishonest or highly dishonest.[3] An official report published in 1991 stated that 60 per cent of the French people and 70 per cent of French judges considered the reform of the justice system a 'priority matter'. Both citizens and judges agreed that the courts were 'overwhelmed'.[4]

Scientific papers and official reports diagnose the same disease everywhere and warn of its dire consequences: growing caseloads; rising costs, and longer delays; scarce financial and human resources; an inefficient work organisation. A state of 'crisis' is explicitly identified and described in large and small, rich and poor regions, regardless of their level of political and legal development, such as Puerto Rico,[5] Italy,[6] the United States,[7] Spain,[8] Quebec,[9] Chile,[10] Brazil,[11]

[1] See 'Am Rande des Infarkts', in the German weekly magazine *Der Spiegel*, Hamburg, 20 September 1993, pp. 72–87.

[2] See 'Justicia de otro siglo. En casos en que no llegan a delito, meras cuestiones civiles, es donde las leyes españolas son más inoperantes', in *El País*, Madrid, December 19, 1993.

[3] See 'Entre abogados te veas', in *Voz y voto*, Mexico, no. 41, July 1996, pp. 23–7. Interestingly, persons who had had prior contact with the justice system (7%) usually had a better opinion of it than those who had not. This was true regarding the honesty of judges, although far more people in the first group than in the second considered judicial proceedings to be slow or extremely slow and costly (70% vs. 53%).

[4] See *Le Monde*, Paris, 16–17 June, 1991, reprinted in Bernard (1996: 194 ff.). The official report, for which two senators were responsible, declares the abandonment of the justice system by the executive power a 'disaster' (*justice sinistrée*). See also Faugeron (1981).

[5] Amadeo Murga (1993), regarding appellate justice in Puerto Rico.

[6] Ferrarese (1988/89), Denti (1986).

[7] Kaufman (1990), on the US federal courts.

[8] Consejo General del Poder Judicial (1997).

[9] Garant (1994).

[10] Peña González (1993: 348 ff.).

[11] Faria (1996).

England and Wales.[12] The introduction to a book published in 1999 and significantly titled 'Civil Justice in Crisis', points out that a 'sense of crisis in the administration of civil justice is by no means universal, but it is widespread', and goes on to say that most of the countries represented in the book (three common-law countries and ten civil-law countries) 'are experiencing difficulties in the operation of their civil justice system'.[13] In many other places, this diagnosis is compounded by other, more insidious evils: widespread corruption; lack of independence; politicisation; inadequate legal training of judges, court employees, and attorneys; extremely limited or no access at all for the majority of the population, etc.[14] A sense of urgency is insistently communicated by this literature: judicial reform is more than overdue in view of the important social functions that the courts are universally acknowledged to have.

Such a worrisome panorama raises a number of questions. Is this alleged state of crisis new and real? If so, what are its indicators and manifestations? Or is it merely the result of distorted media attention and the public's traditional lack of confidence in the courts? Are there new social expectations behind such interest? If so, where do these expectations come from and why are they being expressed so intensely now? Do they imply that the courts should assume a new social role and perform new functions? Or do they simply require that they operate 'better'? What is the meaning and scope of social and professional concerns over court efficiency? Does it demonstrate a renewed yet still narrow social dominance of economic rationality, for example, because an efficient legal system has proved to be a condition for a developed market economy? Or does it express the conviction that efficiency is a more fundamental component of institutional performance and legitimacy in a world that is becoming increasingly globalised?

These are difficult questions indeed, and any attempt to answer them is undoubtedly an ambitious task. This chapter is of an introductory nature, intended as an initial approach to our general topic. It merely attempts to provide a tentative exploration of these issues, in preparation for the following chapters.[15] In any case, we can safely assume that these and similar concerns somehow reflect certain current developments that deserve serious consideration.

[12] Michalik (1999).

[13] Zuckerman (1999: 12).

[14] This would seem to be the prevailing situation in many Latin American countries. See, for example, Ilanud-Fiu (eds) (1987), Rico *et al.* (1988), Salas/Rico (1989a and b), Burgos (1992), Faria (1992), Fried (1995: 92 ff.), Buscaglia/Dakolias (1996), Nemogá Soto (dir.) (1996), Dakolias (1996), Binder (1993), regarding criminal justice, Pérez Perdomo (1985; 1996) on Venezuela; Hammergren (1998: 3 ff.), Prillaman (2000). See also the seven national reports (Argentina, Chile, Colombia, Costa Rica, Mexico, Peru, and Venezuela) in Correa Sutil (ed.) (1993), as well as the essays on change in the legal cultures of Latin countries in Europe (France, Italy, Spain) and America (Argentina, Brazil, Chile, Colombia, Mexico, Puerto Rico, Venezuela) in Friedman/Pérez Perdomo (eds.) (2003).

[15] For an excellent account of the new prominence of courts, see the first chapter in Santos *et al.* (1996: 19–56), Santos (1999) and Garapon (1996: 29 ff.).

Courts before the Court of Public and Professional Opinion

The truth is that the administration of justice has never fared very well in *public opinion* in most countries. For many years, opinion polls have consistently presented a largely unfavourable or deteriorating image of the courts, as seen through the eyes of the public. To give just a few examples, among recent and less recent polls, and to show that the situation in the past was not necessarily better than it is today:

—*Germany*: in 1979, 78 per cent of German citizens thought that court expenses were high or too high. 52 per cent of those who had had experience with the courts judged this experience to be mixed or rather negative. Asked why people who are financially wronged do not go to court, 79 per cent mentioned the uncertainty about the outcome; 60 per cent referred to the possibility of an unfair decision; 78 per cent cited the incomprehensible legal language; 75 per cent found courtrooms intimidating; 59 per cent expected class justice and 55 per cent anticipated authoritarian behavior; while 84 per cent found proceedings too slow.[16]

—*Portugal*: a questionnaire submitted to litigants in the early 1990s yielded the following percentages of persons who agreed with particular statements: 51 per cent felt that judges are influenced by personal preferences and friendships; 41 per cent believed that courts are intimidating; 30 per cent thought that costs discourage people from going to court; 60 per cent, that anybody can obtain anything they want from the courts with money and a lawyer; 25 per cent felt that an accused person is always convicted by the courts; 56 per cent believed that decisions are so slow that it is not worth going to court while 49 per cent thought that courts do not convict persons with power or money.[17]

—*Spain*: several opinion polls conducted during the 1980s show, for example: that around 48 per cent of those polled regarded court performance as bad or 'fair'; 25 per cent viewed courts as 'scarcely just and scarcely efficient', while 21 per cent found them 'more just than efficient'; 61 per cent agreed partly or completely with the assertion that court decisions were so unpredictable that it was preferable to avoid going to court; about 40 per cent considered that Spanish courts were not very independent, or that they were barely independent, from the government.[18]

[16] Kniffka (1981).

[17] Santos *et al.* (1996: 553 ff.).

[18] These figures are reported in Toharia (1987: 48 ff.). The public image of the courts in Spain has since further deteriorated. According to data reported by the Consejo General del Poder Judicial (1997: 18 f.), the percentage of persons who consider that the justice system works poorly, as compared to those who hold a positive opinion, was 28% in 1987, 33% in 1990, 38% in 1992, 46% in 1995 and 51% in 1997. In 2000, this percentage had slightly diminished to 46%. However, if we include here the ambiguous category of 'fair' or 'so-so' ('*regular*'), it may turn out that as much as 76% of the Spanish population were not satisfied with their justice system (Toharia 2001: 83 f.). As

—*United States*: a national opinion poll on state courts, conducted in the late 1970s, reached the following conclusions: there was a profound difference in views between the general public and community leaders, on the one side, and judges and lawyers, on the other, regarding what the courts do or should do; the general public and community leaders were dissatisfied with the performance of courts and ranked them lower than many other major American institutions; while those with knowledge and experience of the courts voiced the greatest dissatisfaction and criticism.[19]

These data and the other figures cited earlier should not be taken at face value as indicative of a (permanent) state of crisis in the administration of justice, or as proof that court performance is actually bad or worse than before. A number of cautionary considerations should be taken into account first, in order to interpret poll results of this kind.

Without going into the technicalities of poll design, it is reasonably clear that the administration of justice presents special difficulties as a subject for an opinion poll and as an indicator of actual developments in this field.[20] First of all, people are not always able to distinguish courts from other governmental institutions, as a result of which the former tend to be judged by the same criteria as those applied to the latter.[21] Courts do not always have a profile of their own and are not clearly separated from other state bureaucracies in the mind of the ordinary citizen, and this may be particularly true in civil-law countries.[22] Such lack of awareness is also favoured by the fact that in any given country, only a small portion of citizens have actually had contact with the courts.[23] Thus, the few who have had this contact can be said to be expressing a judgment; while those who have not, are merely expressing a social prejudice.[24]

regards the level of public confidence, the courts came thirteenth out of 15 institutions. In another poll conducted in 1996, courts received a mark of 3.67 out of 10 and came last out of all the institutions evaluated.

[19] National Center for State Courts (1978). For a very recent poll see also National Center for State Courts (1999). According to the executive summary, the 'survey results indicate that the American public gives an average grade to the performance of the courts in their communities'. However, respondents 'overwhelmingly believe cases are not being resolved in a timely manner', with 46% agreeing strongly with this statement (at 7).

[20] On the use of opinion polls as an instrument to evaluate the performance of justice institutions, see Toharia (2001: ch 3).

[21] This explanation is advanced by Toharia (1987: 51 ff.).

[22] Toharia (1987: 52 f.).

[23] Toharia (1987: 97) estimates this proportion at 25% of the Spanish population (1982), a percentage that does not seem to have changed over the years (see Toharia, 2001: 136).

[24] Kniffka (1981: 226). This difference sometimes has an impact on opinion but not always. First-hand experience leads frequently to a worse opinion. By contrast, a recent survey conducted in England and Wales found a generally positive assessment of experiences with the courts. However, it is noted that such positive responses are not entirely consistent with other recent research on litigants' experiences of court and are somewhat at odds with findings relating to the negative effects of dealing with justiciable problems through the legal system (Genn, 1999: 222 f.).

Prejudices result in contradictions[25] and distortions. Distortions, in turn, are due, for example, to media coverage of extraordinary or scandalous cases,[26] but also to the contamination that the image of other branches of the justice system may suffer from their association with criminal or administrative courts.[27] For many people, the mere idea of having to go to court awakes unpleasant feelings.[28] And finally, for the individual citizen, the likelihood of appearing before a court as a defendant, and losing, may be higher than that of appearing as a plaintiff, and winning.

Given all these considerations, is there any need to worry? If a poor public image is the 'normal' state of affairs, should the courts proceed with 'business as usual'? A cynic might suggest that the time has come for a good press campaign and for the courts to implement a public relations policy of their own. In fact, one of the challenges currently facing judicial institutions in many parts of the world is undoubtedly the need to create a favourable public image. This is but one aspect of the minimal degree of social legitimacy that any institution requires to operate effectively, as is the need to handle the strenuous but increasingly important day-to-day relationship with the media.[29]

Public opinion and social expectations are an extremely powerful force. They may indeed be the factor that ultimately determines whether or not people use the legal system.[30] In the long run, they become a diffuse but strong pressure for change and reform of the system.[31] Conversely, courts derive part of their legitimacy and authority from not having to yield to social pressures and transient opinions. Instead, they are supposed to depoliticise and rationalise social conflict, and to act, if need be, as a countermajoritarian institution.

In conclusion: public opinion, as reflected in surveys and polls, may be used as a tool for capturing the general social climate surrounding public institutions, including the courts. This climate will undoubtedly be favourable to those

25 For example, according to the German data cited above, a large number of citizens consider that the courts are too expensive. However, when asked if they had ever avoided filing suit because it might prove too costly, only 6% answered affirmatively. Kniffka (1981: 232).

26 Zemans (1991). Nowhere is this coverage as extensive as in the United States, where so-called 'court TV' ranks as popular entertainment.

27 Kniffka (1981: 227).

28 According to poll data reported in Kniffka (1981: 230), in Germany 29% considered that 'going to court is at least as unpleasant as a visit to the dentist' and 43% favoured the view that 'a suit is unpleasant, but a very normal thing.' For examples of traumatic court experiences, see Genn (1999: 223 ff.).

29 Kniffka (1981: 229) reflects on the difficulties of establishing such favorable image by fighting ignorance and prejudice; Rozenberg (1995: 96 ff.) examines the difficulties that the (English) judiciary experiences in dealing with the media (press and television). See also Canon/Johnson (1999: 138 ff.) on the media and the public as 'secondary populations' with respect to the implementation of judicial policies.

30 This is suggested by the concept of 'legal culture', that is, values and attitudes towards the law and legal institutions. For Friedman (1975: 193 ff.), legal culture is virtually the key to the effectiveness of the law. For a contrary view, which holds that institutional factors (the actual operation of the courts) are primarily responsible for the level of access to the courts, see Blankenburg (1989a).

31 Cf Zemans (1991). In the United States, this seems to have been the case with the movement for the establishment of small claims courts and alternative dispute resolution (ADR) institutions.

institutions that are perceived as efficient and accountable. But public opinion may be less than useful for diagnosing a situation of crisis and for identifying the specific circumstances that surround it.

If we turn to *professional opinion*, we find that judges, attorneys, policymakers, and public officials have also proved extremely effective in promoting and disseminating the discourse on a 'crisis' in the administration of justice.[32] As interested parties, they are supposed to know better and, as such, they should enjoy the necessary credibility for drawing attention to the problems besetting judicial institutions, as well as for proposing the changes that they consider most likely to solve them.[33] However, it is for this very reason that both diagnosis and remedies will tend to be biased. Moreover, their different positions in the justice system will prevent them from developing a single, consistent view on the existing situation. Judges and attorneys, in particular, will have a different perception of problems and their possible solutions. Understandably, they will tend to be somewhat self-indulgent towards themselves and critical of each other, or of other institutions.[34] Thus, without underestimating the valuable contributions that they may make to this discussion, the truth is that a more demanding and impartial approach is needed, an approach that goes beyond a narrow definition skewed by professional interests. In this respect, only a rigorous empirical analysis of both problems and solutions will be able to place the whole discussion on a surer footing.

Since at least the 1960s, the discipline known as sociology of law has expressed a keen interest in the courts.[35] On the one hand, although the courts are extremely important legal institutions, their study by social science is by no means evident. On the other hand, empirical research on the courts has not limited itself to an analysis of their operational problems. This analysis has usually been coupled with broader theoretical, ideological, political and policy considerations.

Take, for example, the problems of 'litigation'. Socio-legal research has not only taken up legal science's traditional preoccupation with delay and court overload. In addition to trying to determine whether these alleged problems exist, as well as their immediate causes and actual dimensions,[36] it has also attempted to link caseloads and litigation to broader processes of social change

[32] Of course, these actors may also dispute the notion that a crisis exists, and with good reason. See, for example, the results of a questionnaire for Brazilian judges: only 15.8% agreed completely with the assertion that the judiciary was in a crisis; 20.5% agreed partially with this statement; while 54.4% agreed with only a few aspects of it. See Sadek (1997: 393).

[33] See, for example, President's Council on Competitiveness (1991). It is this professional circle, for example, which has most enthusiastically endorsed 'alternative dispute resolution' and other relief measures for the courts. See Röhl (1982).

[34] See, for example, a survey of attorneys conducted in Chile (Peña González, 1991). Brazilian judges attributed the main problems of the courts to external factors, over which the judiciary exerts little control, such as material resources. See Sadek (1997: 393).

[35] See, for example, the impressive research project, started in the early 1960s by the *Centro Nazionale di Prevenzione e Difesa Sociale*, on 'The administration of justice and Italian society in transformation', which published ten volumes after 1968.

[36] See, for example, Borucka-Arctowa (1989) and Röhl (1987).

and their impact on the courts. For example, the study of litigation rates, especially in their historical evolution,[37] seeks to establish a correlation with social factors such as the level of economic activity, population growth, general social and cultural trends, etc. Of course, this knowledge may also provide a more comprehensive perspective on present-day developments and may even be of some help in planning for the future.

The issue of 'access to justice', a prominent topic among legal reformers not so many years ago, has also prompted intense socio-legal scrutiny. In this respect, research has not only tried to determine who actually has access to the courts, but has also explored other issues, such as who wins and why,[38] and more generally, what the real functions of courts in contemporary society are. Similarly, the 'alternative-dispute-resolution' reform movement helped focus attention more rigorously on the advantages and shortcomings of the courts as dispute-settlement institutions,[39] while also enabling the very notion of 'alternative' dispute 'resolution' to be criticised.[40]

In short, in studying the courts, socio-legal research has attempted to develop a broader analytical framework which is not dependent on specific institutions,[41] and which, even when it has adopted a strong policy orientation, does not lose sight of the larger political and social implications.

This has been the general situation in the United States and Western Europe. In Latin America, socio-legal research has assumed a somewhat different profile. A cursory glance at Latin American socio-legal literature shows that it is not the courts—and generally, formal legal institutions—that elicit the greatest interest among socio-legal scholars.[42] The reasons behind this are manifold. On the one hand, it is a reflection of the reality of Latin American official legal systems, which are almost completely irrelevant to the majority of the population. Plagued by corruption and inefficiency, courts, as part of those legal systems, are usually avoided in favour of more informal, effective alternatives.[43] On the other hand, it is also a by-product of the predominantly political orientation of most of the region's socio-legal scholars, many of whom adopt a 'critical' stance (and a denunciatory style) which sometimes feels justified in dispensing with solid empirical evidence. And last but not least, empirical research is expensive and requires researchers who are well trained in empirical methodologies, a rare quality among members of a traditionally-minded legal profession.[44]

[37] So-called 'longitudinal studies of courts'. See the essays on this subject published in the *Law and Society Review*, vol 24, no 2, 1990.

[38] The classic reference here is Galanter's 'Why the Haves Come Out Ahead . . .' (1974).

[39] See, for example, Falke/Gessner (1982).

[40] Abel (1982a).

[41] See Abel (1973) and the justification for a dispute-based approach for the Civil Litigation Research Project in Trubek (1980–1).

[42] Cf Correas (ed) (1991), and especially Cappeller (1991).

[43] See, for example, two case studies on Mexico (Gessner, 1976) and Brazil (Henckel, 1991).

[44] Sociologists and political scientists have generally shown little interest in the legal system and legal institutions, although this is rapidly changing.

Despite all these factors, which certainly do not enhance the special attention that courts have obtained elsewhere, there is an important body of empirical research on the way courts operate, at least in those Latin American countries with an established tradition in this respect, such as Colombia, Peru, Argentina, and Chile.[45] Thus, Latin American courts have also been studied from the perspective of the problems that affect courts elsewhere, such as costs, delay, and widespread inefficiency. At the same time, those studies have also incorporated other pressing realities of the judicial system which—while not exclusive to the region—assume dramatic dimensions there.

Perhaps the unprecedented challenges that globalisation poses for national legal systems have fostered a renewed interest in the courts. And it appears that justice administration faces the same, or at least similar, problems in seemingly very different regions and countries of the world. The social expectations that contribute to this common ground between countries can be summed up in the concepts of 'efficiency' and 'effectiveness'. Whatever their political, social and economic background, and regardless of other important requirements, such as independence, courts are universally expected to be efficient and effective.

What does being 'efficient' and 'effective' involve? At first sight, efficiency and effectiveness seem fairly simple to define: efficiency is the best use of resources;[46] effectiveness, the achievement of goals. When translated into the judicial arena, this means that courts should settle disputes in a 'just, speedy, and inexpensive manner', as a well known formula has it. However, trouble begins as soon as we attempt to define terms such as 'dispute settlement', 'just', 'speedy' and 'inexpensive' with more precision. And matters are further complicated by the realisation that the simultaneous fulfillment of these values requires trade-offs and compromises: 'speediness' may come at the expense of 'justice' (for example, if 'speediness' benefits one party and disadvantages the other); unlimited access to the courts may result in considerable backlogs and delay; 'justice' may demand the possibility of a slow, costly appeal process; while a court proceeding, even if it is regarded as just, speedy and inexpensive, may not be able to 'settle' the underlying dispute at all. Evidently, complex social choices are at stake here.

[45] The national reports on these countries in Correa Sutil (ed) (1993) have a descriptive section on the main studies and surveys conducted in this area. Some of the scholars who participated in the 'law-and-development' research program in the early 1970s subsequently made significant contributions to an empirically oriented sociology of law in their respective countries. See Merryman *et al.* (1979: v ff.). Mexico seems to be the only major Latin American country with no tradition of empirical socio-legal studies. For further references on the development of socio-legal studies in Latin America, see the corresponding reports in Ferrari (ed.) (1990a).

[46] Buscaglia/Dakolias (1999: 1 f., 7 f.) define 'court efficiency' in terms of 'how well resources are used in generating court output'. 'Court output', in turn, can be measured 'in terms of the elasticity of supply of court services, procedural time, and clearance rates'. 'Cost elasticity of supply' is further defined as 'the percentage change in the number of cases disposed per court that would be produced by a 1% change in the allocation of budget resources to that court', while 'clearance rates' are determined by 'the proportion of cases filed per year per court that are disposed during that same year'.

Regardless of whether or not these issues can be sorted out, the problem of finding a workable definition of such terms for the purposes of research and policy recommendations remains. When can a judicial decision be considered 'just'? How does one measure 'case processing time'? What are the causes of 'delay' and how do we fight them? What are the cost components of judicial proceedings? How can they be calculated? What are the likely effects of reducing certain costs for the 'demand' and 'supply' of court services? How does one evaluate court performance? These are operational questions which science must tackle, if our courts are to become (more) 'efficient' and 'effective'. Only rigorous empirical evaluation, however difficult this may prove to be, will help provide an answer to these questions.

Nevertheless, sociology of law enjoys no monopoly over the study of courts. Other social disciplines have expressed their interest, such as economics, political science, social psychology, the sociology of professions and organisations, and anthropology. Certainly, competition and cooperation between these disciplines can only be productive. An inter- or trans-disciplinary approach may result in a less ideological, one-sided analysis. And observation from multiple points of view increases the possibility of a more comprehensive examination of complex issues.

Is there a 'Litigation Explosion'?

As seen from an internal perspective, the alleged crisis in the administration of justice has been dramatically condensed in a two-word formula: the 'litigation explosion'. The litigation explosion is apparently a shorthand explanation for the main problems faced by the courts in many countries. 'Litigation explosion' usually means a dramatic and disproportionate increase in caseloads that severely affects the courts' capacity to handle them efficiently. But has there really been a 'litigation explosion'? If so, what are its causes and consequences? This section does not attempt to provide a rigorous, exhaustive answer to these questions. It can only provide a few points of reference and a brief examination of some of the existing evidence. But before exploring this terrain, a number of qualifications and clarifications are in order.

The evidence on a supposedly irresistible litigation explosion and its serious consequences is insufficient and unconvincing. Data from several countries show a steady growth of caseloads, particularly after 1970, although the situation differs significantly from country to country.[47] However, this fact alone

[47] For a contrasting study on the roots of the avoidance of litigation in a developed country (Japan), which is attributed to its distinctive legal culture, see Wollschläger (1997). Cf Ishikawa (1998), who contends that the current situation is due to a deliberate policy consistently followed by Japanese governments for one hundred years in favor of a 'small judiciary'. According to critics of this policy, the judicial system is not performing its proper function in society. Therefore, it is now necessary to increase the number of lawyers and the material resources available to the judiciary ('large judiciary'). For a review of recent developments that point to a larger role of litigation and lawyers in Japanese society see Goodman (2001).

hardly amounts to a litigation explosion. It is necessary to show that not only has there been an increase in the number of cases, but that longer delays and a general decline in the quality of judicial services, as indicated, for example, by an increase in the number of appeals, are precisely the consequence of growing caseloads. In other words: it must be proved that increasing litigation levels cannot reasonably be absorbed by the courts and other alternative mechanisms[48] without a severe reduction in the efficiency and quality of adjudication.

On the other hand, perceptions of overload, inefficiency, delay and the like are relative and subjective. They depend on the point of view adopted and the criteria used for evaluation.[49] And even when objective indicators are available, such as statistical data, significant methodological difficulties arise as to their degree of accuracy and their appropriateness for scientific explanation,[50] not to mention the fact that many countries have only recently been able to compile relatively complete, reliable judicial statistics.[51] Furthermore, even if complete, reliable statistics were available, there would still be the problem of defining the point of comparison that would lend support to the claim that a litigation explosion exists.[52] Let us now consider some specific evidence from various countries and regions.

In the *United States*, a considerable increase in caseloads before the federal courts has been observed in recent decades.[53] This growth is due to circumstantial, fairly transitory factors, such as the increase in criminal prosecutions in the context of the 'war on drugs' begun in the 1980s,[54] as well as to long-term shifts in litigation patterns, such as the rise of public law litigation and the increasing involvement of courts in specific policy problems.[55] This has undoubtedly contributed to longer delays and rising litigation costs.[56]

However, this does not make the existence of a 'litigation explosion' conclusive. Marc Galanter[57] and Lawrence Friedman[58] carefully examined this problem in the early 1980s. Both dismissed the 'excessive litigiousness' of the population as the primary source of growth in court caseloads. First of all, litigation rates did not seem to be substantially higher than in other industrialised countries. And secondly, the courts had been able to absorb the moderate shock of growing caseloads without dramatic adjustments, through enhanced

48 See Blankenburg (1989a).

49 Borucka-Arctowa (1987: 47).

50 Friedman (1985: 16 f.).

51 On the problems of interpretation and comparability, see also Wollschläger (1989: 22 ff.).

52 'There is no standard for deciding how much litigation is a lot or a little'. Friedman (1985: 17).

53 See, for example, Dungworth/Pace (1990), President's Council on Competitiveness (1991), Clark (1981), Posner (1996: 53 ff.). Friedman (1985: 17) points out that, although 95% of cases filed begin and end in state and local courts, these courts have been understudied and their work, until recently, inaccurately measured.

54 Kaufman (1990: 5).

55 Clark (1981).

56 Kaufman (1990). See also Hurst (1980–81), Posner (1996).

57 Galanter (1983a; 1988).

58 Friedman (1985: 15 ff.).

productivity and managerial techniques.[59] Thus, for example, in the 1990s the situation of the US federal courts could be described as challenging, but not critical.[60]

With respect to *Western Europe*, an impressive comparative survey of litigation rates in twelve countries since the mid-nineteenth century places the problem of growing caseloads in a broader social and temporal context.[61] The study shows that the present era has not experienced the highest historical rates of litigation. Germany during the economic crisis of the 1920s, and the Scandinavian countries before the beginning of industrialisation in the 19th century, are examples of the highest levels of litigation to date. Thus, the long-range perspective does not allow for a definitive evaluation of the recent trend towards higher litigation rates.

Fairly recent studies on individual countries offer a more differentiated but otherwise consistent panorama. Growing litigation rates have been systematically identified and described in Germany,[62] Spain,[63] France,[64] Belgium,[65] and Portugal.[66] In all these countries, litigation has increased considerably over the past two decades, with perceptible effects on delay and costs, as well as significant variations both in time and across the different branches of jurisdiction, Belgium being perhaps the most extreme example of increased delay in the area of civil justice.[67]

In *Latin America* we also consistently find the familiar picture of growing caseloads, particularly in the area of criminal justice, within the context of a chronically under-funded and understaffed judiciary, that is therefore structurally unable to perform many of its functions.

Generally speaking, the evidence on growing caseloads and their consequences in Latin American countries is more fragmentary than in the United States or Western Europe.[68] Many countries in the region have no systematic

[59] An economic study by Gillespie (1976) had already found considerable idle capacities in the federal district courts.

[60] For the second edition of his impressive study on the US federal courts (1st ed. 1985; 2nd edn 1996), Richard Posner changed the subtitle from 'Crisis and Reform' to 'Challenge and Reform', in view of the 'success of the federal courts in coping with a caseload that ten years ago I would have thought wholly crippling, and the recession of caseload in all but the courts of appeals . . .' However, although it was inaccurate to describe the situation of the federal courts as critical 'it may become so in the future, perhaps the near future; elastic will stretch only so far'. Posner (1996: xiii).

[61] Wollschläger (1989). 'Social context' means that a relationship is established between litigation rates and variables such as population growth and Gross National Product. The twelve countries considered include: the Netherlands, Belgium, Denmark, Prussia and the Federal Republic of Germany, Austria, England and Wales, France, Italy, Sweden, Finland, Norway, and Spain. For an English-language overview of the research project on European litigation rates see Blankenburg (1992).

[62] Röhl (1987).

[63] Pastor Prieto (1993) and Toharia in Friedman/Pérez Perdomo (eds) (2003).

[64] Ietswaart (1989), based on a survey of four courts of first instance.

[65] Van Loon/Langerwerf (1989).

[66] Santos *et al.* (1996).

[67] Van Loon/Langerwerf (1989: 249 ff.).

[68] For an overview of litigation trends in several European and Latin American countries since 1945, see Clark (1990).

studies on the subject. Where such studies do exist, they are not usually based on a comparative approach, ie, they do not establish, for explanatory purposes, a relationship between litigation rates and other significant social and legal variables,[69] or else they fail to identify a 'litigation explosion' in the sense defined above.

Nevertheless, some studies describe a situation where growing caseloads undoubtedly have the crippling effects attributed to the litigation explosion elsewhere. Thus, for example, Mexican federal courts have been experiencing a steady growth in caseloads for a long time. Although this increase may not qualify as an 'explosion' (among other reasons, because their relationship to social and demographic variables has not been systematically analysed), a severe lack of resources which prevented the establishment of a significant number of new courts until the 1980s, meant that judges could only fight backlog through an increasing rate of dismissals for procedural reasons.[70] A study on recent transformations in the Brazilian legal culture also shows that disputes in relation to the population have grown disproportionately in almost all branches of jurisdiction between 1990 and 1998. Thus, for example, ordinary matters almost doubled before the ordinary courts of first instance and appeals, whereas disputes before the federal courts of first instance grew almost three times during the same period. Filings before the High Court of Labor increased almost six times.[71]

In Argentina and Ecuador, the work of the civil trial courts has also steadily grown during the last decade, resulting in increasing backlogs and delay.[72] Interestingly, these increases have also resulted in a *relative decrease* in the use of the courts. Discounting for both population and economic growth, the number of filings per court has been decreasing, which means that litigants 'are either solving their disputes informally or are writing off their losses'.[73] In the case of Argentina, there is also a detailed study on dispute behavior in the province of Córdoba between 1968 and 1999. The starting assumption was that democratisation and growth in the administration of justice would translate into higher litigation rates. On the contrary, the general litigation rate followed a rather declining trend between 1970 and 1999,[74] which confirms again the idea that the relationship between litigation rates and other social, political and economic variables is more complex than is usually assumed.

[69] This is also the case with many European and American studies. For an interesting, and in this respect exceptional study, which tries to establish such relationship in the case of Colombia, see Rubio (1997: 363 ff.). This study examines the negative impact of legal rules in general, and more specifically, of legislative inflation, the diminishing life span of legal rules, and the increasing degree of discretion they embody, on economic growth.

[70] CIDAC (1994).

[71] Junqueira, in Friedman/Pérez Perdomo (eds) (2003).

[72] Buscaglia/Dakolias (1996: 8 ff.).

[73] Buscaglia/Dakolias (1996: 13–14).

[74] Bergoglio (2001, 43 f.).

In short, there seems to have been a considerable rise in litigation in many countries, which often translates into increasing costs and delay. However, neither from a historical perspective, nor in relationship to other social and economic variables, is there any reason for this increase in caseloads to be considered exceptional or critical. In fact, the opposite may be true: higher court caseloads may be just another manifestation of general growth processes in modern societies.[75] Supply and demand of court services is a dynamic phenomenon. Courts have usually been able to adjust to growing caseloads through an increase in productivity and other strategies, but in view of growing costs and delay, litigants may also choose to avoid the court system and resort to more efficient alternatives.

Therefore, we must consider the alleged 'litigation explosion' and the 'crisis' in the administration of justice as a discourse that, while reflecting an actual phenomenon, ie, a substantial growth of caseloads over a prolonged period of time, can undoubtedly be attributed to the position and interests of the actors declaring it, but also to other significant social developments, such as the new social prominence of the courts. Qualitative reasons that support this discourse include the following:

—The interest of socio-legal research in alternative dispute resolution mechanisms, primarily as a result of dissatisfaction with the 'antagonistic' nature of the judicial process and distrust of state institutions.[76]

—The movement towards the privatisation of justice and dispute-settlement, since public institutions are regarded as inherently inefficient.[77]

—Perceptions by the legal and political elites (judges, professors, practitioners, politicians) that are not necessarily in touch with the general conditions prevailing in the legal system.[78]

—The heightened symbolic presence of litigation in society through media coverage of spectacular or simply unusual cases;[79] which reinforces the perception of a 'litigious society' where 'everybody is suing everybody else.'[80]

[75] Wollschläger (1989: 83) contends that a small increase in contractual relations gone sour may result in a large, disproportionate increase in litigation.

[76] Röhl (1982) and Galanter (1980).

[77] See, for example, Benson (1990).

[78] Galanter (1983a: 61) cites this as a further symptom of the weakness of contemporary legal scholarship (at 5).

[79] Galanter (1983a: 49).

[80] See, for example, Lieberman (1981) and Olson (1991). This perception may vary with the social characteristics of citizens. The analysis of a statewide poll of Louisiana voters, in which two out of three responded that Americans are too quick to sue, found that the race of the respondent had an incidence on the response. Whites overwhelmingly agreed that 'people are too quick to hire a lawyer and go to court', whereas blacks overwhelmingly agreed that 'anyone should be able to use the legal system to their advantage'. The authors conclude: 'those with status appear quick to blame those with low status for filing too many suits'. Neubauer/Meinhold (1994: 1).

—Moral disapproval of the recourse to litigation and the courts, which are viewed at best as a necessary evil rather than as a normal 'service' capable of satisfying socially legitimate needs.[81]

—The existence of recent, largely unfulfilled social expectations regarding the courts.

These reasons make it necessary to refer to the larger political and economic context of judicial institutions in the contemporary world.

THE THIRD BRANCH OF GOVERNMENT? THE CHANGING ROLE OF COURTS IN SOCIETY

Courts in the Welfare State and the Paradoxes of Globalisation

If anything else, the twentieth century, particularly since World War II, has witnessed a considerable expansion of the state's functions, giving rise to what has come to be known as the 'welfare state'. The welfare state not only guarantees its citizens the most basic rights—such as physical integrity and liberty—, but also seeks to ensure them minimal conditions of well-being, such as education and health, as well as to protect them from the consequences of other social risks, such as unemployment and old age. To this end, the state intervenes actively in all social spheres, formulating a wide array of public policies and implementing them through its most important instruments: money and legislation.

The expansion in the size and scope of administration and legislation has not merely generated *more* business for the courts. It has also expanded the scope and meaning of adjudication itself, so that, in addition to the traditional fields of criminal and civil law, the courts have become involved in new areas of the law and public policy in general.[82] Consequently, courts are not merely supposed to apply and enforce existing laws any more. They have also been granted law-making powers[83] and the capacity to formulate and implement policies—most visibly so in the United States[84]—sometimes supplementing, at other times replacing, and even opposing the policies of executive agencies and legislative bodies. The courts—or at least some of them—participate openly in the constitutional and political process by controlling and monitoring the actions of the legislative and executive branches.[85] They have become a third, real branch of

[81] See, for example, Carrington (1979). Galanter (1983a: 67 f.) also speaks of a loss of communal feeling and of the concern for the moral balance of society.

[82] See Cappelletti (1989: 11 ff.). See also Hurst (1980–81), a study of the functions of the courts in the United States between 1950 and 1980, precisely the period when the welfare state developed and began to decline.

[83] Cappelletti (1989: 3 ff.; 1990).

[84] See Hurst (1980–81: 446 ff.). On policy making as a distinct mode of judicial action see Feeley/Rubin (2000: 1 ff.).

[85] See Vallinder (ed.) (1994), Tate (1995), Vallinder (1995) and Jacob *et al.* (1996).

government, at least in the sense that they now play an important role in shaping the general direction of society.

But the new prestige and powers enjoyed by the courts also entail disadvantages. Not only do the courts have to cope with growing caseloads and more complex questions of law and public policy. They also run the risk of losing impartiality and legitimacy. Not only is the law increasingly used as an instrument of politics, but the courts themselves are utilised by minorities and other social groups who see them as a means of achieving particular goals and policies.

If the courts exercise such important powers and are the ultimate guarantors of citizens' rights, it is only logical that the welfare state also grant the widest possible access to the courts to all individuals and disadvantaged groups in society. State policies aimed at ensuring this access are conceived of as a contribution to social justice, consistent with the welfare state's goals. These policies can be summarised under the heading 'access to justice.'

During the 1970s and 1980s, however, the welfare state underwent a severe crisis in many advanced industrial societies, and the optimistic belief in unlimited prosperity began to falter. The origins and development of this crisis, which has lasted until the present, are well known and, therefore, will not be examined in detail here.[86] For example, the 'fiscal crisis of the state,' ie, the growing inability of the state to pay for ever increasing expenses, required, in the view of many, a complete restructuring of government, through deregulation, privatisation and drastic reductions in public spending. This recipe for economic recovery was either enthusiastically endorsed, or grudgingly accepted, by developing countries, which were experiencing crises of their own, as a result of a crushing external debt, inflation, and weak growth. At the same time, many of these countries were undergoing a transition to a more democratic rule. After 1989, the former socialist countries started their own transformation towards the Western model of a liberal democracy and market economy.

The crisis of the welfare state has had significant implications for the courts. The most visible impact was the need to reconceptualise judicial reform in a context of relative fiscal austerity. This means, in short, that the promises of unlimited access to the justice system and its steady expansion have been forced to give way to efficiency-enhancing strategies.[87] Other impacts of this crisis on the justice system include, according to some observers:[88]

—The over-legalisation of social practices continues, exacerbating the loss of coherence and unity in the legal system.
—The drastic increase in litigation levels during the previous period has begun to stabilise.

[86] See, among others, Rosanvallon (1981) and García Cotarelo (1986).

[87] This goal was explicitly incorporated into the 'Structural Analysis of the Administration of Justice', a research program begun in the 1980s by the German Federal Ministry of Justice. See Van Raden/Strempel in WIBERA (1991: 7 ff.).

[88] Santos *et al*. (1996: 27 ff.).

—The increasing complexity of certain controversies is not matched by the routine practices and the inadequate training of judges.
—New areas of litigation emerge, for example, regarding third-generation human rights.
—A crisis in political representation, an increase in the levels of corruption and the activities of organised crime mobilise the social control function of the courts.

After nearly two decades of drastic adjustment and despite a seemingly unchallenged consensus that only political democracy and a market economy can lead to free and prosperous nations, the world is currently facing problems that go well beyond the cadre of the nation-state: regional wars, environmental destruction, financial crises, unemployment, drugs and arms trafficking, money laundering, migration, etc. All these challenges are not merely a sign of crisis but a manifestation of new developments which are increasingly linked to 'globalisation'.

'Globalisation' is a term generally used to describe the reality of a world market, with integrated processes of production, distribution and consumption that flow over and across national borders. In this respect, the most impressive manifestation of globalisation are integrated, 24-hour financial markets, which move billions and billions of dollars around the world each day and which are able to cripple a national economy in a matter of hours, should investors decide to withdraw their capital.

For our purposes, however, we shall use a broader concept with reference to the traditional notion of the sovereign state. Thus, globalisation can be understood as the existence of integrated social fields across the segmented space defined by the borders of sovereign states.[89] Accordingly, it is not only the market that is increasingly globalised (including the illegal activities of organised crime), but also, to a greater or lesser extent, politics, law,[90] and culture. In any case, the novelty lies in the compression of time and space that makes communication processes in and across such fields an instant reality. It should be noted that globalisation in this sense is a differential process, which means that not all these fields are integrated in the same way or to the same extent in the various countries.[91]

The most visible consequence of globalisation for the sovereign state is the existence of social activities that increasingly seem to escape its influence and control.[92] Old and new actors alike take advantage of new spheres of inter-

[89] This concept of globalisation is formulated in Fix-Fierro/López Ayllón (1997) and López Ayllón (1997b: 27 ff.). A different yet related concept, which is presupposed by the idea of globalisation, is that of 'world society.' See Luhmann (1986).

[90] On the 'globalisation of law' see, for example, Shapiro (1993) and Röhl (1996).

[91] See McGrew (1998: 328 ff.).

[92] This is, of course, a dynamic process. With regard to legal globalisation, the empirical studies in Gessner/Budak (eds.) (1998) provide examples of what the editors call 'complete state control', 'autonomous globalisation' and 'mixed models,' with dramatic changes in some of these areas, 'either in the direction of increasing state control or in the direction of decreasing state control' (7). See also the essays by Zürn and Scheuerman in Appelbaum/Felstiner/Gessner (eds) (2001).

action. They acquire new skills for exerting pressure on the state and other state-based actors. The state is thus subjected to multiple tensions and contradictions, both from above and below.[93] In response, the state has developed various strategies for coping with these developments, such as its increasing participation in the establishment of international and transnational structures for cooperation and governance,[94] which then develop virtually autonomous links with the domestic sphere.

From the perspective of globalisation, however, the courts seem to undergo a paradoxical process of simultaneous *strengthening* and *weakening*.[95] The weakening of the state under the market's pressure and 'the symbolic failure of democratic man and society'[96] converge and reinforce each other. Both phenomena are hidden beneath the growing relevance and power of the courts.[97]

> The irruption of judicial activism cannot be understood if it is not linked to a deep movement of which it is only a manifestation. It is not a transference of sovereignty to the judge, but rather a transformation of democracy. Judges would not enjoy such popularity if they did not satisfy a new political expectation which they have come to champion, and if they did not embody a new manner of understanding democracy.[98]

The courts have thus become a means of addressing political and especially moral demands. Courts are expected to 'tell right from wrong and to fix injustice onto the collective memory' in a world deprived of a higher authority.[99] They have become the last refuge of a disenchanted, democratic ideal. This explains why in certain countries, like Italy and Spain, previously anonymous judges suddenly became prominent actors in the fight against political corruption,[100] or why judicial reform has become a priority in countries which only recently experienced a democratic transition, as courts are expected to play an important role in consolidating political and economic reform.[101]

[93] Röhl (1996: 2 f.) identifies the following 'contradictory' developments:

—Universalisation vs. particularisation;
—Homogenisation vs. differentiation;
—Integration vs. fragmentation;
—Centralisation vs. decentralisation;
—Coexistence vs. confusion.

[94] Knieper (1991) insists, for example, that economic globalisation requires the establishment of international governance structures, because the state's functions cannot be restricted to specific territories.

[95] See also Pérez Perdomo (1993).

[96] Garapon (1996: 21 f.).

[97] Garapon (1996: 21 f.). Santos *et al.* (1996: ch 1) and Santos (1999) also explore the reasons behind the new protagonism of the courts. Both Santos and Garapon explicitly link this prominence to the problems of contemporary democracy.

[98] Garapon (1996: 35). 'Law has become the new language for formulating political demands, which, having been disappointed by a retreating state, are being massively addressed to the courts' (translation by HFF).

[99] Garapon (1996: 22).

[100] For a journalistic account of this phenomenon, see Tijeras (1994).

[101] Correa Sutil (1993), Domingo Villegas (1995).

However, this new role entails considerable risks. The images of an all-powerful judiciary may turn against the courts themselves,[102] because it is all too easy to disappoint social expectations.[103] The courts become increasingly politicised, but their effectiveness and legitimacy is still dependent on the *apolitical* exercise, in each individual case, of their political power.[104]

The interplay between the new relevance and potential weakness of the courts is clearly visible in the central arena of globalisation: the economy. Provided they do perform their role *efficiently*, courts are regarded as institutions of central importance for guaranteeing a *general climate of stability and predictability* that encourages investment and trade.[105]

Why Efficiency? The Economic Dimensions of Adjudication

Courts obviously play an economic role when deciding economic matters, as, for example, when they settle business controversies and make legal rules with direct economic consequences. However, their current economic functions have a much broader scope, since courts are supposed to facilitate the whole range of exchange relationships in society. Courts belong to the set of institutions which, according to Douglass C North, winner of the Nobel Prize for Economics in 1993, 'structure incentives in human exchange, whether political, social or economic' and influence fundamentally 'the differential performance of economies over time . . .'.[106]

Institutions influence human exchange relationships by helping to reduce so-called '*transaction costs*'. Transaction costs are the costs 'of measuring the valuable attributes of what is being exchanged and the costs of protecting rights and policing and enforcing agreements'.[107] Since in a complex society, where impersonal exchange predominates, contracts and agreements are usually not self-enforcing, some form of third-party enforcement should accompany exchanges, to 'provide information for individuals to police deviations'.[108] However, nothing guarantees that institutions in this sense will also be efficient. In any case, institutions are not efficient in the terms of Paretian allocative efficiency, but in an adaptive sense. Adaptive efficiency is concerned

[102] Garapon (1996: 23).

[103] So-called 'transitional justice', ie, the involvement of judges and courts in the reparation and punishment of wrongs and injustices committed during a dictatorship seems to be particularly problematic. See the essays compiled by McAdams (1997).

[104] Santos *et al.* (1996: 34).

[105] See, for example, Boza/Pérez Perdomo (1996) and Zamora (1993).

[106] North (1990: 3). North defines institutions as 'the rules of the game in a society' or more formally, as 'the humanly devised constraints that shape human interaction.'

[107] North (1990: 27).

[108] North (1990: 57). Of course, third-party enforcement also works when it is *not* used and exists only as a potential possibility that helps shape interaction in a certain way. It should be noted that criminal courts also help reduce transaction costs by raising the 'price' of engaging in illegal activities, that is, the price of avoiding the voluntary exchange of goods and services.

'with the kinds of rules that shape the way an economy evolves *through time*'.[109] It is also concerned

> with the willingness of a society to acquire knowledge and learning, to induce innovation, to undertake risk and creative activity of all sorts, as well as to resolve problems and bottlenecks of the society through time.[110]

The problem is, in North's view, that we are still a long way from understanding how to achieve adaptively efficient economies 'because allocative efficiency and adaptive efficiency may not always be consistent'.[111] Moreover,

> institutions are not necessarily or even usually created to be socially efficient; rather they, or at least the formal rules, are created to serve the interests of those with the bargaining power to devise new rules.[112]

Despite such theoretical difficulties, policymakers around the world seem to agree more and more that, in view of the ruthless struggle for markets and investment opportunities that economic globalisation imposes, judicial reform, and consequently court efficiency, are increasingly important. Thus, for example, international financial institutions like the World Bank and the Inter-American Bank for Development now consider judicial reform as an important component of economic structural change and have already given support to reform projects in many countries.[113] The underlying notion is that the lack of an effective and efficient court system generates significant costs that hamper economic growth. Such costs derive from three main sources: the loss in property-right value due to the lack of predictable enforcement of legal rules; the added transaction costs of contracting in an environment with dysfunctional third party adjudication, and corruption.[114]

Of course, the importance of judicial reform goes beyond its immediate economic implications, because it can also be regarded as a way of enhancing the general institutional and governance capabilities of embattled nation-states. Thus, many policymakers, especially at the national level, have understood that not only economic *but also* democratic reform require, *both*, effective justice institutions and that this coincidence offers the unprecedented and perhaps unique opportunity to push for real judicial reform.[115]

[109] North (1990: 80). Emphasis added.

[110] North (1990: 80).

[111] North (1990: 81).

[112] North (1990: 90).

[113] See for example the papers presented at the two conferences on justice and development sponsored by the Inter-American Development Bank, in Banco Interamericano de Desarrollo (ed) (1993) and Jarquín/Carrillo (1997). On the involvement of international development agencies in legal and judicial reform in Latin America see Thome (2000). A few studies (Prillaman, 2000; Hammergren, 1998) come to a rather skeptical assessment of the reform projects carried out so far.

[114] Buscaglia/Dakolias (1996: 1).

[115] This is explicitly expressed by Binder (1993). See also CIDAC (1994) and Domingo Villegas (1995).

Another problem of judicial reform—and court efficiency—is that the factors that have led to the conviction that courts are important for economic growth are increasingly international in character. International economic transactions can therefore be expected to give rise to a certain number of legal disputes which the courts could, if necessary, settle appropriately. But it is also a fact that economic controversies of an international character—especially high-stakes legal disputes related to trade and investment—tend to be taken away from the domestic jurisdiction and transferred to international *fora*, and in particular to *ad hoc* arbitration panels. To what extent are domestic courts avoided because they are unable or unwilling to *efficiently* handle cases with international components? And to what extent does the process of global economic competition also require a process of competition between legal and judicial systems as a factor that helps attract (or at least, does not discourage) trade and investment?

There is some evidence that domestic courts handle only a small portion of the potential number of international cases and that these cases tend to have a longer duration and be more costly than comparable domestic cases A recent research project on international civil litigation in the courts of New York City, the northern German cities of Bremen, Bremerhaven and Hamburg, as well as in the city of Milan, Italy, yielded some interesting results that will be briefly summarised here.[116]

It should be noted, first of all, that these are all large cities with a special significance for trade and business. New York, in particular, is a major marketplace for international legal services. This attracts foreign companies, which in turn fosters the development of a solid legal infrastructure, in the form of legal firms which also possess expertise in foreign law, usually by employing foreign lawyers. Therefore, courts in these cities might be expected to handle a relatively large proportion of international cases, but, in fact, this is not the case.

In New York, Germany and Milan, the percentage of international cases fluctuated between 1.5 per cent and 3 per cent.[117] As far as costs and duration were

[116] Gessner (ed) (1996a).

[117] In *New York*, about 30 thousand general civil matters were filed in the court of first instance in 1986. A sample of 2,200 cases yielded only 34 (1.5%) cross-border cases, ie, cases which involve a foreign party. A database research of all civil judgments rendered in New York state in 1992, including judgments by the federal courts, led to a similar result: of a total of 23,181 judgments, only 353, or about 1.5%, concerned international cases. However, the percentage was significantly higher (10.6%) in the Federal District Court for the Southern District of New York. Freyhold (1996: 57, 64).

In *Germany*, the picture was not that very different from the New York panorama. In Bremen, 4,438 cases were initiated in 1988 and decided by the civil and commercial chambers of the court of first instance. 3,605 cases were general; 45 of these, or 1%, were international. A total of 833 cases were commercial, 91 of which, or approximately 11% being international. The total proportion of international cases was 3% (136 cases). In Hamburg, 7,591 cases were begun in 1988 in the special 'international chamber' and the civil and commercial chambers. 6,661 cases were general, of which 110 (about 2%) were of an international nature. 930 were commercial cases, 99 of which (11%) were international. The total proportion of international cases was less than 3%. In Bremerhaven, the research focused solely on family cases. 2,534 cases were initiated in 1988, of which only 59, or about 2.3%, were international. However, 19 cases were related to the presence of a US Army base

concerned, in New York, international cases had a longer duration and were more costly than comparable domestic cases.[118] In Bremen and Hamburg, international cases showed a clear tendency towards a significantly longer duration, which could be partly attributed to the difficulties of serving process abroad and the higher number of hearings required.[119]

The study shows that even if, in absolute terms, domestic courts handle a large number of international cases (100 to 200 thousand cases a year are estimated for the fifteen countries in the European Union),[120] this only accounts for a small proportion of the total number of international civil disputes. This again raises the issue of the role of *domestic* courts in the global economy, but in any case, it means that courts (and nation-states, for that matter) are *relatively weakened* if a significant number of cases that can be potentially handled by these courts are resolved by other means.

Regarding the second question, ie, competition between legal systems[121] and the role of courts in such a process, legal rules obviously serve as an important instrument for attracting foreign trade and investment by creating comparative economic advantages. After all, this is the logic that lies behind the impressive transformation that the legal systems of many countries experienced in the 1980s and 1990s towards economic and political liberalisation, with considerable success.[122]

In this context, and as has already been stated, domestic courts play an important role as a factor in the general climate of economic and political stability, as well as of legal certainty, that favors investment, trade and, ultimately, growth. In fact, the perception that domestic courts are ineffective and inefficient, or that their judgments and interpretations may reduce economic opportunities, will weigh heavily on the decision-making process of foreign (and domestic) economic actors.[123]

nearby, so the actual percentage of international cases was much lower (about 1.5%). Gessner (1996b: 155, 190 f.).

In *Milan*, 20,036 files were registered in the civil court in 1988. A total of 546 prospective cross-border cases were selected. Of these, nearly half, or 286 files, were still open after five years. The group of 260 closed files had to be reduced for other reasons (lost files, mistaken register, etc). The final group of cases fitting the research guidelines consisted of 197 cases, or 189 if only one of the nine Japanese-Italian files is included. The proportion of international cases was estimated at around 2%, on the basis of the 546 prospective cases, assuming a similar percentage of error due to the cleansing of the closed files. Olgiati (1996: 221 ff.).

118 Freyhold (1996: 119 ff.).

119 Gessner (1996b: 177).

120 Freyhold *et al.* (1996: 269). The estimate should be much higher (from 200 to 300 thousand cases) now that the corresponding figure for Germany has been calculated with some precision (64 thousand international cases per year) (Volkmar Gessner, personal communication).

121 See, for example, Reich (1992).

122 See, for example, López Ayllón (1997a and b).

123 Zamora (1993). See, for example, Walch (1994) who claims that an incorrect interpretation of New York State's personal jurisdiction statute might threaten New York's position as the headquarters for the international recording industry. On the competition between legal orders, see Reich (1992).

Courts may be relevant in the process of economic competition in another sense. They may *attract* international disputes (and indirectly, business opportunities) that might also have been resolved elsewhere. In principle, the potential for competition between courts in this respect is limited. There is no unrestricted possibility of bringing legal action before any court, unless there is a justifiable point of contact with a case, such as the defendant's domicile or the existence of assets within the court's jurisdiction. A desirable degree of legal certainty precludes the possibility that the choice of jurisdiction be completely arbitrary. However, there are some jurisdictions which have a 'long arm' and are generous about admitting international cases (for example, New York and Germany).[124] Moreover, parties to a contract may insert a clause determining in advance the competent forum in the event of a controversy, which may be arbitration or the regular courts.[125]

All this means that, for a variety of reasons, foreigners may still bring suit abroad with some frequency. How many actually use foreign courts, though? What are their chances of overcoming the natural barriers of language, legal culture, the likely application of foreign laws, and the higher duration and costs of proceedings? The research project just cited also offers some interesting evidence in this respect.

In New York's international cases and judgments, an equal distribution was found between foreign and US plaintiffs.[126] The success rate of plaintiffs in all decisions was not very high: 21 per cent, of which 53 per cent corresponded to foreign plaintiffs and 7 per cent to foreign and US plaintiffs. The success rate of plaintiffs in final decisions was 24 per cent, 57 per cent of which corresponded to foreign plaintiffs and 7 per cent to foreign and US plaintiffs.[127]

In Germany, nearly 80 per cent of international files failed to mention foreign or unified law and/or the parties argued in favor of the application of German law. 86 per cent of judgments were actually based on German law.[128] As to the number of foreign plaintiffs, out of a total of 320 cases in Hamburg and Bremen, the plaintiff was foreign in 209 cases (approximately 65 per cent).[129] The plaintiff won totally or predominantly in 67 per cent of international cases, while the comparable rate in domestic cases was 60 per cent.[130] Plaintiffs who were not resident in Germany were significantly more successful in German courts than German residents in either domestic or international cases (69 per cent to 61 per cent, respectively). However, this advantage disappeared if requests by non-

124 Freyhold (1996: 84 ff.) and Gessner (1996b: 169).

125 Freyhold (1996: 92 ff.) points out that such clauses are not nearly as frequent as usually assumed, and that they may face enforcement problems, since some countries do not accept derogations from their courts. In the study on German courts, forum selection clauses appear in only 25% of cases. Gessner (1996b: 170).

126 Freyhold (1996: 90).

127 Freyhold (1996: 116).

128 Gessner (1996b: 179 f.).

129 This is deduced from table D–21. Gessner (1996b: 186).

130 Gessner (1996b: 187).

German residents for the enforcement of foreign judgments were eliminated from the sample. Then the chance of winning was about equal, but slightly 'more than could be expected'.[131] By contrast, in international family cases, plaintiffs were nearly all German residents.[132]

In Italy, in 80 out of 170 cases, the plaintiff was resident abroad, whereas in 90 cases the plaintiff's residence was in Italy. Defendants were foreign in 80 cases and resident in Italy in 85 cases.[133] In seven out of 189 cases (3.7 per cent), a foreign plaintiff and foreign defendant seem to have chosen Italian jurisdiction voluntarily.[134] With respect to the contents of the controversy, in 116 cases (65 per cent) it was business-related. In 64 of these 116 cases (73 per cent), the plaintiff was foreign.[135]

These data show that even if domestic courts handle a relatively small portion of international cases, and even if such proceedings will be more expensive and last longer than comparable domestic proceedings, those courts may still be more attractive to foreign parties in comparison with *their* own courts.[136] In international cases, foreigners are as likely to be plaintiffs as domestic residents. Foreign courts may also be attractive from a business perspective, because of the adequate legal infrastructure or even because such courts will apply their own law, not foreign or uniform law. Furthermore, plaintiffs do not fare badly in foreign courts, since they win in roughly the same proportion of cases as domestic plaintiffs in both domestic and international cases.[137] Thus, if courts are perceived as fair and/or efficient by foreign parties, they may also contribute, albeit marginally, to international competitiveness. The predominant picture, however, indicates that domestic courts 'still do not provide this institutional security for long-distance and cross-cultural trade, or for any other global legal interaction'.[138]

Obviously, the fact that this is so at present does not mean that it will remain so. Therefore, we should now turn to the question of whether domestic courts are willing and able to participate in the process of internationalisation, given the absence of strong international adjudicative institutions. The authors of the study cited above, for example, are somewhat sceptical of the likelihood that a complex legal cultural environment will be established around the domestic judicial process, thereby creating a generalised expectation structure of trust and predictability. Such an environment would, for example, require widespread information among judges, legal professionals, and business actors, on international rules and practices.[139]

[131] Gessner (1996b: 188 f.).
[132] Gessner (1996b: 191).
[133] Olgiati (1996: 230).
[134] Olgiati (1996: 229 f.).
[135] Olgiati (1996: 233).
[136] For a study of choice between jurisdictions in the US domestic context, see Bumiller (1980–1).
[137] Cf conclusions by Freyhold (1996: 148) and Gessner (1996b: 206).
[138] Freyhold *et al.* (1996: 279).
[139] Freyhold *et al.* (1996: 280).

Nevertheless, domestic courts are making a modest but visible effort to achieve internationalisation. One could cite the unusual sensitivity of New York judges that allows them to grant truly international cases special treatment,[140] but also the increasingly frequent international contacts between judges and justice institutions, including the establishment of formal ties and cooperative organisations.[141] The real problem is not that domestic courts and judges are incapable of adjusting to internationalisation, but rather the structural limitations that the domestic institutional framework imposes on them. This raises the issue of the need for supranational adjudicative bodies that will perform, at this level, the same functions that domestic courts accomplish within the national sphere.[142]

At present, there are not many supranational courts in this sense. The most highly-developed example is the European Court of Justice at Luxembourg, which occupies a prominent place within the European Union. It is widely recognised that the construction of European integration has largely been achieved through the law and that in this respect the European Court has played a major role. What is interesting about the European Court is that it does not replace domestic courts, but constitutes the head of a court system charged with the application and interpretation of Community law which also relies on domestic courts and incorporates them into the system.[143] However, for supranational courts or quasi-judicial bodies to be established, such an advanced integration process is perhaps unnecessary. The binational panel system established by chapter 19 of the North American Free Trade Agreement (NAFTA) between Canada, Mexico and the United States for the resolution of controversies deriving from unfair trade practices is an example of a dispute settlement institution with an international composition but which applies domestic laws.[144]

In short: the need for an adequate international legal infrastructure does not imply that either domestic or international courts will eventually be able to provide this service alone. On the contrary, it is more likely that an extremely diverse set of judicial and quasi-judicial institutions, both domestic and international, will be developed for such purposes. Whether or not they are used will depend on various factors, such as those mentioned above: rules of jurisdiction, perceived fairness and efficiency, the nature of the parties' claims, the degree of international orientation of judges and attorneys, the general business climate, etc.

140 Freyhold *et al.* (1996: 271).

141 See, for example, the '*International Judicial Observer*', jointly published by US Federal Judicial Center and the American Society of International Law (1995–). In the second number of this publication (January 1996) the creation of the Organisation of Supreme Courts of the Americas is reported. The Charter of this organisation was voted in Washington, DC in October 1995 by the representatives of the supreme courts of 25 countries of the Western Hemisphere.

142 Such supranational courts are all the more necessary insofar as private arbitration does not usually perform the crucial function of public rule-making.

143 See Hartley (1994: 64 ff., 195 ff.).

144 López Ayllón/Fix-Fierro (1999).

As will be shown later, the general economic role of adjudication outlined above is also inextricably linked to the nature of courts as an *organised apparatus* which employs scarce resources that always have alternative uses.[145] This means that the organisational efficiency of courts is a component of their overall efficiency as social institutions.

As North suggests, third-party enforcement is costly,[146] and part of the costs generated by it are linked to the need to devise incentives and guarantees for making such enforcement impartial:

> The enforcer is an agent and has his or her utility function, which will dictate his or her perceptions about the issues and therefore will be affected by his or her own interests.[147]

From the perspective of transaction costs, courts could be said to be both part of the problem and part of the solution, since, on the one hand, courts should help reduce transaction costs in society; while on the other, courts also generate transaction costs.[148] Courts will then be socially efficient institutions if the gains from facilitating exchange relationships are not offset by the costs associated with the operation of the judicial process as a whole. It should be borne in mind, however, that it is precisely at this point that social and individual utility may diverge. While individuals may find it worthwhile to litigate, the overall social costs may still be higher than the overall social benefits. Nevertheless, if and when this occurs is in itself a difficult—and costly—question to answer.

Adjudication—the operation of the courts—is costly and its resources cannot be expanded indefinitely. Given rising caseloads, courts are under pressure to rationalise and make more efficient use of their resources; otherwise, the price of adjudication will rise in the form of longer delays. Litigants, for their part, have to evaluate whether resorting to the courts is the best alternative in terms of costs, or whether other solutions are less expensive, including settlement and even the abandonment of their claims. This is what is usually meant by 'court efficiency'.

Towards an Effective Judiciary

Of course there is much more to court performance and judicial reform than just 'efficiency'.[149] There are reasons to think that efficiency is just a component of

[145] See Hazard, Jr. (1965).

[146] North (1990: 58): 'Enforcement is costly. Indeed, it is frequently costly even to find out that a contract has been violated, more costly to be able to measure the violation, and still more costly to be able to apprehend and impose penalties on the violator'.

[147] North (1990: 58).

[148] North (1990: 32): it is 'measurement plus the costliness of enforcement that together determine the costs of transacting'.

[149] But see Dakolias (1999: 5 f.) on the advantages of choosing efficiency as a starting point for the evaluation of a court system: first, 'most indicators can be quantitatively measured using objective data', thus providing a sound basis for comparison; second, 'congestion, cost, and delay are the most

a broader concept that indicates the social adequacy of courts. One could call this broader concept 'effectiveness',[150] meaning, as defined above, the capacity to achieve the goals for which courts have been established.[151]

When are courts effective? When they fulfill at least the following requirements:

—*Institutional design*: courts should be organised and vested with powers in a way that is appropriate for the performance of their functions.
—*Judges and judicial employees*: judges and other judicial personnel should be properly trained and selected, and given attractive job and career incentives.
—*Selectivity*: courts should be able to select and handle cases considered 'relevant' from a social point of view.
—*Processing capacity*: courts should have sufficient capacity to handle cases in a timely fashion.
—*Legal profession*: the adequate performance of courts requires both trained attorneys and lawyers capable of interacting with them and evaluating their work.
—*Legitimacy*: courts require a minimum degree of social credibility and visibility.

'Selectivity' and 'processing capacity' are the two requirements which have the most direct implications for court efficiency. Other requirements, however, also have such implications, since they demand the efficient use of resources. These include, for example, 'institutional design' and 'judges and judicial employees'.

'Legitimacy' may be regarded as a requirement of court effectiveness, because social expectations towards the judicial system act as an incentive for better performance, provided other conditions, such as adequate resources, are met. In this respect, visibility is nowadays a significant component of the institutional legitimacy of courts, as shown by a study on mass attitudes towards high courts and constitutional courts in eighteen countries.[152] This study concludes that, generally, 'to be aware of a court is to be supportive of it' and that 'courts generate specific support by becoming salient, by making their policymaking activity known to the mass public'.[153]

The opposite is also true: effectiveness is a requirement of legitimacy. This is so because contemporary societies rely on a kind of legitimacy that can be termed 'functional': legitimate is

often complained about by the public in most countries', and third, 'efficiency is a promising starting point for the study and design of judicial reform because of its relatively apolitical nature.'

[150] In Buscaglia/Dakolias (1999: 1 f.), court efficiency is explicitly defined as a single yet important aspect of 'judicial effectiveness'.

[151] 'Effectiveness', ie, the measurement of the degree to which legal rules are obeyed and applied or the extent to which their goals are realised, has a long tradition in socio-legal studies.

[152] Gibson *et al.* (1998).

[153] Gibson *et al.* (1998: 356).

> whatever is effective and effective is whatever fosters and guarantees technical and economic development under specific environmental conditions and in given circumstances, since this is, in the last resort, a condition for the effectiveness of any values whatsoever.[154]

A recent study on Mexican state courts shows why an evaluation of judicial performance with respect to a specific sector of adjudications—the enforcement of money debts—should include indicators that go beyond narrow efficiency criteria and encompass effectiveness indicators.[155] Besides the evaluation of efficiency aspects such as 'duration of commercial and mortgage proceedings', 'enforcement of judicial decisions' and 'sufficient level and efficient use of human and material resources', the 'institutional quality' of the respective judiciary is also assessed on the basis of 20 indicators, such as the following: 'professional quality of judges', 'quality of judicial decisions', 'judicial independence', 'judicial career and civil service', 'homogeneity and consistency of judicial decisions', 'number of courthouses', 'file consultation service', 'technical quality and corruption in the provision of auxiliary services', 'quality of procedural rules', etc.[156] Interestingly enough, both qualitative and efficiency indicators include the performance of other governmental bodies and agencies that do not belong to the judiciary but make an important contribution to its overall operation.

PURPOSES, SCOPE, AND METHODOLOGY

Purposes and Scope

This study attempts to discuss at some length the meaning and relevance of the concept of efficiency for the operation of courts and court systems. It seeks to provide some elements for answering questions such as the following. In what sense can we say that the adjudicative process works efficiently? What are the relevant criteria for the measurement and assessment of court efficiency? But also: should the courts try to operate efficiently and to what extent is this viable? What is the proper relationship between 'efficiency' and 'justice' considerations in a judicial proceeding?

The concept of 'efficiency' belongs unquestionably to economics. In the economic view of the world, or at least in mainstream economics, 'efficiency' constitutes the universal parameter by which the proper allocation and use of scarce resources is evaluated. In so far as the law and legal institutions affect such allocation or use, they are inevitably subject to economic efficiency

[154] García Pelayo (1991: 1423) (translation by HFF). A similar formulation can be found in Calsamiglia (1988: 307; 1993), for whom legitimacy through efficiency and effectiveness is added to the traditional concept of legitimacy through legality.

[155] Sarre/López Ugalde (2002).

[156] Sarre/López Ugalde (2002: 28).

judgements. Economists and lawyers with an economic background or an interest in economic thinking have ventured into the field of the law and attempted to apply economic tools to legal problems. They have proposed economic models for the differential consequences of different legal rules. They have critically assessed the efficiency of particular legal institutions, and they have suggested substantive or policy changes on the basis of their insights. These efforts have led to an identifiable 'school' or movement, the 'economic analysis of law' or, more simply, 'law and economics'.[157] Although not all law-and-economics scholars may share to the same extent the concern for efficiency, or for a particular concept of efficiency, it does not look, at first sight, as if it could be completely ignored when evaluating legal institutions from an economic point of view.[158]

Economics is not the only social science seeking to examine and evaluate the performance, however it may be defined, of legal institutions. Sociology, or perhaps more accurately, sociology of law, has enjoyed a long tradition in which the critical examination of the behaviour of legal institutions in their social context plays an important role. Since the 1960s, sociology of law has devoted considerable effort to the empirical and theoretical analysis of conflicts and dispute-settlement and has therefore paid a great deal of attention to the working of the courts and other justice institutions. For this purpose, it has resorted to widely differing perspectives that have sometimes been either akin to, or directly influenced by, an economic approach.

This apparent concurrence of economic and socio-legal perspectives, both seeking to examine the performance of the social institutions called courts and to eventually provide the policy-maker with criteria and insights for reforming them, seems to call for a systematic consideration of the relationships between the two approaches. Such consideration is not only required by the imperatives of systematic analysis, but also because it does not seem to have received the amount of attention it deserves. From the standpoint of a scientifically based legal or judicial policy (in itself not an entirely unproblematic notion), the question of the comparative advantages of, or the contributions to be expected from, different social sciences should first be clarified, before trying to draw specific lessons or recommendations from empirical research. As it happens, both approaches converge and diverge with respect to several, identifiable points.

[157] For a very competent 'reconstruction' by two Continental scholars of this mainly American intellectual movement, see Chiassoni (1992) and Mercado Pacheco (1994). See also Deakin (1996), who distinguishes between economic analysis of law and the broader perspective of the law-and-economics movement, and Cossío Díaz (1997), who attempts to determine the uses of economic analysis of law in the civil-law tradition. This is carried out on the basis of a conceptual delimitation between normative legal science, legal sociology, the science of legal policy, and economic analysis of law proper. For an introduction see Cooter/Ulen (1988), Hirsch (1988), Polinsky (1989), Pastor (1989), Veljanovski (1990), Lemennicier (1991). Mercuro/Medema (1996) provide a useful overview of 'schools' and approaches.

[158] See Coleman (1980: 510ff.) on the relevance of the concept of efficiency for the economic analysis of law and the various efficiency-related notions used by economists and proponents of this analsysis ('productive efficiency', 'Pareto optimality', 'Pareto superiority', 'Kaldor-Hicks efficiency' and—controversial—'wealth maximisation').

The practical consequence is that we may combine and compare both socio-legal and economic studies to produce a more complex and accurate picture of adjudication in contemporary societies.

In the light of these remarks, the main purpose of this study is to systematise and discuss:

—The concepts and theories of what efficiency means for the law, adjudication and the courts, and more specifically, the place of efficiency in the legal system, as well in the context of court performance.
—The relationship between sociology of law and economic analysis of law; and
—Empirical (socio-legal) research that can be considered relevant for clarifying the relationship between court operation and efficiency.

These three aspects are also interrelated in the sense that the conceptual and theoretical discussion was partly suggested by, and oriented towards, available research. There was no *a priori* conceptual framework for organising existing empirical studies. On the contrary, this framework evolved out of an attempt to give a meaningful structure to the wealth of studies produced in many countries on the most diverse aspects of the operation of courts.

The empirical studies on the courts described and summarised here, including many which are perhaps not easily accessible, are also interesting for other reasons:

—The substantive results they have obtained.
—Their methodological approach, including methods for measurement and performance indicators.
—Their theoretical insights.
—Their usefulness as inspiration for further research.

Although this study focuses on the courts and their operation, other justice institutions are taken into consideration insofar as they have an impact on the operation of the courts themselves, such as alternative dispute resolution (ADR).

For carrying out this research, mainly scientific publications were taken into account, although other relevant materials were occasionally used, such as official documents and reports. These materials refer basically to research conducted in the United States—by far the most productive source of socio-legal knowledge—and Western Europe. References to materials from Latin America have also been made as far as possible, despite the fact that such materials are more scattered and that Latin American socio-legal research is not always formally published.

This study does not intend to be an exhaustive overview of existing surveys. Instead, it aims to examine relevant studies for their contribution to the understanding of our general topic. There are a significant number of other relevant studies, but I believe that those included here help sufficiently to illustrate the main problems and concepts associated with court efficiency, as well as the complexity of the issues involved. Obviously, it has not been possible to discuss fully each and every one of the studies.

It is important to note that many of these studies do not directly address the problems of 'court efficiency'. They may have a quite different scope instead. However, I have chosen to *read* and *interpret* them from the perspective of judicial efficiency. In this way, one particular study may be used to illustrate several of the aspects examined here.

Finally, the general purpose of this study significantly limits the scope of the conclusions that may be drawn from it. The diversity of legal systems and traditions, of procedural and substantive features that affect court operation, do not favor a certain type of generalisation. Furthermore, many studies remind us constantly that court operation is affected by local conditions. In this respect, for example, the concept of 'local legal culture' has been used to explain the pace of litigation in the courts, emphasising that it is the particular relationships established between the participant actors (judges, attorneys, prosecutors) which largely determine the operation of a particular court. For this reason, the reader should be able to draw useful lessons only against the background of a particular judicial context.

The study seeks to qualify as a *socio-legal* study. Although the central concept it examines—efficiency—is clearly an economic concept, the study's approach is predominantly sociological insofar as it will be examining the *social* operation of legal institutions, ie, its main interest lies in finding out how a basic concept of efficiency can be related to different social dimensions of the legal system (including legal science) and court operation, from the level of society as a whole to the level of individual judicial proceedings and decisions. In other words: the study explores *the socio-legal context of economic rationality in the legal and judicial systems.*

Thus, it is necessary to examine the relationship between sociology and economics *vis-à-vis* the law, or more precisely, the relationship between 'sociology of law' and 'economic analysis of law'. Both disciplines share certain features, in addition to the fact that the law is their particular object of study. This fosters a certain degree of competition and 'rivalry' between both approaches and raises the issue of their relative explanatory power. Some law-and-economics scholars, for example, have unabashedly proclaimed the superiority of the economic over the sociological approach, both in terms of pure explanatory power and in terms of the range and depth of the issues that have actually been analysed by these two disciplines.[159]

Without wishing to take sides in this 'dispute', we assume that, in theory at least, the confrontation between both approaches can only result in a richer knowledge of the law. However, the combination of both approaches may not

[159] Posner (1995) explicitly uses a law-and-economics perspective to examine the relative contributions of both disciplines to the study of the law. Other essays in the same issue of the *European Journal of Law and Economics* compare the economic and the sociological approaches to the law (regarding crime, for example).

necessarily enrich them if this is attempted at a low common denominator. It may be then preferable to begin with either an economic or a sociological approach and subsequently incorporate insights from the other discipline.[160]

As stated earlier, this study purports to be basically rooted in a sociological approach. In addition to the concepts and theories of the economic analysis of law, it takes contributions from other disciplines into consideration, such as those from social psychology or the sociology of organisations.

Legal Traditions and Branches of Jurisdiction

Courts and court systems are very different in organisation and functioning. Besides the inevitable local differences, there is a basic, general difference rooted in the two major legal traditions of the West: common law and civil law. Legal tradition has a significant influence on the central features of the judicial system, such as the role of judges and attorneys; the basic characteristics of procedure; the nature of appeal; the legal force of judgments and precedents, etc.

Mirjan R Damaška has written an extraordinary comparative study on the judicial process in both legal traditions.[161] Damaška not only identifies and describes the major differences existing in the judicial process between both traditions. He goes beyond them in order to uncover their deep roots in the organisation and philosophy of political authority.[162] In his view, such differences are the manifestation of two basic ideals of officialdom: the hierarchical and the coordinate ideals.[163] The first ideal corresponds essentially to Continental civil-law systems. The second is typical of the Anglo-American legal tradition. If this is so, there are more differences between both traditions than usually meet the eye, since many of these differences 'lurk behind superficial similarities and can be discerned only on close inspection'.[164]

An important consequence of this for judicial reform would be, for example, that one has to be extremely cautious about recommending the adoption of features and devices of one tradition, where they operate satisfactorily, by the other, where they might turn out to be disruptive in a different socio-legal context.[165] Of course, this does not mean that comparisons are not useful as a point of reference for analysis and criticism, as well as a source of inspiration.

160 See, for example, Ellickson (1991), and Trubek (1980–1) on the Civil Litigation Research Project.

161 Damaška (1986).

162 Damaška (1986: 8 ff.).

163 Damaška (1986: 16 ff.).

164 Damaška (1986: 1). He goes on: '. . . a consensus is sometimes proclaimed on points where agreement is mainly a rhetorical achievement. Virtually all states subscribe to the view that judges should be independent and that the accused should be presumed innocent until proven otherwise, but the unanimity begins to break down as soon as one considers the implications of these views and their operational meaning in the administration of justice of various countries.'

165 See, for example, Langbein (1985) and the response by Gross (1987).

In this study, such differences will be taken into account and addressed explicitly whenever they may have a particular relevance. For one thing, they imply that efficiency will have a different significance and occupy a different place in the two legal traditions. And in terms of scientific analysis, such differences may also prompt the question of whether economic analysis of law, officially originated and developed in the United States, is also equally applicable to civil-law systems. The difficulties which the reception of this type of analysis has encountered in Continental Europe and other civil-law countries may point in the direction of a negative answer.[166] However, such difficulties appear to be more of a (legal) cultural type, ie, related to the ways in which the law is learned, interpreted and conceived of, than of a theoretical nature. From a general *theoretical* point of view, there is no obstacle to the scientific use of economic tools to analyse the law. An entirely different question is related to the appropriate means of doing this with respect to a particular legal system and its particular methods of operation, as is the scope and validity of the conclusions which may thus be obtained.[167]

The latter consideration is confirmed and reinforced if a more comprehensive perspective on the role of courts in modern legal systems is adopted. It then becomes clear that differences between legal traditions should not be unnecessarily exaggerated. We should not lose sight of the fact that civil law and common law share deep historical and philosophical roots, which makes it possible to speak about a *Western* legal tradition encompassing both.[168] Both legal traditions share, for example, the idea that law builds a rational and integrated system or body of rules, whose institutions are separated from other social institutions and which is administrated by a specially trained group of professionals.[169] On the other hand, the demands that a complex, technologically sophisticated society places on legal institutions, especially now that globalisation tends to remove all barriers to communication, fosters homogenisation and convergence processes between legal and judicial traditions. Indeed, such homogenisation and convergence processes have been visible for some time now

[166] See Pardolesi (1990).

[167] This problem is examined at some length by Cossío Díaz (1997: 263 ff.). He proposes the same general conclusion. In order to explore the theoretical functions and the explanatory possibilities of economic analysis in the context of a civilian system (here, the Mexican legal system), he first reviews the origins and development of Law and Economics in the United States. He considers that the economic approach can be a useful tool for the instrumental interpretation of legal rules and for legal policy in general (what he terms the 'context of possibility' of economic analysis). However, the likelihood (the 'context of probability') that this will occur varies, depending on the type of legal operation being considered. This likelihood may be higher for legislation, subject to the general dynamics of legal systems and the prevailing abstract conceptions on law-making, while the application of legal rules seems to be more affected by legal-cultural factors (353 ff.).

[168] Berman (1983).

[169] See Berman (1983: 7 ff.). Berman points out that some of the characteristics of the Western legal tradition are in a state of crisis, precisely at a time when this tradition has achieved an extraordinary, almost universal, scope and influence.

with respect to the administration of justice. We shall mention them occasionally and emphasise their significance.[170]

Another important distinction that should also be taken into account is that between civil justice, in a broad sense, and criminal justice. There are significant differences in organisation and procedure between both branches of jurisdiction. For example, in the criminal justice system, besides the judge and the parties, other official actors, like the police and the prosecutor, play a key role in the operation of the courts and influence the outcomes of cases. This circumstance, and the nature of the public and private interests involved in criminal proceedings, seem to make efficiency a much more pressing issue here than in a civil court. Society demands the swift and certain punishment of crimes, while accused persons have also an interest in speedy proceedings, in order to avert the unfavourable consequences that derive from being subject to prosecution, such as provisional detention.

This increased relevance of efficiency appears to be counteracted by a heightened interest in justice and due process in criminal cases. It is here that the alleged trade-off between justice and efficiency—frequently discussed in the literature—is most visible and compelling. But apart from this particular consideration, empirical studies on civil and criminal courts will be used indistinctly to illustrate some of the main issues that will be examined in the following chapters.

[170] Posner (1996) repeatedly indicates that the judicial process in the US federal courts tends to adopt a few features of Continental systems, such as the interventionist role of the judge or the beginnings of a rudimentary judicial career. The same can be said of the English judiciary. See, for example, Rozenberg (1995: 104 ff.).

2

Litigation, Justice, and Efficiency

LITIGATION FROM AN ECONOMIC AND SOCIO-LEGAL PERSPECTIVE

As HAS BEEN the case with other legal fields, scholars have applied the tools of economic analysis to civil and criminal litigation and have gradually developed an economic model of the judicial process.[1] Such a model is generally concerned with the costs and benefits that influence the litigants' and other actors' decisions, such as, for example, the decision to go to trial or to settle (or to accept a plea bargain in the criminal process); the amount of money the parties are willing to invest in litigation; the decision to appeal, etc. The model has induced, and its development has been often accompanied by, a variety of efforts to empirically test its assumptions and implications.

The starting point of the economic analysis of litigation is the assumption that 'the rules and other features of the procedural system can be analysed as efforts to *maximise* efficiency'.[2] However, from an *operational* point of view, efficiency is achieved through the *minimisation* of the *sum* of two types of costs:[3]

—*Error costs* (EC), ie, 'the social costs generated when a judicial system fails to carry out the allocative, or other social functions assigned to it'; and[4]
—*Direct costs* (DC), ie, 'the costs (such as lawyers', judges' and litigants' time) of operating the dispute-resolution machinery'.[5]

[1] See Landes (1971), Posner (1973), Rhodes (1976). See also Forte, in Forte/Bondonio (1970), for a general consideration of the costs and benefits involved in the operation of the justice system and the particular aspects to be taken into account by an economic approach.

[2] Posner (1973: 400).

[3] Posner (1973: 399). Forte, in Forte/Bondonio (1970: 11), proposes a possible explanation of why the *maximisation* of efficiency requires, in an apparent contradiction, the *minimisation* of certain costs: 'If the standard of justice is fixed [ie, the most exact application of substantive law possible], the process of maximisation in the construction of procedural codes cannot follow the normal criteria of comparison between an additional unit of cost and an additional unit of production, but must develop only as minimisation of costs, assuming that the product to be obtained is fixed' (translation by HFF). In other words: if the product of the application of judicial codes of procedure is 'justice', then efficiency can only be maximised *within* the boundaries defined by justice considerations.

[4] An approach concerned with minimising not only utilitarian costs but also the considerations of other values in procedure (such as the respect for rights) may distinguish between 'economic' and 'moral' costs within the category of error costs. The moral cost approach would not differ very much from the economic approach, since monetary value can also be used to compare both types of costs. For example, moral costs can be indirectly priced: their monetary value would then be the amount one is willing to pay to avoid moral costs. See Bayles (1990: 120 ff., 125).

[5] Obviously, any direct cost in this sense, is also an *opportunity cost*, ie, costs deriving from the alternative uses to which resources have *not* been applied.

EC and DC are related to and interact with each other,[6] sometimes in a complex manner,[7] meaning that it is difficult to predict the *a priori* overall effect of changes in the relevant variables.[8] In other words: the minimisation of either EC or DC without taking into account their interaction may yield unexpected or unfavorable overall results.

Take, for example, the allegedly 'unmitigated' and 'universal' problem of delay.[9] Delay is in reality both a source of error and of benefits. Court delay can increase the probability of an erroneous decision, for example, because of the decay of evidence over time; but it can also increase the settlement rate or permit the reduction of expenditures for the court system (judges, judicial personnel, courthouses).[10] Therefore, its reduction (for example, through procedural reforms that facilitate the admission of evidence or through an increase in the number of judges) may be offset by a lower settlement rate and increased litigation.[11] Note that, without having introduced any consideration about the consequences of the reduction of delay for the assessment of a judicial proceeding as fair or unfair (consider, for example, the common claim that such a reduction impairs the procedural opportunities of a defendant), the economic approach itself precludes simple, unilateral, 'efficiency-enhancing' measures. Thus, it can be concluded that delay minimisation alone is not an appropriate formulation of the goal of judicial reform and that the problem of delay must be defined within the larger framework of the minimisation of the sum of EC and DC.[12]

The possible negative consequences of partial efficiency-enhancing measures has also been discussed in terms of a trade-off between 'justice' (or 'equity') and 'efficiency'. Such a trade-off may be intuitively plausible,[13] but the relationship

[6] This relationship is already suggested by the formula that proposes the minimisation of the *sum* of EC and DC, rather than the minimisation of each category independently. An alternative definition (Cooter/Rubinfeld 1990: 537) states that a legal dispute is resolved efficiently 'when legal entitlements are allocated to the parties that value them the most, legal liabilities are allocated to the parties who can bear them at least cost, and the *transaction costs of dispute resolution are minimised*' (emphasis added).

[7] Posner (1973: 441) summarises this relationship in a loss function having three terms: a) EC (which is a function of the probability of error, in turn a function of the fraction of cases litigated, as opposed to those settled, the amount of private expenditures of litigation, and the amount of public expenditures); b) the sum of the private and public expenditures in cases that are litigated (equal to the total of those expenditures in all cases multiplied by the fraction of cases litigated); and c) the total private expenditures on cases that are settled (equal to the total private expenditures in all cases multiplied by the fraction of cases settled multiplied by the fraction cost of settling rather than litigating).

[8] Posner (1973: 441 f.).

[9] Posner (1973: 445 f.). Posner offers other examples of the interaction of EC and DC, such as discovery, the jury, *res judicata*, etc.

[10] Posner (1973: 446).

[11] Posner (1973: 447 f.).

[12] Posner (1973: 448).

[13] Such a trade-off may be intuitively plausible simply because the two parties to a judicial proceeding have contradictory interests and also because private and social utility tend to differ. It becomes more plausible whenever an issue of fundamental or human rights is involved. Such rights have a 'pre-emptive' effect, subjecting any other value to an increased pressure for justification. See, for example, Smith (1995: 69 ff., 79), criticising the US Supreme Court for its policy of increasing the

between both values is much more complex and highly differentiated than initially suggested by such intuition. The complexity stems, first, from the different levels in the operation of justice administration that have to be taken into account; secondly, from the relevance, if any, of the particular concept of efficiency used; and thirdly, from the reference system (law, economy, politics or science). However, this is not only a theoretical or abstract question. It has significant implications for both empirical research and policy-making.

The following sections will attempt to develop the assumptions and implications of Economic Analysis of Law (hereinafter EAL) for the judicial process on two levels: *judicial decisions* and *litigation behaviour*. It should be recalled that EAL purports to be both a descriptive (positive) explanation of the law and legal institutions as well as a criterion for their assessment (normative approach), and that these perspectives are not always easily distinguishable.[14]

Such an economic approach will be compared with alternative theoretical and empirical perspectives (in the latter case, mainly socio-legal research), particularly regarding the place of efficiency considerations (for example, in the form of settlement, plea-bargaining or alternative dispute resolution—ADR—mechanisms) for the operation of judicial institutions. It is hoped that this comparison will provide a better picture of the questions involved, and yield further elements for the clarification of the relationship between the economic and sociological approaches to law and legal institutions.

The Efficiency of Judicial Decisions

Contrary to a widely-held perception, EAL is not a homogeneous movement.[15] Various theoretical and methodological perspectives coexist under the same label.[16] Nevertheless, all its proponents largely share the conviction that microeconomic theory serves as an effective tool for analysing, explaining and even predicting how people behave under rules of law.[17] This conviction is based on the assumption that individuals are rational maximisers in all their activities, not just in economic exchanges, and that they are capable of responding to the

efficiency of the federal courts at the expense of an affordable, thorough review of criminals' convictions (conveniently exemplified by capital cases). Cf also the controversies concerning the efficiency proposals of the Royal Commission on Criminal Justice (Field/Thomas 1994).

[14] On the distinction between the positive and normative perspectives of EAL and their relevance for jurisprudence, see Posner (1990: 353–92, 362 ff.)

[15] A common perception, not entirely unjustified, identifies EAL with the Chicago school of economic thought and with conservative political positions, hostile to government economic regulation and intervention. The most prominent and prolific representative of the Chicago school of law and economics is Richard A Posner, a professor at the University of Chicago Law School and currently a judge of a US federal court of appeals. Chiassoni (1992: 152 n 57).

[16] See, for example, the excellent review essay by Johnston (1990), that can also serve as an introduction to the main problems of EAL, Mercado Pacheco (1994: 58 ff.) and Chiassoni (1992: 113 ff.).

[17] See Kornhauser (1986: 237 f.) and Cooter/Ulen (1988: 9 ff.).

incentives incorporated into legal rules.[18] This, in turn, implicitly asserts an instrumental view of the law, according to which it is the task of economic analysis to show and model the various consequences attached to different rules in view of a particular social goal.[19] An instrumental conception of EAL as a sort of 'policy science' of the law shares several features with other schools of legal thought, particularly in the United States,[20] and will provide a number of points of reference for comparing the economic approach with the socio-legal perspective in connection with the problems of legal policy.

Two theories of EAL regarding the economic relevance (efficiency) of judge-made law will be examined here:[21]

—A *descriptive theory*, ie, the explanation of why the common law (or judge-made law) *is* efficient or *tends* towards efficiency; and
—A *normative theory*, ie, the reasons why judges should pursue efficiency as a desirable *goal* in their decisions.

As already noted, it is not always easy to distinguish between both dimensions, as will be evident in the following discussion, where a normative claim is implicit in a functional explanation. However, a distinct normative dimension revolves around the question of whether justice should prevail, completely or partially, over efficiency considerations, and whether efficiency is in fact an appropriate criterion for the evaluation of the law. We shall deal with the normative approach again later when the relationship between justice and efficiency has been explained in more detail.

Why is the Common Law Efficient?

Some proponents of EAL have made a strong claim that the common law, ie, the rules of (mostly) private law (for example, torts and property) developed by (Anglo-American) judges largely conform to the dictates of economic efficiency and the needs of a market system. It is not claimed that judges have consciously pursued the goal of efficiency, but simply that the outcome of judicial rule making, whatever the doctrines and justifications supporting it, has tended to be compatible with economic efficiency.[22]

[18] There is some dispute as to the scientific status of these assumptions. For some of the proponents of EAL they do not have to correspond to verifiable phenomena; their truth lies in their potential for explanation and prediction. For others they cannot be completely severed from reality. See Johnston (1990: 1229 ff.).

[19] Kornhauser (1986: 238).

[20] Some versions of EAL show strong parallels to the formalist and realist conceptions of legal reasoning. See Johnston (1990: 1221 ff.), Chiassoni (1992: 275 ff.) and Mercado Pacheco (1994: 181 ff.).

[21] Both claims are strongly stated and defended in Posner (1990).

[22] 'It is as if the judges *wanted* to adopt rules, procedures, and case outcomes that would maximise society's wealth'. Posner (1990: 356).

Regardless of its truth or empirical content, this functional theory seems to be at best a restatement of old, respectable ideas,[23] and at worst, tautological, if not trivial.[24] What, then, is its purpose? It appears to have a strong polemic value, and herein lies its implicit normative attitude, in at least two respects:

—It purports to become a new language of legal analysis, by transforming, or even replacing, the language in which legal doctrine is usually expressed and justified;[25] and

—It strives to reduce judicial and legislative interventions ('redistribution') in the existing law to a minimum.

The possibility of adopting economic tools for examining and solving legal problems has an evident affinity with the balancing and weighing up of interests that contemporary, policy-oriented, utilitarian legal doctrines advocate and that judges frequently apply.[26] The adoption of economic tools is intended to make legal doctrine more precise, simple and scientific. At the same time, if judges, lawyers and legal clerks adopted the economic perspective, it could become a theory for the prediction of individual outcomes in concrete cases;[27] it would become, so to speak, a self-fulfilling explanation. Nevertheless, the economic modeling of legal rules is also capable of discovering new problems and of drawing attention, in a systematic, controlled way, to the different implications, perhaps even of a counter-intuitive nature, of a variety of legal solutions.

The second point clearly stems from a sympathy towards market solutions or, rather, from a deep-seated distrust of governmental, including judicial, efforts at wealth redistribution. Clearly, an efficient division of labor is favored in which the legislative branch can

> concentrate on catering to interest-group demands for wealth distribution and the judicial branch on meeting the broad-based social demand for efficient rules governing safety, property and transactions.[28]

[23] One is reminded of the Weberian investigation of the connections between law and modern capitalism. Obviously, modern law must be functional to capitalism in a general sense (Marxists claim just as much). The problem is to determine how and why, as well as what consequences derive from such determination for both the law and the economy. If it does not want to remain on a superficial or trivial level, functional explanation must take problems already solved by society as a starting point in order to show other possibilities and make comparisons possible. See Luhmann (1984: 83 ff.). For a critical examination of the relationship between capitalism and a legal order based on clear general norms and relatively formalistic modes of legal decision making, see Scheuerman (1999).

[24] Johnston (1990: 1233) points out that '*any legal rule can be shown to be efficient under appropriate background modeling assumptions*' (emphasis in the original) and this would be a direct and fundamental implication of Coase's Theorem.

[25] Johnston (1990: 1224 ff.). Mercado Pacheco (1994: 200 ff., 211 ff.) speaks of EAL as a new form of 'legal rhetoric'.

[26] Johnston (1990: 1224).

[27] Johnston (1990: 1226 f.). Another related topic is the importance of judges' economic training, or their lack thereof, for the solution of legal conflicts with economic consequences. See Raiteri (1991).

[28] Posner (1990: 361).

In other words: the common law is almost efficient *per se* and superior in this respect to statutory or legislated law. If a judge is called upon to solve a legal conflict, he or she has to follow the economic logic already embedded in existing rules, or, if such rules do not exist or are not found to be efficient, that same judge should mimic a market solution. This latter proposal derives from the Coase Theorem. In his essay on 'The Problem of Social Cost', Ronald H Coase tried to demonstrate that state intervention in the case of market failure was not automatically necessary if transaction costs allowed for an efficient exchange of property rights. Hence, when deciding a legal conflict, courts should prefer the solution that the parties themselves would have arrived at through voluntary exchange if transaction costs had not prevented them from doing so.[29]

The notion that judge-made law as almost automatically efficient and superior to legislated law is highly debatable. It would be just as easy to argue instead that the inefficiencies inherent in common law decision-making have contributed to the codification of Anglo-American law.[30] However, the thesis of the greater efficiency of common-law rules as compared to statutory law, together with the postulate of the desirable prevalence of market logic in judicial decision-making, should give way to the application of truly comparative criteria to the performance of the three institutions, that is, the market, the legislature, and the courts. In fact, it makes little sense to say that courts, the political process or the market, achieve a particular social goal, such as efficiency, better if only one institution is considered.[31] No necessary policy or institutional action can be derived from a social goal without first examining the relative advantages of those institutions for the achievement of that particular goal:[32]

> The proponents of law and economics believe its insights derive from the importance of the social goal of resource allocation efficiency. But resource allocation efficiency is connected to law and public policy through institutional choice, and its implications for law and public policy can only be realised through comparative institutional analysis.[33]

For these reasons, Neil K Komesar has attempted to develop a model of the comparative performance of the market, the political and the judicial processes, and to apply it to specific instances of public policy.[34] It is a simple economic model of institutional participation ('participation-centered approach'). In this model, the interaction of the benefits (distribution of stakes) and the costs of participation determine the nature of institutional participation.[35] The analysis

[29] Coase (1988: 95–156)
[30] See Yale Law Journal (1983: 863).
[31] Komesar (1994: 28, 133).
[32] Komesar (1994: 4f.).
[33] Komesar (1994: 10). Such a comparative analysis would be in the spirit of Coase, who tried to show the incomplete nature of an economic analysis that points to the existence of market imperfection as a sufficient condition for government intervention (29).
[34] Komesar (1994).
[35] Komesar (1994: 8).

is unfortunately complicated by the fact that the three institutions are not merely complementary. Instead, their performance is enhanced or diminished in a parallel fashion.[36]

In the judicial process, participation takes a binary form (plaintiff/defendant), while three distributions of stakes are considered in connection with it: uniform high, uniform low, and skewed distribution.[37] The three distributions mentioned affect the likelihood of litigation in the following terms:

—*Uniform low stakes* make litigation very unlikely, particularly if the higher threshold costs of access to the courts is taken into account;
—*Uniform high stakes* make litigation easier, but not necessarily more likely, considering that the three institutions work better in a parallel manner;
—A *skewed distribution* is affected by the availability of class actions and makes litigation more likely up to the point where the dispersion of the parties, especially of plaintiffs, raise the costs of access.

Nevertheless, in Komesar's view, the comparative advantage of adjudication lies rather in a 'shifted distribution'.[38] A shifted distribution occurs when an *ex ante* low distribution of stakes becomes a high uniform distribution *ex post*, as, for example, in accidents. Before an accident occurs, a high number of potential victims may face a low probability of injury. However, the actual occurrence of an accident usually entails a significant loss (high stakes) for a small number of victims.[39]

A shift also occurs in certain types of public decisionmaking that translate into statutes and administrative actions.[40] In building a majority and a minority, the decision has the effect of transferring stakes. It is usually a concentrated minority that challenges the decision against the state, which concentrates the majority's stakes. Litigation is less likely in the opposite direction, that is, a majority against a concentrated minority interest. However, in both cases, adjudication may counteract and deal with malfunctions of the political process. The higher threshold costs, the limited scale and the structural independence of adjudication isolate judges and juries. This gives adjudication an advantage for the correction of minority or majority bias, but it can also keep courts from deciding on a given social issue or on large sets of social issues.[41]

At this point, it is important to remember that the competence and scale of courts affect the institutional performance of adjudication when they interact

[36] Komesar (1994: 23).

[37] Komesar (1994: 128 ff.). The same binary form of participation (majority/minority) and stakes distribution is characteristic of the political process.

[38] Komesar (1994: 128 ff., 134 ff.).

[39] A shift does not always accompany actual injury. This is true, for example, of water or air pollution. Komesar (1994: 136).

[40] Komesar (1994: 136 f.).

[41] Komesar (1994: 128).

with the stakes and costs of participants.[42] Thus, the comparative advantages that the adjudicative process enjoys when shifted distributions occur may be less so in the context of substantive issues that severely strain the abilities of judges and juries or that require large allocations of scarce resources, since there are definite limits to the possibility of increasing resources affecting the competence and scale of the courts.[43]

The relatively detailed account of Komesar's model on the institutional performance of the adjudicative process has been necessary to qualify and contextualise the simple claim that judge-made law is more efficient than legislated law. While this model may coincide with the latter claim in certain respects (for example, the advantage of courts in the field of torts or in the enforcement of property rights), it also helps explain the phenomenon of public and constitutional law litigation, a central and pervasive feature of modern political life in many parts of the world. Secondly, the model raises the issue of a general framework for the analysis of political and legal institutions in modern society, not just those of the Anglo-American tradition. Finally, the model is also interesting in that it establishes a link between the relative efficiency of judicial decision-making and the resources available to the judicial machinery.[44] Thus, whatever its merits or faults, the functional explanation seems to be incomplete. It fails to give an account of *how* efficient legal rules are selected within the judicial process over inefficient, or less efficient, rules.

Some EAL scholars have attempted to answer this question.[45] Essentially, they give an invisible-hand explanation. They posit that the common law tends toward efficiency *in the long run*, since inefficient judicial outcomes would invite more litigation than efficient ones. Inefficient rules would be challenged and relitigated more often, until they were replaced by efficient rules. This thesis can, in turn, be linked to an equilibrium theory of judicial precedent,[46] according to which the existence of abundant, recent and informative precedents in an area of the law discourages litigation and promotes settlement. However, the informative value of precedents decays with time, meaning that litigation will rise again, producing more precedents, which, in turn, will cause a further reduction in the rate of litigation.

This theory has been subject to various criticisms. It has been argued, for example, that even if the value of overturning inefficient laws exceeds the value of overturning efficient laws, the party that values an allocation the most, that is, the efficient outcome, has to spend more on litigation, both intensively and

[42] Komesar (1994: 138 ff.). 'Competence' is defined as the ability of trials and triers to investigate, understand and make substantive social decisions. 'Scale' refers to the resources available to the judiciary and the constraints on the expansion of the size of the adjudicative process.

[43] For this reason, courts usually resort to a variety of methods to reduce excess demand. See Komesar (1994: 146 f.).

[44] This is another formulation of the relationship between error costs (EC) and direct costs (DC) indicated above.

[45] See Kornhauser (1986: 244 ff.), Cooter/Ulen (1988: 492 ff.).

[46] Posner (1990: 358 ff.).

extensively. Thus, the bias towards social efficiency may well be offset by the inclination of plaintiffs to challenge laws only when they can capture a large part of the precedent's value, without considering the social costs that the continuation of an inefficient law will impose on other parties.[47]

Other scholars have maintained, on the assumption that both parties have equal future stakes, that rather more litigation is to be expected in areas of the law where there is already a tendency toward efficiency. Such a tendency 'will be further strengthened by litigation creating additional precedents,' whereas areas 'dominated by inefficient rules will tend to become dormant in terms of litigation activity.'[48] With asymmetrical stakes, however, the conclusion that there will be little litigation in legal areas dominated by inefficient rules is considerably weakened.

In the same line of reasoning—ie, assuming that litigants have a future stake in litigation—the invisible-hand explanation may lead to the very visible interests of attorneys. Based on a study of the evolution of products liability law, Paul H Rubin and Martin J Bailey have developed a model that also takes the (financial) interest of lawyers into account.[49] According to this model, not only will the law 'come to favor the more concentrated class of parties with an interest in the law', but 'the same litigation process that leads the law to favor concentrated parties will also lead, at least in some branches of law, to favor attorneys.'[50] Consequently, the theory predicts how attorneys will behave and the impact of such behaviour on the law.

Rubin and Bailey marshal some evidence to support their predictions. They show, for example, how attorneys have organised themselves as an interest group that has been active in giving the law its current shape; how changes in the law favourable to lawyers have resulted in an increased demand for their services and in higher (greater-than-equilibrium) earnings; or the extent to which the reduced consideration given to private agreements by the courts has translated into increased uncertainty and unpredictability (inefficiency) of the law.[51]

All these considerations suggest that even if the common law (judge-made law) tends towards efficiency over time, it will not do so in a general, unqualified manner. If the unconscious forces favouring efficiency are present, they are nevertheless weak, and additional assumptions are necessary to explain whether and how efficient rules will prevail more often than inefficient rules.[52] But inefficiency may also be the result of the law's evolution through litigation, either because attorneys' interests will have a strong impact on it, or because inefficient rules will become dormant. Both circumstances would invite legislative intervention in the last resort.

47 See Cooter/Ulen (1988: 495 ff.) and Kornhauser (1986: 245 f.).
48 Landes/Posner (1979: 261).
49 Rubin/Bailey (1994).
50 Rubin/Bailey (1994: 807).
51 Rubin/Bailey (1994: 814 ff., 821, 823 ff.).
52 See Cooter/Ulen (1988: 495 ff.).

These criticisms and considerations notwithstanding, the evolutionary theory being discussed here seems to have a significant potential for helping explain the forces and incentives that influence legal change and evolution and for linking them with related socio-legal research and theory. Thus, for example, the implication suggested by the evolutionary explanation that litigants may be able to shape legal rules regardless of the preferences of judges and legislators could be linked to Komesar's analysis of the relative costs and stakes of resorting to litigation,[53] or to Luhmann's proposition of a circular relationship of mutual observation between legislation and adjudication.[54] The assumptions about the incentives to litigate and relitigate in a certain legal area could be compared, for example, with Galanter's idea of litigation having 'a life of its own,' partly independent of underlying events,[55] or with other socio-legal explanations of the social factors that govern litigation rates.[56] The equilibrium explanation of precedents could be tested through specific research on the incentives social actors have to litigate and the legal precedents they have to produce to solve uncertainties and guide their future exchanges.[57]

The Uses of Efficiency, or Judges as Economists?

A much-debated issue in connection with EAL as a *normative* approach has been the usefulness of the concept of efficiency as a criterion for evaluating the law and judicial decisions,[58] particularly when compared with the value of justice.

Some EAL proponents have not only made the claim that judge-made law conforms to the requirements of economic efficiency, but have also explicitly demanded that judges decide according to its postulates, although not necessar-

53 Komesar (1994).

54 Luhmann (1993: 302).

55 Galanter (1990).

56 See some of the contributions in vol 24, no 2 of the *Law and Society Review* (1990), on the longitudinal study of courts and litigation. In an essay included in this issue, two economists, Cooter and Rubinfeld (1990: 533) argue that socio-legal research on this topic has not paid sufficient attention to the more rigorous economic models, which would be relevant for such a purpose.

57 A study on the London reinsurance market shows how, after a period of informal dispute settlement businessmen began to increasingly resort to litigation. See Stammel (1998).

58 On the various concepts of efficiency applied to the evaluation of the law, see the general discussion in Coleman (1980). See also Margolis (1987), who discusses two definitions of efficiency, which are implicit or explicit in the law-and-economics literature. The two definitions are as follows:

Definition 1: 'An efficient legal system is one in which property rights are assigned and liability rules are formulated so as to duplicate the allocation of rights obtained by a market in a world in which transaction costs are zero' (at 472).

Definition 2: 'An efficient legal system is one in which property rights are assigned and liability rules are formulated so that the value of the things present in society, as measured by willingness to pay, is maximised over alternative legal environments, given the costs of transacting' (at 473–474).

He concludes that the first definition is easier to say 'but both impossible and undesirable to achieve'. The second definition 'is more awkward to specify, but it is more attractive as a norm' and provides a more useful positive paradigm. It requires that the court 'minimise the losses due to transactions and foregone gains from trade' and that it takes account 'of transaction costs it is unable to affect' (482).

ily as an exclusive or explicit goal.[59] This has elicited strong opposition from those who consider that *justice*, rather than efficiency, is the proper goal for judges to achieve. The best example of such opposition can be found in Ronald Dworkin's polemic against utilitarianism and other policy-oriented legal doctrines, including EAL.[60]

Of course, it is always possible to deny efficiency *any legal relevance* without making reference to the concept of justice, arguing that the law is inefficient by nature and design, meaning that any effort to make it efficient must be doomed to failure.[61] While this position seems appropriate for sparking a lively debate, it is so drastic that it borders on self-defeat, since it seems to deny the law any possibility of meeting certain legitimate social expectations.

A far more productive approach, because it is much more restricted, is to deny a *particular concept of efficiency* its usefulness for evaluating the law. Thus, for example, Guido Calabresi has argued that Pareto efficiency and similar concepts are useless, not only because they disregard the problem of the initial distribution of entitlements or the subjective feelings of individuals when a comparative change in their situation occurs.[62] More importantly, such concepts view efficiency-enhancing changes as a movement towards a boundary previously defined, *as if transaction costs did not exist*. However, since transaction costs *do* exist, any movement *towards* the boundary also constitutes a movement *of* the boundary. It is then obvious why such a point could have important implications for our topic. If courts are regarded as institutions that have their origin in the existence of transaction costs in society and if their operation has an impact on these costs, any attempt to make them more efficient will involve a movement *of* the boundary and will therefore have to take into account the serious difficulties that arise from trying to measure and evaluate such a change.

Finally, others have raised the problem of the *authority* judges could possible have to impose certain desirable social polices, such as efficiency or distributional justice, on the litigants' interests in a private dispute. Although defensible and justified in economic arguments, global interests and social goals run counter to the common sense view of law as being concerned with rights and obligations, which it is the court's duty to enforce, rather than to create.[63] However, this argument seems to overlook the fact that adjudication is never solely concerned with private interests. Furthermore, to the extent that judges

[59] Posner (1973: 399 ff.), Cooter/Ulen (1988: 497 ff.), Cooter (1995: 57 ff.).

[60] See Dworkin (1980a and b).

[61] Cf for example, Seagle (1952: 1), from which the following quotation has been extracted: 'The most striking characteristic of law as it has existed in democratic societies has been its inefficiency. This statement must not be understood in the sense merely that the law of such societies represents a system which is designed to work efficiently, but which unfortunately breaks down in practice as the result of the ineptitude of judges, lawyers, and executive officers of government. By its very nature, law is doomed to be inefficient; its innermost structure and basic machinery produce inefficiency; and particularly in democratic societies it is often made or kept inefficient with painstaking deliberation. Law may be described, indeed, as the science of inefficiency.'

[62] Calabresi (1990, and especially 1991).

[63] Coleman (1980: 550 f.).

should decide according to the existing law, the law itself (for example, in the form of a statutory provision) may incorporate efficiency as a criterion or as an explicit authority, on which judges can rely in order to decide legal conflicts from an economic point of view.

This point leads us to the issue concerning the *training* and the *ability* of judges to decide according to economic principles. While the answer to this question should not be problematic when economic matters are directly involved,[64] the debate provoked by the use of efficiency as a general criterion for evaluating the outcomes of adjudication suggests the need to consider this issue from a broader perspective. We should ask a more general question about the penetration of economic rationality in the law and about the crisis and evolution of court functions in the light of economic realities.[65] From this point of view, EAL would not only be a manifestation of an intellectual movement or of particular legal developments in specific countries, but also a sign of the closer interdependence between law and economy in contemporary society.

Efficiency in Litigation and Settlement: An Economic Model

This section will present some theoretical and empirical contributions of EAL to the analysis of litigation. Such contributions concern, for example, the factors that influence the decision to litigate or to settle, the implications of this decision for the outcome of a judicial proceeding, as well as the incentives and constraints faced by the participants that affect the speedy and efficient disposition of a case. These contributions will then be compared with other social science perspectives.[66] The goal at this point is not to criticise the law-and-economics approach from such perspectives, resorting to the all-too-easy argument that individual decisions are not merely influenced by cost or economic rationality considerations. Instead, the aim is to show similarities and differences in approach. The contrast should allow us to clarify the place and significance of efficiency in the judicial process, particularly with respect to its conflictive coexistence with 'justice' as a legal value, as well as to examine the theoretical and methodological relationships between both perspectives.

Before proceeding to examine certain relevant examples of economic and other social science research on litigation, a preliminary question should be clarified. EAL, in its Anglo-American version, has established a necessary connection between the decision to litigate a dispute and the decision to settle it. In conventional terms, settlement is the decision to enter into an agreement with the other party that will dispose of the underlying dispute short of an authoritative judicial decision on the merits. Thus, both decisions spring from the same

[64] See the preliminary remarks of Remiche (1985). See also Rescigno (1985) and Raiteri (1991).

[65] See Raiteri (1992).

[66] Socio-legal research on dispute resolution and litigation is already so vast, that I shall concentrate on a few representative essays and studies.

decision-making process, forming mutually excluding choices. It is further asserted by the proponents of this model that settlement costs are normally much lower than litigation costs, meaning that the fraction of cases settled is an important determinant of the total direct cost of legal dispute resolution.[67]

The question is whether this link between litigation and settlement (and the concomitant proposition that settlement is usually less costly and, therefore, more efficient than litigation) reflects only a particular feature of a specific procedural model—the Anglo-American adversarial trial, both civil and criminal—which would render it inapplicable to a different procedural model, or whether it is a general assumption, applicable to any form of litigation.

This is not an irrelevant question, given the pervasiveness of settlement and plea bargaining in the United States legal system. It is a well-known fact that an extremely high percentage of civil and criminal cases in that country (around 90 per cent or even more) never go to trial. Settlement in civil cases, both in and out of court, as well as plea bargaining in the criminal process, are the established, accepted and even consciously promoted mechanisms for avoiding a costly trial. However, settlement (and likewise plea bargaining) has been strongly criticised as a 'problematic technique for streamlining dockets'.[68] Among other criticisms, it is argued that settlement may be unfair to the weaker party, who is forced to accept less than her due, and that courts have other important functions, such as authoritative rule-making, which go beyond the resolution of private disputes. Thus, if justice fails to be served, society may unwittingly be paying a price.[69]

In my view, the economic approach is capable of offering a general model of the conditions and factors that affect the decision to litigate or to settle a dispute at any stage, both before and after a formal suit has been filed. In the economic model, settlement is not defined as a decision that is necessarily obliged to identify with a particular institutional practice. Settlement can simply be described as a form of termination of a legal dispute other than through final judgment. In a hypothetical procedural system, in which any case termination other than through final judgment were prohibited, the rational calculation for deciding to litigate or to settle out of court would just have to be made *before* the filing of any formal suit. In fact, in civil-law countries, the termination of cases through means other than final judgment is also common,[70] so even a judgment by default in a non-contested case is regarded as a 'settlement' in this sense.

On the other hand, it is true that, in economic terms, and by definition, agreement is the most efficient form of exchange. In a world without transaction costs, no agreement would come into being if it did not make both parties better off than before. However, in a world where transaction costs make

[67] Posner (1973: 417).

[68] Fiss (1984: 1075).

[69] Fiss (1984: 1085).

[70] See, for example, the data offered by Blankenburg (1980: 54) on different types of civil proceedings in Germany.

agreements difficult, bargaining is frequently carried out under the 'shadow of the law'. This means that the terms of an agreement will be influenced by the perception parties have of the entitlements or rights granted them by the law. Whenever the parties have an inconsistent view of their respective entitlements, their dispute will lead to litigation not because of uncertainty about the law, or because an agreement might still not be mutually advantageous, but mainly because *divergent* expectations about the *potential* outcome of litigation and the stakes involved preclude such an agreement. This is the basic assumption underlying the general economic model of litigation.

The Selection of Disputes for Litigation

In 1984, George L Priest and Benjamin Klein, professors of law and economics, respectively, published a highly influential paper on 'The Selection of Disputes for Litigation.'[71] In this essay, Priest and Klein take the problem of the representativeness of appellate cases for the systematic knowledge of the legal system as their starting point. If appellate cases were representative of the number and type of legal disputes in society, their study would enable inferences to be drawn about how legal rules affect behaviour or about the generation of legal disputes. However, the authors contend, most legal scholars 'either ignore the problem of the representativeness of appellate decisions or presume representativeness', generally assuming that the facts of disputes that reach trial or appeal 'resemble the facts of disputes that are settled'.[72]

Furthermore, it is also very common 'to infer the influence of a legal standard or the attitudes of judges or juries toward plaintiffs or defendants by observing the proportion of cases in which plaintiffs recover verdicts'.[73] Such inference, however, cannot be accurate if litigated disputes are not representative of the entire class of underlying disputes.[74] And although legal scholars have expressed concern about the peculiar sample of cases that reach trial and appeal, none has been able to develop an accepted means of adjusting the analysis in response to the problem.[75]

Therefore, Priest and Klein attempt to develop a model of the litigation process that clarifies the relationship between the set of disputes settled and the set litigated. According to their model, the determinants of settlement and litigation are solely economic,

> including the expected costs to parties of favorable or adverse decisions, the information the parties possess about the likelihood of success at trial, and the direct costs of litigation and settlement.[76]

[71] Priest/Klein (1984).
[72] Priest/Klein (1984: 3).
[73] Priest/Klein (1984: 3).
[74] Priest/Klein (1984: 4).
[75] Priest/Klein (1984: 2).
[76] Priest/Klein (1984: 4).

The most important assumption is that potential litigants form rational estimates of the likely decision, 'whether it is based on applicable legal precedent or judicial or jury bias'.[77] The model shows that the disputes selected for litigation, as opposed to settlement,[78] constitute neither a random[79] nor a representative sample of the set of all disputes.[80]

Thus, disputes are selected for litigation in a specific way. They will be concentrated more heavily among disputes where the probability estimates of the parties of a plaintiff victory, assuming their error as equivalent, lies closer to the decision standard, and the difference between those estimates is likely to increase. When the difference is likely to be small, the parties will be more able to agree on settlement terms in order to save litigation costs.[81]

Priest and Klein derive an interesting implication from their model: the so-called 50 per cent 'rule'. This rule states that

> the individual maximising decisions of the parties will create a strong bias toward a rate of success for plaintiffs at trial or appellants at appeal of 50 percent, regardless of the substantive standard of law,

as the parties' error in their estimates diminishes and the litigation rate decreases.[82] To put it more simply:

> the process of negotiation tends to weed out the extremely weak or extremely strong cases through settlement, thereby pushing the win rates on those cases that are ultimately adjudicated toward 50 percent.[83]

This tendency remains if symmetrical stakes between the parties are assumed.[84] Differential stakes will affect the rate of litigation and the proportion of victories

[77] Priest/Klein (1984: 4).

[78] A dispute is defined as 'any occasion in which a plaintiff asserts a claim for some injury against a defendant'. A dispute is regarded as litigated only if a verdict is rendered, and all terminations of the dispute short of a verdict are regarded as a settlement. Priest/Klein (1984: 6).

[79] The model proposed by Priest and Klein derives from the economic approach developed by William Landes and Richard Posner. According to the approach suggested by Landes and Posner, the principal determinant of litigation is the absolute difference in the parties' estimates of the likelihood of success. It is assumed that litigated cases are a random sample of the underlying disputes, an assumption that is challenged and corrected by Priest and Klein. Priest/Klein (1984: 4–5, footnote 16).

[80] Priest/Klein (1984: 4).

[81] Priest/Klein (1984: 14 ff.).

[82] Priest/Klein (1984: 5, 17 ff.).

[83] Siegelmann/Donohue III (1995: 428).

[84] Other simplifying assumptions of the model are: the distribution of initial disputes is determined exogenously; litigants do not engage in strategic behavior; standards exist for resolving disputes and juries or judges apply specific standards consistently in disputes of one type or another; provided it is consistent, a decision may be based on precedent or personal bias; stakes are symmetrical to the parties when described solely in terms of expected judgment; thus, it is assumed that the judgment will not have an effect on the subsequent behavior of potential litigants and therefore may be particularly inappropriate with respect to the settlement of disputes considered for appeal, litigation costs to parties greater than settlement costs, a restriction that only implies that the parties can gain more by settling than by litigating a dispute, and will do so unless they differ to an extent greater than D Priest/Klein (1984: 7, 12 f.).

for either party. Attitudes of litigants towards risk can be analysed in the same fashion.[85]

Priest and Klein then present empirical evidence related to the selection hypothesis. This evidence comprises data they themselves have compiled, together with a review of empirical studies that offer information on the outcomes of contested civil cases.[86] They caution the reader not to draw the conclusion that the hypothesis has been confirmed by the data, since definitive measurements of the variables that are relevant to the theory are missing.[87]

Nevertheless, they manage to provide a fairly convincing account of a wide variety of data and empirical studies, ranging from the data of plaintiff verdicts in contested civil actions tried to juries between 1959 and 1979 in Cook County, Illinois, to the discussion of the six- or twelve-person jury in the 1970s in the United States. When compared with empirical data, the selection hypothesis allows Priest and Klein to criticise the methodology of certain studies, such as those that attempt to measure the impact of judicial attitudes on case outcomes. Priest and Klein argue that the parties themselves will incorporate judicial bias into their calculations.[88] In this respect, the standard of decision operates neutrally, while the terms on which cases are settled may reveal powerful judicial biases.[89]

The selection hypothesis of Priest and Klein has been the subject of a continuing debate, most of it directed at finding support or counter-evidence for the 50 per cent rule in different areas of litigation.[90] I shall just mention two of these that essentially confirm and extend the Priest-Klein model.

The first study concerns the selection of employment discrimination disputes for litigation.[91] Using a time-series record of all employment discrimination litigation in US federal trial courts over a 20-year period, the study demonstrates that the plaintiff win rate is not the same across the business cycle, but varies 'systematically with the health of the macro-economy, falling during slumps and rising during booms'.[92] Since the win rate fluctuates significantly less than the settlement rate, this means that only a *partial* selection is at work. However,

[85] Priest/Klein (1984: 24 ff., 27).
[86] Priest/Klein (1984: 30 ff.).
[87] Priest/Klein (1984: 30).
[88] With respect to this point, see, for example, Ashenfelter *et al.* (1995), who examine the impact of judges' characteristics and political background in three American federal trial courts on the basis of the mass of randomly assigned civil rights cases in a particular year, rather than of published opinions. They find that the individual judge has a more modest influence on the outcome of the mass of cases than on the subset of cases leading to a published opinion. They conclude that characteristics of the 'judges or the political party of the judge's appointing president are not significant predictors of judicial decisions' (at 257). Read in light of the Priest/Klein hypothesis, this result would seem to be more indicative of the selection effect by litigants than of the actual influence of the judges' ideology on their opinions.
[89] Priest/Klein (1984: 37).
[90] See the literature listed in Appendix A to Kessler *et al.* (1996: 258 f.).
[91] Siegelmann/Donohue III (1995).
[92] Siegelmann/Donohue III (1995: 431).

although the Priest-Klein model is slightly modified, there is strong evidence that, as predicted, the weak cases are weeded out through settlement.[93]

The second study, based on data from 3,259 cases decided by the US Seventh Circuit Court of Appeals between 1982 and 1987, tries to demonstrate that violations of the assumptions implicit in the model by specific case characteristics can account for divergences in the win rates of plaintiffs.[94] The seven case characteristics are:

—Differential stakes.
—Differential sophistication of the parties.
—Inaccurate measurement of plaintiff victory, or damages vs. liability.
—Legal standards favor one side.
—Settlement costs are high in relation to litigation costs.
—High awards (risk aversion).
—Agency effects.

The study concludes that 'among the cases that conform more closely to the assumptions underlying the simple divergent expectations model, the plaintiff win rate is closer to 50 per cent.'[95]

The Priest-Klein hypothesis is certainly not the only available economic model for explaining the selection of disputes for litigation. A competing view, for example, describes a trial as an outcome of the parties' strategic behavior, not of their inconsistent predictions on what the court will do.[96] But regardless of the issue of which is the more accurate model,[97] it is clear that the Priest-Klein hypothesis has been successful in sparking a scientific discussion and in suggesting new problems and avenues for scientific inquiry.[98] In any case, it shows that disputants will usually settle their disputes out of court, because a rational consideration of their reciprocal chances for success will lead them to prefer a mutually advantageous agreement. Thus, the courts will deal only with a small (if biased) sector of legal disputes, where a significant degree of uncertainty prevails, a result that may be viewed as socially efficient.

[93] Siegelmann/Donohue III (1995: 432).

[94] Kessler *et al.* (1996).

[95] Kessler *et al.* (1996: 233).

[96] Cf Gross/Syverud (1991: 321). The classic reference here is the essay by Mnookin/Kornhauser (1979).

[97] Four essays that qualify and modify the Priest-Klein model are those of Eisenberg (1990), Hylton (1993), Thomas (1995) and Siegelman/Waldfogel (1999). See also Stanley/Coursey (1990). Gross/Syverud (1991: 321 f.) analysed a sample of civil jury trials in California that included data on settlement negotiations and the size of the jury award. They conclude that the Priest-Klein model provides a useful starting point for examining actual litigation, but that strong evidence of strategic bargaining could also be found. Moreover, there was 'more than a hint that such bargaining is a major force in determining which cases fail to settle' (at 322).

[98] Whether inspired by Priest-Klein or not, an interesting problem for research is the 'selection of cases for publication'. Published decisions normally constitute the official face of the law. However, it can be shown that such publication is biased, that the relationship between published and unpublished decisions follows regular and predictable factors and has consequences for a scientific study of the law. See, for example, Siegelmann/Donohue III (1990), Atkins (1990) and Serverin (1993).

The Economics of Criminal Justice

An economic model of criminal behaviour and criminal law is also based on the principle of the rational calculus of costs and benefits and on the assumption of maximising behaviour by human beings who are capable of responding to the incentives and disincentives contained in legal norms. Such a model focuses primarily on *enforcement*.[99] It therefore seeks to explain the deterrent effects of punishment, which can simply be regarded as the price for engaging in non-market activity designed to reduce the level of that activity to what it would be if it were provided in a reasonably efficient market, as well as the optimum severity of sanctions.[100] The deterrent effect is partly dependent on the probability of prosecution and conviction, ie, the adequate operation of the criminal justice system. The economic model therefore also has to explain the incentives and choices faced by criminal defendants, prosecutors and judges once criminal proceedings are underway, as well as their outcomes.

Taking advantage of the obvious parallels between civil litigation and the criminal justice process in the Anglo-American legal tradition, the most visible being the parallel between settlement and plea-bargaining, law-and-economics scholars have provided an economic analysis of the criminal process with empirical tests.[101] Not surprisingly, they have found that the plea-bargaining process can be characterised as a 'market transaction' in which the prosecutor 'buys' guilty pleas in exchange for the promise of sentence leniency.[102] Plea-bargaining regulates the number of trials and helps explain the severity of sentences when defendants are tried and convicted. Overall, the same variables that are at work in civil litigation operate here: plea-bargaining as the less costly option as compared to a trial;[103] the effect of the defendants estimate of the probability of being convicted by trial in relation to the prosecutor's estimate; the role of the defendant's aversion to risk, etc.[104]

[99] Panther (1995: 367) and Miceli (1991: 3).

[100] Posner (1979: 136), Panther (1995: 366 ff.) and Savona (1990).

[101] See Landes (1971), Rhodes (1976), and Elder (1989).

[102] Rhodes (1976: 311 f.).

[103] This means, for example, that defendants not released on bail show a lower propensity to go to trial, and much more so if the opportunity costs of a trial are increased by court delay. Landes (1971: 99 ff.).

[104] This model once again raises the question of its generality and applicability to the Continental legal tradition, which officially ignores the practice of plea bargaining, although this may be changing in some cases. The reply is similar to the one given when an equivalent problem was mentioned with respect to civil litigation: if actors in the Continental criminal justice system also feel under pressure to regulate the number of trials, on the one hand, and a need to predict a certain outcome, on the other, they will resort to practices that accomplish a function similar to plea bargaining, perhaps at an earlier stage of the proceedings and in an informal way.

Litigation from a Socio-legal Perspective

Access and Outcomes

Sociology of law (hereinafter, SL) has developed what one could call, in a parallel formula to the economic approach, a model of the *social selection* of disputes for litigation. Such a model tries to identify and explain the social factors that attend the emergence of disputes in society, their successive stages and transformations, including their framing or otherwise in legal terms. It purports to describe the multiple courses of action available to the disputants, particularly the conditions that govern the likelihood of resorting to legal dispute-resolution institutions, such as the courts. And finally, it seeks to establish the influence of social factors and conditions on the outcomes of judicial proceedings. In short, such a model would consist of three interrelated pieces of theory: a theory of social conflicts, a theory of the mobilisation of law, and a theory of legal disputes in the courts.[105] In so far as such a sociological model has been able to overcome an over-narrowly defined concern with access to the law or access to justice,[106] it would have to show evident points of contact, as well as visible differences in conception and scope, with the economic approach.

The most evident point of contact may lie in the idea that the law normally has to be mobilised or set in motion by either state officials or citizens.[107] Whether this is viewed from the standpoint of social control[108] or from the perspective of citizens, who may consider the law and legal institutions as a resource and an instrument for the attainment of individual or collective goals, the theory cannot fail to frame the problem, to a greater or lesser degree, in terms of a *decision*, or of several decisions, whether or not to mobilise the law.[109] If we say 'decision' or 'choice', we almost invariably imply other concepts that have a close affinity with or are shared by the language of economics, such as self-interest, rationality, costs, stakes, alternatives, expectations, etc. This is particularly true of civil or private law litigation, where such affinity may stem from the fact that the law itself follows an *entrepreneurial model*,[110] either because it relies on self-interested individuals who are free to act according to social concepts of rationality or because it is more directly conceived of as an extension of market activity.

[105] Blankenburg (1980: 37). Van Loon/Delrue/van Wambeke (1995: 379) distinguish three approaches in research studies on civil litigation: the social process of disputes and its dynamics; the role and functions of the different actors; the longitudinal analysis of court activities.

[106] The almost inescapable conclusion is that disadvantaged members of society are such partly because they are not able to effectively claim their legal rights. See Zemans (1982: 989 ff.).

[107] Black (1973). See also Blankenburg (1980; 1994a).

[108] As Black (1973) does explicitly.

[109] Cf Zemans (1982: 992 ff.). Griffiths (1983: 174): 'The theory of the litigation process is, in short, a *theory of choice*, specifically applicable to normative conflict' (emphasis added).

[110] Black (1973: 16), Zemans (1982: 993 f.).

There are many important socio-legal studies that implicitly or explicitly adopt an economic or rational decision-making approach to the mobilisation of law and the social selection of disputes for litigation.[111] These include, for example, the Civil Litigation Research Project (CLRP)[112] or the so-called 'longitudinal studies of litigation.'[113] The CLRP adopted a 'disputes-focused approach', within which it was possible to analyse, in an explicit manner, the costs of civil litigation (litigation as an investment process) and the available alternative *fora* to the civil courts. More specifically, the concern with costs had two dimensions: a description of the amount and nature of expenditures made by individuals and organisations in civil-dispute processing settings, and an explanation of the factors, such as stakes and outcomes, that affect the level of investment in civil controversies.[114] Longitudinal studies of litigation, by contrast, examine the factors (for example, economic growth) that explain the behaviour of litigation rates over time.[115] They deal with aggregates of decisions, trends, and variables that refer, explicitly or not, to the kind of problems that lie at the core of economic reflection, such as growth or static and dynamic equilibria.[116]

The rational decision-making assumptions that apply to the mobilisation of the law should also help explain the behaviour of the parties once a judicial proceeding is underway and, most importantly, the outcomes of such proceedings. A significant proportion of socio-legal studies on litigation concern the relationship between the social characteristics of litigants and case outcomes, focusing on those characteristics that influence litigants' success rates in civil litigation (or, likewise, the probability of being given a conviction in a criminal trial). In this respect, socio-legal studies have taught us that social class, gender, race, etc, but also the previous relationship between the parties, do matter.[117] More generally, we know now that the likelihood of various social groups appearing and winning as plaintiffs or defendants before the courts is also different (for example, it is more likely for a business actor to sue an individual and win, than vice versa) and that these probabilities are linked to the interests of litigants and the nature of their involvement in the judicial process.

Similarly, organisational studies of the judicial process have attempted to observe directly the incentives and constraints that affect the production of judicial outcomes. Some of these studies coincide with the basic assumptions of and the empirical evidence supporting the economic approach. Thus, for example, the prevalence of plea-bargaining in American criminal courts as a cheaper,

[111] It is not suggested that all socio-legal research on litigation follows or is akin to a rational-choice model.

[112] See the Final Report by Trubek *et al.* (1983).

[113] See Trubek (1980–1).

[114] Trubek (1980–1: 486).

[115] See Friedman (1990).

[116] Cf Cooter/Rubinfeld (1990: 540 ff.).

[117] See, for example, Douglas (1994) and Black (1989).

speedier alternative to trial can be traced back to the informal norms and practices that ensure the smooth disposition of cases by the courtroom workgroup.[118] Defendants who dare disturb the smooth operation of the courtroom workgroup by demanding a trial risk a harsher punishment if convicted, thereby effectively reducing the 'price' of settlement.

In short: litigants' differential success rates linked to organisational advantages, longer-term strategies, and economies of scale ('one-shot vs. repeat players')[119] can also be easily accommodated in the economic model as asymmetric stakes that modify outcomes in a predictable fashion.[120]

An interesting consequence of the adoption of the rational decision-making approach to the explanation of judicial outcomes is that the law itself must be seen, to a large degree, as *indeterminate*, ie, as having no real influence on the resolution of the dispute.[121] Both the economic and the socio-legal model seek to explain outcomes in terms other than as an effect of the legal standards that govern dispute resolution. However, whereas rational decision-making in the economic model means that litigants *internalise* (or know about) all factors affecting their decision to litigate or to settle, including the applicable legal standards and judicial or jury bias, the socio-legal model tries to identify *individual exogenous* factors that contribute to a *particular* outcome.

Thus, socio-legal accounts of litigation can and actually do differ in many ways from the assumptions of the economic model. A sociological model of litigation is subject to different scientific requirements, which to a certain extent are more demanding than those that an economic approach must satisfy.[122] While economic analyses begin with simple (and often unrealistic) assumptions that allow them to 'assume away' the elements studied in sociology,[123] the sociological model, for example, will not treat conflicts as exogenous,[124] since it is extremely interested in observing and explaining the emergence and transformation of social conflicts, nor will it necessarily accept a linear continuum in the development of disputes or, for that matter, the existence of homogenous

118 See, for example, Eisenstein/Jacob (1977) or Nardulli (1978).

119 Galanter (1974). See also the special issue of the *Law and Society Review*, vol 33, no 4, 1999 revisiting the impact and implications of Galanter's classic essay. For a study that contributes evidence to the so-called 'party-capability theory,' see MacCormick (1994). For another study that found that political factors, rather than litigation resources, explained litigation success in abortion cases decided by US federal district courts between 1973 and 1990, see Yarnold (1995).

120 As in Priest/Klein (1984: 28), who refer explicitly to Galanter's classic essay.

121 When socio-legal scholars have qualms at the thought that the law may actually *govern* the outcome of cases, ie, that plaintiffs and defendants may win because the law is on their side, they rely on statistics and probability to somehow neutralise such a disquieting possibility. See, for example, Bender/Schumacher (1980: 11). The economic model has an explanation for this: the selection process.

122 See Griffiths (1983: 159), who defines the requirements that a sociological theory of litigation has to fulfill in order to be scientifically satisfying.

123 De Geest (1995: 305).

124 One of the assumptions of Priest/Klein (1984: 7).

conditions of rationality across social fields.[125] Cost-benefit analysis is regarded as important for explaining decisions related to dispute-processing, either as an appropriate model for shedding light on certain issues[126] or as a factor that despite being active throughout the decision process,[127] is not viewed as a sufficient basis for a comprehensive explanation.

This is again exemplified by the CLRP. The initial framework was an economic model of decision-making as determined by the costs and stakes involved in a dispute. It was felt, however, that the economic model would not fully predict disputant decisions, so other factors which could cause disputants to deviate from dispute trajectories predicted by the economic model were added, such as the past and future relationship between the parties or the nature of the dispute itself.[128] Likewise, several studies that examine the practice of plea-bargaining in the criminal justice process do not accept 'case pressure' as the sole or even predominant explaining factor.[129] It is also hardly surprising to learn that the decision to appeal is not exclusively governed by cost-benefit considerations.[130]

Procedural Justice

The label 'procedural justice' covers a rich, thought-provoking body of research in the field of social psychology, which is also increasingly being taken into account by socio-legal scholars in the field of litigation and alternative dispute resolution.[131] Research on procedural justice is especially interesting for the purposes of this section. Since it has managed to empirically implement a distinct concept of justice as it applies to judicial and other legal proceedings, it allows one to examine the relationship between the procedural values of 'efficiency' and 'justice' as an empirical problem too, rather than just on the basis of abstract speculation. It should be noted that procedural justice studies focus predominantly on subjective attitudes, values and opinions, although some of its proponents have also investigated the objective consequences of these beliefs. Similarly, the economic approach is based on the assumption of maximisation

[125] Cf Griffiths (1983: 174 f.) who criticises the linear, court-centered approaches to litigation and links the specific trajectories of disputes to the features of semi-autonomous social fields.

[126] Griffiths (1983: 188 ff.).

[127] Zemans (1982: 999 ff.).

[128] Trubek (1980–1: 498 f.). See also the factors discussed by Zemans (1982: 1003 ff.).

[129] See, for example, Heumann (1978), Feeley (1979). An empirical study conducted in Germany on informal negotiations in the prosecution of general and economic crimes (Bussmann/Lüdemann 1995: 5 ff., 149 f., 163 ff.) attempted to link these practices to time problems and found some overall relevance (*i.e.* for prosecutors, judges and defenders considered as a group) for this factor, together with material and legal problems, interests in restitution or procedural climate. The degree of relevance changed or was actually found to be non-existent when the different actors and the type of procedure were analysed separately.

[130] Barclay (1997).

[131] See Röhl (1993a; 1997), who gives an overview of this field of research and establishes connections with related issues and research in the sociology and philosophy of law, especially in the German language.

as an unchanging motivation for the individual, which also allows for the prediction and assessment of objective behavior.

Research on procedural justice encompasses a broad variety of problems, results, interpretations and theories at the interface between different approaches and disciplines.[132] As already noted, however, its common initial problem generally lies in the attitudes and evaluations of persons who participate in legal and other procedures. While procedural justice theorists may disagree as to the specific factors that are important in explaining the fairness of procedures, they all agree 'that people are remarkably sensitive to the process and procedures they experience in encounters with the law'.[133] Thus, if a central proposition had to be drawn from the large body of empirical research on procedural justice, it could be as follows: the process for reaching social decisions has a value of its own for participants,[134] and this value is independent, to a degree that can be subject to measurement, from the value of the outcome for such participants.

This central proposition of procedural justice theory can be used to discuss, and contradict, three assumptions about the efficiency of judicial procedures, as they might be advocated by a purely economic approach:

—The 'inquisitorial' style of judicial procedure, because it places a higher degree of control in the hands of the judge, is more efficient and therefore to be preferred over the 'adversarial' model of litigation.[135]

—Settlement and other less formal mechanisms of dispute resolution, such as arbitration, mediation and conciliation, are more efficient in terms of costs and delay and, therefore, to be preferred over formal adjudication.

—The expected value of a judgment, as well as the costs and delay associated with judicial proceedings, are the sole, and certainly the most important, factors affecting litigant satisfaction;[136] therefore, efficiency, defined as the minimisation of the sum of error and direct costs, prevails over procedural justice considerations.

John Thibaut and Laurens Walker, two pioneering researchers in the field of procedural justice, proposed a theory which claims that, in specifically legal settings, the procedural model best suited to the attainment of distributive justice

[132] Röhl (1993a: 5) distinguishes at least three broad approaches: a social-psychological approach, a sociological approach, and a normative-philosophical approach. See also Arts/van der Veen (1992: 163 ff.) on the points of contact between procedural justice and sociology of law.

[133] Lind *et al.* (1990: 947). For a comprehensive introduction to the rich, empirical research conducted in the field of procedural justice and the theories and explanations derived from it, see Lind/Tyler (1988).

[134] For a general theoretical discussion of the independent value of procedure, see Summers (1974).

[135] For a thoughtful characterisation of the 'inquisitorial' and the 'adversarial' styles of procedure see Damaška (1986: 3–6).

[136] Cf Lind *et al.* (1990: 955).

in disputes entailing high conflict of interest is, on both subjective and objective grounds, the Anglo-American adversarial model.[137]

Thibaut and Walker first made a distinction between the objectives of 'truth' and 'justice' in conflict resolution. The objective of dispute resolution is 'truth' if the conflict involves determining the most accurate view of reality according to a standard, as in scientific disputes. On the contrary, its objective will be 'justice' if the conflict revolves around the apportionment of outcomes, such as inconsistent claims to the division of assets or losses. Distributive justice is supposed to be attained whenever

> the ultimate outcomes are distributed to contending parties in proportion to their respective contributions or inputs to the transaction underlying the dispute.[138]

The legal process, for example, is primarily concerned with the apportionment of outcomes, ie, with the resolution of conflicts of interest.[139]

Thibaut and Walker then claim that a procedural system designed to achieve distributive justice will function best if *process control*[140] is assigned to the disputants, because 'the disputing parties themselves are best qualified to describe their respective inputs or contributions to the transaction'.[141] These parties typically have more information than a third party would. Third-party decision-makers interpret and evaluate the behaviour of disputants differently from the disputants themselves, and such differences affect their conclusions regarding causality.[142] The freedom of disputants to control the statement of their claims 'constitutes the best assurance that they will subsequently believe that justice has been done regardless of the verdict.'[143] On the other hand, control over the decision should remain in the hands of a third party, because the disputants are in no position to evaluate the relative importance of rival claims.[144]

As one would expect, the strong thesis of Thibaut and Walker in favour of the Anglo-American adversarial model has elicited equally strong criticisms, particularly against their claim concerning the *objective* superiority of this model.[145] Thus, for example, the validity of their conclusions was contested on the grounds that they were based on experiments, rather than on real-life

137 Thibaut/Walker (1978: 551 f.). Thibaut and Walker based their theory on experimental work, the initial results of which they published in *Procedural Justice: A Psychological Analysis* in 1975. The experiments and their implications are described and discussed in Lind/Tyler (1988: 12 ff., 17 ff., 39 f., 117 ff.).

138 Thibaut/Walker (1978: 541 f.).

139 Thibaut/Walker (1978: 541, 543).

140 Thibaut/Walker (1978: 545 ff.) regard the distribution of control among the procedural group participants as the most significant factor in characterising a procedural system. A distinction is made between 'control over the decision' (outcome) and 'control over the process'. The latter 'refers to the control over the development and selection of information that will constitute the basis for resolving the dispute' (at 546).

141 Thibaut/Walker (1978: 549).

142 Thibaut/Walker (1978: 549).

143 Thibaut/Walker (1978: 551).

144 Thibaut/Walker (1978: 551).

145 Röhl (1993a: 10).

situations.[146] It was argued that the preference for an adversarial procedure might be rooted in cultural bias rather than in universal preferences, and that the inquisitorial model was misrepresented because it did not correspond to its reality. And, indeed, some of Thibaut and Walker's experiments on the accuracy of evidence and decisions could be interpreted as being in favor of the inquisitorial system, since it was demonstrated that the information gathered and presented by lawyers and witnesses in adversarial settings could be incomplete or biased.[147]

These criticisms can be answered fairly convincingly, and Thibaut and Walker actually anticipated the response to some of them. Thus, while experiments may not have been ideal from a certain point of view, they had strong theoretical and practical justifications.[148] To counter the objections of cultural bias, their experiments were replicated in England, France and Germany, with similar results.[149] The characterisation of the adversarial and inquisitorial systems was based on the variable 'process control' and did not necessarily purport to reflect particular real-life procedures.[150] Finally, although Thibaut and Walker expressed their preference for the adversarial system, despite its possible shortcomings in terms of accuracy or costs, they did so because they assumed that fairness was more important than accuracy if the conflict was, as most legal controversies were in their view, about the distribution of outcomes, and outcomes, it should be remembered, were fair if they reflected the relative inputs of the parties to the underlying relationship.[151]

Subsequent research to the work of Thibaut and Walker has focused on the identification and interpretation of the so-called procedural justice 'effects', in other words, the factors that are likely to be viewed by participants to a procedure as contributing to its fairness. Interpretation mainly concerns the relative importance of these factors in relation to each other, and their influence on the degree of acceptance of specific outcomes by these participants.[152] These studies have generally confirmed the finding that procedure matters as regards the perceived fairness of an outcome. Recently, they have gone even further, suggesting that procedure accomplishes an expressive function, which is not outcome-related,[153]

[146] For a critical discussion of the evaluation of procedural systems in laboratory experiments, see Hayden/Anderson (1979).

[147] These experiments, and similar studies by other researchers that are also unfavorable to the adversary procedure in this respect, are described in Lind/Tyler (1988: 19 ff., 114 ff.).

[148] See Lind/Tyler (1988: 41 ff.).

[149] Despite the experimental results, the influence of cultural bias continues to be questioned. Röhl (1993a: 14) argues that the sample of German students was too small (30) and that the diffusion of popular notions about the Anglo-American legal process by the media (television) might have played a role. See also Vidmar (1993: 43 ff.).

[150] Thibaut/Walker (1978: 552) expressly point out that they had not adopted a 'game' or 'combat' concept of the adversarial system.

[151] Cf Lind/Tyler (1988: 113).

[152] See Tyler (1988) and (1990) for a discussion of the connection between procedural justice effects and the legitimacy of law and public institutions.

[153] For another view of the value of procedure as procedure and of its symbolic significance see Summers (1974) and Garapon (1985; 1997).

and that procedural fairness responds to the more fundamental and universal dilemma of the relationship between the individual and the collectivity.[154]

This has implications for the design and evaluation of dispute-resolution mechanisms and, particularly, for the place of efficiency considerations within such a context, as shown, for example, by the so-called court-ordered arbitration in the United States. Court-ordered arbitration programmes involve a mandatory referral of a particular class of civil suits to an arbitration hearing.[155] Since such programmes offer the possibility of an adversarial proceeding but with a lesser degree of formality than a normal trial, they have often been adopted by US state and federal courts as an efficiency-enhancing mechanism designed to speed up disposition and decrease costs.[156]

However, empirical evaluation of court-ordered arbitration programs has produced mixed results as regards efficiency.[157] It has determined that such programs are not necessarily faster or cheaper than normal adjudication proceedings,[158] since in most cases they do not provide an alternative to trial but rather to a settlement reached without a hearing.[159] Considering also that litigants have generally expressed their satisfaction with this type of procedure, regardless of whether it achieves its intended efficiency-enhancing goals, it should be clear that both the absence of a formal procedure and excessive time-consuming and costly formalities must be reassessed if judicial reform in this area is to be successful.[160]

Thus, the three efficiency-oriented assumptions about judicial procedure cited at the beginning of this section would have to be rejected, or at least qualified, if procedural justice, ie, the intrinsic value of a fair procedure, is seriously regarded as a social goal. This is not to say that efficiency considerations or other desirable objectives are not important for the design and performance of actual judicial proceedings. In fact, the best solution would lie in 'hybrid procedures' which, while retaining the beneficial effects of procedural justice, would accommodate those other objectives.[161]

Thus, for example, the traditional Anglo-American adversarial style of procedure in civil matters has been criticised both for its incentives to distort evidence and for the expense and complexity of its modes of discovery and trial.[162] To solve this problem, it has been proposed that the responsibility for investigating facts and for the gathering of evidence should be taken out of the hands

[154] Lind (1994).

[155] Hensler (1990: 400).

[156] Hensler (1990: 401 ff.).

[157] Hensler (1990: 407).

[158] Hensler (1990: 408 ff.). See also McCoun (1991).

[159] Hensler (1990: 407). However, an economic analysis of ADR would predict precisely this consequence.

[160] Hensler (1990: 415).

[161] Thibaut/Walker (1978: 559 ff.) recognised the possibility of 'mixed disputes', where elements of truth and interest were difficult to distinguish, and for this eventuality they recommended a two-pronged procedure.

[162] Langbein (1985: 823). See also Kagan (1991).

of the parties involved and placed with the judge, as practiced in Continental legal systems.[163] But to be socially successful, such a proposal would have to attend to procedural justice considerations by respecting and safeguarding the parties' interest in being given a proper hearing.[164]

However, a compatible arrangement of inquisitorial and adversarial elements cannot often be achieved without changes in the broader institutional context of adjudication.[165] Such changes can be more costly and problematic than a mere concern with the procedural dimension might suggest. They may lead to the conclusion that inefficiency may be desirable or even inevitable if other aspects of the *particular* social and political environment of judicial institutions are taken into account. Thus, for example, it has been argued that the 'advantage' of Continental procedural models, such as the German system, rests on an efficient judicial bureaucracy, with high standards for training and performance. Such specialisation implies concentration and centralisation, which would be very difficult to achieve in the United States, given its extreme social diversity and political fragmentation.[166] These reasonable allegations against legal transplants notwithstanding, it turns out that case management in the Anglo-American judicial process is nothing less than an attempt to wrest some degree of control from the parties and transfer it to the judge. This has been rightly perceived, and criticised, as a form of bureaucratisation. Thus, procedural models can be actually transplanted . . . under a different guise.

LAW, ECONOMICS, AND SOCIOLOGY

The first section of this chapter left two interrelated sets of questions unanswered. The first set of questions concerns the relationship between EAL and SL. We have described an economic and a socio-legal model of litigation. Their comparison shows evident concidences and divergences. The coincidences seem to involve the use of a rational decision-making model, and the reliance on empirical tests. Both approaches seem to consider the law as an indeterminate influence on the access to the courts and on litigation outcomes. The divergences appear to derive from the results of empirical research and their interpretation, particularly from the identification of social factors that modify or supersede the role of individual maximising behaviour. What, then, is the general meaning of such coincidences and divergences? Some elements for answering this question are given below.

[163] Langbein (1985: 824 f.).

[164] Langbein (1985: 855).

[165] Langbein (1985: 855) advocates creating incentives that resemble those of the judicial career in European countries as a change that must accompany the transference of control to the judge.

[166] Gross (1987: 748 ff.), who responds directly to Langbein's essay (1985). Another reasoned attempt to link the style of procedure to political and ideological variables can be found in Damaska (1973; 1986).

The aim, however, is not to give the relationship between EAL and the socio-legal perspective an impartial consideration, so to speak, for two reasons. The first reason is that this study does not concern the purely technical aspects of court performance, since it also seeks to link it to the general role of courts in the legal system and society at large, thus consciously placing itself within the context of socio-legal interest. Secondly, the relationship between both perspectives is ultimately rooted in the organisation of social knowledge, which also calls for a sociological explanation. Questions about the meaning of EAL for the sociological approach to the law or, about its contribution to the assessment of court operation, for example, through the concept of efficiency, are subject to sociological analysis.

Two particular aspects come to mind with respect to these questions: the use of economic assumptions or models in empirical socio-legal research and the methodology of EAL. As already shown, many socio-legal studies have implicitly adopted, either by virtue of their language, assumptions or results, or as a consequence of an explicit choice, a framework derived from an economic decision-making model. The question is whether this adoption is tantamount to a tacit recognition of the fact that the economic approach generally offers better theoretical and methodological tools for the analysis of litigation processes, as claimed by some economists,[167] or simply that economic analysis can be fruitfully applied to any field of social action, provided its assumptions, methodologies or results are accepted as being subject to criticism or modification in the light of the specific concerns and perspectives of other disciplines.

If the economic approach has any advantage at all, it appears to lie more in the *way* it defines a problem and makes it operational for a fruitful analysis and less in the intrinsic or empirical validity of its underlying assumptions. The economic approach works through the definition of simple starting assumptions about variables and constraints. These assumptions can subsequently be modified and made more complex in a controlled manner. The purpose of formal (mathematical) analysis is essentially to provide a rigorous definition of the relationships between the assumptions and the conditions that apply to them. The model thus defined allows for further consequences and implications, which in turn can be subjected to empirical testing. For this reason, SL can validate and incorporate empirical results offered by EAL, but it can also be induced to conduct further empirical research of its own and reflect, for its own purposes, on the fact that economic and sociological explanations tend to diverge.

The second set of questions concern the relationship between the concepts of justice and efficiency as goals of the adjudicative process. I shall attempt to give the problem a more general formulation in terms of the functioning of the legal and economic systems in modern society.

[167] See Cooter/Rubinfeld (1990).

SL and EAL as Autonomous Disciplines

Before attempting to clarify the relationship between the economic and sociological approaches to law, it is necessary to address the scientific status of both types of analysis. Specifically, this status is defined by their relationship to their respective mother disciplines—economics and sociology—as well as by the nature and problems of their object, the law.

In order to approach this problem, we shall begin with a discussion of the scientific status of SL, which will provide a useful framework for conducting a similar analysis of EAL. These discussions will lead to a useful comparison of the two disciplines.

SL as an Autonomous Discipline

Much of what has been recently said and written about the scientific status of SL reflects a state of dissatisfaction with the empirical, theoretical and practical achievements of the discipline. Certainly, SL has attained a certain degree of autonomy *vis-à-vis* legal science and sociology. It defines itself by a relative separation from both intellectual traditions and by the construction of an original conceptual and thematic apparatus. On the other hand, the very autonomy SL enjoys has contributed to the 'double ostracism' it suffers from both lawyers and social scientists. SL, so it seems, is unable to escape a cyclical polemic with social science, which it has selectively incorporated and 'corrected', or with the internal legal culture of lawyers, to which it regards itself as an alternative.[168]

SL has developed an ambiguous relationship to both disciplines, oscillating between sociological culture and legal culture,[169] between a sociology of law of sociologists and a sociology of law of lawyers,[170] between the modest role of a hand-maiden of legal science and the more demanding task of explaining the social functions of legal regulation.[171] To make matters worse, just as it has become an institutionalised and recognised discipline, SL is said to have entered into a state of crisis, defined by the inability to face the challenges posed by new scientific paradigms and to overcome the debates that accompanied its birth.[172]

To have a clearer idea of what the scientific status of SL might be, I propose to view it as endlessly oscillating between *three* poles, not just two, against the irradiating background of general sociology and legal science. Accordingly, SL can also be defined:

[168] Ferrari (1990b: xxix ff.).
[169] Ferrari (1990b: xxxiv f.).
[170] See Arnaud/Fariñas Dulce (1996: 18 ff., 119 ff.).
[171] See Commaille/Perrin (1985).
[172] Arnaud/Fariñas Dulce (1996: 51 ff.).

—As an *instrument of a policy-oriented legal science and theory*: the critique of legal 'formalism' and a reform-minded social research using empirical methods have increasingly penetrated the field of law and legal institutions. However, it is by no means clear that SL has been successful in incorporating social-science concepts into legal science or in translating them into broad legal policies and reforms.[173]

—As an *alternative to legal science and theory*: SL has asserted a claim to being an *alternative explanation* of the law's nature and functions in society *vis-à-vis* the jurists' intellectual constructs. According to this conception, SL has to distance itself from the legal system, although at the same time, it must understand and take legal doctrine seriously.[174]

—As *sociology*: although a SL which is primarily rooted in sociological concepts and theories is perfectly legitimate and possible,[175] many socio-legal scholars do not find it satisfactory, because the law is regarded as an ordinary object, easily confused with politics and power phenomena attached to the state.[176]

The ambiguity and dissatisfaction caused by SL is rooted in each of those poles, which drives it towards the other two. This very oscillation allows for middle-ground positions, which are nonetheless unable to overcome the basic ambiguities that define the 'autonomy' of the discipline. Additionally, one should recall that people matter and that the SL has been strongly attracted to the legal pole partly because it has been cultivated more by lawyers than by sociologists.

EAL as an Autonomous Discipline

EAL, as it has developed mainly in the United States since the 1960s, also enjoys a certain degree of autonomy from both its parent disciplines.[177] Because it has generally adopted a rather narrow economic approach to legal problems,[178] it cannot be said to be suffering from the same ambiguities and identity problems that seem to beset SL. We shall now analyse whether the three poles between which SL oscillates are also useful for placing EAL within its intellectual context and scientific ambitions.

[173] See Teubner (1989). See MacLean (1993) and the papers collected in Gessner/Thomas (eds) (1988). For a case study, cf for example, Tanford (1991) where, interestingly enough, it is the courts who offer the most resistance to recommendations by empirical research and are even prepared to go in the opposite direction. Cf Luhmann (1990: 409). See also Ietswaart (1984).

[174] Cotterrell (1995: 27 f.).

[175] Luhmann (1988b: 1989) exemplifies this possibility. See the table showing the differences between the jurisprudential and the sociological models of the law in Black (1989: 21).

[176] Commaille/Perrin (1985: 99) As Roger Cotterrell puts it, in this version of SL, legal doctrine, i.e., the institutionalised operation of legal rules, principles, concepts and modes of reasoning, will not be compared. Cotterrell (1995: 28).

[177] See, for example, Cooter/Ulen (1988: 11 ff.) and Deakin (1996: 66, 93).

[178] Deakin (1996: 66 ff.), who, for this reason, distinguishes it from the broader movement of 'law and economics'.

—EAL as an *instrument of a policy-oriented legal science and theory*: EAL has the explicit goal of becoming a new policy science of the law or, more modestly, of clarifying the alternative consequences that attach to different courses of legal action.[179] The validity of such an approach is guaranteed by an instrumental conception of the law, by the assumption that individual maximisation also occurs in the field of legal behavior, and by the explicit normative nature of economics. Ultimately, however, this type of economic analysis goes against the autonomy of traditional legal science,[180] and the question is whether the project of an 'economicisation' of legal science can be successfully accomplished, even in a limited area of the law.[181]

—EAL as an *alternative to legal science and theory*: until now, the economic approach has been applied to a rather narrow set of legal problems, but nothing precludes its extension to all kinds of legal activities, in the same way as it has been applied to other types of social behaviour.[182] Despite this, it will be unable to dispense entirely with more traditional legal categories and concepts, which in turn will make it gravitate towards the legal pole, more so than an autonomous SL, because of the tendency of economic analysis to address preferably instrumental issues and to offer normative solutions. On the other hand, if economic analysis tends to consider the law as indeterminate, because it has been internalised by rational decision-makers, then EAL should gravitate towards economics instead. A middle, autonomous pole for EAL should tend to disappear.

—EAL as *economics*: EAL was partly born out of economists' concern with the role that institutions and legal rules play in favouring or obstructing economically efficient solutions.[183] The famous Coase Theorem simply states that in the absence of transaction costs, the market will arrive at an efficient allocation of legal entitlements regardless of the initial allocation.[184] In

179 Cooter/Ulen (1988: 10).

180 And this attack on the autonomy of traditional legal science, which some versions of EAL share with the Critical Legal Studies movement, is intentional, rather than accidental. See Chiassoni (1992: 141 ff.) and Mercado Pacheco (1994: 173 ff.).

181 EAL can also be subject to criticism from the economic side. Its approach is seen as too narrow, even in economic terms. Apparently, it has failed to incorporate recent developments in mainstream economics or show interest in developments in other social sciences. Deakin (1996: 66, 93 ff.) Even the technical level of economic analysis displayed by some of its proponents is considered as utterly insufficient. Frank (1986: 207 ff.).

182 See Becker (1986). Posner (1995) contends precisely that economic analysis is being applied to a wider range of problems than socio-legal analysis.

183 Ronald H Coase, one of the acknowledged founders of the modern law-and-economics school, did not incorporate the operation of legal rules and institutions into economic analysis with the purpose of making a contribution to *legal theory*. On the contrary, he intended to criticise the economic notion that market failure is a sufficient reason for state intervention. Intervention is itself costly, so it will only be efficient when the removal of obstacles to market exchange is more costly than state intervention. See his well-known essay on 'The Problem of Social Cost' in Coase (1988: 95–156). See also Chiassoni (1992: 51 ff.).

184 See Cooter (1989: 64 ff.).

this view, law has no independent meaning *as law*. The role of legal regulation will be interpreted, for example, in the light of its impact on transaction costs, and the initial allocation of legal rights becomes irrelevant if they can be freely exchanged.

The Coase Theorem shows that, like sociology, economics is capable of analysing law in response to its own internal theoretical needs,[185] and such an analysis will not correspond to the conception law has of itself or to its immediate practical concerns. Legal sanctions, for example, can be seen merely as a price imposed on behaviour,[186] rather than a necessary consequence of the violation of a *valid* obligation designed to prevail over any other motive or consideration. Behaviour is subject instead to a cost-benefit analysis, so that a rational economic actor may arrive at the (economically plausible) idea that the breach of a contract may be efficient.[187] And even when economic theory uses concepts such as 'contracts' or 'property rights,' they will not necessarily correspond to their normal legal uses.[188]

Rival or Complementary Approaches?

The examination of the scientific status of EAL and SL on the basis of a common framework reveals some interesting similarities and contrasts. Both disciplines seem to enjoy a certain degree of autonomy *vis-à-vis* their target discipline, legal science and theory, as well as their respective mother disciplines, economics and sociology. However, such autonomy, while undoubtedly an advantage, exposes them to criticism and impels them towards an oscillatory movement of cyclical reassurance and feedback.

In the case of SL, the identity problems of sociology itself and its reflexive competence for society as a whole, may perhaps contribute to a higher degree of autonomy as an alternative explanation of the law. This would seem to be less true of EAL. Economics could certainly provide an alternative explanation of legal behavior. However, the application of economic assumptions and tools to legal problems will not necessarily yield an autonomous explanation of the law in the same sense that SL intends to provide it, because economics seems to lack the 'external-reflexive' qualities of sociology with respect to all social behaviour.[189] In other words: the core behavioral assumptions of economics,[190] which

[185] Coase (1978: 205) suggests that economic 'imperialism' will be fruitful and durable only if it is dictated by the demands of economic explanation. 'To the extent that it is necessitated by their subject matter, we may expect the range of studies undertaken by economists to be permanently enlarged'.

[186] For Veljanovski (1990: 7) the law is nothing more than a giant pricing machine which places incentives or disincentives on human behaviour.

[187] See Teubner (1992: 128 ff.) for examples of the different values the economic system can place on legal measures, including indifference.

[188] See, for example, Barzel (1989: xi).

[189] By 'external-reflexive qualities' I mean the fact that sociology, despite being part of society, observes and reflects on it as if it were outside it.

[190] See Becker (1986) and Cooter (1995: 54 ff.).

sociology seems to lack, have more of a *methodological value* than explanatory power in terms of causality.[191] If relentlessly applied to 'non-economic' behaviour, this assumption will help to generate more or less powerful models, while leaving little room for an autonomous 'value' of the behavior that is the object of explanation.

Consequently, one would expect EAL to be dependent on inputs (problem definition, unresolved issues) from legal science, economics, or even SL.[192] In its explanatory dimension, EAL would be attracted either to the legal pole or the economic pole.[193] Its autonomous core would lie in its methodology for the analysis of the problems proposed to it or motivated by other disciplines.[194] This should open the door to a fruitful interdisciplinary cooperation, or else to the much-resented 'imperialism' of economic science.

At this point, we should examine more fully the claim that economic analysis is in itself more powerful than either legal science or SL. Thus, for example, Robert Cooter claims that EAL has been so successful (at least in the United States) because it was able to find 'a vacant niche in the intellectual ecology' by providing a behavioural theory to predict how people respond to changes in laws.[195] Richard Posner claims that EAL has already addressed (at least in the United States) a wider range of problems, with more interesting results, compared with the methodological, theoretical and empirical limitations of SL.[196] For both, the success of EAL is much more than circumstantial. It is founded on the assumptions of maximisation, equilibrium and efficiency which lie at the heart of economic theory.[197] These assumptions are crucial to explaining behaviour in institutions that co-ordinate interactions among people, not just market interactions, and they cannot simply be rejected by pointing to other motivations that people actually have in social life besides, or in the place of, a narrowly defined self-interest.

These assumptions, and their relative immunity from superficial critique, *do* make economic analysis more powerful in the following sense: it is more abstract, general and straightforward. It finds support in the observation that, *over time*, all social behavior will tend to follow the principles of economic

[191] See Johnston (1990: 1228 ff.).

[192] See, for example, the study in Castellano *et al.* (1970) to determine whether litigants were discriminated against on the grounds of their socioeconomic status. Discrimination was measured in terms of delay and operationalised as the difference between the average duration of the proceedings in which litigants have an objective interest in delaying them, and the duration of proceedings in which they have an interest in speedy disposition.

[193] Another consequence would be a much clearer distinction between the groups of economists and lawyers who cultivate EAL. History, and existing work on EAL so far, seem to confirm this observation.

[194] It should be remembered that the essay of Priest/Klein (1984) on the selection of disputes for litigation was motivated by the problem of the representativeness of appellate judicial decisions for the study of the law.

[195] Cooter (1995: 51, 53).

[196] Posner (1995).

[197] Cooter (1995: 54 ff., 57, 59 ff.).

rationality with a certain degree of *probability*. This may explain why economic analysis would seem capable of reconstructing and generalising other social science models.

However, reconstruction and generalisation of other social-science models will only go so far, at the expense of simplifying and assuming many other factors away.[198] The economic approach is reductionist not in the sense that it reduces all behaviour to economic behaviour, but in that it has so far been unable to account for other important dimensions of behaviour. As Robert Cooter puts it, economic analysis has 'X-ray vision,' rather than 'peripheral vision,' and he argues that the incompleteness of economic theory 'prevents researchers from perceiving facts that psychologists and sociologists regard as central to the law.'[199] Economics has to 'thicken' self-interest by taking into account developments in other social disciplines, such as psychology and sociology (for example, by incorporating the internalisation of norms), *but without abandoning the core of economic theory*.[200] In other words: the core of economic theory should serve as the basis for a unified social theory.

Quite apart from the question of whether a unified social theory can or should use economics as its basis,[201] and consequently, of whether SL can or should begin with rational decision-making assumptions (which in fact, it sometimes has), the relationship between these two disciplines can be also established on more practical grounds. EAL and SL can fertilise and criticise each other under three conditions: first, that they be able to identify problems that can be of mutual interest; secondly, that they profit from the tools of empirical analysis, and third, that they become capable of learning reflexively from each other's assumptions and theoretical interpretations. In particular, this implies that sociology should not limit itself to the rather sterile role of the critic bent merely on explaining and correcting the insufficiencies of economic theory.[202]

The wide world of norms—their emergence, evolution, enforcement and decay—seems to be a common, fertile ground for the convergence of sociological and economic analysis of the law.[203] Unfortunately, the two communities of socio-legal and law-and-economics scholars do not seem to be aware of the possibilities of collaboration since they take little notice of each other's intellectual achievements.[204]

Hardly any studies seem to have made direct reference to socio-legal and economic assumptions for the purpose of analysing the emergence and use of social

[198] Panther (1995: 373) gives the example of anomie theory, which would seem to be merely a version of a general economic model of crime. However, to the extent that anomie theory introduces a hypothesis about preference change, it goes beyond the economic approach.

[199] Cooter (1995: 54).

[200] Cooter (1995: 60).

[201] Cooter (1995: 66).

[202] See Cella (1990), Gephart (1995).

[203] See, for example, Cooter (1995: 63 ff.).

[204] See Donohue III (1988) and Ellickson (1991: 7).

norms. One exception is Robert Ellickson's study of dispute settlement among cattle owners in Shasta County, California.[205] Ellickson discovered that, contrary to the Coase Theorem's assumptions on transaction costs, people are often able to resolve disputes without paying any attention to their legal entitlements, that is, the presence of transaction costs was not a sufficient condition to make the law matter.[206]

The conclusion may seem trivial from a socio-legal point of view, but Ellickson attempts to go beyond this. He also criticises sociological theories that are unable to provide a convincing account of the content of norms, and generally, all current theories of social control in so far as they fail to offer a widely accepted explanation of the interplay between informal social controls and the legal system.[207] Therefore, he develops and tests, with the help of game theory, a hypothesis about the emergence of welfare-maximising norms among the members of a close-knit group and about the incentives they are offered for engaging in cooperative behaviour.[208]

Another promising avenue of mutual interest may derive from so-called 'neo-institutionalist economics' or NIE. In its various versions, NIE attempts to incorporate into economic analysis, either as endogenous or exogenous variables, phenomena such as property rights, organisations and political decision-making, traditionally neglected by neo-classical economics.[209] One approach that seems to be particularly close to the sociology of law is the theoretical concern of certain NIE proponents, such as Douglass C North,[210] with the interplay of formal and informal rules that create incentives or disincentives for institutional change and economic growth over time.[211]

Finally, another field of possible fruitful reflection, this time under the aegis of sociology, may lie in today's interest in culture and values as factors that affect legal interaction and economic behaviour. The process of globalisation, it appears, has drawn new attention to the cultural embeddedness of social action by pointing out regional differences in attitudes and values that affect legal and economic exchanges, especially across borders.[212] The problem is very similar to the one addressed by some of the NIE proponents, ie, how to analyse and explain the impact of informal (here: 'cultural') elements on cross-border

205 Ellickson (1991). See the review essay by Brigham (1993).

206 Ellickson (1991: 281).

207 Ellickson (1991: 149 ff., 137 ff.).

208 Ellickson (1991: 167 ff.).

209 For a comprehensive introduction into this intellectual field see Eggertsson (1990). See also Chiassoni (1992: 67 ff.) for a summary of the efforts by several economists to analyse property rights, legal regulation and political processes in economic terms.

210 North (1990).

211 See Ferrarese (1995).

212 See Clegg (1990: 107 ff.), Holton (1992: 179 ff.) and Gessner (1994). An example of the influence of cultural norms on economic transactions can be found in the literature on *guanxi*, ie, connections, in Chinese business practices. See Chung/Hamilton (2001).

exchanges governed by a common formal framework, as well as the interplay and evolution of both informal elements and formal framework.[213]

What about litigation? What degree of interplay of sociological and economic analysis is appropriate for the various dimensions of court operation? Here, we must distinguish between different levels of analysis.

If the general relationships between the legal and economic systems are involved, including the generation and diffusion of economic or legal knowledge, a sociological explanation would seem to provide an appropriate approach.

If the point of interest is rational decision-making in the field of law and litigation, including its effects on legal change and evolution, an explicit or implicit economic model,[214] perhaps with sociological or psychological qualifications, will serve as the starting point. The scope and meaning of such qualifications will be an interesting subject for reflection. In this respect, one could perhaps describe EAL as the core of a '*rationality-oriented sociology of law*.'[215]

There is still another dimension of the courts that we have not yet examined: the dimension of *organisation*. Courts are organisations of a particular nature. As such, they constitute a point of confluence for sociological and economic analysis. Courts 'produce' a particular kind of 'service'. Access to and use of the courts can be characterised in terms of 'demand' and 'supply'. Their operation can be measured and evaluated in terms of costs in time and money, as well as of productivity and service quality. And we have already explained why economic language has permeated the everyday running of the courts and the scientific analysis of the judicial process.

The Legal System and Economic Rationality

Justice vs efficiency?

In the course of this chapter we have made several allusions to a much debated point between EAL and legal philosophy: the relationship between 'justice' and

[213] This is the challenge facing, on the socio-legal side, the concept of 'legal culture', which has long been used to refer to the attitudes, values and opinions, either of the lay population or of legal professionals, towards the legal system (Friedman 1975: 193 ff.). For the purposes mentioned above, it would have to be adjusted to a comparative analysis of local settings (for example, international commercial arbitration) and above all, be able to explain evolution and change of specific legal cultures. See the essays collected in Nelken (ed) (1997), especially the strong critique of this concept by Cotterrell and the rejoinder by Friedman. For a case study (on NAFTA's binational panel system) which gives an account on how institutional and time constraints placed upon the interaction of lawyers from two countries induces a learning process that transforms legal culture's normative expectations into cognitive expectations, see López Ayllón/Fix-Fierro (1999: 29 ff.).

[214] According to Luhmann (1988a: 272 ff.), the almost automatic referral to economics whenever rational decision-making is concerned, is partly due to the failure of sociology to provide a theory of decision. A sociological theory of decision would not have to coincide with an economic explanation. Therefore, Luhmann leaves the element of rationality aside and suggests instead to view as a decision any behaviour that reacts towards an expectation directed towards it.

[215] Cf Eder (1986) and the critique by Frank (1986).

'efficiency' as values to be achieved by the law. Depending on the answer, certain conclusions may be drawn on the usefulness of the concept of efficiency for evaluating courts as legal institutions. It should be noted that economists speak of 'equity' rather than of 'justice'. By equity they mean the (equal) distribution of income among individuals.[216] Since justice as a legal value can be considered, in at least one of its meanings, in terms of equality ('treat like cases alike'), for our purposes we will substitute justice for equity and treat them as interchangeable.

We must further ask whether the apparent conflict depends merely on the point of view adopted (the legal or the economic perspectives) or whether it is a matter of Solomonic pragmatism. We shall also try to determine whether the three positions mentioned below are as clear-cut as their formulation seems to imply.

At first sight, and on the basis of some of the arguments encountered in our discussion of the economic model of litigation, three distinct positions are possible:

—The *prevalence of justice*: there seem to be strong reasons to believe that justice prevails over efficiency considerations in both judicial decision-making and judicial procedure. This position is represented by Dworkin's polemic against utilitarianism and other policy-oriented legal doctrines, including EAL,[217] but even some EAL scholars, like Guido Calabresi, concede that justice has the power of veto, meaning that efficiency can only be maximised within the boundaries marked by justice considerations.[218] Research on procedural justice also seems to provide a strong argument for the prevalence of justice over efficiency, which becomes even stronger if people's perception of fairness is actually more dependent on procedure than on outcomes, as initially assumed by procedural justice theorists.[219]

We have here, in fact, two different distinctions—procedure/outcomes and justice/efficiency—and there is no obvious reason why they should behave towards each other in a parallel fashion. Perhaps this point can be demonstrated if we interpret the central finding of procedural justice research solely in terms of either justice *or* efficiency. If so, we may then realise that this finding also concerns the conflict (trade-off) between two concepts of justice (distributive vs.

[216] See Polinsky (1989: 7–10).

[217] See Dworkin (1980a and b). Dworkin's central argument is that if individual rights have any meaning at all for the resolution of legal conflicts, they prevail over any utilitarian or instrumental considerations.

[218] Calabresi (1980; 1990).

[219] This is explicitly expressed in Lind (1994: 35). People 'do not think about justice in the allocation-oriented terms that are so often seen in legal, economic or psychological theories of justice'. In a similar line Howard *et al*. (2000): 'If litigation, and the outcomes from litigation, is not fair, then regardless of efficiency, citizens have little incentive to use the court system to resolve disputes or to comply with or obey the results from the litigation if they *have* gone to court' (at 450; emphasis in the original).

procedural justice) and two dimensions of efficiency (private vs social efficiency). If litigants are willing to sacrifice efficiency in terms of both procedure and outcome, because their higher private costs are offset by a higher sense of satisfaction and dignity, the higher social costs thus generated may also be compensated by lower social costs in terms of lower social conflictivity and higher legitimacy and acceptance of institutions.[220] Certainly, the problem of social choice becomes even more complex.

—The *trade-off between justice and efficiency*:[221] this position has a strong intuitive plausibility, especially when applied to adjudication and criminal judicial proceedings, which have to strike a difficult balance between the competing interests and values of the parties and of government, such as speediness and the thorough consideration of the claims and defenses raised during the proceedings. As seen above, this trade-off may also come about not because efficiency is in conflict with justice, but because different conceptions of justice may be at odds with each other (procedure vs outcome). Although the conflict may be real and the trade-off unavoidable, we also find here complex contradictions between different conceptions and levels of justice as well as different perspectives of efficiency.[222]

—The *prevalence of efficiency*: Richard Posner has proposed the much criticised, and, as he himself argues, not always well understood, idea of wealth maximisation[223] as a more convincing *moral basis* for the (common) law, and alternative to both utilitarianism and Kantianism.[224] In this view, not only is efficiency an important component of justice, but a particular concept of efficiency[225] is raised to the category of foundation for the law and

[220] See, for example, Paternoster *et al.* (1997), which states that fair procedures on the part of police officers called to the scene of a domestic assault inhibits subsequent assault, if compared with the cases in which the police did not act in a procedurally fair manner when arresting assault suspects.

[221] See, for example, Savona (1990) in relationship to criminal justice, Herrero (1993), Polinsky (1989: 9f., 119ff.).

[222] See Howard *et al.* (2000), who examine four possible types of equilibria between efficiency of outcome and fairness of process: fair equilibria that are inefficient; efficient equilibria that are unfair; equilibria that are neither fair nor efficient; equilibria that are both fair and efficient. However, this last type of equilibria is difficult to achieve: it occurs when litigation costs are zero, or where litigation costs are 'moderate', at the .50 level. If litigation costs were to deviate slightly from either hypothesis, 'fairness or efficiency would cease to exist' (at 450). So, they conclude that 'going to court is always a non-efficient outcome because of the cost of going to court'; the loss of efficiency that arises by going to court 'often results in greater fairness' (at 436).

[223] Posner (1979; 1990: 356). 'Wealth' refers to 'the sum of all tangible and intangible goods and services, weighted by prices of two sorts: offer prices . . . and asking prices'. As such, it is not a simple monetary measure.

[224] Posner (1979: 119ff.).

[225] Coleman (1980: 521) contends that not only is wealth-maximisation not an alternative efficiency criterion but that it is not an efficiency criterion at all.

legal policy.[226] Notice, however, that wealth maximisation is proposed here as a new concept of *justice* and that if it is to serve as a guiding principle or value for the law, it cannot simply be accepted as an *economic* category.

To say that either justice or efficiency should be the prevalent value in the legal system, or that there is a necessary trade-off between them, may also mean *that each is a component of the other.* That economic efficiency is a component of justice and legitimacy[227] has already been suggested in the introductory chapter to this study. Efficiency has become indeed an important value for assessing the performance and legitimacy of social institutions in modern society, so that there can be no justice without some degree of economic efficiency.[228]

The inverse proposition—that justice is an element of economic efficiency—may also hold true. It is advanced by those who consider the initial distribution of rights as an important issue that cannot be divorced from an efficiency-oriented economic analysis,[229] but it is also reflected in the importance accorded to the concept of 'equity' in economic theory.

Thus, a *circular relationship*, that is, the reciprocal remission of one to the other, is actually established between justice and efficiency. Such relationship can perhaps be exemplified by the discussion around the welfare state. Historically, the welfare state was born when social justice concepts were introduced into the operation of non-regulated markets. It can be said, therefore, that justice was used as a corrective for economic efficiency. But lately, the opposite has been true. Efficiency considerations have been proposed as a necessary

[226] According to Posner (1979: 127), the wealth-maximisation principle implies:

–An initial distribution of individual rights to their natural owners (*i.e.* those who would value them most);
–Free markets to enable those rights to be reassigned;
–Legal rules that simulate the operations of the market when the costs of market transactions are prohibitive;
–A system of legal remedies for deterring and redressing invasions of rights;
–A system of personal morality that serves to reduce the costs of market transactions.

In a more recent statement, however, Posner has somewhat diluted his moral claim and seems to favor a more pragmatic argument instead: 'wealth maximisation may be the most direct route to a variety of moral ends', considering that people in societies where markets are allowed to function more or less freely are not only wealthier but 'have more political rights, more liberty and dignity, are more content . . .' And while it is not clear that some of these rights could find their justification in a wealth-maximising perspective, particularly those deriving from an individualistic stance, they seem to be 'too deeply entrenched in our society for wealth-maximisation to be given free rein'. At the same time, society might not be willing to pay an infinite or a very high price for freedom. This is another way of saying that rights are inseparable from an economic valuation. They cannot be had without a price or at any price. See Posner (1990: 374 ff.: quotations at 382, 380 and 379). Cf. also the following quotation by Adams (1981: 45): 'the contents of a right can only be correctly and usefully assessed, when besides its nominal value, as determined by the substantive law, the costs of enforcement and the risks of litigation which such rights carries are known, as is the response of the obligated person towards such costs and risks' (translation by HFF).

[227] Calsamiglia (1988; 1993) and García Pelayo (1991).

[228] See Rawls' (1973: 65 ff.).

[229] See Calabresi (1990).

corrective of welfare principles. Thus, justice and efficiency can be alternatively viewed as a corrective of the other. Even more: the respective arguments are conducted using the opposite concept. This is the case, for example, when it is argued that the level of public expenditure in the welfare state is not only *inefficient* in economic terms but also *unjust* for the same reason. This circular relationship seems to suggest that justice and efficiency accommodate and enhance each other *over time*.

In short: there can undoubtedly be a conflict between justice and efficiency considerations in legal settings, but this may cover a more complex relationship than is suggested by an intuitive contradiction. In particular, those contradictions may be expressed in terms of justice or efficiency alone, or there may be a reciprocal remission between both values. In any case, in so far the legal system is concerned, justice is the prevalent value. It appears that demands addressed to the legal system, for example, in terms of economic rationality, must be transformed into a legally acceptable language, the language of justice. However, it is not just a question of rhetoric, or of competing interpretations of justice. The conflict, the circular remission and the prevalence of justice as a legal value can be explained by the circular nature of both the legal and the economic systems and their reciprocal relationship at the level of society.

Law in the Collision of Discourses

In the previous section we examined the place and significance of efficiency in the legal and judicial system through the analysis of its relationship to justice as a legal value. To complete the picture, the relationship between the legal and the economic systems, considered as functionally differentiated subsystems of society, must also be explored.[230] To this end, I shall provide a brief summary of an essay by the German legal theoretician Gunther Teubner.[231]

Teubner begins his essay, titled 'Altera Pars Audiatur: Law in the Collision of Discourses', by asking whether economic rationality represents the new universality of law and whether 'the emaciated concept of justice' is being replaced by the ideal of the economic efficiency of the law.[232] According to this view, law and economics would be 'the new victorious paradigm which eliminates older moral-political orientations of law', with no tolerance of any other paradigms alongside it. After all, law and economics find strong support in the society-wide and almost worldwide institutionalisation of economic rationality and in the demands it places on the law for providing market-adequate, economy-adequate legal forms.[233]

[230] The theory of functionally differentiated social systems is a core element of Luhmann's sociological approach. For an introduction, especially with respect to the legal system, see King/Schütz (1994).

[231] Teubner (1997a and b).

[232] Teubner (1997a: 149). A displacement that would be happily applauded by many an EAL defender.

[233] Teubner (1997a: 150).

To answer these questions, Teubner redefines the problem, placing it within a broader perspective. The problem is not about the replacement of one form of rationality by another, or about the substitution of one ideal of justice for another, with the consequences that for the law might derive from this replacement. It is about the demands that *multiple rationalities*—not only economic rationality, but also truth, political legitimacy, and moral criteria—place on the law and about the responses they expect from the legal system. Those rationalities are particularistic in the sense that they are institutionalised at the level of specific social systems or interactions. At the same time, they manifest society-wide claims and they contain features of social effectiveness which render their influence on the law almost irresistible.[234] These rationalities, values, and discourses collide within the law not as simple ideals but as real social practices with an inner logic that has an enormous potential for destruction.[235]

While the law is protected against immediate competition from other universalities by its formal binary code, the other discourses will nevertheless rule as the criteria that govern the distribution of the legal/illegal values at the level of programs (norms).[236] The consequence is a legal pluralism in a more radical sense than just a plurality of coexisting laws and rule-systems. Legal pluralism here also refers to a plurality of incompatible rationalities with a claim to universality within the law, as well as to a multiplicity of conflicting moral, political and economic theories about the law.[237] How can the law decide and choose between them?

Teubner proposes to accept this conflict, not as a symbol of decay but as a productive opportunity, and suggests the need to work out the concept of a new law of conflicts.[238]

> Instead of trying once more to declare one of the particularistic rationalities as the very deepest fundament of law and justice, jurisprudence should develop a theory of discourse collisions which calibrates law precisely to the plurality of social rationalities.[239]

To accomplish this, Teubner sees two possibilities: either to incorporate the collisions in the operations of the internal *forum* of the law through legal reasoning, or to externalise them into the operations of other social subsystems, into social non-legal *fora* for dealing with social conflicts.[240]

234 Teubner (1997a: 150 ff.). These characteristics are as follows: a material base consisting of manifest social practices; the development of self-concepts and reflexive theories; presence in legal theory and jurisprudence; influence on legal practice in the form of simulation of the logic of law's social environments ('politicisation', 'economisation', 'scientification', 'moralisation'), and the independent production of social norms as legal norms in the various subsystems of society.

235 Teubner (1997a: 154 f.).

236 Teubner (1997a: 156 f.).

237 Teubner (1997a: 157).

238 Teubner (1997a: 158 f.).

239 Teubner (1997a: 160 f.).

240 Teubner (1997a: 161 f.).

According to the first solution, which is the one that interests us more here, *external* rationalities are deconstructed and reconstructed as *local* rationality by the law. The law subjects them to the local practice of equal and unequal treatment in view of past and present legal practices. 'To treat what is equal equally and what is unequal unequally is not only a fundamental legal norm but also a dynamic process of law-making which triggers off a self-propelling series of distinctions'.[241] Law neutralises and legalises the non-legal discourses, but only insofar as the internal realm of legal discourse is concerned.[242]

The solution comes at a cost, however. The legal system has no way of knowing what the external consequences of its way of treating the colliding discourses are. Teubner examines here the problem of 'legal consequentialism' as a mode of reasoning, ie, the choice of legal alternatives contingent on their outcomes,[243] and the need to identify and reduce the number of relevant consequences for legal decision-making. Teubner suggests that the law should 'hear the other party', that it should consider the 'back translation' of the effects that legal decisions have on the other discourses.[244] In other words: the issue is not the prediction of real consequences (particularly in view of the limited capacity of social science to provide it), but the evaluation of the process of 'translation' and 'back translation' between legal and non-legal discourses.[245] Thus, for example, the law should make use of the sociological insight that legal norms are reconstituted by other discourses and 'translated' into costs, positions of power or instruments of education.[246]

In the context of the two solutions envisaged by Teubner, the role of law no longer consists of the final, authoritative solution of social discourse conflicts. It is limited to participating in the infinite game of *renvoi* between closed discourses and to minimising their destructive tendencies when they collide. In Teubner's words:

> the current task of the law cannot be to reconstitute the lost unity of society but to designate borders of plural identities, protect them against domination by other discourses and limit damage from the fallout of discourse collisions.[247]

A Preliminary Conclusion

At this point in our investigation, particularly after the last section, a number of important preliminary conclusions may be drawn.

241 Teubner (1997a: 164).
242 Teubner (1997a: 167).
243 Teubner (1997a: 168 ff.).
244 Teubner (1997a: 170 ff.).
245 Obviously, we are thinking of SL and EAL as a relatively autonomous manifestation of this process of translation and back translation between systems.
246 Teubner (1997a: 170).
247 Teubner (1997a: 175).

First, in the conflict between justice and efficiency within the legal arena, justice prevails. It prevails not because it is the superior value but because it is the specific *modus operandi* of the legal system for solving the conflicts submitted to it. To treat the equal equally and the unequal unequally, which is the specific legal form of justice, is a fundamental norm that emerges from the circular, recursive operation of the legal system itself.[248] The consequence is not that efficiency and economic rationality are rejected as alien values to counter a much-feared 'economicisation of the law'. Rather, the consequence is precisely that they are subject to a process of legalisation. Therefore, the degree of relevance of these non-legal values within legal discourse cannot be determined *a priori* by their discourse of origin ('economic analysis').

Secondly, EAL and SL have an important role to play in the process of 'translation' and 'back translation' between law, economy and society. They can serve, so to speak, as an organ of perception, learning and reflection of the legal system through their influence on legal science and theory, which, nevertheless, remain separate from economic and sociological analysis.[249] This also applies to the *actual consequences* (for example, effectiveness or discrimination) of law in social life—the traditional *raison d'être* of SL—to the extent that they can be reformulated in terms of 'back translation' (for example, as a problem of political or moral justice).[250]

Thirdly, the two previous conclusions are relevant for the functioning of courts as the *center* of the legal system.[251] Courts perform multiple functions in society—mainly political and economic—besides their specific role in the legal system, but never, and this is sometimes easily forgotten, *without* reference to and mediation by the law. Thus, efficiency and economic rationality will be

[248] See Luhmann (1993: 214 ff.).

[249] Luhmann (1993: 543 f.) suggests the possibility of a structural coupling between the legal and the scientific systems at the level of theories.

[250] Niklas Luhmann was always extremely critical of the idea that the legal system can learn anything from sociology (see for example Luhmann 1988b). Needless to say, most socio-legal scholars, who consider that socio-legal research has to be useful in some way for legal practice, reject his position. Take, for example, the interesting issue raised by Donald Black in his book *Sociological Justice* (1989). Black considers that the central discovery of a truly scientific sociology of law, ie, that the legal process is fundamentally unequal and discriminatory, will re-enter the legal system as a conscious exploitation of such a discovery by those that benefit from the law's inequality (but this is a reality, with or without scientific sociological knowledge). Black himself does not seem to favor this consequence and many a liberal-minded socio-legal scholar will think that the legal system surely cannot accept this without trying to counteract discrimination. Then again, it could be argued that both the starting point and the solution are more of a political question (the use or the change of the law) than a strictly legal problem.

[251] Luhmann (1993: 297 ff.) considers the courts to be the 'center' of the legal system, as opposed to the 'periphery', formed by contracts and legislation. They are the center of the legal system, not because of their greater importance compared to other sources of the law, but because they perform various unique *legal* functions: they accomplish the closure of the legal system; they manage the hidden paradoxes of the system; and they are the only organs that control the consistency of legal decisions ('justice').

an important dimension of the social function of the courts depending on the specific exchange situation between legal and economic discourses in society.[252]

Fourthly, if the legal system is autonomous in its handling of economic rationality, so is the economic system in its perception and evaluation of the law and legal institutions, such as the courts. Not only can it develop a different concept of justice with a different place and meaning within the system ('equity')[253] but it seems best suited to analysing (perhaps with the cooperation of sociology) *another dimension* of the courts: their operational and organisational dimension. To the extent that courts are social institutions that use and manage *scarce social resources*,[254] they fall under the jurisdiction of economics and are liable to be described by the language of economics. Thus, courts become relevant in terms of costs (time and money), demand and supply, production and allocation efficiency. And if court operation can be effectively described in economic terms, court reform proposals can be framed in the same language.

In the following chapters, the investigation will examine this dimension of courts in more detail. Despite the acknowledged competence of economic analysis, this approach will not be explicitly used here for several reasons:

—This study is ultimately concerned with the broader issue of the functions of courts in society and with a broader notion of judicial effectiveness, of which efficiency is an important element.

—The problem of costs, delay and the like can certainly be conceptualised in terms of supply and demand, but the factors that affect access to and the use of the courts are so complex, that an alternative socio-legal description might also be necessary. However, the difficulty is not only scientific. Attempts to regulate the demand and supply of judicial services based purely on economic assumptions may not always produce the desired results.

—Guido Calabresi's rejection of the concept of efficiency for the evaluation of the law because it does not take the existence of transaction costs into account, may mean that although we can measure changes in court performance over time, we cannot assess those changes in terms of social efficiency without an external criterion that tells us whether the boundary has moved, and in which direction.

—Most of the empirical studies that will be used to illustrate the analysis are not economic studies, although they could be read in economic terms.

Chapters 3 and 4 will examine and systematise empirical research which is relevant for the operation and organisation of the courts under two variables: *selectivity* and *processing capacity*. At first sight, these concepts seem to run parallel

[252] Raiteri (1992) examines the process of evolution in the functions of courts with respect to the economy.

[253] The difference between the legal (and political) and the economic concepts of justice is examined in Raiteri (1988).

[254] Cf Hazard, Jr. (1965).

to the economic categories of demand and supply.[255] However, if they are seen as variables that can be manipulated for the purpose of enhancing the efficiency and effectiveness of courts and court systems, it soon will become clear that, in both cases, such manipulation can be accomplished from both the supply-side *and* the demand side. Instead, the distinction refers to a multiplicity of dimensions: the 'pyramid' of disputes; the filter effects of ADR on judicial procedures; the internal organisation of the courts; the role of procedure, the importance of administration and management, etc. For the same reason, the distinction is only analytical. Selectivity and processing capacity have many points of contact that will become readily apparent.

[255] Stock (1995) employs a similar distinction ('caseloads' and 'disposition capacity'), that also seems to run parallel to the economic concepts of supply and demand.

3

Selectivity

THE DISPUTE 'PYRAMID'

THE SELECTION PROCESS of disputes for litigation has been often depicted as a 'pyramid'. The base of the pyramid is formed by a particular universe of social conflicts, which is considered relevant for a specific research purpose, such as family conflicts that may lead to judicial divorce. Disputes are the result of the rejection of a perceived grievance or of the assertion of incompatible claims to the same resource. In order to be recognised as such, disputes must first have undergone a transformation process. It is necessary, for example, for injurious experiences to be considered as a legitimate cause for a dispute.[1]

This does not mean, however, that a dispute will always result in judicial proceedings. The dispute would have to be defined first as a *legal controversy* or a *case* capable of being resolved by a legal mechanism. Even then, it may not reach the judicial stage. Other possibilities are always open, such as abandonment, settlement, or resolution by alternative dispute mechanisms (ADR). In any case, only a minute proportion of disputes in society reach the courts, since they are filtered out at each successive stage of transformation.

The Civil Litigation Research Project (CLRP), for example, has documented this process by trying to determine when and how experiences are perceived as injurious, as well as the factors that contribute to their developing into a dispute, including their definition as a *legal* dispute.[2] It has also attempted to quantify the 'dispute rate', as measured against a pre-established baseline, and, most importantly, the 'litigation rate', or at least, the degree of participation of lawyers and courts in the relevant disputes.[3] Thus, according to a survey of American households that sought to identify the occurrence among the general population of civil disputes of the type that might be brought before the courts or non-judicial alternatives, as well as the way in which these disputes were handled,[4] found that only in a small proportion of cases (one fourth, or less, with exceptions) did the disputants resort to lawyers' services, while they took the dispute to a court (generally between 3 per cent and 20 per cent, depending on the type of problem) even less frequently.[5]

[1] See Miller/Sarat (1981: 527) and Abel (1973).
[2] Felstiner *et al.* (1980–1).
[3] Miller/Sarat (1981).
[4] Miller/Sarat (1981: 534 ff.).
[5] Miller/Sarat (1981: 537, 543).

A similar survey, conducted in the late 1990s in England and Wales, found that, among a random sample of 4,125 adults, about 40 per cent reported having experienced one or more 'justiciable problems' during the previous five years.[6] A second sample of 1,134 individuals was then selected among those who had experienced a non-trivial justiciable problem. 5 per cent did nothing about the problem; about a third (35 per cent) tried to resolve the problem without help; the rest (60 per cent) tried to obtain help or advice from an outside adviser.[7] About 20 per cent of respondents had either commenced legal proceedings or had to defend themselves against legal action taken by others, but only in about 14 per cent of all cases was the matter concluded on the basis of a court, tribunal or ombudsman's adjudication. Of course, such percentages would vary across the types of problems concerned. Involvement in legal proceedings was most common in cases concerning divorce and separation (62 per cent), DSS and education tribunal matters (38 per cent), owning property (37 per cent), employment problems (21 per cent) and accidental injury (14 per cent). Involvement in legal proceedings was least common in neighbor disputes (2 per cent) and consumer problems (5 per cent).[8]

A similar phenomenon may be perceived in the criminal area. Here, the 'selectivity of criminal prosecution' means the phenomenon whereby only a fraction of the total number of crimes committed in society are brought before the criminal justice system and ultimately result in a sentence. Thus, for example, out of a total of 4,072,000 crimes reported or otherwise made known to the authorities of the Federal Republic of Germany in 1981, only 1,845,000 were solved (46 per cent); of which only 1,065,000 (26 per cent) led to a judicial proceeding; and, finally, only 385,000 sentences and penalties were decreed (less than 10 per cent of the total number of reported crimes).[9] For many observers, the selectivity of criminal prosecution is tantamount to social discrimination, to the extent that poor and marginalised persons are more likely to be prosecuted than the members of the wealthier social classes. While this perception is not unfounded, in reality it is the complex interplay of several factors and multiple stages, such as the type of crime, the criminal record of defendants, the willingness of the population to report crimes, the degree of police effectiveness,[10] the prosecu-

[6] Genn (1999: 21 ff.). A 'justiciable problem' or 'event' was defined, for the purposes of this survey, as a (non-trivial) 'matter experienced by a respondent which raised legal issues, whether or not it was recognised by the respondend as being "legal" and whether or not any action taken by the respondent to deal with the event involved the use of any part of the civil justice system' (at 12 f.).

[7] Genn (1999: 68).

[8] Genn (1999: 150 f.).

[9] Rottleuthner (1987: 123). The more complex the intervening factors, the more socio-economic status is diluted as an explanation of selectivity. This observation has been made by studies seeking to relate SES (socio-economic status) of defendants to outcomes in criminal cases. Douglas (1994: 99): 'After all, if one controls for virtually all the processes whereby SES might affect outcome, one would scarcely expect to find that SES continues to be related to outcome.'

[10] According to the data cited, German police were able to solve only 46% of crimes, that is, where a suspect is identified and arrested. In other places, such as Mexico City, police are much less

tor's and the courts' policies, that ultimately determines the extent of the criminal justice system's selectivity.[11]

The image of a pyramid and the marginality of court involvement become clearer in certain areas, such as tax matters, where possible disputes are almost exclusively of a legal nature and where, for the same reason, the appropriate mechanism for resolution is primarily of a legal character. Thus, for example, in 1974 American taxpayers filed a total of over 121 million federal tax returns. Out of the more than 2 million returns examined, 18,569 civil cases were received by the appellate division of the Internal Revenue Service; of which only 9,932 civil cases were docketed in trial courts; the courts of appeal decided only 363 cases and, finally, the US Supreme Court, at the apex of the American judicial hierarchy, had to decide just four cases.[12]

The model of the litigation pyramid has been criticised for being too simple and linear, and for failing to take account of the complex paths that disputes may take.[13] The pyramid model implies a court-centered approach that does not hold true in reality. From the perspective of the methods that exist for handling disputes, courts represent just one of many possibilities, and the complex factors that influence the course of a dispute do not warrant considering judicial proceedings as their natural 'goal'. And even if the problems and disputes confronted by ordinary persons are defined, from the outset, as 'justiciable problems', ie, matters which raise legal issues capable of being resolved by the courts, it can clearly be shown that they may take many paths that do not necessarily involve a final court order or decision.[14]

A court-centered approach, however, is precisely what is intended here, since we are examining social and other factors that affect court performance. However, partly because of the need to recognise the effect of other dispute resolution mechanisms on the demand for court services, I propose to modify the idea of vertical selectivity implicit in the pyramid model through the addition of a 'horizontal'-selectivity criterion. Accordingly, the demand for court services would be the composite result of both vertical and horizontal selectivity.

It is also claimed that the pyramid model is flawed in that it suggests a continuous, seamless progress of disputes up the pyramid and the judicial hierarchy. Indeed, there are significant formal barriers to access to the courts, ie, access to the courts is surrounded by certain formalities and subject to specific

successful. There, in 1995, according to official statistics, 218,599 crimes were made known to the public prosecutor's office, but only 5,479 suspects were formally charged before the courts (2.5%). See Ruiz Harrell (1996: 18 ff.). But even if the police are utterly ineffective, the factors that influence selectivity may produce similar results to those elsewhere.

[11] Cf Rottleuthner (1987: 125 ff.).

[12] Hurst (1980–81: 429).

[13] Cf Griffiths (1983: 174 ff.).

[14] Genn (1999: 150 ff.).

requirements that stress the difference between the internal and external dimensions of courts. Besides economic, social, cultural and organisational barriers, access to the courts is governed by the corresponding rules of jurisdiction. In particular, such rules have to define the appropriate 'point of entry' to the judicial system: the appropriate type of court and the appropriate type of procedure. This means, in fact, that the way disputes are treated by the system also *defines* the dispute itself, the existing possibilities for, and the limits to, its resolution. A good example of this would be the 'small claims' discussion.

Finally, the demand for court services may be subject to a limited degree of feedback. Litigation levels may also be affected by the way courts deal with disputes; by the social effects of their decisions, including their economic consequences; by their rate of compliance and implementation, etc. One would expect—as a general economic principle postulates—that supply and demand would eventually find a state of equilibrium. The continuing debate on the 'litigation explosion', where demand always seems to exceed supply, shows that this is not so. It should be borne in mind that, although several options and possibilities for resolving disputes exist, they do not constitute a competitive market in a strict sense, nor are citizens, strictly speaking, consumers who influence the level of supply through their power to choose the quantity and quality of the 'justice services' available. It is true that selectivity and efficiency require that the judicial system select only the number and type of cases it can adequately process. However, the manipulation of either the demand for, or the supply of, court services will seldom introduce fundamental changes into a dynamic process affected by complex factors.

Selectivity

As already stated, selectivity means the degree of discrimination between social disputes that may potentially go to court and the actual number of disputes that reach them. Ideally speaking, the selectivity process should operate in such a way that only 'relevant', 'important' or 'real' disputes, however defined, are handled by the courts, whereas all 'non-relevant' disputes are dismissed or left out.[15] There are many reasons why such process does not work like this in real life, such as the following:

—The general, abstract, and formal formulation of the rules of jurisdiction.
—The social, economic, and cultural barriers to the courts, which exert pressure in favor of the abandonment or settlement of claims (hence, the problem of access to justice).
—The multiple functions performed by the courts.

[15] For a similar formulation, see Simsa (1995: 18). This makes for the relevance of extra-judicial settlement mechanisms and their 'filtering effect'.

—The necessary intervention of courts in certain kinds of disputes or for the achievement of certain outcomes (for example, the enforcement of debt payment).

The attempt to increase the degree of selectivity in favor of the 'relevant' disputes is a never-ending process. Different strategies—both internal and external to the courts—are available for this purpose. Changes intended to relieve the judicial system (for example, through the introduction of no fault divorce) almost always have a real and positive effect, at least for some time. But the final (ideal) goal of selectivity may be illusory. If we look at selectivity in dynamic terms, as if it were a problem of balance of supply and demand, we would probably find that such an equilibrium never materialises. 'Excess' demand may prompt continuous supply adjustments, but changes in supply also affect demand levels.

Selectivity has two dimensions: a vertical and a horizontal dimension. *Vertical selectivity*, as defined here, corresponds closely to the 'pyramid' model of dispute resolution, ie, the proportion of disputes that survive various stages of development and transformation always gets narrower and narrower. Within the judicial hierarchy, the progress of disputes is subject to more precise and controllable criteria (appeal). Vertical selectivity also refers to the appropriate type of court and procedure for the entry of disputes into the court system.

On the other hand, *horizontal selectivity* concerns the continuum of procedures and dispute settlement mechanisms that range from traditional adjudication and other forms of third-party dispute-settlement resolution, such as arbitration, mediation and conciliation, to negotiation and settlement of disputes between the parties. There is, in Martin Shapiro's words, a 'mediating continuum' comprising different forms of triadic conflict resolution. Judges and courts 'are simply at one end of a spectrum rather than constituting an absolutely distinct entity'.[16] The discussion on 'alternative dispute resolution' (ADR) has also made it clear that there is no essential difference between adjudication by the courts through a formal proceeding and other dispute settlement procedures. For this reason, ADR may either coexist with formal adjudication within the same court (for example, in court-annexed arbitration),[17] or stand as an alternative outside the court system, which will be mainly the situation considered here.[18]

In both cases ADR helps regulate the demand for court services (such as through a 'filtering effect'), in so far as the duration and costs of adjudication are comparable to the duration and costs of ADR procedures. In other words: court efficiency is affected by ADR efficiency. For this reason alone, ADR

[16] Shapiro (1981: 2ff., 8).

[17] Here, we find a point of contact between the aspect of selectivity and the problem of 'processing capacity,' which is addressed in the next chapter.

[18] See also the distinction drawn by Shavell (1995a) between *ex ante* and *ex post* ADR agreements.

warrants analysis as a component of court selectivity. It should also be considered that selectivity is a dynamic process and that the discussion on court efficiency is centered partly on the transference of dispute treatment from the formal court system to ADR.

Even if a continuum exists between adjudication and other 'alternative' dispute resolution mechanisms, a formal boundary or threshold between both types of procedures will necessarily be present. The boundary is marked by the formal requirements established for access to the courts. The advantages that less formal procedures are supposed to have over formal adjudication indirectly show that such a boundary can have a significant effect. Moreover, although the existence of ADR devices within the courts themselves (mediation, conciliation, arbitration) may lower access barriers to the judicial system and increase litigation levels, it does not make the formal entry threshold irrelevant.

Another important boundary/threshold exists between the social and legal fields. As will be discussed later, disputes do not progress in a continuous way from non-legal to legal and subsequently to adjudicated disputes. Many disputes never reach a formal legal stage, but not because they are incapable of becoming legal disputes. The legal nature assumed by a dispute may partly depend on the person, instance or agency to which it is channeled in the first place (attorney, information center, etc.). Such persons, organisations or agencies may be partially isolated from each other, which would translate into a small number of referrals between them, as shown by a study conducted in four German cities, summarised later.

Rules of Jurisdiction and Court Functions

Rules of jurisdiction define which disputes can be heard by which court.[19] Disputes have to be framed in legal terms. They have to be formulated as a legal problem and their scope narrowed in a way that can be processed by a court. This requirement has the important consequence of partially severing the link between a legal controversy and the underlying social dispute. In fact, the vast majority of disputes processed by the courts are only such in formal terms. They are not necessarily 'real' disputes, for example, where the parties are already in agreement or where defendants choose not to contest a suit. Thus, the formal definition may have a significant impact on the functions performed by the courts themselves. Other formalities and requirements that accompany the concept of a legal dispute and that have a considerable selective effect on them, include requirements such as the legal interest of the parties, the ripeness of the controversy, etc.

[19] Of course, *substantive* legal rules also play an important role in terms of selectivity. But we assume this to be a case of self-selectivity, so to speak, by the disputants themselves, ie, their decision to go to court will be affected by their estimates as to the outcome. Cf the economic model of the selection of disputes for litigation described in the previous chapter.

Rules of jurisdiction are normally defined by legislative bodies. However, in applying them, the courts exercise significant interpretative powers. Thus, even if they are supposed to be 'passive' organisations waiting to be called upon by citizens or governmental agencies, courts have the ability to determine and 'manipulate' their workload to a certain degree, by deciding which cases they will hear and which ones they will dismiss. Such a decision often takes place after a suit has been filed with and admitted by the court. The court may find some formal requirement missing, which enables it to dismiss the suit. In other cases, courts, particularly those with the highest hierarchy, enjoy considerable discretion in choosing the cases they will hear when they satisfy certain relevance criteria.

In short, rules of jurisdiction, as well as the courts themselves through their interpretations, exert a powerful selective influence on litigation. For that reason, and because of the relative ease with which rules of jurisdiction can be changed, they are the first target of reform efforts aimed at curbing excessive demand. A slight modification of the rules means that whole categories of cases will be transferred to other courts, to alternative dispute-resolution mechanisms or even cease to be an appropriate object of judicial proceedings. This seems to be a recurrent strategy whenever certain types of cases become a mass phenomenon, often because they are not backed by 'real' disputes. Under such circumstances, rules of jurisdiction are changed in order to transfer cases or take them out of the courts entirely. Disputants, particularly institutional parties, may also develop strategies and mechanisms that effectively avoid the recourse to litigation.

There is an inevitable tension between the ideal criteria of selectivity, as embodied in the rules of jurisdiction, and the real functions that courts are called upon to perform in society. The four-function model of courts proposed by Erhard Blankenburg[20] may be helpful in visualising this tension. The model is based on two variables: 'predictability of outcomes' and 'agreement between parties.' Each of these two variables, in turn, may present itself as 'high' or 'low,' as shown in the following table:

Table 1
Four-fold model of court functions
(Blankenburg 1981–2)

	Predictability of outcome	
Agreement between Parties	*Low*	*High*
Low	I. Adversary litigation	III. Enforcement
High	II. Mediation	IV. Notary

[20] See, for example, Blankenburg (1981–2: 613).

Cell 'I' consists of 'real' litigation, where the parties do not agree on questions of fact or of law, and they therefore rely on a third party to resolve them. Cell 'II' implies a partial accord between the parties, which leaves room for mediation. In the case of cell 'III', plaintiff and defendant are well aware who will win, as a result of which the proceeding started by the plaintiff (but perhaps provoked by the defendant) has the purpose of enforcing or providing him or her with a legal title, as in the case of a debt which, for some reason, the defendant is unwilling or unable to repay. In the case of cell 'IV', the intervention of the court is meant to certify an agreement previously reached by the parties, to lend it formality and validity. This happens, for example, in uncontested cases such as most divorce suits, where the court plays a formal but necessary role to make a previous arrangement legally valid.[21]

From the point of view of ideal selectivity, the order of functions (I–IV) also reflects their presumptive degree of priority for the courts. Thus, rules of jurisdiction should preferably allow the entry of type I and II cases, and filter out, as far as possible, type III and IV cases. Paradoxically, from a numerical standpoint, type III cases seem to predominate in most jurisdictions. Does this mean that rules of jurisdiction should be changed in order to achieve 'ideal' selectivity?

Such outcome does not seem desirable or even possible, in view of other important considerations. First, it should be remembered that while it is advisable that 'real' disputes be settled or treated by the courts, the formality of the rules of jurisdiction and, more generally, the separation between the legal and other social fields, do not make 'real' and 'legal' disputes equivalent. Courts may use this distinction for the purposes of higher selectivity, but this may be perceived as problematic or even arbitrary. Secondly, courts, like any other institution, perform many other functions besides dispute resolution,[22] which has traditionally been viewed as their central task. Enforcement is particularly important as a primarily economic function of the courts, even if it does not involve 'real' adjudication. The same can be said of rule-making. And finally, court functions are subject to a dynamic process of redefinition. Thus, instead of expecting courts to concentrate ideally and exclusively on a particular function, the compromise that has to be found between the various functions they perform leaves room for such a process of redefinition, which can justifiably follow efficiency concerns, among other criteria.

Small claims courts offer an interesting example of the complex interplay between (1) the rules of jurisdiction defining which disputes are to be considered 'small'; (2) the basic justification of such institutions, which is to give the common citizen access to speedy, inexpensive justice; (3) the functions they

[21] Cf Blankenburg (1981–2: 613).

[22] See, for example, Galanter (1983b).

effectively perform, and (4) the continuum that exists between formal judicial proceedings and other less formal dispute-resolution mechanisms.[23]

In the United States, small claims courts emerged basically in response to the perception that the ordinary justice dispensed by the courts was too cumbersome and costly for the 'poor' citizen, who was thereby deprived of the opportunity to assert his or her legal rights.[24] The solution was seen in the establishment of courts with claim limits, a simplified and less formal procedure, and with little or no need for attorney representation.

However, a series of empirical studies conducted in the 1960s and 1970s, in the wake of the consumers' rights movement, found that small claims courts were not really performing the functions for which they had been created.[25] It appeared that they were mostly used as debt collection agencies by business plaintiffs, frequently with attorney representation, against individual debtors.[26] Consequently, the victory rate for plaintiffs was high, as was the default and losing rate for defendants.[27] Additionally, the assumption that 'small' claims were 'simple' claims was shown to be plainly wrong in many cases.[28] Thus, one was left with the impression that small claims courts had been really established for the purpose of either eliminating cases under a specific amount from the dockets of the formal court system, and/or of creating or preserving professional opportunities for attorneys.[29]

As a consequence of these findings, many proposals have been advanced with the aim of making small claims courts more effective *as courts*, even if this implies introducing many features of ADR into their mode of operation.[30] However, regardless of whether this aim is attainable, small claims courts cannot escape a fundamental economic constraint. The cost of resolving a dispute is normally inversely proportional to the amount at stake, so that, notwithstanding the merits of small claims and the advisability of having them heard and decided by a court, disputants will generally *not* resort to them if, as measured in monetary terms, such claims are indeed too 'small'.

[23] Small claims courts are fairly typical of common-law countries, but other systems have roughly equivalent institutions (for example, justices of the peace). See the essays compiled in Whelan (ed.) (1990).

[24] See Yngvesson/Hennessey (1975) and Steele (1981).

[25] For a summary and criticism of some of these studies, see Yngvesson/Hennessey (1975: 228 ff.). See also Weller/Ruhnka/Martin (1990), summarising a study conducted in the late 1970s on fifteen small claims courts in various cities in the United States.

[26] Cell III instead of cells I or II in Blankenburg's model cited above.

[27] Yngvesson/Hennessey (1975: 247 ff.) discuss different explanations for this finding. See also Weller/Ruhnka/Martin (1990: 9 ff.), who contend that this fact alone does not justify prohibiting collection agencies from making use of these courts. For a different concept of what winning and losing means in a small claims court, which avoids framing it in terms of 'all-or-nothing', see Vidmar (1984).

[28] Yngvesson/Hennessey (1975: 226, 258).

[29] Yngvesson/Hennessey (1975: 258, 226 f., 256 f.).

[30] Yngvesson/Hennessey (1975: 262 ff.).

Justice as a 'Market'? The Dynamics of Supply and Demand

One of the central tenets of economic theory holds that supply and demand will reach equilibrium, ie, a state where the marginal cost of producing and consuming a good are the same. The state where the marginal social cost equals the marginal social benefit is efficient.[31] An efficient equilibrium is only reached if certain conditions are met, such as the existence of a competitive market, where information flows to all agents equally, and where transaction costs are negligible. In the real world, however, few of these conditions are fulfilled. Thus, the concept of equilibrium is useful as an analytical tool or as a criterion for economic evaluation, rather than as a description of the actual operation of the economic system.

We shall not concern ourselves here with the problems of economic theory in this respect. Instead, we shall briefly examine the problem of selectivity in terms of the supply and demand of court services. We shall assume that the courts are 'producers' of one or more 'goods' (actually, 'services'),[32] and that their quantity and quality are somehow affected by the level of demand for such goods and by the capacity of the courts to provide them.[33] In this section three questions will be specifically considered. The first question is whether the operation of the courts and similar institutions can be conceptualised in terms of a 'market', that is, whether, and to what extent, this operation responds to the laws of supply and demand, as in a competitive market. The second and third questions deal with a related yet more specific problem: how do courts respond when demand for their services increases? Why is excess demand not only possible but also a common occurrence? The latter question is quite relevant from the point of view of court efficiency. Regardless of whether or not we accept the existence of a 'litigation explosion,' it is easy to observe that almost everywhere caseloads are tending to increase, rather than decrease. What is the efficient response to this growth?

At first sight, nothing seems to be further from a competitive market than the way courts operate. First of all, court operation is heavily subsidised, which means that the parties do not pay the full price of their services, either because, as happens in many countries, court fees do not exist or are extremely low, symbolic.

Then there is the issue of *choice*. Do people really have the choice of going to court? If they want to obtain a *binding* and *enforceable* resolution to their disputes, they seem to have little choice but to go to court, because courts provide a (quasi) monopolistic service. However, if their interest lies rather in dispute *settlement*, the question is then: how do the many forms of the 'mediating

31 Mercuro/Medema (1996: 14 ff.).

32 On justice as a service, see Gravelle (1995: 279 ff.).

33 Landes/Posner (1979) contend that courts produce two basic goods: dispute resolution and rule-making, and that such goods are intermediate goods, in the sense that they can be used as inputs for the production of final goods. See also Posner (1996: 88 ff.).

continuum'—adjudication, arbitration, conciliation, mediation, and the like—relate to each other in terms of choice? Do citizens, at least in their capacity as claimants, have the freedom to choose the mechanism that is best suited to their disputes, needs and budgets? And if so, does competition between those mechanisms therefore ensue as a consequence, resulting in a more efficient 'service'? In other words: is there a 'market' for justice, where citizens, like consumers, buy (and sometimes sell) a specific service which consists of dispute resolution?

Beginning in the 1960s, but particularly in the 1970s and 1980s, the inadequacies of the judicial process as a provider of 'justice' were rigorously exposed and criticised. Justice, as rendered by the courts, was deemed too costly, slow, cumbersome, formal, exclusive, and antagonistic.[34] For these reasons, among others, ADR mechanisms were proposed as an alternative to the formal judicial system that was not plagued by the evils attributed to adjudication. ADR was supposed to be speedier and cheaper; less formal and therefore more accessible; less antagonistic and consequently more favourable to the survival of ongoing social relations; it could even be more attractive from a technical or expert point of view (as, for example, in the case of commercial arbitration).

We know better now: ADR is not necessarily cheaper or speedier than adjudication; it may also result in second-rate justice; its political and ideological shortcomings should not be overlooked; and it tends to substitute the 'ideology of community' for the notion of legal rights.[35] Nevertheless, ADR mechanisms, both inside and outside the courts, continue to proliferate, thus increasing the apparent diversity of options available to the 'consumer' of dispute-resolution services.

ADR marks a profound change in the way the law and its use in society are viewed, a change that goes well beyond the failures of the court system. As Mauro Cappelletti points out in connection with the 'access-to-justice' and 'consumer-justice' movements,[36] modern law has undergone a shift in perspective: from the perspective of the 'producers' of law (legislative bodies, judges, public administrators) to the perspective of the 'consumers' of law; from the 'supply side' to the 'demand side'.[37] Such a shift is hardly surprising. If the law is an instrument in the hands of individuals and groups for the realisation of their particular goals, rather than just a necessary evil, it is to be expected, as in other fields of social life, that people will search for instruments and institutions that satisfy their legal needs. In this respect, citizens' legal needs can be said to foster the creation of a 'market' for justice.

[34] See, for example, Galanter (1980) and Röhl (1982).

[35] See, for example, Abel (1982a) and Edelman/Cahill (1998).

[36] Cappelletti (1993: 145 ff.).

[37] At least, from the point of view of the goals and legitimacy of the justice system. Further on, we shall argue that the demand for court services is decisively shaped by the available supply, which comprises the services provided by alternative mechanisms.

Nevertheless, the existence of a market implies that the unfettered freedom to buy determines, in the long run, the type and price of services that will be offered, because supply will adjust as long as there is a profit to be obtained upon entry into the market of new producers. This is not always so in the 'market' for justice. As we have seen, citizens are not as free to choose between the many dispute resolution mechanisms available to them while supply does not necessarily adjust to a competitive equilibrium. Consider, for example, the following aspects:

—Plaintiffs may voluntarily go to court, but they cannot always go to a court of their choosing (rules of jurisdiction prevent overlapping jurisdictions); defendants do not have this freedom. It is true that they may decide not to appear, but this, in turn, may have negative consequences for them.
—Some ADR mechanisms are not voluntary or binding (for example, court-annexed arbitration; certain forms of conciliation), which may subsequently result in judicial proceedings (for constitutional reasons, in many countries the right to resort to the state courts cannot be waived or denied).
—Some legal acts require court intervention to acquire legal validity.

In short, adjudication can be considered as a 'private good'[38] only in a limited sense, not only because the parties do not have the complete freedom to choose between various providers of 'adjudication services' in a competitive market, but also because private adjudication cannot offer other goods that derive from court activities, such as precedents. Public legal precedents are also necessary for the operation of private adjudication itself, since this form of adjudication cannot work with complete independence from state legal systems.[39] Moreover, adjudication cannot be wholly transformed into a private business, since judges competing with each other would always have the incentive to decide in favor of plaintiffs, who are the ones that choose to go to court.[40] Thus, the social legitimacy of adjudication would suffer if courts and judges were no longer perceived as impartial and independent.[41] For both reasons, ADR operates under the 'shadow of the law,' in the sense that it cannot completely exclude the intervention of the official court system.

On the other hand, even if there is no real market for justice, the existence of alternatives to the courts *does* affect the size and composition of judicial business. Any attempt to improve on court efficiency must consider the fact that the quantity and quality of adjudication is affected to a certain extent by the operation of these alternative mechanisms.

[38] Cf Landes/Posner (1979) and the comment by Carrington (1979).

[39] The main point of Landes' and Posner's analysis of adjudication as a private good (1979) is that private adjudication may be more efficient in some respects when compared with state adjudication, but that it lacks the necessary incentives to accomplish the function of rule-making.

[40] Landes/Posner (1979: 254).

[41] Shapiro (1981: 1 ff.) examines at length the problem of the collapse of court adjudication into a relationship of 'two against one'. The central justification for forcing a defendant to appear before a court is that a third party will be impartial and independent.

The very reasons that discourage the operation of the justice system as a market also prevent the supply and demand of court services from achieving equilibrium. Normally, a rise in the demand for goods or services in a private market may have two effects: the price of such goods or services will rise, which should help curb demand by discouraging those buyers who find the new price to be above the value of the particular goods or services (another consequence is that the buyer will start looking for substitute goods); and/or supply will rise, usually in the longer term, so that it achieves a new equilibrium with the higher level of demand.

Court systems can use either strategy to accommodate a rise in demand for their services. They can raise the 'price' of their services, for example, through longer delays, since they do not usually charge a fee for them. Alternatively, courts can expand the supply of their services by hiring more judges or other judicial staff, by increasing 'productivity' in the handling of cases, for example through case management, or by higher selectivity.[42]

These strategies, however, cannot operate in the same straightforward, uncomplicated manner in which they may work in a market. The supply of judicial services cannot be expanded at will, either in the form of more judges and judicial staff or through the speedier disposition of cases. A higher level of productivity may be achieved at the expense of the 'quality' (justice) of the product. An increase in the 'price' of court services, in the form of longer delays, may discourage some litigants although not enough of them to really operate as an equilibrating mechanism (some of those discouraged will resort, for example, to ADR). Alternatively, the dismissal of an increasing proportion of cases that do not fulfill certain criteria of relevance may not be effective enough in preventing litigants from filing suit anyway.

Because of the quasi-monopolistic and subsidised position of courts, but also because they may serve other purposes of the parties (for example, they may be useful as a means of pressure for reaching a settlement or the abandonment of a claim), the demand for judicial services does not seem to be able to reach a point of equilibrium. Instead, courts seem destined to face ever rising caseloads and to search for mechanisms that will enable them to cope with increased demand without seriously compromising the social functions they perform.[43]

Economic, Social, and Legal-institutional Factors

The economic model of litigation, as described in a previous chapter, is based on the idea that costs alone, of whatever kind, are the sole determinants of the decision to bring suit before a court. The socio-legal model, on the other hand, identifies a varied set of social factors that bear on that same decision. The two models are not

[42] Cf Pastor Prieto (1993: 235 ff.).

[43] On the problems and consequences of excess demand for judicial services, see Pastor Prieto (1993: 231 ff.).

incompatible, insofar as social factors can be easily translated into the language of costs. However, because the economic model is more abstract and general, individual social factors still have to be identified, analysed and understood first

There are various types of socio-legal studies that examine such social factors. One of these is 'longitudinal studies', which seek to establish a statistical relationship between caseloads and social variables, such as population or economic growth, over a long period of time.[44] Other empirical studies attempt to identify the specific factors that affect litigation levels in a certain place and time. Thus, for example, a study on the prediction of future caseloads in Germany identifies and systematises the factors that influence court caseloads.[45] Those factors are divided into *social factors*, *legal system factors*, and *factors deriving from the 'filtering level'*.

Social factors include:

—Complexity of life conditions.
—Social forms of behaviour.
—Marginal economic conditions.
—Introduction of new technologies.
—Demographic and socio-structural developments.

Legal system factors include:

—Legal costs.
—Attractiveness of courts as dispute resolution institutions.
—Certainty of the law.[46]
—Acceptance of the law.

Factors deriving from the 'filtering level' include:

—Behaviour in relation to legal issues.
—Dispute advice in the pre-court field.
—Influence of legal insurance.
—Influence of extra-judicial forms of dispute resolution.
—Behaviour of attorneys.

In several studies, Erhard Blankenburg[47] has attempted to identify the factors that influence the supply and 'demand' of court services. His most illustrative

[44] See *Law and Society Review*, vol 24, no 2, 1990, and the observations on this issue by Pellegrini (1992), who stresses the impact of 'endogenous' variables, such as procedural reforms and court organisation, on litigation rates.

[45] See Stock (1995: 117 ff.).

[46] And of judicial decisions! There is an interesting empirical study by Hanssen (1999) that links the recruitment method of judges to the uncertainty of judicial decisions and litigation rates. Using three different sets of statistical data on US state courts, the study concludes that greater judicial independence—itself a consequence of appointment methods as compared to the election of judges—has a net positive effect on decision uncertainty (here, in disputes over public utility regulation) and, therefore, on higher litigation rates in high courts (but not trial courts).

[47] See, for example, Blankenburg (1981–2, 1994b).

study is a comparison between the 'litigation cultures' of the Netherlands and the neighbouring German state of North-Rhine-Westphalia.[48] Both regions display strong similarities in a number of social, economic and cultural indicators. Thus, one would expect to find similar litigation rates. However, litigation rates were significantly lower in the Netherlands. In his search for an explanation, Blankenburg demonstrates the extent to which the lower number of caseloads in the Netherlands is influenced by all sorts of non-judicial institutions and mechanisms that filter out disputes and help avoid formal litigation. This result is brought about by the complex interplay of several institutional levels, of which the courts are just one factor. Therefore, his study suggests that institutional factors may be more decisive in explaining litigation rates than either social values or attitudes towards the courts.

These studies indicate, on the whole, that caseloads are not an irresistible force of nature, but are influenced in predictable ways by economic, social and legal-institutional factors that operate outside the courts. It is true, on the other hand, that the supply and demand of court services cannot be regulated as easily as that of other services, due to the complexity of the factors involved and to the fact that this supply and demand does not create a completely free consumer 'market.'

VERTICAL SELECTIVITY: THE PROCESS

Cases and Controversies

Formal requirements provided for in procedural laws concerning access to the courts establish a degree of social and legal relevance for such cases to be heard. They also seem to have an important economic function to fulfill: to avoid a costly flood of lawsuits. The scarce resources of the judiciary are much too precious to be squandered on lawsuits that are not sufficiently relevant in legal terms or that will bring little benefit to the parties or to society. Efficiency demands that potential plaintiffs be discouraged from resorting to the courts without 'real' cause. At the same time, the courts' doors should be sufficiently open to them for redressing the harm and violations they have suffered or are about to suffer.

For example, Article III, Section 2, of the United States Constitution extends the federal judicial power to 'cases and controversies' (regarded as synonyms) of specified types. Judicial doctrine has interpreted this expression to imply a set of requirements that admissible lawsuits must satisfy, such as standing and ripeness,[49] which mean that the plaintiff must have been directly injured or have a personal stake in the outcome. Cases must also be concrete and adverse, ie,

[48] Blankenburg (1994b).

[49] See Currie (1990: 6 ff.) and Landes/Posner (1994: 683).

no hypothetical cases or 'friendly' lawsuits are allowed. Thus, the 'cases-and-controversies' clause has been construed as preventing the US federal courts from giving so-called 'advisory opinions,' whereas administrative agencies are not.[50]

A detailed analysis of so-called 'anticipatory adjudication', where plaintiffs seek an opinion of the court on the hypothetical legality or illegality of prospective behavior, rather than the resolution of an actual dispute caused by previous events, may help to better understand the purposes, in terms of selectivity, of the 'cases and controversies' requirement. In attempting to uncover the economic rationale behind the general ban on anticipatory adjudication, Richard A Posner and William M Landes conclude that part of the answer may lie in the risk of increased costs:

> It would consume enormous resources by requiring courts to decide hypothetical, contingent, inchoate, premature, abstract, not yet fully developed disputes that, left alone by the courts for a time, might not require judicial resolution at all.[51]

It appears that anticipatory adjudication may also increase the amount and, therefore, the cost of judicial error. Anticipatory adjudication carries a greater risk of incorrect decisions because of the lack of a factual record, with questions of injury, damages, social costs and benefits being largely of a hypothetical nature. Thus, the court does not have the benefit of deciding on the information generated by the act itself.[52]

It should also be considered that the private incentive to seek anticipatory adjudication is greater than the social incentive. Thus, if the private cost of litigation were not considerable, courts would be flooded with requests for anticipatory adjudication by persons deterred from acting by the prospect of being sanctioned. If courts are guided by efficiency concerns, they will turn down requests for anticipatory adjudication, at least whenever the private gain is positive but the social gain negative. Ripeness, mootness, and related doctrines provide courts with convenient categories for refusing anticipatory adjudication when it is unlikely to be socially beneficial.[53] In short, anticipatory adjudication is unlikely to be worthwhile when all it does is replace private legal advice.[54]

[50] Landes/Posner (1994: 684 f.). On the other hand, courts in several countries, including many states in the US (Posner and Landes mention ten), have the power to render advisory opinions. This possibility seems especially useful and interesting for international courts, in view of the fact that states are rather reluctant to bring suit or to appear before them.

[51] Landes/Posner (1994: 685).

[52] Landes/Posner (1994: 685, 690). It should be noted that the abstract questions of legality and constitutionality that courts in the European legal tradition may sometimes resolve resemble anticipatory adjudication, in the sense that plaintiffs are not required to demonstrate a direct and personal legal interest or harm. Perhaps for this reason, the circle of persons and organs entitled to raise them is very restricted. Nevertheless, such questions are never purely hypothetical. They may derive from a real conflict and a general social interest must be affected in order for the courts to intervene.

[53] Landes/Posner (1994: 694).

[54] Landes/Posner (1994: 715).

Economic reasons are of central importance here, because—it should be recalled—judicial systems encounter severe diseconomies of scale beyond a certain size:

> Increases in demand for judicial services, unlike other services, cannot readily be accommodated by creating new 'firms' without undermining consistency of legal doctrine or by enlarging existing courts without greatly increasing decision costs.[55]

Efficiency concerns regarding the use of judicial resources are particularly significant because of the position and role of courts in the legal system: courts have the final say in legal matters, and, for this reason alone, their decisions and opinions always have some precedential value. It is rather odd, however, that although anticipatory adjudication is generally rejected by judicial systems, precedents—which we shall discuss later—may play precisely this role for third parties.

Procedural Stages and Anticipated Disposition

Despite a common perception to the contrary, few cases are actually resolved by a final decision of the courts. Selectivity continues to operate once a case has been admitted by the courts and is being processed by them. A certain proportion of cases is filtered out at each stage of proceedings, with ever fewer cases surviving into the next stage. Cases that are selected out are disposed of or terminated in an anticipated manner. Thus, the pyramid is reproduced at each procedural stage and at each judicial instance.

To illustrate the extent to which this may happen, I shall summarise a Colombian study on the performance of so-called 'regional justice' (*justicia regional*).[56] In Colombia, regional justice was a special branch of criminal jurisdiction established in 1984 to combat particularly violent or socially disturbing crimes, such as kidnapping, extortion and terrorism.[57] The study is interesting for several reasons. First, it shows how selectivity operates in the criminal courts. Besides self-interest and costs, more rigorous due process requirements and heightened technical demands in the application of the criminal laws make it difficult to reach the sentencing stage. Secondly, the study offers revealing data for each stage of criminal proceedings. Third, regional justice was established for the specific purpose of becoming especially effective, but this was seldom the case. And finally, the study also illustrates how the problem of *backlog* is created when the selectivity process does not result in *final* dispositions.

The *first stage* in criminal proceedings is the investigation carried out by the prosecutor's office to determine whether certain facts qualify as criminal behavior and who may be the alleged violators. A total of 15,688 cases were under

[55] Landes/Posner (1994: 712).
[56] Nemogá Soto (dir.) (1996).
[57] Nemogá Soto (dir.) (1996: 37).

investigation during the period between July 1992 and 1993. This resulted in an overall disposition rate of only 16.5 per cent (2,588 cases or about 46.7 per cent of new cases). Of these 2,588 cases, 43.7 per cent (or an overall rate of 7.2 per cent) reached the 'pre-trial' stage (*instrucción*); while 56.4 per cent were disposed of by inhibitory determination or lack of jurisdiction.[58]

The *second stage* is the pre-trial stage. In the period between July 1992 and July 1993, a total of 15,897 cases were pending before the courts. 2,123 cases were disposed of (13.4 per cent of total cases or 25.9 per cent of new cases), but only 512 cases resulted in a formal accusation and a trial (3.2 per cent of total cases and 24.2 per cent of dispositions). The remainder were disposed of on other procedural grounds, including lack of jurisdiction (31.7 per cent).[59]

The *third stage* is the trial stage. Between June 1993 and July 1994, a total of 6,041 cases were pending before the courts. Some 3,336 cases were disposed of, or about 55.5 per cent of the total number of cases and 88.8 per cent of new cases. Only 2,327 cases were terminated by sentence (38.5 per cent of total cases and 70 per cent of dispositions). Some 533 cases were terminated by 'normal' sentence (about 22 per cent of total sentences), while the remaining 1,794 sentences (78 per cent) were anticipated terminations, ie, negotiated sentences.[60]

In short: this example shows how selectivity by the courts and official agencies *themselves* operates in the first instance of a criminal trial, reproducing the overall pattern of a pyramid, and how the inability to produce final dispositions results in increasing levels of backlog. It also provides us with an insight into the complex interplay between selectivity and other efficiency criteria. While the increased selectivity of cases undoubtedly operates as a necessary efficiency device, it may have other undesirable (inefficient) consequences at the social level. In this example, the relevant question is whether selectivity does not go so far as to nullify the deterrent effects of the criminal process and its legitimating role with respect to the institutional apparatus of social control.

Appeal

Appeal, that is, the possibility of challenging a judicial opinion or a judgment in order to get a review before another, usually higher, court, appears to be a universal or at least a widely accepted feature of legal systems which have attained some degree of development.[61] Appeal implies a structured hierarchy of two or more tiers of courts, each one hearing a smaller number of cases the higher up they are in this hierarchy.

The scope of appeal, ie, the issues that will be examined on review, may also vary at each level of the judicial hierarchy. We find here an important distinc-

[58] Nemogá Soto (dir.) (1996: 42).
[59] Nemogá Soto (dir.) (1996: 46 f.).
[60] Nemogá Soto (dir.) (1996: 53).
[61] The most visible exception being Islamic law. See Shapiro (1981: 194 ff.).

tion between *de novo* and *limited* appeal. *De novo* appeal means that a case can be reviewed anew, in all its factual and legal aspects, while a limited appeal restricts the issues that may be raised for the purpose of such a review. In civil-law countries, a *de novo* review is usually granted at a first level of appeal, whereas in common-law systems, appeals tend to be limited.[62]

Another important distinction is that between appeal *as of right*, normally at a first level, and *discretionary* appeal. The latter gives a court (for example, a Supreme or Constitutional Court) the power to admit or to reject an appeal. It is also important to realise that nowadays a common form of appeal concerns decisions made by administrative agencies and bodies, either before ordinary or specialised courts ('judicial review of administrative action').

Appeal is a form of vertical selectivity within the judicial hierarchy. At each successive level, a decreasing but variable portion of the cases initially filed are heard. The decrease in the number of cases at each level and the variable portion of cases appealed (rate of appeal) are due to many factors, such as the following:

—The functions and scope of appeal, especially the increasing rigor and selectivity of the standard of review.
—The increasing difficulty of arguing a case that has already been examined, and consequently, the diminishing likelihood of prevailing at a higher level (the reversal rate).
—The increasing costs of continuing to pursue a case.
—The pyramidal structure of the court system, where a decreasing number of judges at each level can only consider an increasingly limited number of cases.

What the *efficient* level of selectivity on appeal might be depends again on the functions and scope of appeal. Appeal is seen as performing a multiplicity of functions and purposes, such as political control, error correction and prevention, harmonisation of the law, selection of issues for judicial lawmaking, a new opportunity to be heard, etc.[63] Assuming that a fundamental (economic) objective of judicial decisions is *accuracy*, the primary function of appeal would therefore be *error correction*. Steven Shavell[64] has developed an economic analysis of the appeals process based on the assumption that error correction is the main purpose of appeal.

If error correction is accepted as the central purpose of appeal,[65] then the appeals process can be explained as a low-cost, effective means of achieving this

[62] This is probably due to the power the jury alone has to determine the facts, a decision that cannot be changed by a higher court. In general, common law systems continue to attach to the ideal of 'one-level decision making, upon which bits and pieces of hierarchical quality controls have been grafted.' Damaška (1986: 58 ff.).

[63] See Shavell (1995b), Shapiro (1980) and Barclay (1997). See also the list of functions cited in Gilles (1992: 140).

[64] Shavell (1995b).

[65] The problem with the notion of error correction is that it may imply a subjective perception. Shavell (1995b: 424).

end in a legal system. Despite efforts that can be made to achieve accuracy in judicial decisions, error is always possible and correcting it costly. Thus, an alternative exists between investing more resources to improve accuracy and prevent or correct error at trial level (for example, through better-trained judges or by lengthening the time available for consideration of cases), and granting the possibility of appeal.[66]

If investment in enhanced decision accuracy at the trial level is chosen, such investment will only be marginally productive at a certain point. Consequently, installing an appeal process may turn out to be cheaper. This is so because, firstly, no matter how accurate trial courts are, it is still desirable to correct errors that do occur at trial, which is accomplished by the appeals process. Secondly,

> investing an additional dollar in trial court accuracy to reduce errors means that the dollar cost is incurred in every case, whereas investing a dollar in the appeals process means that the dollar cost is incurred only with the probability that an error is made.[67]

In short, there is an underlying advantage to investment in accuracy in the appeals process rather than in the trial process.[68]

What is the Efficient Level of Appeal?

Generally speaking, the appeals process will be efficient if the costs of providing it are less than the costs that would otherwise be incurred by the parties and society in its absence. In other words:

> the appeals process will be desirable if and only if the social harm from certain error exceeds the social cost of an appeal plus the expected harm from failure to reverse error, that is, the probability of failing to reverse error multiplied by the harm from error . . . (I)n general, the appeals process is more likely to be socially desirable the lower the cost of the appeals process, the greater the chance of reversing error, and the greater the social harm from error.[69]

There are a number of circumstances and problems that affect the efficiency and the value of the appeals process:[70]

[66] Shavell (1995b: 383).

[67] Shavell (1995b: 387).

[68] Shavell (1995b: 387). The optimal accuracy of the trial court is lower when an appeals process is utilised than when trial courts alone are relied on and there is no second chance to correct errors. Social harm from error at trial is less than the harm deriving from certain error. Social harm from error at trial is instead measured by what follows trial court error, namely, the cost of the appeals process plus the expected harm from failure to reverse error. This amount is less than the certain harm from error (386). On the other hand, an appeals process gives trial judges an incentive to be more accurate in their decisions, in order to avoid reversal (390 f.).

[69] Shavell (1995b: 386).

[70] Shavell (1995b: 388 ff.) addresses most of these problems as extensions of the basic economic model of error correction.

The first concerns the process of 'separation of disappointed litigants.'[71] The appeals process takes advantage of the information that litigants possess about likely errors. Consequently, it is the litigants who decide if an appeal will be brought or not. Thus, not only errors will be corrected, but also this will be done cheaply, 'for the legal system will be burdened with reconsidering only the subset of cases in which errors were more probably made'.[72] But in order for this to be effective, it is necessary to find some means of ensuring that victims of error find it more worthwhile to bring appeals than those who are not. In other words: 'there will be separation if the private cost of an appeal is less than the expected return given mistake but exceeds the expected return given correct decisions'.[73]

If separation does not occur naturally due to the private costs of appeal, the state can ensure that separation occurs by selecting an appropriate fee or subsidy. If fees or subsidies for separation are introduced, the social value of appeals may be diminished but may still be positive.[74]

Another problem is that the information that litigants may possess about error is imperfect, ie, they may not know beforehand what the appellate court will define as an error, which may somewhat diminish the value of appeal. On the other hand, when litigants are able to predict appeals court outcomes, the appeals system may become either more or less valuable, depending on whether the trial court's decision was correct or incorrect.[75] Moreover, errors in appeal are possible, ie, correct decisions can be reversed.[76] To counter this possibility, multiple levels of appeal will be established, and the extension of the basic model to them is straightforward.[77]

Going beyond the economic model, the question is now: how efficient is the appeals process in the real world? An indication of the cost of the appeals process is the *frequency of appeal*.[78] If appeals are too frequent, it may mean one or both of two possibilities: the lower courts in fact make too many errors, or, litigants bring more appeals than are really warranted. In the latter case, there may be a variety of explanations:

—The appeals process is too inexpensive (disappointed litigants are not sufficiently 'separated').

—The appeals process is also uncertain (for example, there are many appellate courts, all of which maintain different positions on a legal issue) or prone to error, meaning that litigants wish to take advantage of even the slightest probability of winning.

[71] Shavell (1995b: 384).

[72] Shavell (1995b: 381). An implication of this is that the appeals process is superior to the random selection of cases for review by a higher court (388).

[73] Shavell (1995b: 385).

[74] Shavell (1995b: 385, 388).

[75] Shavell (1995b: 390, 413).

[76] Shavell (1995b: 389). The *accuracy* of appeals courts is described by the probability of reversal given trial court error and the probability of reversal given correct trial court decisions (383).

[77] Shavell (1995b: 389).

[78] Shavell (1995b: 380, footnote 3).

—Litigants wish to delay the final decision on a lawsuit, raising the stakes and the cost to the other party.
—Litigants do not accept losing and bring appeals regardless of the need or cost of doing so.
—Appeal is regarded as little more than the continuation of the first instance and only the appellate court will give a 'real' decision.[79]

The frequency of appeals can be measured by the proportion of lower court cases that go before a higher court.[80] This proportion can be shown to greatly vary across countries and jurisdictions. Thus, for example, the rate of appeals filed to civil and criminal cases terminated between March 1992 and March 1993 before the US federal courts was about 16 per cent.[81] In France, approximately 42 per cent of cases brought before the *tribuneaux de grande instance* were appealed in 1990. In Germany, about 16 per cent of cases brought before the *Landgerichte* (regional courts of first instance) were appealed in 1991. In Japan, the likelihood of appeal was about 10 per cent from district courts in 1989. In Mexico, about 32 per cent of final judgments rendered by the High Court of the Federal District (itself an appellate court of second instance) were further challenged before the federal courts in 1992.

Nevertheless, the appeal rate does not in itself clearly indicate that there are in fact 'too many appeals'. An appeal rate of 50 per cent (one out of every two cases, a rate approached by the French example) might arguably be considered too high, but then again, much depends on the purposes and conceptions that lie behind the appeals process. Therefore, a more reliable and objective indicator would be the *overload* of appellate courts. By overload we not only mean that the court has a growing backlog of pending cases but also that it cannot adequately fulfill the purpose or purposes for which appeals exist (purpose or purposes that are not necessarily those of the individual litigant).[82]

Obviously, isolated figures for appeal rates in different countries tell us nothing about *trends* in the appeals process. Nevertheless, there are reasons to believe that the rates of appeal in different countries have been increasing for some time.[83] The perception of a 'litigation explosion' seems to be linked to the perception of an 'overload' of the appellate courts as well, as suggested by the title of two general reports presented at the 8th World Conference on

[79] Jolowicz (1989: 76).

[80] The following figures for the US, France, Germany and Japan are reported in Shavell (1995b: 380 f., footnote 3). For Mexico, see CIDAC (1994: 61).

[81] See the somewhat different rates of appeal presented in tables 4.2 and 4.5 in Posner (1996: 100 f., 114 f.) for the same period. Posner also examines the difficulties of computing appeal rates, especially the 'real' rates, based on the number of appealable decisions rather than on the number of cases filed in the lower courts (1996: 113 ff.).

[82] Jolowicz (1989: 73).

[83] For the US, this is confirmed in Posner (1996: 92 ff.). See also Krafka *et al.* (1996). This study found that the increased volume of civil appeals resulted firstly from the increased volume of filings in the district courts and secondly from an increased proclivity to appeal prisoner and non-prisoner civil rights cases.

Procedural Law in 1987.[84] The reports examine the procedural techniques that have been adopted or have been under consideration with a view to keeping caseloads of appellate courts under control.[85] These techniques fall into two main groups: those intended to control the number of appeals ('restriction on the right to or content of appeal') and those intended to enable appellate courts to dispose more expeditiously of their caseloads ('efficiency devices').[86]

Below is a list of these occasionally overlapping techniques and measures, intended to control the number of appeals by limiting the right to or the content of an appeal:[87]

—The sanction of costs for the losing party.
—The use of discretionary appeal, usually after the first appeal.
—The finality of first instance decisions.
—The upgrading of first instance trials.
—The exclusion from appeal of certain cases or decisions (for example, small claims; non-final decisions).
—The restriction of the admissible grounds for appeal.
—Raising the level of importance of cases as measured in monetary terms.
—The circumscription of appeals to questions of public importance or to the existence of special reasons.
—The restriction of appeal to issues of law.[88]
—The claimed error should make a difference to the judicial outcome.
—The issues on appeal should have been ordinarily raised at the trial.
—The imposition of penalties for abuse of the appeals process.

An interesting twist to the problem of growing appeal caseloads and of the overload of appellate courts is that this phenomenon sometimes goes hand in hand with the diminishing value of appeal, either because the rate of reversal of lower court decisions is also decreasing or because the rate of cases that are not dismissed and granted review is also declining. Thus, for example, the reversal rate for US district courts and administrative agency decisions on appeal has fallen considerable since 1960, from 17.7 per cent to 5.3 per cent.[89] Moreover, in 1993, only 1.47 per cent of the cases on the US Supreme Court's docket were granted review, but the number of applications had been steadily growing, from 870 in 1960, to 2,841 in 1982 and to 5,156 in 1993.[90] In Germany, the following success rates on appeal were reported for the '*Landgerichte*', '*Oberlandesgerichte*' and

[84] See the general report by Jolowicz (1989: 71 ff.) on 18 'Western' countries. A report on the socialist countries of Europe can be found in the same volume, pp 95 ff.

[85] See Jolowicz (1989: 74).

[86] Jolowicz (1989: 74 ff., 87 ff.). This distinction is virtually equivalent to my distinction between 'selectivity' and 'processing capacity'.

[87] Jolowicz (1989: 74 ff.) and Shavell (1995b: 418 ff.).

[88] The problem is here the fluid distinction between questions of fact and questions of law. Jolowicz (1989: 82).

[89] Posner (1996: 70, table 3.5).

[90] Posner (1996: 83, footnote 23, 122).

'*Bundesgerichtshof*' in civil matters during 1989: nullification and remand 1.7 per cent, 1.8 per cent, and 12.7 per cent; modification or own decision on the merits 20.3 per cent, 19.6 per cent, and 5.3 per cent, respectively.[91]

Growing appeal rates, however, suggest that appellants do not seem to be discouraged by their rather dim probability of success. So why do people appeal? Again, such figures may indicate that people are less interested in winning their case than in pursuing other goals, such as making sure that they are being treated fairly, or simply increasing the stakes for the opponent party. Thus, the economic model may be useful as a starting explanation of the appeals process as error correction and as a predictor of long-term developments, but it will hardly help us to interpretate fragmentary figures from various countries.

The Role of Political and Institutional Constraints

In principle, the problem of the overload of the appellate courts could be also solved by an adequate increase in the resources assigned to them. However, this is not always possible for several reasons that derive from particular institutional, economic and political constraints, thus making the optimisation of the limited resources available the most viable alternative, ie, through higher selectivity and productivity.

Consider first the difficulty of increasing certain resources. For example, where there is only one Supreme Court, increasing the number of justices may diminish its political clout, or, if it is divided into several chambers, increasing their number may result in more inconsistencies between their opinions. Instead of appointing more judges, another possibility is to hire more clerks and staff, although there is always a limit to the number of cases that a judge can adequately handle or oversee.

Two examples, the first of which refers to the Mexican federal judiciary, and the second to the US Supreme Court, may illustrate the role that political and institutional constraints play in this sense. They show that the alternative between growth and higher selectivity depends on the institutional position of the court in question and the political functions it performs.

The Mexican federal judiciary has a double jurisdiction: an ordinary jurisdiction in federal matters, and a constitutional jurisdiction in '*amparo*' matters.[92] '*Amparo*' is a judicial procedure originally established around the middle of the nineteenth century following the model of American judicial review. It was originally designed as a simple, expeditious procedure before the federal courts for the protection of the fundamental constitutional rights of citizens when encroached upon by public authorities, but subsequently developed into a highly complex device for the final review of all kind of decisions by public authorities, including courts, both local and federal. This development resulted

[91] Gilles (1992: 134).

[92] See CIDAC (1994), Taylor (1997) and Fix-Fierro (1998).

in what a scholar at the beginning of the twentieth century called the 'impossible task' of the Supreme Court.

The composition of the Mexican Supreme Court changed several times during the twentieth century with the aim of helping it cope with its growing caseload and backlog.[93] The Court was composed of eleven justices in 1917. In 1928, the number increased to sixteen, and the Court also started working in three chambers. In 1934, the number of justices jumped to twenty-one. In 1951, a fifth or auxiliary chamber, composed of five justices, was incorporated into the Court. Additionally, new courts, modeled on the US Circuit Courts of Appeals, were established to take over some of the Court's business.

These changes were purely palliative. Clearly, the only way to solve the problem was for the Court's jurisdiction to be redefined and for it to specialise in constitutional matters (this was finally achieved to a large degree between 1987 and 1999). However, this would have given it a degree of political power that would have been at odds with the existing authoritarian regime. That the federal judiciary was weak is further demonstrated by the fact that the number of lower federal courts grew at a very slow pace until the mid-1980s, lagging far behind population and other social growth processes.[94]

Unable to grow because of the lack of political clout to negotiate a satisfying budget and facing increasing caseloads, the federal courts resorted to higher selectivity in the form of a growing proportion of '*amparo*' suits dismissed for procedural reasons. The federal courts began to rigorously interpret the statutory grounds for dismissal of suits, such as 'lack of standing' or 'lack of legal interest', 'non-exhaustion of ordinary remedies', 'irreparable consummation of the harmful act', 'lack of proof of the challenged action' etc.[95]

A statistical study on the workload of the Mexican federal district courts shows that, in general terms, the percentage of cases dismissed for procedural reasons, which reached almost 79 per cent in 1992, closely correlated to the average number of cases the courts handled, against the background of a relatively low, constant backlog rate.[96] However, despite the growth of the number of federal courts since the early 1980s, the rate of dismissal for '*amparos*' has remained relatively high and few such determinations are further challenged (approximately 11 per cent). This indicates that the '*amparo*' does not always serve its purpose as a review procedure for error correction, but has become a

[93] Taylor (1997: 145 ff.) and Fix-Fierro (1998).

[94] For example, in 1930 there were only forty-six single-judge district courts and six single-judge appeals courts, for a total population of fewer than twenty million inhabitants, mostly in rural areas. Twenty years later the number of courts remained virtually unchanged, with the exception of the five new collegiate courts to be established the next year. In 1970, there were only fifty-five district courts, nine appeals courts and thirteen collegiate courts, but the population had grown to almost fifty million inhabitants, in a country undergoing a rapid process of industrialisation and urbanisation. The federal judiciary's share of the federal budget decreased from 1.33% in 1930 to 0.06% in 1980 (by contrast, it was 0.42% in 1996). See Cossío Díaz (1996: 54 ff.)

[95] A similar strategy is confirmed for the overburdened courts in the Mexican state of Jalisco by Zepeda Lecuona (1997).

[96] See CIDAC (1994: 74 ff.).

device for delaying and creating additional costs during a judicial proceeding, since it is very likely that a higher court will confirm the lower court's decision to dismiss the suit.

The other example concerns the 'New York University Supreme Court Project',[97] which conducted a two-year empirical study between 1982 and 1984 with the two-fold purpose of developing a theory of the US Supreme Court's role and of how it should select cases for plenary consideration, and of subsequently applying that theory to the cases brought to the Court in a term in which a serious workload problem was alleged. In particular, the study sought to determine whether 1) on the basis of the theory developed, all the cases heard by the justices that year truly demanded their attention, and 2) there were cases the Court did not hear that it should have heard.[98]

The study is based on what the authors call a 'managerial model' of the Supreme Court's responsibilities. The basic ideas underlying this model are that the Court has a finite capacity to hear cases, that it cannot act as the ultimate 'error corrector,'[99] and that the objectives it should follow in selecting cases for plenary consideration 'should be to establish clearly and definitively the contours of national legal doctrine,' once the issues have fully 'percolated' in the lower courts; 'to settle fundamental inter-branch and state-federal conflicts', and 'to encourage the state and federal appellate courts to engage in thoughtful decision-making'.[100] In other words, the Court should not select cases because of the presence of error or because of the importance of the substantive issues involved, but because there is some structural basis 'for suspending the strong presumption of regularity that should ordinarily attach to the decisions of subordinate actors in the judicial system.'[101]

The study's findings for the 1982 term indicate that, under the proposed managerial model, 'a significant portion of the time and energies of the Supreme Court (was) being misdirected'.[102] In particular:

—Only 48 per cent of cases granted review in 1982 *had* to be reviewed; meaning that over half of the Court's docket was discretionary.
—Nearly a quarter of the cases granted review did not have a legitimate claim on the Court's time and resources.
—Less than 1 per cent of the cases denied review during 1982 were cases that should have been heard by the Court that year.

[97] See Estreicher/Sexton (1984, 1986).

[98] Estreicher/Sexton (1986: 4).

[99] Estreicher/Sexton (1986: 1 ff.) argue that the Court has consciously ceased to play this role at least since 1925. They also reject the proposal of an Inter-Circuit Tribunal that would hear cases referred to it by the Court, because with or without this Tribunal, the Court could never intervene in a sufficient number of cases to eliminate incoherence from federal law.

[100] Estreicher/Sexton (1986: 4 f.).

[101] Estreicher/Sexton (1986: 4–5).

[102] Estreicher/Sexton (1986: 6).

In short, according to the managerial model, during the 1982 term the US Supreme Court was unnecessarily overburdened.

Obviously, the persuasiveness of these findings depends on the acceptance of the theory and of the managerial model behind them, which might not go unchallenged if a different perspective were adopted. The NYU Project uses a 'legal' model of case significance, but other models—such as the policy, the market, and the statist models—which imply other roles for the Court, might yield different results. Those other models show that the Court selects cases that are of significance to different constituencies, none of which dominates the Court's agenda.[103] Consequently, a new consideration of the cases granted review reaches the conclusion that most cases were significant according to two or more of the other models, and that far fewer cases could clearly be categorised as 'agenda mistakes.'[104]

The first example shows that higher selectivity in a situation of political and institutional weakness of the courts, which prevents them from obtaining resources that are minimally sufficient, is more of a desperate strategy than a policy for the rational management of judicial resources and of the judicial process as a whole. It may result in an unacceptable degree of formalisation of the legal criteria that the courts apply to resolve cases and, ultimately, in injustice.

Regarding the second example, and assuming that the US Supreme Court was actually overburdened,[105] the unique position and power it enjoys exclude any changes that may diminish such a position. Other solutions must be envisaged, such as, for example, the establishment of an Inter-Circuit Tribunal,[106] or, if this is not accepted, through a different definition of the criteria by which the Court selects the cases it will hear, since most of its business is discretionary.[107] And such criteria depend, in turn, on the conception one may have on the role played by the Court, for example, as 'manager of the federal judicial process.' Paradoxically, such a definition, while theoretically opening up more maneuvering room for the Court to select its cases, would in fact impose greater constraints on it, as it is based on a single—the legal—agenda, thus preventing the Court from flexibly responding to a variety of social agendas and concerns.

In short, it is difficult to strike a balance in the complex interplay between the size of available resources and selectivity, relative to the functions performed by the courts in a given political system. We may cite, as a last example of this assertion, the case of the Federal Constitutional Court of Germany and the 'constitutional complaint' (*Verfassungsbeschwerde*), a remedy available to citizens

[103] Cook (1994: 146).

[104] Cook (1994: 144 f.).

[105] The number of Supreme Court decisions on the merits during one term has steadily declined, from 163 in the term that ended in 1983 to 86 in 1995! Posner (1996: 80 f., table 3.9).

[106] As already mentioned, Estreicher/Sexton (1986: 2 f.) explicitly reject this proposal, which is one of the motivations behind the development of their managerial model.

[107] Abraham (1998: 187 ff.).

for challenging unconstitutional actions or laws issued by public authorities.[108] The number of constitutional complaints has steadily grown since 1951 (423 complaints were filed that year) and 1996 (5,117 complaints filed).[109] This has required the introduction of a previous selection procedure. As a result, on average, only 2.57 per cent of complaints are granted review.[110] However, since the complete suppression of this remedy is a 'political taboo,' the Court will be only able to operate effectively in the future if the selectivity of complaints is further increased and if the Court is able to freely decide which constitutional goals and policies it will pursue.[111] Thus, the likelihood that individual complaints will be granted review will further decrease, but at least the legal system as a whole may profit from the overproduction of complaints and from the possibility of selecting only new legal issues with an 'evolutionary potential'.[112]

VERTICAL SELECTIVITY: THE PRODUCTS

The outcome of courts' activities undoubtedly has an impact on what we have called vertical selectivity: decisions, precedents, and judicial law-making can affect the volume and type of business the courts will handle, by either encouraging or discouraging litigation. Nowadays, litigation is a mass phenomenon, so it is extremely important to distinguish clearly between 'judicial activities', that is, the production of individual actions and decisions under certain procedural conditions, and 'jurisprudential activities' of courts, ie, the production of information about legal reasoning and its dissemination.[113]

While any judicial action or decision, separately considered, may fall into either of these two categories, the distinction is necessary because they form two sets of activities that are constituted and interpreted in different ways.[114] 'Judicial activities' can be analysed from a statistical point of view, as well as from procedural and pragmatic perspectives.[115] The 'jurisprudential activities' of the courts, on the other hand, depend on the institutional conditions that govern the production and the formal legal force of precedents, but also on the activities of the legal community, which affect their dissemination and exert an influence in defining their formal or informal authority.

In this section, we shall simply consider some aspects of these court activities to the extent that they may affect vertical selectivity. It should be noted that

108 See Blankenburg (1998).
109 Blankenburg (1998: 40 f.).
110 Blankenburg (1998: 49).
111 An inquiry commission of the Federal Ministry of Justice recently recommended that the Court should enjoy broader discretion in accepting or dismissing complaints. Blankenburg (1998: 58).
112 Blankenburg (1998: 58 f.).
113 This distinction is taken from Serverin (1993: 339 ff.).
114 Cf Serverin (1993: 340).
115 Serverin (1993: 341 ff.).

there seems to be a shortage of empirical studies that examine this particular perspective in detail. For example, there are studies that deal with the selection processes for the dissemination and publication of judicial decisions, rather than their effect on the demand for judicial services. Nevertheless, we shall at least mention the issues involved.

Decisions

Judicial decisions (in general, not only final judgments) are relevant from the point of view of selectivity in connection with at least two aspects: *accuracy*, and *enforcement* and *implementation*. Accuracy is relevant because, as we assumed earlier, inaccurate or incorrect decisions generate unnecessary social costs and may even have an impact on future levels of litigation. Implementation is relevant because judicial decisions that are not enforced or complied with also generate unnecessary costs. It may well be that they discourage litigation in the short term, thus relieving the courts of some of their workload, but in the longer term they contribute to the social inefficiency of the judicial institution as a whole.

Accuracy

We have already established that legally accurate, or correct, decisions are also economically efficient, at least in the long term, for the parties, the judicial system, and society in general.[116] Accurate decisions may be more or less likely to be challenged and re-litigated, but regardless of this possibility, it remains to be determined when a decision can be regarded as accurate. One possibility is to look at the rate of appeals and the way appeals are handled. Specifically, the percentage of decisions that are reversed in the various instances can be used as an indicator of the level of (legal) accuracy or inaccuracy of the judicial system.

A groundbreaking study on the efficiency of the Italian judicial system, carried out in the late 1960s, sought to determine the *general probability* that judges and courts would make accurate decisions, so as to calculate the same probability for particular courts.[117] This was done in two ways. The first approach involved the analysis of a sample of judgments rendered in civil matters by the *Corte di Cassazione* in 1962.[118] The analysis tried to determine, first, the degree of concordance or discordance between the decisions of the three levels of courts (*Corte di Cassazione*, court of appeals, district court) respecting the same matters.[119] For example, it was found that complete agreement between the three levels of

[116] For a detailed economic analysis of accuracy in adjudication, see Kaplow (1994).

[117] Pace (1970).

[118] Pace (1970: 172 ff.).

[119] Each court was regarded as if it were a single judge, and the three levels of courts as if they were a panel of three judges. This was done so as to avoid a systematic distortion in the calculation, because the voting numbers of each decision were not generally known. Pace (1970: 177).

courts occurred in 41.9 per cent of cases.[120] Next, the probability of concordant decisions was calculated, considering that decisions could be rendered either by unanimity or by majority. Finally, the probability of rendering accurate decisions was calculated for each court and for each judge. Thus, the corresponding probability was 60 per cent for district courts, 82 per cent for courts of appeals, and 83 per cent for the *Corte di Cassazione*, while the equivalent rates for individual judges were 56 per cent, 68 per cent and 67 per cent respectively.[121]

The second approach consisted of analysing judgments rendered by two collegiate courts (*grandi tribunali*) in 1965–6.[122] Here, the unanimity or majority vote for each decision was recorded. It was observed that an extremely high proportion of civil judgments and criminal sentences were rendered by unanimity, meaning that the probability of obtaining an accurate decision was also very high, almost 100 per cent.[123] Why the significant differences between both approaches? Although the two approaches were not comparable, it could be assumed that the first probability estimate was more realistic than the second. 98 per cent or 99 per cent probability can be more readily explained by the fact that most decisions are not reached through full analysis and discussion by the members of a panel, but are the result of the adherence to a judge's draft opinion by their colleagues.[124]

The *probable* level of accuracy may not be the *actual* level of accuracy corresponding to society's and litigants' expectations. Appeal is also a matter of perception, information, and predictability. Litigants will decide to challenge a judgment (or otherwise) partly on the basis of the perception or information they have on what the higher courts will do. This perception may be incorrect, so the higher court will confirm the correct (or incorrect) decision.[125]

But there is more to this than just misperception by the individual litigant. This misperception could have been instigated by the courts themselves, for example, through an inconsistency between their decisions, or because they have indicated a change in policy or interpretation. In any case, an incorrect decision by the highest court can only be corrected, at a later moment, by legislative intervention or by the court itself, provided litigants keep insisting.

The last point is linked to another possible indicator of judicial inaccuracy: *public* and *professional opinion*. Notwithstanding the fact that a final judgment cannot be changed, public and professional opinion may view one or more judicial decisions as incorrect and exert some pressure towards a change in that particular interpretation of the law. In this respect, no judgment will ever definitively settle a legal issue. The lawyers' community, which cites, uses and criticises those decisions may further shape judicial policy.

[120] Pace (1970: 176).
[121] Pace (1970: 187).
[122] Pace (1970: 188 ff.).
[123] Pace (1970: 190).
[124] Pace (1970: 191). A third analysis was carried out to evaluate concordance of judgments over time. See Pace (1970: 191 ff.) and the following chapter, by Carla Esposito (197 ff.).
[125] The perception that too many appeals are brought stems partly from the fact that only a small percentage of judgments are overturned on appeal.

Finally, a further indicator of judicial inaccuracy may be found in *ADR*, in so far as alternative mechanisms may yield a different solution in disputes that might otherwise have gone to court and where citizens show a preference for the non-judicial alternative.

Enforcement and Implementation

Court efficiency depends largely on the enforcement and implementation of judgments, not only on their accuracy. Non-existing or deficient enforcement of judgments may mean, for the winning party, a loss of money, time, and legal rights. When this kind of deficiency accumulates, it becomes dysfunctional for society as a whole. The judicial system itself may start to become irrelevant, and would-be litigants face the choice of either 'lumping it' or turning to other alternatives, which are not always available. Litigation may effectively be discouraged, thus reducing costs for the judicial system, but generating other socially diffuse costs.

Socio-legal studies on litigation have seldom focused on this problem.[126] They either give the impression that the judicial process ends when the final judgment of the trial or first instance court is issued (apparently, the appellate process is not as sociologically interesting), or they analyse the social consequences of judicial intervention in disputes. Except perhaps for a few exemplary studies, which will be mentioned later, they fail to discuss the impact of the enforcement and implementation of judgments on the efficient operation of the judicial system or, for that matter, the costs that may be imposed on the parties or on society by the lack thereof.

The main problem arising in this area is often that enforcement and implementation of judgments is highly dependent on the cooperation of non-judicial agencies (for example, those subordinated to the executive) because, technically speaking, the courts lack enforcing authority and means of their own. Such agencies normally pursue their own interests and agendas, meaning that the enforcement and implementation of judgments will be carried out under their terms, if at all, unless the courts enjoy considerable institutional weight and social legitimacy of their own.[127] In some proceedings, though, it is the parties who are primarily responsible for moving the enforcement process forward.

[126] For an exceptional study in this sense, although it analyses the implementation and impact of judicial decisions as a *political process*, see Canon/Johnson (1999). The study reviews much of the relevant research in this area and provides a model of the implementation and impact of judicial policies (16 ff.).

[127] This is a severe problem in many countries. To cite an example: in 1996, over 900 incidental petitions regarding the non-enforcement of '*amparo*' judgments (*incidentes de inejecución de sentencia*) were filed with Mexico's Supreme Court. This means that public authorities, which must comply with these judgments, often fail to do so, and not always for illegal reasons. It should be noted that Mexico's Supreme Court has, on paper at least, the power to remove from office and prosecute any official who repeatedly and unjustifiably refuses to comply with the judgment of a federal court. However, this power has almost never been used and petitions are either settled through a monetary compensation or languish for years on the Court's docket. See Fix-Fierro (1998).

The term 'implementation' might sometimes be more appropriate than 'enforcement' or 'execution'. It suggests a rather complex process, not unlike the process for public policy making and implementation, whereby one or several court decisions undergo different stages of interpretation, negotiation and partial realisation, rather than strict application.[128] Even the use of a higher court's precedents by the lower courts can be viewed as a problem of implementation.[129] So, in most cases the judgment itself will not be final, in the sense that it is likely to serve as the basis for further activities.[130]

In particular, there are significant differences in the implementation process of court judgments, depending on the area of the law involved. The implementation of a criminal sentence, entrusted to agencies that are formally part of the justice system, is not the same as that of a civil monetary judgment, where much depends on the activity of interested parties and the relationship existing between them. The implementation of an administrative court's judgment will certainly differ from a labour judgment, and so on.[131]

Here, some empirical findings related to this problem area shall be described. We shall select two examples from a series of studies conducted in Germany on the implementation of different types of judgments (recovery of money debts, divorce, labour, criminal sentences, administrative and constitutional judgments).[132]

One very common, even massive, type of judicial procedure concerns the enforcement of private money debts. This kind of proceeding makes up a large proportion of the civil courts' business in many countries,[133] but it hardly represents a legal problem, since, in most cases, the plaintiff has an enforceable document and the defendant does not contest the suit. The execution of the judgment, however, often entails a major practical obstacle, as shown by a German study on the collection of money debts, which is entrusted to a court official, the '*Gerichtsvollzieher*' ('court executor').[134]

The author of this study accompanied court executors on their rounds in their judicial district for several months. In addition to this, the court executors' files were assessed in connection with the behavior observed. Also, debtors were asked about the reasons why execution proceedings were initiated or why the

[128] See Blankenburg/Voigt (1987b: 10, 15 ff.). See also the essays collected in Raiser/Voigt (eds) (1990), Canon/Johnson (1999: 62 ff.) and the discussion, with regard to the US prison reform cases, in Feeley/Rubin (2000: 299 ff.).

[129] Cf Gottwald (1990: 71 ff.).

[130] Blankenburg/Voigt (1987b: 12).

[131] Blankenburg/Voigt (1987b: 10 ff.).

[132] Blankenburg/Voigt (eds.) (1987a).

[133] We have pointed to this phenomenon in connection with small claims courts.

[134] Klein (1987). See also the essay by Hörmann (1987) in the same volume, which offers a statistical analysis of civil courts caseloads in relationship to execution proceedings (between 1957 and 1981). No dramatic increase in money debt cases occurred, although a medium-sized increase in the enforcing activity of courts was detected.

debt was not paid. The study offers some interesting insights, which can be briefly summarised as follows:[135]

—There is a sort of debtor's (negative) career, comprising five stages, as defined and known to the executor. Court executors know the stage a debtor is in and arrange their work according to this knowledge.
—Workers, employees, unemployed persons and women in domestic activities, are over-represented in relationship to the execution rate in a district.
—70 per cent of executions concern enforceable titles; 13 per cent are based on judgments.
—Creditors belong mainly to the following categories: 18.4 per cent are large mail order stores; 71.4 per cent are small and middle-size businesses; 5.1 per cent are public utilities, and 5.1 per cent are private creditors.
—In 15 per cent of the cases the following reasons are given for non-payment: non-collected income or lack of money, 20.7 per cent; contractual violations attributable to the other party, 31.7 per cent; forgetfulness, 11 per cent; own fault, 11 per cent; fault of third persons or of family members, 13.4 per cent.
—The court executor's efforts to collect money debts (501 cases) yielded the following results: in 8 per cent of cases, the debtor promised to pay; in 55.5 per cent of cases, such efforts were unsuccessful;[136] in 19.4 per cent of cases, payment was effected, and in 11.4 per cent of cases, some property was successfully attached.

In short, there was only about a 40 per cent chance of recovering any amount of money at all. Where this probability is known beforehand to potential plaintiffs, it has to be taken into account in the calculation of litigation costs and expected judgment value. It should be noted that, in many cases, debt was incurred by persons who would never be able to repay the debt. In such cases, the affected businesses were either incapable of assessing this situation beforehand or else they factored a certain rate of default into the normal cost of doing business (this seems to be more the case for the larger businesses).[137]

In times of financial crisis, when payment default becomes a mass phenomenon that affects particular economic sectors, such disputes rapidly acquire social and political overtones that exceed the possibility of dealing with them effectively through the court system. Therefore, it is not surprising that, sooner or

[135] First stage: an enforceable title is served for the first time (27% of cases). Second stage: debtors have been served before and are known to the court's executor (21%). Third stage: titles accumulate over time and are regularly served (20%). Fourth stage: the debtor gives the '*Offenbarungseid*', that is, a solemn statement that he or she is not solvent (13.7%). Fifth stage, the debtor is officially known not to have seizable property (17.6%). Klein (1987: 52 ff.).

[136] This percentage corresponds roughly to the debtors that are included in the three last categories of a debtor's 'career'.

[137] For a highly detailed analysis of the legal and economic problems of consumer credit, see the study by Holzscheck/Hörmann/Daviter (1982) on Germany, especially sections XIII and XIV, on the judicial enforcement of consumer debts.

later, a tendency will emerge for such disputes to be resolved out of court, while institutional arrangements will be developed to deal with default as a matter of routine. An alternative here is, of course, the emergence of private debt collection. It has been reported, for example, that the annual amount of debts collected by commercial debt collection agencies in Germany in the late 1990s was three times the amount collected by court executors. Collection methods used by these agencies may include not only enforcement measures proper, such as attachment, but different 'persuasion tactics,' such as warning letters, telephone calls and personal visits, in order to put a certain degree of pressure on the debtor.[138]

The second German study refers to judgments pronounced by administrative courts on the validity of urban zoning plans approved by municipal governments and challenged by citizens.[139] One part of the study concerns the reaction of these local governments to the judgments rendered by the administrative courts, either where such courts had declared the invalidity of a local zoning plan or where a regional or a higher administrative court had issued an opinion with possible general consequences for them, but without immediate binding force.[140] In the first case, the rate of compliance was fairly high, with the occasional occurrence of evasion or delay tactics, whereas in the second, tactics involving evasion, non-compliance or ignorance were more frequently observed. Zoning plans that would be otherwise invalid were still being officially treated as valid.

Part of the explanation for the difference in reactions may lie in the varying constellations of actors and interests that participated in the implementation process. In the first case, citizens, local public opinion, attorneys and architects can be said to have had a high influence potential. In the second case, this potential diminished considerably, although the possible influence of certain actors, such as the representatives of professional or technical opinion, may have been greater. In both situations, however, the internal influence of local authorities remained high.[141]

Policy Making

There seems to be no doubt that courts are capable of pursuing certain identifiable policies when applying and interpreting the law. The larger role that courts play in contemporary society, which we discussed in a previous chapter, as well as the instrumental use of the law, explain and justify this possibility. However, pursuing certain policies when deciding individual cases may be somewhat different from general *policy-making*. In a recent, remarkable study on the intervention of the US federal courts in prison reform after 1965,

[138] Budak (1998: 34 ff.).
[139] Schäfer (1987).
[140] Schäfer (1987: 295 ff.).
[141] Schäfer (1987: 296).

Malcolm M Feeley and Edward L Rubin make this particular point convincingly.[142] They maintain that courts are capable of making policy as a distinct mode of judicial action that cannot be explained in terms of interpretation of existing laws. When making policy, the courts use the law as a broad basis of authority and, in this respect, judicial policy-making is not essentially different from policy-making by other branches of government. US prison reform cases are an excellent example of how the courts may define a larger social problem to be solved and choose and implement an appropriate solution.[143]

After a prolonged period characterised by a 'hands-off' approach to the handling of prisoners' complaints, the US federal courts began, quite abruptly after 1965, to play an increasingly active role in the running of state prisons. In the five-year period after 1965, federal courts declared prisons in Arkansas, Mississippi, Oklahoma, Florida, Louisiana and Alabama unconstitutional, either in whole or in part. Five years later, 28 more jurisdictions (and at present, 48 out of 53) had had at least one facility declared unconstitutional.[144] Alternatively resisted or welcomed by prison officials, intervention by the federal courts lasted many years, and, in at least ten states, their decisions and orders were directed at virtually every aspect of every institution in the state, ranging from due-process opportunities that had to be granted to inmates to the wattage of light bulbs in the cells or the caloric contents of meals.[145]

Prison reform cases are interesting on several counts. Feeley and Rubin use them as an opportunity to explore in depth the operation of courts in modern society. Here, we shall briefly discuss the effectiveness and the social efficiency of judicial policy-making in the prison reform cases, as well as its connection with selectivity.

How successful were the courts in reforming state prisons? Feeley and Rubin state that any assessment of success will be relative, but that the impact of judicial policy making in this area can be readily summarised.[146] In their view, the courts accomplished at least the following:[147]

—The extension of well-recognised constitutional rights to prisoners.
—The abolition of the South's plantation model of incarceration.
—The acceleration and consolidation of larger reform trends in correctional institutions.

These trends were visible in the professionalisation and bureaucratisation of prison administration, the emergence of a new generation of correctional

[142] Feeley/Rubin (2000).

[143] Feeley/Rubin (2000: 4 ff.). Feeley and Rubin examine and interpret this process using and combining the 'classic', the 'incremental-intuitive', and the 'hermeneutic' models of policy making.

[144] Feeley/Rubin (2000: 39 f.). The courts' first target was the 'plantation' model of incarceration prevailing in most southern states and which the judges had come to view as seriously deviant from the perspective of the national penal standards of the time.

[145] See Feeley/Rubin (2000: 41).

[146] Feeley/Rubin (2000: 362).

[147] Feeley/Rubin (2000: 366 ff.).

administrators, and the development and implementation of national standards. In particular, the bureaucratisation of prisons led, according to Feeley and Rubin, to a more efficient and accountable running of the prison system. On the other hand, courts were unable to prescribe new alternatives to prison, because their reform approach involved incremental changes to existing institutions.[148]

Was the reform process accomplished by the courts institutionally and socially efficient? According to a traditional model of adjudication, it could be argued that the courts were not the most suitable institutions for carrying out this process. However, the courts behaved more or less as any other policy-making body would have, regardless of their judicial nature, and were quite effective in this. It should also be noted that the courts became involved with prison reform partly because the legislature and the executive, both state and federal, had shown little interest in the subject. The courts were clearly responding to their own particular notions of social morality that made their efforts appear both necessary and legitimate. This also facilitated the rapid acceptance of their decisions at the appellate level, including the Supreme Court. Thus, we could safely say that the courts' intervention was socially efficient because it was necessary, effective, and legitimate.

Court behaviour in the prison reform cases is also interesting from the point of view of selectivity. Initially, the federal courts routinely dismissed prisoners' complaints on the basis of technical arguments, but also as a reflection of their own perceived role.[149] Despite these routine dismissals, prisoners were not discouraged and complaints kept pouring in, since the two main factors that deter people from litigating (time and money) meant little to them.[150] Gradually, the judges felt the need to provide a different response to these complaints, which also implied the need to view their role in a different light and to overcome traditional notions of federalism and separation of powers.[151] This new response naturally prompted further litigation. Once their task was seen as essentially accomplished (although other factors have also played an important role), the reform movement began to decline.[152]

At least two things can be learned from this example. First, selectivity is clearly a function of the 'technical' interpretation of legal rules by the courts as much as of their perceived institutional role. Courts may then modify both in response to changing social views. And second, the admission or dismissal of

[148] Feeley/Rubin (2000: 375 ff.).

[149] See Feeley/Rubin (2000: 30 ff.). Feeley and Rubin quote a significant statement in an opinion of the United States Court of Appeals for the Seventh Circuit: 'We think it is well settled that it is not the function of the courts to superintend the treatment and discipline of prisoners in penitentiaries, but only to deliver from imprisonment those who are illegally confined' (at 30–1).

[150] Feeley/Rubin (2000: 34 f.).

[151] Feeley/Rubin (2000: *passim*).

[152] Feeley/Rubin (2000: 46 ff.).

complaints may not necessarily have an impact on the volume of cases courts handle when certain marginal conditions obtain; for example, when access to the courts carries little or no costs (as was the case with prison inmates), or where it is expected that they may provide the most effective, and perhaps the only, response, especially if demands addressed to them are being formulated in the language of 'constitutional rights'.

Precedents

The effects of individual judicial decisions are, in theory, restricted to the parties to the controversy. In reality, however, they tend to spill over the case at hand. They serve as a kind of signal about how the courts may handle similar cases in the future. This is true in so far as the courts follow the fundamental principle of justice (the legal system's 'contingency formula', in Niklas Luhmann's terms), to 'treat like cases alike', which is also the source of another very basic value—that of certainty—that the law is supposed to guarantee. Therefore, judicial decisions always have some precedential value. It is worth noting that even though 'anticipatory adjudication' is not, as a rule, accepted by the courts, this is precisely the effect that their decisions may have on non-parties. Non-parties may profit at no cost from decisions that plaintiffs and defendants have provoked and for which they have incurred expenses. Adjudication is a 'public good' in this sense.

Judicial decisions also have an impact on selectivity. They may encourage or discourage litigation. Such an impact is related both to the formal legal authority and to the informal force of precedents, their dissemination, and to the degree of consistency between them.

Force and Dissemination

We have ascertained that judicial decisions naturally spill over the specific case at hand. Although this does not necessarily mean that a particular legal force must be attached to these decisions, legal systems have sometimes developed doctrines and principles that confer formal legal authority on judicial decisions beyond the specific case at hand.

A well known example is, of course, the doctrine of *stare decisis* developed and followed by the courts in common-law countries. *Stare decisis* means that the courts are bound by their own past decisions or by decisions of the higher courts in their jurisdiction when deciding similar cases, in other words, when the facts cannot be distinguished.[153] It is interesting to note that this doctrine could not have developed without an effective system for reporting and publishing cases, a situation that did not really exist before the nineteenth century

[153] Kempin (1990: 102 ff.).

and could not have developed without some notion of substantive law.[154] Today, *stare decisis* seems to be in a process of decline, apparently as a result of mass litigation and computerised information systems. As one commentator puts it:

> The judiciary has declined in influence while increasing in size; *stare decisis* is described as self-destructing, since if all the decisions are correct the bad ones must be drowned with the good in the process of attempting harmonious statements of law.[155]

To put it another way: the law is to be found, if at all, in large groups of decisions, rather than in the individual case.[156]

On the other hand, there are legal systems, belonging mostly to the civil-law tradition, where judicial decisions, at least in theory, affect only one particular case and lack any formal legal authority beyond this. Even judgments by the highest ordinary courts only have binding force respecting the individual case. They may invalidate a decision of a lower court, giving directions to a court of the same jurisdiction and hierarchy, where the case is sent for further consideration, as to how to apply the law correctly (which it can follow or not), as happens, for example, with the *Cour de Cassation* in France.[157] However, the nature of this court's judgments as a rational reasoning on how the law is to be correctly applied, and the fact that they are published, commented on and cited by lawyers through a network of communicating channels, confers on them a legal authority of their own that extends well beyond the individual cases that gave rise to them.[158]

The legal authority of court judgments, especially of appellate courts,[159] appears to rely heavily on existing channels for their publication and dissemination, and such publication is biased, in the sense that cases and judgments are selected according to certain criteria of relevance. The transformation of a Supreme Court's decisions into jurisprudential references is not automatic. Far from being a rational and neutral selection process, legal professionals (editors, judges, professors) participate in the dissemination process by selecting, reproducing, reducing and commenting on decisions on the basis of criteria that are never made explicit.[160] Publication, in particular, seems to play a central role in

[154] Kempin (1990: 103) and Glenn (1995).

[155] Glenn (1995: 270).

[156] As the medieval conception appears to have been ! Kempin (1990: 103). A similar view is also held by Feeley/Rubin (2000: 28 f.) in connection with the US 'prison reform cases'. These cases are not about single decisions that involve a 'purely self-contained dispute between two equal, fully competent parties . . .', but about 'narratives describing a complex, ongoing interaction between a court and a prison or prison system . . .'. They conclude that 'these extended cases are the real source of insight into modern law' (at 29).

[157] Cf Vincent *et al.* (1996: 408 ff.).

[158] See Serverin (1993: 345 ff.).

[159] It is mainly in appellate decisions that a rule-making role is acknowledged. This may be due to the fact that appellate decisions not only *apply* the law but also *reflect* on the process of the correct application of the law on the basis of a first-instance decision.

[160] Serverin (1993: 347 ff.). See also Siegelmann/Donohue III (1990) and Atkins (1990).

this process. In the United States, for example, not all opinions of federal courts of appeals are published any longer, but merely those that meet various criteria intended to identify an opinion likely to have precedential value.[161] Unpublished opinions are still available, but they cannot be cited by counsel as precedents in the circuit that issued them, nor will courts cite them as precedents in their own opinions.[162]

Obviously, non-published opinion is a useful adaptation to caseload growth, since it is not as carefully prepared as published opinion. However, there is plenty of room for discussion about the usefulness of having a class of appellate opinions that cannot be used as precedents, considering that the criteria for publication are vague and that significant precedents may be accidentally suppressed.[163] More seriously, a court's unpublished opinions are not a random sample of all its opinions, so the court's published opinions alone 'give a misleading impression of the judges' views': for example, reversals are more likely to be published than affirmations, which constitute the vast majority of decisions appealed.[164] So, for example, according to a study on discrimination complaints filed in US federal courts, 80 per cent to 90 per cent of cases fail to produce a published opinion. A direct comparison of published and unpublished cases shows that the two sets differ in significant and predictable ways (for example, cases with published opinion tend to be more complex), and that an understanding of the operation of employment discrimination law will change, sometimes dramatically, if all cases are considered rather than just those with a published opinion.[165]

Furthermore, institutional litigants may benefit from unpublished opinions, to which they have easier access, and also influence the decision to publish those opinions that are favourable to their litigation interests.[166] From this example, it is easy to see that the decision whether or not to publish an opinion may affect the litigants' behaviour in ways that are not necessarily desirable or efficient. On the other hand, there seems to be no alternative to limited publication.[167]

In civil-law countries, the discussion on the law-making powers of judges has made it clear that the judicial application of the law is far more complex and richer than the mechanical operation it was supposed to be, according to the ideology espoused by the French Revolution. Such law-making powers have often been recognised to be of a quasi-legislative nature, in the sense that statutes and codes depend on judicial and especially scholarly interpretation for their application.[168] Sometimes such interpretations serve as the basis for

[161] Posner (1996: 162 ff.), with further references to the relevant literature.
[162] Posner (1996: 165).
[163] Posner (1996: 165).
[164] Posner (1996: 167).
[165] Siegelman/Donohue III (1990).
[166] Posner (1996: 167).
[167] Posner (1996: 168 f.).
[168] See, for example, Shapiro (1981: 136 ff.).

changes in those very statutes and codes.[169] In any case, the law-making powers of the judge are not equivalent to those of the legislator.[170]

There are courts, however, that have been directly, explicitly and formally vested with legislative powers, albeit of a special nature. Such is the case of constitutional courts, which have been established in increasing numbers in European, Latin American and other countries since the end of World War II.[171] Such courts act as a sort of 'negative' legislator when they invalidate, with so-called general or *erga omnes* effects, a law, statute or regulation they have deemed to be unconstitutional. In other cases, they will not invalidate the unconstitutional legal rule, but instruct the legislator to change it according to specific guidelines and limitations.

We shall not concern ourselves here with the theoretical underpinnings of these special judicial institutions or with the source of their power to invalidate general rules. It is clear, however, that such power can be supported on the grounds of both justice *and* efficiency: justice (here: 'equality before the law'), in so far as it does not seem to be fair that only those that seek the court's protection will enjoy it, especially in view of the fact that the case concerns a general rule that will be declared unconstitutional; efficiency, to the extent that one ruling makes hundreds, if not thousands, of suits seeking the same protection unnecessary.[172]

There are other means for extending the effects of a judgment to a greater number of persons than those who actually appear in court. *Class actions* in the United States, for example, permit the representation in a judicial proceeding of a group of plaintiffs or of defendants who will not necessarily appear in court, but who will be affected by its judgment, provided that the court certifies that certain requirements have been met. As Mauro Cappelletti has put it, this and other similar procedural devices seek to 'provide a flexible, efficient protection of group and collective interests against the abuses of mass economy and a big government . . .'.[173]

Here, again, such devices seem to be justified in terms of both justice and efficiency: a group of persons who would not otherwise have filed a claim, obtain access to judicial redress and at the same time avoid the comparatively high costs of either organising for a collective appearance before the courts or of

[169] Luhmann (1993: 302, 320 ff.) postulates that the relationship between the legislator and the judge is not asymmetrical, with the latter subordinated to the former, but circular: the judge observes the legislator and develops interpretation criteria and doctrines (for example, the principle of the 'rational legislator'), while the legislator, in legislating, has also to observe the judge and to anticipate how judges will interpret and apply the laws.

[170] Cf Cappelletti (1989: 30 f.).

[171] See Cappelletti (1989: 185 ff.).

[172] Here again, the Mexican case may be paradigmatic. When private citizens seek protection against the application of general rules they consider unconstitutional and the Mexican Supreme Court grants such protection, it may only do so in favour of the claimant without making any general declaration regarding the rule or measure concerned. So, the force of its judgment will not benefit other citizens, unless they also file for protection and prevail in court. See Taylor (1997: 156).

[173] Cappelletti (1989: 290).

bringing to them a multitude of individual suits. However, it is doubtful that this form of representation also saves the judicial system expense. In fact, the reverse may be true: class actions may foster the propensity to litigate (we have assumed, for example, that isolated plaintiffs would not otherwise have filed suit), and the dispersion of the parties, particularly of potential defendants, translates into considerable enforcement and other costs.[174]

In conclusion, it may be more efficient to find ways to attribute broader legal effects to court judgments or to enhance the mechanisms of publication and dissemination of judicial decisions than to promote class actions and other similar procedural devices. Nonetheless, there are obvious limits to the effects that court judgments may have, if the distinction between legislation and adjudication is not to be blurred altogether and if the decision to litigate, driven mainly by self-interest, should still make a difference *vis-à-vis* the decision *not* to litigate.

Consistency

In general terms, judicial decisions should be consistent with each other. Contradictory judgments by the same or different courts concerning the same or a similar legal issue may create a state of uncertainty that will result in increased social (transaction) costs. Although such divergences are inevitable to a certain point, given the multiplicity of judicial bodies and the objective possibility of having different interpretations of the law, judicial systems have developed a variety of means for avoiding them.[175]

Before considering some of these solutions, note first, however, that changes in judicial interpretations and doctrines over time do not necessarily constitute an inconsistency in the sense mentioned above. It is an unavoidable fact that courts will give different answers at different times, as they seek to remain open and responsive to changing social needs.[176] On the other hand, courts should not change their interpretations in a way that is surprising, erratic or unwarranted.[177] On the contrary, new solutions will often be slowly introduced by the courts and explored as to their various consequences, before they form an identifiable, accepted jurisprudential trend.

Hierarchy and the binding force of *precedents*, where they exist, are the principal means by which the consistency between judicial decisions has traditionally been controlled. Another possibility is to centralise the decision over

[174] See Komesar (1994: 130 ff.).

[175] Luhmann (1993: 327) points out that the courts are the only institutions in the legal system charged with monitoring the consistency of legal decisions, including their own.

[176] For many years, it was held in common-law jurisdictions that the doctrine of *stare decisis* prevented the courts from changing their own decisions, although this position was later gradually abandoned. The English House of Lords only did so in 1966! Kempin (1990: 102).

[177] Or, as Luhmann (1993: 338 ff.) would have put it: not without first generating a sufficient amount of redundancy!

contradictions in a higher court or in a special body or committee set up for that purpose, as is the rehearing of a case by a larger number of judges.[178]

In Mexico, for example, the Supreme Court resolves the contradictions between the decisions of its chambers, between its own decisions and those of other lower federal courts, and between the decisions of these lower courts.[179] In Germany, the highest court in each of the five branches of ordinary jurisdiction (civil and criminal, labour, social security, fiscal, and administrative) is normally composed of several chambers ('*Senate*'). For example, when the civil and criminal chambers of the *Bundesgerichtshof* (BGH) render inconsistent judgments, the contradiction is resolved by the corresponding 'great chamber'. If an inconsistency has arisen between a civil and a criminal chamber, including a great chamber, the contradiction is then resolved by the 'united great chambers'.[180]

This latter solution depends as much on the effectiveness of the mechanism for identifying inconsistencies and for bringing them to the attention of the competent court or judicial body, as it does on the time it will take for the contradiction to be resolved. Usually, the power to bring an inconsistency to the attention of the courts is conferred on the courts themselves, the parties or certain officials, such as the Attorney General. In view of the massive increase of possible contradictions between judicial decisions, it could be argued, for example, that a technological solution for their identification, such as a computerised system, might be more effective.

But what is the use of resolving inconsistencies that have not posed any challenge or affected any legal interest as yet? It may then be preferable to leave the resolution of judicial inconsistencies to the selective filter of self- or public interest. Thus, only litigants who have stakes in future litigation will have a clear incentive to challenge inconsistencies between judgments, while in the long run, the resolution of such contradictions will tend to favor their interests.

HORIZONTAL SELECTIVITY

We have already briefly stated what is understood by 'horizontal' selectivity. Horizontal selectivity mainly concerns the existence of alternatives to adjudication, such as ADR and other non-judicial mechanisms. From a dynamic point of view, it also comprises the *transference* of certain types of cases to different courts or agencies (for example, from ordinary first instance courts to small claims

[178] Scholarly doctrine may also play an important role, by analysing court decisions and exposing their inconsistencies.

[179] The decision that resolves a contradiction is binding on all lower courts for the future, but the decisions that led to the contradiction in the first place are left unchanged.

[180] See §§ 132, 136 and 137 of the German '*Gerichtsverfassungsgesetz*' ('Organic Law of the Civil and Criminal Courts'). Similarly, § 11 of the '*Verwaltungsgerichtsordnung*' ('Organic Law of the Administrative Courts').

courts), as well as the partial or complete *dejudicialisation* of certain conflicts. Such conflicts are dejudicialised insofar as they are not brought to court any longer, either because of the existence of alternative modes of handling them or because, legally speaking, they are not the object of judicial proceedings any more (the decriminalisation of certain behaviours would be a good example).

In this section we shall first examine the reasonable economic intuition that ADR is cheaper than ordinary adjudication. Then, certain relevant empirical socio-legal studies will be summarised. These studies show the existence of the 'filtering effect' of ADR and other structural or institutional arrangements that keep a higher or lower proportion of potential suits out of the courts. Several studies essentially confirm the economic model in its basic assumptions.

The second subsection offers some examples of empirical research that attempts the difficult but necessary task of comparing the cost, speed and other characteristics of judicial proceedings with those of alternative mechanisms. In the same order of things, other studies show the consequences that the transference and dejudicialisation of certain types of disputes have on litigation rates.

Alternative Dispute Resolution (ADR) and the Infrastructure for Avoiding Litigation

An Economic Analysis of ADR

Basic economic intuition tells us that settlement (and, to a large extent, other non-judicial, 'informal' dispute settlement mechanisms, such as conciliation and mediation) are cheaper than formal adjudication in the courts,[181] thereby establishing a *reciprocal economic relationship* between the costs of both types of dispute resolution. Settlement and the other dispute resolution alternatives (ADR) help set the 'price' of adjudication by acting as a substitute that helps regulate the demand for court services (the reverse may be also true). This reciprocal link mandates that an assessment of the efficiency of *either* the courts *or* of ADR be carried out as a comparison between *both* types of institutions.[182]

Steven Shavell provides a general economic analysis of ADR.[183] Its starting point is a basic distinction between *ex ante* and *ex post* ADR. *Ex ante* ADR concerns arrangements to use ADR made before a dispute arises; *ex post* ADR refers to the use of ADR once the dispute has arisen.[184] The distinction is important because the costs and benefits of both kinds of ADR may be different.

[181] One might ask why, if the cost of settlement is less than the cost of trial, not all cases settle. One answer lies in the uncertainty over the outcome of litigation for both parties. Posner (1996: 89 f.).

[182] Cf Komesar (1994).

[183] Shavell (1995a).

[184] Shavell (1995a: 2).

Ex ante ADR may be mutually beneficial to the parties to a dispute because:[185]

—ADR may lower the cost or risk of resolving disputes, although the possibility of a lower cost admits an important qualification: the parties do not at present pay the full cost of the public service of adjudication, but they do pay the full cost of ADR. ADR may thus appear more expensive in comparison to the courts than it really is, so its use may be less frequent than it should be.[186]
—ADR may create greater incentives through more accurate results or other characteristics.
—ADR may result in greater incentives either to engage in disputes or to refrain from them.

Such benefits cannot generally be obtained by means of *ex post* agreements to use ADR, especially because it is too late to incorporate its positive incentives into the parties' behaviour.[187] Nevertheless, *ex post* ADR would produce mutual gains through the promotion of settlement and the reduction of dispute resolution costs. Two regimes are possible in this respect: in the first one, the use of ADR, both binding and non-binding, is voluntary; in the second, the use of non-binding ADR is required before there can be a trial.

The main conclusions regarding *ex post* ADR are as follows:[188]

—The tendency to bring suit is not affected by ADR where its use is voluntary: the defendant can always refuse to use it, so the plaintiff must be willing to go to trial to have a credible threat.
—The tendency to sue may be both higher or lower in the case of non-binding ADR: higher, because a party who is unwilling to go to trial would be willing to engage in non-binding ADR, which is cheaper, and thus, to bring suit;[189] lower, because in order to go to trial, a party must incur ADR costs plus trial costs rather than just the latter.[190]

[185] Shavell (1995a: 2, 5 ff.).
[186] Shavell (1995a: 8).
[187] Shavell (1995a: 3, 9 ff.; formal analysis at 21 ff.). It should be noted that *ex post* ADR may be the most frequent form of alternative used, since *ex ante* ADR may be confined to certain contractual relations that choose it as the best way to resolve disputes (for example, international commercial arbitration).
[188] Shavell (1995a: 3 f.).
[189] In other words: filing suit is the key to having access to ADR.
[190] 'The propensity to sue is the same in regimes without ADR and with voluntary ADR, for under both the plaintiff must be willing to go to trial to have a credible threat against the defendant. But when non-binding ADR must precede trial, the tendency to sue is different; the plaintiff will sue if he would be willing to engage in non-binding ADR. This means that the tendency to sue is greater than otherwise if ADR would be followed by settlement, something that is likely if ADR predicts trial outcomes. But it means that the tendency to bring suit will be less than otherwise if ADR would not be followed by settlement and would therefore merely add costs to the litigation process; this is likely if ADR does not predict trial outcomes very well'. Shavell (1995a: 19).

—Given that suit has been brought, the availability of ADR tends to reduce the frequency of both trial and immediate settlement;[191] ADR is both a substitute for trial and cheaper than trial, so parties may elect it rather than go to trial, but they may choose ADR rather than settle, since ADR constitutes an inexpensive form of legal combat.[192]

Shavell is critical of voluntary ADR. In principle, it is not clear to him that it enhances individuals' welfare. He does not find any apparent basis for the state's requiring non-binding ADR before trial, since mandatory ADR can have the perverse effect of increasing the cost of litigation, by adding another layer to it without promoting settlement.[193]

The Filtering Effect

We have already cited a study by Erhard Blankenburg which attributes the significant differences in litigation rates between two otherwise similar regions (the Netherlands and the Western German state of North-Rhine-Westphalia) to the existence of institutions and mechanisms that filter disputes out and keep them from reaching the court system.[194] There are many other studies that demonstrate the working of this mechanism in a more specific area of the law. Such is the case of a study on the judicial and extra-judicial resolution of disputes deriving from traffic accidents in Germany and the Netherlands, an area where significant similarities between the two countries also exist.[195]

On the basis of interviews with experts and a file analysis, the study concluded[196] that, in the Netherlands, not only did a smaller percentage of all reported traffic-related injuries ever reach the courts in comparison to Germany (0.1–0.2 per cent as opposed to 1–2 per cent), but also that there are fewer disputes in the settlement of traffic accidents. The most important explaining factors lie in the differences between both countries regarding the practice of legal advice and negotiations by insurance companies.

In *Germany*, attorneys enjoy a monopoly on legal advice established by law, whereas in *the Netherlands* the most varied professions and institutions are allowed to provide this type of advice. Consequently, the intervention of attorneys in the settlement of traffic injuries is the rule in Germany and the exception in the Netherlands. Specifically, the file analysis showed that the likelihood of an accident resulting in a court case was a function of the degree of attorney intervention. Judicial proceedings resulted mostly from disputes concerning liability,

[191] The latter point has been confirmed by some empirical studies on court-annexed arbitration, which will be examined in ch 4.

[192] Shavell (1995a: 4, 19). The costs of ADR are lower than those of trial, but may not be high enough to discourage the parties from the use of ADR.

[193] Shavell (1995a: 4).

[194] Blankenburg (1994b).

[195] Simsa (1995).

[196] Simsa (1995: 294, 298 ff.).

which attorneys could not or would not settle. This means that attorneys do not act as conflict preventers, at least if not only the amount of damages is at stake.

The way traffic accidents are handled is also different in these two countries. In Germany, settlement occurs predominantly between participants in the accident and the insurance companies, with assistance from their respective lawyers. In the Netherlands, instead of having claims being formulated by attorneys, injuries resulting from traffic accidents are usually settled by employees of insurance companies, who sometimes also give legal advice to the parties. This fosters more professional procedures and less conflictive outcomes.[197] In Germany, settlement becomes 'legalised' at a very early stage, not only because of the intervention of legal insurance, but also because the parties themselves start worrying about the legal consequences immediately after the accident. Moreover, the accident report is almost never signed by both drivers. In the Netherlands, on the contrary, agreements, including acknowledgement of responsibility, are frequently signed. German drivers also call the police more frequently than Dutch drivers do.[198] In conclusion: the emergence of disputes is not only favored by the early legalisation of traffic accidents but also by the involvement of attorneys, who direct the conflict into legal channels that may more easily result in court proceedings.

Another empirical German study analyses the intersections between various extra-judicial legal advice services and formal adjudication by the courts.[199] The central point of concern is the long-term reduction of growing caseloads in the German courts as well as the preservation and enhancement of the quality of the administration of justice in view of those growing caseloads.

Specifically, the study examined the situation in four urban judicial districts: two in Western Germany (Lübeck and Nuremberg) and two in the territory of the former German Democratic Republic (Rostock and Leipzig). The legal areas taken into account were mainly housing, consumer and debt problems, as well as business disputes. Various legal services, including conciliation and arbitration, were provided by public and private agencies. They were classified according to the intensity and depth of the legal advice offered.[200]

[197] Simsa (1995: 299).

[198] Simsa (1995: 300).

[199] Stock *et al.* (1995: summary at 11–19). The study belongs to the 'Structural Analysis of the Administration of Justice' series, financed and published by the German Federal Ministry of Justice.

[200] This is the typology of legal services proposed (Stock *et al.* 1995: 12–13):

—*Orientation*: indicates which office might be most suitable for the solution of the legal problem at hand; may include information material and general advice;
—*Legal information*: limited information and references for providing the affected person with a provisional assessment of the legal situation;
—*Legal advice*: complete analysis and discussion of the legal problem, for which the adviser is liable; recommendation as to appropriate further steps or strategies;
—*Representation*: frequently linked to legal advice; both extra judicial and judicial;
—*Extra-judicial settlement offers*: conciliation and arbitration services, including enforceable agreements before attorneys.

The findings on the use of the services, measured as the number of cases per 1,000 inhabitants, show that the greatest potential corresponds to attorneys and notary publics. Institutions and agencies in the 'pre-court' field ('*Vorfeld*')[201] handled a smaller but not insignificant number of cases. Quantitatively speaking, conciliation and arbitration services played an insignificant role. The relationship between attorneys and courts confirms the high participation of attorneys in out-of-court settlements. In the former East Germany, the number of cases was generally lower. The intensive use of legal services provided in the pre-court field there may indicate the existence of a high demand for simple, inexpensive services, but it could also be a manifestation of a different legal culture.

Referrals between services were significant and routine in both the pre-court field and between attorneys. Quantitatively speaking, the number of referrals was low in all cities, although somewhat higher in the pre-court field than between attorneys. The pre-court field and the attorneys' field constitute relatively closed fields, between which few referrals take place. This also means that both fields offer predominantly independent legal services and settlement possibilities. Almost no cases went directly from the pre-court field to the courts. The filtering potential of the pre-court field is therefore as high as 90 per cent. Consequently, this field has little importance in the generation of business for attorneys.

The study identifies two *intersections* which are relevant from the point of view of legal policy:

—The first intersection is located between the primarily technical and the primarily legal handling of problems. It is mainly situated outside the organs of the administration of justice, ie, it concerns the choice of legal means, which makes it necessary to reduce the whole problem to its legal aspects, which in turn influences the possible dispute solution.

—The second intersection is located between resolution inside and outside the court. It involves the choice of the judicial solution, and consequently, it falls mainly within the sphere of influence of attorneys.[202]

The two studies just summarised are conveniently complemented by another study on the dispute—or litigation-preventing and—settling behaviour of German attorneys.[203] This study also sheds some light on the factors that influence the choice in favour of either a judicial or an extra-judicial solution. The study explores both the quantitative and qualitative aspects of these activities.

[201] Attorneys are not part of the 'pre-court' field because they are regarded as agents of the administration of justice.

[202] The study offers a graphic depiction of both intersections: it consists of a pyramid and its area is irregularly divided between the field of influence of attorneys, who possess key access to the courts (apex of the pyramid), and the pre-court institutions and professions. The influence and participation of the latter diminish the greater the legal component and depth of the service, and vice-versa. Stock *et al.* (1995: 16).

[203] Wasilewski (1990).

The results refer to the total number of cases (both contested or requiring only advice) handled and settled during 1985 by the attorneys surveyed:[204]

—The general average for all attorneys was 236 cases (184 for sole practitioners and 315 for law firms); between 78 per cent and 82 per cent were civil law cases.
—Excluding divorce, labour and debt injunctions ('*Mahnverfahren*') pending in court, 70 per cent of those civil law cases were settled out of court; accordingly, only 30 per cent went to court.
—More out-of-court settlements were reached by law firms than by sole practitioners.
—The relationship between the increasing size of the law firms (measured by number of cases and the amount of fees billed) and the higher proportion of out-of-court settlements is positive but not uniform.
—No positive linear relationship was found between professional experience and the extra-judicial resolution of disputes; apparently, sole practitioners with growing experience prefer more the judicial option, whereas law firms prefer extra-judicial settlement.
—Only a very tenuous link exists between the opinions and attitudes of the attorneys themselves and the actual handling of cases.
—In the extra-judicial resolution of disputes, 40 per cent of the cases were terminated to the complete or virtual satisfaction of the client's interest; in 25 per cent of the cases, counseling was sufficient to reach a solution; in 15 per cent of cases it was necessary for the attorney to explain to the client that the other party was in the right.
—The legal areas especially amenable to extra-judicial settlement were: intellectual property and partnerships; traffic accidents (around 75 per cent); disputes deriving from insurance contracts (more than 70 per cent); conflicts between neighbours, commercial agency; material damages and personal injury; family and inheritance; real estate and housing property (around 50 per cent). By contrast, conflicts relating to the buying, exchange or leasing of movable property and to services and building contracts were predominantly adjudicated.
—The client's interest was not insignificant for the type of resolution achieved: in 14 per cent of cases, the client sought advice or an opinion, especially in family and inheritance matters, or intervention in disputes with a neighbour.
—The rate of extra-judicial settlement also increased in proportion to the amount of money at stake.
—A higher rate of litigation where legal services were covered by insurance was not confirmed (57 per cent of extra-judicial settlements).[205]

[204] Wasilewski (1990: 91–5).

[205] Blankenburg (1981–2) did not find that legal insurance, by taking away the financial risk of litigation from the insured's shoulders, fosters greater litigiousness.

—If the relationship between parties was personal, the likelihood of extra-judicial resolution was also higher.
—When the other party is represented by an attorney, the rate of extra-judicial resolution is considerably lower than when he or she is not.

Attorneys and judges were asked about the causes of and reasons for civil litigation and about the possibilities of avoiding them. Two-thirds of the attorneys surveyed considered that in Western Germany there was too much litigation, due to:

—The diffusion of legal insurance.
—Unwillingness to compromise on the part of the client.
—The higher fees that can be collected in judicial proceedings.
—The views and attitudes of attorneys towards extra-judicial settlement.

For their part, judges blamed this on the training deficits and attitudes of attorneys; as well as on the client's behaviour.

A study on social and legal conflict conducted in a very different society and time (Mexico in the early 1970s)[206] also reveals the existence of the filtering effect in the complex interplay between the courts and extra-judicial dispute settlement institutions. Here, a comparison was made between the judicial and extra-judicial resolution (conciliation) of labour and property conflicts on the basis of several indicators.[207] As might be expected, conciliation was both speedier and less expensive than judicial proceedings. In fact, the majority of conflicts settled through the intervention of a third party were caught in a dense conciliation filter situated before the court system.[208] Depending on the type of dispute involved, this filter worked in three ways:

—Some disputes were resolved exclusively through conciliation (such as family conflicts and insurance claims).
—Other disputes went through conciliation first and were subsequently followed by a suit (such as certain employment disputes).
—Still other disputes were only solved through adjudication (such as disputes regarding commercial paper).

The empirical research summarised so far coincides in demonstrating the existence of a filtering effect in the interplay between judicial and extra-judicial dispute settlement mechanisms. This filtering effect works in different ways and may be more or less powerful, depending on factors such as the legal area concerned, the previous relationship between the parties, the existence of routine settlement and negotiation practices by institutional actors, and the role played by attorneys.[209]

[206] Gessner (1976).
[207] Gessner (1976: 138 ff.).
[208] Gessner (1976: 147 ff.). See also Henckel (1991), a study on the wide variety of judicial and non-judicial mechanisms for the enforcement of civil obligations in Brazil.
[209] See also Stock (1995).

The role of attorneys is especially interesting. The German studies cited earlier suggest that the early legalisation of the conflict through the intervention of attorneys, especially if they enjoy a monopoly over the provision of legal advice, fosters litigation. It is true that attorneys exercise considerable influence on the use of the courts. However, if seen from their perspective, it may well be argued that attorneys also filter and prevent litigation, since not all the cases they handle actually go to court and they also participate actively in the negotiation of out-of-court settlements. Much also depends on the fee system, the legal areas concerned, and the client's behaviour. For example, an empirical study on the effects of the contingent fee system on the behaviour of attorneys regarding the screening of potential cases in the United States basically finds that 'gatekeeping is an important part of the role played by contingent fee lawyers' and that they 'carry out this function in large part as an exercise in economic self interest'.[210] However, it is also argued that the American contingent fee serves to ameliorate some of the problems of access to civil justice for the average citizen.

> By shifting the burden of the role of economic incentives in gatekeeping from the potential litigant to the contingent fee lawyer, the system has made it possible for 'one shot' litigants with minimal resources to take on wealthy, experienced 'repeat players'.[211]

Of course, these divergent perspectives are not inconsistent with each other. Attorneys may effectively prevent many cases from going to court. In aggregated terms, however, it is safe to assume that if a dispute is initially brought to an attorney and is consequently framed in legal terms, the *likelihood* of litigation is higher than if the case is first handled by some other agency or institution.

The study on the four German cities also indicates that the effectiveness of the filtering level is *enhanced* by the relative isolation of the 'pre-court' field from the agents of the administration of justice, including attorneys, and consequently, by the low rate of referrals between the two fields. Under these particular circumstances, as already stated, it is the *initial* handling of a legal dispute which largely seems to determine its fate in terms of whether or not it goes to court. This isolation may be achieved, however, at the expense of a bias or imbalance in the outcome of those cases, since the initial treatment may prevent their referral to the most appropriate institution or mechanism for their resolution.

Finally, all these studies contribute evidence to the hypothesis that it is the institutional framework, the 'supply side', rather than legal culture (defined as a set of attitudes, values and opinions about the law and legal institutions), or 'demand side', which largely influences the existing rates of litigation in a given society.[212]

[210] Kritzer/Pickerill (1997, 19).
[211] Kritzer/Pickerill (1997, 21).
[212] Blankenburg (1989b; 1994b).

Litigation and its Alternatives Compared

Speed, Costs, and Satisfaction

Empirical studies that compare the costs and effectiveness of adjudication and ADR (mostly, *ex post* ADR) generally confirm the assumptions of the economic model. However, considerable difficulties are involved in making such a comparison:[213]

—Only a small portion of cases that enter the legal process remain until the end, which makes it necessary to monitor and compare cases with different points and times of exit.
—It is also necessary to take into account the idiosyncratic practices of local legal culture.
—The criteria used to evaluate effectiveness (or efficiency) are unclear, given that different participants will have different expectations and goals.
—It is difficult to ascertain whether the advantages of either mechanism are attributable to the process itself or to the characteristics of the cases and the parties.[214]
—The comparability of the cases is also problematic, since some informal mechanisms offer services involving a broader set of disputes than are admissible by a court.[215]

Despite such difficulties, there are a number of interesting studies that attempt to make precisely this comparison and that provide valuable insights into this problem. Some of them will be summarised here as examples of this type of research.

The first study refers to medical malpractice claims.[216] It examines the experience of a single large hospital with an informal and voluntary resolution process that resolves some cases outside the legal system, in order to avoid high legal costs. The study discovered the following regularities:[217]

—The informal dispute resolution process resolves almost half of all the cases that use it without lawsuits being filed ('filtering effect').
—Cases initiated informally ('complaints') are not resolved in significantly different ways from lawsuits that fail to make use of the informal dispute resolution process, controlling for quality of medical care and severity of damage.
—Complaints that are not resolved and result in lawsuits are significantly more likely to result in compensation for plaintiffs than lawsuits that do not make previous use of the informal dispute resolution process.

213 Ogus *et al.* (1990: 58).
214 Ogus *et al.* (1990: 61).
215 Ogus *et al.* (1990: 63).
216 Farber/White (1994).
217 Farber/White (1994: 778).

—Settlements occur less frequently at the complaint stage than at the lawsuit stage.
—Settlements at the complaint stage, when they occur, are only about one-third as high, on average, as settlements at the lawsuit stage.
—Crude estimates of the hospital's legal expenses are far lower for complaints than for lawsuits.

Patients acquire information about the quality of care during both the complaint and the litigation processes, thus making settlement or abandonment of their claim more likely, to the hospital's advantage. The hospital, in turn, uses the informal dispute resolution process to learn about the litigiousness of specific patients. It uses the filing of lawsuits as a hurdle that patients must overcome in order to convince the hospital that they are sufficiently litigious to justify a high settlement. In conclusion, the informal dispute resolution process is a cost-effective 'front end' for the litigation process.[218]

The second study concerns the use of conciliation in family matters in England.[219] It was commissioned by the Lord Chancellor to evaluate the effectiveness and cost of various types of family conciliation schemes, in order to determine whether a publicly funded national conciliation service should be established, and how such a service should best be organised and funded. After all, family conciliation is an area where the virtues of ADR should be more apparent, so an important issue was to decide whether the services it provided should receive public support.[220]

The study examined four types of service: court-based conciliation, with high and low judicial control (types A and B); independent conciliation linked to a probation service and without a probation link (types C and D). Two control courts without a conciliation service were also chosen.[221]

For the purpose of comparative cost analysis, the study[222] focused solely on cases involving children and in which there was clear evidence of related judicial proceedings. The cost analysis sought to answer two questions: how much does it cost to provide the various types of conciliation? And the most important question for our purposes here: what net impact does conciliation have on the overall cost of settling disputes?[223]

The cost of providing conciliation was measured by referring to the resources actually expended rather than to simple financial flows. Costs included: the parties' expenditure on items specifically related to the dispute and their loss of

[218] Farber/White (1994: 779, 806).

[219] Ogus *et al.* (1990). It should be noted that conciliation here is not a substitute for the court, which always has some form of intervention.

[220] By the mid 1980s, two types of service had proliferated: court-based conciliation (available at approximately two-thirds of the divorce courts in England and Wales) and independent and voluntary organisations (affiliated to the National Family Conciliation Service). Ogus *et al.* (1990: 59).

[221] Ogus *et al.* (1990: 62).

[222] The article cited here (Ogus *et al.* 1990) focuses solely on the comparison of costs. The study itself was much broader in scope.

[223] Ogus *et al.* (1990: 63 f.).

productive output and leisure; the capital and recurrent expenditure of the courts, probation services and independent schemes; and legal costs for advice and representation.[224] The overall social cost per case in court-based conciliation schemes (not including overheads) was between £150 and £200, whereas the cost per case of independent schemes was between £200 and £300.[225]

As to the second question, it was not possible to compare the average cost of conciliated disputes with the average cost of non-conciliated disputes, since the procedures were not identical or sufficiently similar. Instead, significant differences in clientele and type of case, both conciliated and non-conciliated, were taken into account.[226] The analysis was finally carried out through a statistical multiple regression analysis of 1,162 cases, in 219 of which the parties had attended a conciliation service.[227]

The main conclusion was that conciliation in all categories *added* to the cost of settling child disputes.[228] Court-based conciliation added, on average, about £150 to the net cost of settling child disputes; the equivalent figure for independent conciliation for cases proceeding through the county courts being about £250.

This conclusion notwithstanding, the analysis proved that conciliation could be effective in the *relative reduction* of other costs involved in settling a dispute. Thus, a tendency was identified for court-based conciliation to achieve certain cost-reductions in the dispute settlement process, 'but these reductions (were) by no means sufficient to produce anything remotely resembling a *net* reduction in the cost of dispute settlement'.[229] The authors observed that there was nothing in their research to support the hypothesis that court-based conciliation (types A and B) 'pays for itself' in terms of savings elsewhere. In category C conciliation, there was a substantial tendency to generate cost reductions elsewhere. Category D showed only a slight tendency for savings on other costs of dispute settlement.[230]

The third example concerns compliance and satisfaction with judgments in small claims courts. Research on small claims courts in the US state of Maine[231] found that the likelihood that mediation defendants would comply with their agreements 'was almost twice the likelihood that adjudication defendants would fully meet the obligations imposed upon them by the court,'[232] and this likelihood was accompanied by greater satisfaction on the part of the

224 Ogus *et al.* (1990: 64, 70).
225 Ogus *et al.* (1990: 66).
226 Ogus *et al.* (1990: 66).
227 Ogus *et al.* (1990: 63). Questionnaires were also used to obtain information on these cases.
228 This finding is consistent with the more general conclusion suggested by the economic model, in the sense that *ex post* ADR may add to the costs of settling disputes when court intervention is not avoided.
229 Ogus *et al.* (1990: 72).
230 Ogus *et al.* (1990: 72).
231 McEwen/Maiman (1984).
232 McEwen/Maiman (1984: 11).

parties involved.[233] The authors of the study contend that the differences in compliance rates cannot be explained away by variations in defendant or case characteristics.[234]

The prediction that (*ex post*) ADR may both reduce and increase costs (through a higher litigation rate) seems to be further confirmed by this example. Costs may be reduced by the higher degree of compliance with a court's judgments and, on the whole, by the increased satisfaction with and, hence, legitimacy of, the dispute settlement process. However, even if most people and organisations regard negotiation and bargaining as the preferred means of handling a dispute, the only incentive to negotiate, and the only access to bargaining, often comes from a formal lawsuit: 'Threatened use of formal legal processes thus provides a bargaining lever for one party against another and serves to mobilise "informal", consensual justice'.[235] Nevertheless, it is difficult to determine the extent to which this cost reduction offsets the higher costs of the additional litigation.

A final example shows that the choice of alternative forums of dispute resolution has to take into account a complex and sometimes not fully predictable cost structure, in which some costs turn out to be higher than expected but can be offset by other benefits and advantages of the alternative process. In this respect, one can mention the *sui generis* binational panel system initially created by the United States-Canada Free Trade Agreement of 1989 and subsequently incorporated into chapter 19 of the North American Free Trade Agreement (NAFTA) between Mexico, Canada and the United States.[236] These binational panels, which are of an international nature although they apply national law, replace the domestic judicial review of antidumping and countervailing duty (AD/CV) determinations by the national investigating authorities, when either importers, exporters or domestic producers request their establishment. Panels are supposed to conduct their reviews and to render their decisions in a speedy, just and inexpensive manner. Their establishment suggests that they will do so in terms that are comparatively more favorable than those available in the domestic court they replace.

After a few years of operation, first evaluations of the system show, for example, that, in the case of panel reviews of US antidumping determinations, the proceedings were on the average shorter than comparable proceedings in the US

233 'Rates of compliance and satisfaction are quite high in mediated cases and seem consistently higher than those reported in comparable adjudicated cases, although problems of comparability abound'. McEwen/Maiman (1984: 45).

234 For a different perspective on this point, arguing that case characteristics, such as admitted liability, explains more variability in dispute outcomes and compliance than whether the case was mediated or adjudicated, based on an analysis of small claims courts in Ontario, Canada, see the research note by Vidmar (1987).

235 McEwen/Maiman (1984: 46). For this reason, they argue against critics who imply that informal justice deprives parties of the rights they would have had in court, that they 'ignore the symbiotic qualities of informal and formal justice'.

236 López Ayllón/Fix-Fierro (1999).

Court of International Trade. Most decisions were rendered unanimously and not further challenged.[237] Apart from the possible cost savings in time, panel decisions may be more readily accepted and complied with, because of the binational composition of the panels, that translates into a higher degree of impartiality and legitimacy, rather than by virtue of their contents. It should be remembered that panels are supposed to decide in the same way as a domestic court would have decided.[238]

The situation has been different with the panel review of Mexican antidumping determinations. There, the panel review system, which is based on the Anglo-American procedural tradition, has come into contact with a very different legal tradition and culture, and with a far less developed AD/CVD system. Although based on similar facts, the first decisions rendered were extremely inconsistent with each other. Increased costs for the parties have also resulted from the learning process which is inevitable when a new system begins to operate; the unexpected legal issues (for foreign participants) that have arisen during the review proceedings, and other practical constraints, such as translation. Moreover, the Mexican cases have lasted longer on average than cases decided in the United States.[239]

Overall, the first panel reviews of Mexican antidumping determinations would seem to be far more expensive and unpredictable than comparable domestic proceedings, thus making it less likely for foreign exporters to resort to them. However, should the system succeed in consolidating itself, the costs associated with the initial learning process would fall and foreign exporters might still choose the alternative process in view of the lack of experience of Mexican courts with the complex technical issues of antidumping law[240] and, consequently, in view of the possibility that Mexican antidumping jurisprudence may be further shaped by the influence and participation of foreign experts.[241]

Transference and Dejudicialisation

When certain types of cases become too numerous, causing considerable backlog and delay in the courts, it may be time to 'transfer' them to a different setting. Thus, they can be transferred to a more efficient or a different type of court (such as a specialised court or a small claims court)[242] or to an administrative

[237] López Ayllón/Fix-Fierro (1999: 12).

[238] This has at least been so under the Canada-US Free Trade Agreement. López Ayllón/Fix-Fierro (1999: 36).

[239] López Ayllón/Fix-Fierro (1999: 13).

[240] By contrast, panelists should generally be familiar with international trade law.

[241] López Ayllón/Fix-Fierro (1999: 38 f.).

[242] For an initial empirical assessment of the 'judge of the peace' (*giudice di pace*), who replaced the 'conciliation judge' (*giudice conciliatore*) in Italy after 1995, see Vidoni Guidoni (1997). The new judge of the peace should contribute to unburdening the ordinary civil courts and enhancing access to justice for the benefit of citizens, through the use of a simplified, more flexible procedure. The assessment concludes that, in its initial years, the judge of the peace in the city of Torino worked

agency, which may resolve the corresponding disputes through quasi-judicial proceedings. The latter strategy may work effectively as a filter for disputes, but in so far as the action by those agencies is subject to judicial review anyway, such agencies will have an incentive not to apply too much effort to their activities, so that dispute settlement may become more costly without really alleviating the court system.[243]

A different strategy for unburdening the courts from certain types of mass litigation is what one might call 'dejudicialisation'. *Complete dejudicialisation* may be achieved through a change in the courts' rules of jurisdiction and in other substantive laws, so that certain social behaviors are altogether excluded from judicial control. The most evident example may be *decriminalisation*, where certain behaviours are not considered criminal any longer and are instead subject to other kinds of sanctions (of an administrative nature, for example) or to no sanction at all. Decriminalisation has repeatedly been used as a form of providing relief for overcrowded prisons and overloaded criminal courts. Although such a measure has been strongly recommended by criminologists and other experts (particularly in the 1970s), the chances of its being implemented depend largely on society's attitude towards certain forms of crime and on the resistance of organised interests and groups (including criminal organisations themselves!).

This can be clearly illustrated by the current debate on the 'legalisation' of drugs, which does not appear to be a viable possibility at present. In the meantime, prisons will continue to be crowded with small-time drug-traffickers, since the big 'bosses' are almost never arrested and charged. Many countries, however, have decriminalised the *possession* of small quantities of drugs for personal consumption. Another form of decriminalisation involves *de facto* legalisation or social tolerance. This is the case of abortion in many countries, where although it continues to be regarded as criminal behaviour by the existing laws, it is hardly ever reported or prosecuted.

Partial dejudicialisation can also be achieved through the modification of procedural and substantive laws, or can be the consequence of social and institutional practices, ie, certain disputes are legally admissible by the courts, but almost never reach them, since there are powerful incentives that prevent this. Two examples will be given here, on judicial debt collection and the handling of traffic accidents by insurance companies in the United States. There are also parallel studies on similar practices in other countries.[244]

with remarkable efficiency, perhaps due to the need to legitimise the new institution. This concern with efficiency may have led the judge to behave in a manner which the author calls 'isomorphic' in relation to the ordinary courts, with the consequence, among others, of the scarce use of alternative methods of dispute settlement, such as conciliation (p. 135).

[243] Cf Posner (1996: 265 ff.).

[244] Of course these examples are also relevant for the discussion of the filtering effect we have developed above. A parallel study on the handling of insurance claims is that of Simsa (1995), already cited, on Germany and the Netherlands.

Robert A Kagan has attempted to explain a seemingly paradoxical example of dejudicialisation in the United States.[245] He noticed that since the 1950s, despite large increases in the volume of loans and delinquent debts, which should have produced a corresponding change in debt collection litigation, there has instead been a sharp decline in contested debt cases in state supreme courts as well as an apparent decline of such cases in trial courts.[246] Indeed, until the 1950s, recorded data on national business failures, which could be used as a proxy for the incidence of debt delinquency, showed upswings and declines paralleled by less extreme trends in the number of debt cases in state supreme courts.[247] Notwithstanding the incidence of individual and business 'crises' in the 1950s, 1960s and 1970s, which might be expected to lead to a dramatic increase in litigation, debt collection cases continued to *decline* in the 1950s and 1960s, both in absolute terms and as a proportion of state supreme court cases.[248]

Kagan explains this apparent paradox by concluding that 'for both creditors and debtors, litigation has become more costly in relation to alternative course of action such as renegotiating payment terms, declaring bankruptcy, or writing off unpaid debts'.[249] The attraction of the non-litigation-based alternatives is attributed to:

—The 'legal rationalisation' of credit transactions by institutional lenders.
—Increased litigation costs stemming from enhanced debtors' rights;[250] and, most importantly,
—'Systemic stabilisation', ie, welfare state measures, economic regulation, insurance arrangements, and market diversification that facilitates the attenuation and spreading of financial losses.[251]

Kagan's general conclusion is that

> . . . the use of formal decision-making and enforcement processes tends to be extraordinary rather than ordinary. The extent and quality of the justice people experience depends equally, if not primarily, on the operation of nonlegal social and economic institutions that prevent, suppress, or settle most problems and on the broader social, economic, and political factors that affect the incidence and seriousness of harmful acts, accidents, deprivations, disputes.[252]

245 Kagan (1984).

246 Kagan (1984: 323).

247 Kagan (1984: 328f.).

248 Kagan (1984: 331, 335). According to Kagan, increased litigation in small claims courts (a 'transference,' in our terms) would at best account for only a small part of the decline in debt litigation in the general trial courts and courts of appeal.

249 Kagan (1984: 323).

250 As Kagan (1984: 45f.) correctly observes, disputes between creditors and debtors are more than a problem of commercial relations. They reflect politically important cleavages. Among other reactions, debtors have turned periodically to legislatures, in efforts to mitigate the legalistic enforcement of 'settled' creditor's rights.

251 In other words, systemic stabilisation consists of 'the development of large-scale economic and social institutions that ameliorate the conditions that cause individual conflicts or that provide collective administrative remedies (as contrasted to case-by-case legal remedies)'. Kagan (1984: 352).

252 Kagan (1984: 368).

The second example can be found in the classic study by Laurence H Ross on the settlement of injury claims resulting from traffic accidents.[253] The rules of tort law required that compensation be paid to the victim if the injury was caused by negligent behaviour on the part of the person who was responsible for the injury, which had to be proven in court. However, in fact most automobile injury claims were decided in private negotiation between the injured, their lawyers and insurance company adjusters.[254] Ross shows how the formal system of tort law, based on rights and wrongs, is subverted in its stated functions and simplified by the needs of the routine, efficient handling of masses of cases by insurance companies. Thus, liability is understood in mechanical rather than moral terms.[255]

This subversion marked the trend towards no-fault insurance. Many states enacted no-fault insurance laws in the 1970s for the purpose of reforming tort law, suppressing abuses, making claim settlements speedier, and keeping small compensation claims out of the courts. However, no-fault insurance involves the possibility of increased costs for the insurance companies, since compensation is paid regardless of the existence of negligence, and for certain risk groups (for example, motorcycle drivers), because insurance pays for the injury of the insured, not for that of third parties, while the probability of suffering injury, rather than causing it, becomes the basis for calculating premiums. In fact, there seems to be no univocal empirical evidence that no-fault liability prevents litigation, but the pure no-fault principle should at least prevent the claims of injured persons against third parties, since liability becomes completely subrogated in favour of the insurance company.[256]

Both studies describe examples of dejudicialisation 'in the shadow of the law', in two respects: certain disputes are dejudicialised *because* their judicial resolution has become too costly in aggregate terms, and, at the same time, the resulting social and institutional practices are structured in a way that (negatively) *reflects* the existing costs and requirements of the judicial process, the use of which is an ever present *possibility*. A good example of this is 'plea bargaining' in American criminal courts, which is built around the need to *avoid* the jury's intervention in as many cases as possible. Ross rightly points out that 'legal relationships cannot be understood as a product of the formal law alone, but must be understood in terms of the interplay between the formal law and aspects of the situations in which the law is applied' and that informality does not mean lack of structure; on the contrary, regularities emerge that are the result of goals and purposes, pressures and strains.[257]

253 Ross (1980). Ross conducted interviews of insurance adjusters and supervisors, as well as of attorneys for plaintiffs. He conducted a statistical analysis of 2,216 company files on body injury claims (1962), and observed adjusters at work.

254 Ross (1980: 18).

255 Ross (1980: 21 f.).

256 Simsa (1995: 36 ff.).

257 Ross (1980: 232).

4

Processing Capacity

COURTS AS ORGANISATIONS

THE MOST GENERAL proposition that the sociology of law could possibly put forward holds that legal phenomena, particularly legal decisions, such as those adopted by the courts, cannot solely be explained in terms of the rules, procedures, and reasoning processes which have been established or recognised by the legal system as the appropriate basis and method for producing them. In the sociological model of the law, law is not about logic, but about social structures, variables, factors, attitudes and the like, or, more simply, about 'how people actually behave . . .'.[1] What these social structures, variables, and factors that actually influence legal decisions are and how this influence operates, are the questions that provide the raw material for much of the sociological research and speculation about the law.

Judicial decisions, specifically, have been subject to various kinds of social explanation. One approach has attempted to explain judicial outcomes by exploring the social characteristics of participants, such as the judges, including their social background and ideology. This type of explanation has proved to be insufficient for giving an account of judicial decisions *as legal decisions*, which is why it has been called a 'sociology of law without law.'[2] This does not mean, however, that such an analysis lacks merit or interest, but merely that, from a certain socio-legal perspective, it should be seen as more properly belonging to the sociology of the legal profession.

Another approach seeks to identify the *systemic factors* and *structures* that influence judicial decisions. Such an approach

> suggests that the way cases are handled is shaped by the court's own interests and the ways structural factors are manipulated for strategic purposes.[3]

In particular, such a perspective tries to determine more subtle factors of organisation and attitude that cannot be always found through sophisticated quantitative analysis.[4]

[1] Black (1989: 20).

[2] Luhmann (1985: 3). Rottleuthner (1987: 100–6) summarises a few German empirical studies that have tried, rather unsuccessfully, to establish significant correlations between ordinary judicial decisions (such as in labor or civil matters) and the socio-economic background and ideology of judges.

[3] Feeley (1979: 126). See also Eisenstein/Jacob (1977: 9 ff.).

[4] Feeley (1979: 123 f.). In the sense that often no significant connection is found between two or more variables.

A variant of the systemic approach regards *courts as organisations.*[5] Organisations can loosely be defined as a set of structured roles, with common goals and standardised ways of doing things to achieve those goals.[6] Prima facie, this definition seems directly applicable to the most basic concept of what a court, or 'courtness', is[7] and, in fact, a vast, growing number of socio-legal studies have fruitfully, and more or less explicitly, adopted an organisational perspective for the analysis and explanation of the ways in which courts, particularly criminal courts, operate. The organisational nature of courts goes beyond the superficial aspects of internal judicial organisation, such as case assignment and the management of personnel. In the organisational perspective, the focus of analysis is on cases and dispositions, in addition to, and not instead of, administrative procedures.[8]

This chapter also adopts a general perspective on courts as organisations, as a framework for the analysis and discussion, not of judicial decisions as such, but of the concept of 'processing capacity'. 'Processing capacity' implies the means and strategies used by courts and court systems to manage their work and enhance their ability to dispose of cases more efficiently. The concept of organisation is related to our general topic of court efficiency in at least two important ways, which will be further developed in this chapter:

—The organisational perspective has been used both to criticise and to supplement the economic approach; accordingly, cost-minimisation and efficiency-enhancing strategies are not the only factors that explain the behavior of judges, litigants and other actors in the judicial arena,[9] or, at least, it is argued that such rational strategies must be placed in a specific *organisational context* that accounts for variations across different courts.[10]

[5] There is a great deal of literature that analyses court operation using an explicit or implicit organisational perspective. References cited here include: Abel (1991); Ackermann/Bastard (1992; 1993 a and b; 1996); Aumüller/Strempel (eds) (1996); Ballé (1979); Ballé *et al.* (1981); Bauer *et al.* (1983); Bender/Wax (1972); Blankenburg (1982); Blankenburg/Wolff (1972); Church, Jr. (1981; 1985); Church/Heumann (1992); Cisa (1991); Dahlin (1986); Di Federico (1968; 1969); Dixon (1995); Eisenstein/Jacob (1977); Emsellem (1982); Feeley (1973; 1979; 1983); Feeley/Lazerson (1983); Fix-Fierro (1995a and b); Flanders (1980); Flango (1994); Flango/Rottman (1992); Flemming (1990); Flemming *et al.* (1987; 1992); Friesen/Gallas (1971); Galanter (1974); Heumann (1978); Heumann/Church (1990); Heydebrand (1977); Heydebrand/Seron (1990); Jacob (1976; 1983; 1997); Kakalik *et al.* (1990); Koetz (1991); Koetz *et al.* (1992; 1993); Koetz/Frühauf (1996); Lipetz (1980); Luskin (1978; 1988–9); Maggi (1984); Martin/Maron (1991); Matheny (1980); Mohr *et al.* (1997); Nagel *et al.* (1978); Nardulli (1978); Nimmer (1978); Padgett (1990); Posner (1996); Raine/Willson (1993); Reed (1973); Röhl (1991; 1993b); Ryan (1978); Ryan *et al.* (1980; 1981); Saari (1982); Schulhofer (1985); Seron (1990); Sipes *et al.* (1980); Vance/Stupak (1997); Wibera (1991); Zwiesele/Bender (1972).

[6] Cf Jacob (1976: 157).

[7] On the concept of 'courtness,' the essence of what a court means, see Shapiro (1981: 1 ff.).

[8] For a contrasting view, which raises doubts about the usefulness of the organisational approach as applied to the courts, stressing that it will sometimes be more productive to consider behaviour in organisations as being 'decisional' rather than 'organisational,' see Mohr (1976: 622 f.).

[9] See, for example, Matheny (1980).

[10] See, for example, Dixon (1995).

—To view courts as organisations also provides the theoretical and practical underpinnings for the consideration of the *administrative* and *managerial* aspects of court operation.

In other words, the organisational perspective helps define the importance, manifestations, and potential for certain efficiency-enhancing strategies within the courts.

The concept of organisation can be meaningful in another, very important respect, a conceptual avenue which does not seem to have been explored by the literature so far, or only in an indirect manner.[11] By this I mean the consideration of *judicial procedure as a temporary organisation.*[12] Analysing procedure from the organisational perspective has many theoretical and practical consequences. The main implication is that the relationship between courts and procedure can be framed in inter-organisational terms, meaning, for example, that the coupling mechanisms between both organisations must be examined if any changes incorporated into them are to be successful.

This chapter is divided into three sections. The first section seeks to determine what kind of organisations courts are, and what the general consequences that derive from this characterisation are for the idea of 'processing capacity.' The second section examines the gains in processing capacity that might be obtained through modifications of judicial procedure. The third part considers the various dimensions of the administration and management of courts and court systems. The administrative and managerial perspective on the courts, which has been explored and discussed fairly recently in connection with judicial reform, is a further manifestation of the penetration of economic, or rational choice, considerations in the study of the courts.

Organisational Concepts and Images

Organisations are a pervasive feature of present-day society. They are even, as one author has put it, the 'form of our modern condition'.[13] Consequently, social research has devoted considerable effort to the study of organisations and their enormous diversity. Despite these efforts, there is not a single set of propositions that could be said to constitute a unified explanation of what an organisation means and how it works. A single body of 'organisational theory' does not exist, since there are many approaches, together with a multiplicity of 'metaphors' regarding organisations (for example, organisations as machines,

[11] Through concepts such as 'courtroom workgroup' and 'local legal culture.'

[12] This approach has been suggested by Luhmann's analysis of procedure as a social system (1983).

[13] Clegg (1990: 2).

organisms, cultures, political systems, etc.).[14] Therefore, we shall not attempt to derive a comprehensive theory of organisation from them here. For our purposes, it may suffice to recall certain elements and concepts which help explain the organisational phenomenon and, later on, the most relevant organisational aspects of courts.

What are organisations and why are they the 'form of our modern condition'? To answer this question, we shall use a very general, abstract concept of organisation as a starting point. The usefulness of such a concept may become apparent when explaining a variety of problems posed by organisations, but especially when dealing with the issue of how and why adjudication is a social function performed within the framework of formal organisations called 'courts'.

Organisations are supposedly instruments consciously designed and created for the achievement of certain goals with the greatest economy of resources and through the most appropriate means. This is the classic definition of organisational rationality. So, for example, in his well-known analysis of modern capitalism, Max Weber established a firm connection between rationality, science, technology, and economic efficiency. In his view, any instrumental or technical question concerns the most rational means of achieving an optimum result with the greatest economy of effort. Rational means are those applied consciously, according to plan, oriented by experience and, ideally, by scientific knowledge. Economy of effort implies the comparative consideration of costs, ie, the possibility of an alternative use of those means for other ends.[15] According to this conception, capitalism is the social embodiment of instrumental rationality, while bureaucracy represents the highest type of rational organisation, due to its formal, regulated application of specialised professional knowledge. Nevertheless, Weber's views on the relentless process of rationalisation and bureaucratisation in the modern world made him rather pessimistic about the long-term consequences of this form of organisation for society. Thus, he came to speak of an 'iron cage' of rationalisation.

Sociological literature after Weber has documented his pessimistic feelings about bureaucracy by uncovering many of its dysfunctional aspects and pathologies,[16] while in the popular imagination, bureaucracy has become synonymous with inefficiency, dehumanisation, corruption or plain irrationality. Certainly, there are justifiable reasons for such negative images. However, their appropriate target should be less the undoubted evils of bureaucracy than the underlying concept of rationality on which this form of organisation is supposedly based. It can be argued that scientific-technical rationalisation is a central element of modernity, but not the only one,[17] and that technical rationality is

[14] Morgan (1986) offers an account of the theories and explanations of organisational life in terms of metaphors that 'lead us to see and understand organisations in distinctive yet partial ways' (12).

[15] Weber (1984: 47).

[16] See, for example, Crozier (1985).

[17] Touraine (1992: 109 ff.).

not the sole provider of organisational rationality.[18] In other words: that rationality is 'less grandiose than that proclaimed by economists'.[19]

Thus, organisational theory has explored the uses and limits of rationality. It has, for example, coined the concept of 'bounded rationality,' meaning rationality that results from the limited cognitive capabilities of human beings and from the uncertainties that surround decision-making processes in organisations. Accordingly, 'administrative man' does not 'maximise,' as postulated by economic theory, but looks instead for a course of action that is satisfactory or 'good enough.'[20]

Organisational theory has also discovered 'disorder' as an important element in organisational life and has proposed the so-called 'garbage can' model to explain the logic underlying an apparent state of anarchy.[21] More recently, it has attempted to identify and study other social factors that contribute to the functioning of organisations, but which cannot be reduced to rationality and efficiency. 'Culture' is one of the factors that have been made responsible for the variable performance of organisations,[22] while 'organisational culture' has established itself as a research programme that focuses on the symbolic, qualitative, and 'sensuous' aspects of human relationships, and 'upon the central place of these qualities in the operation of organisations.'[23]

The critique of organisational rationality can be generalised as a critique of the relationship between decisions in organisations. Organisations must make decisions not only on means, but also on ends and other organisational aspects. Thus, the problem of rationality is transformed into the problem of establishing an appropriate connection between decisions.[24] For example, *time* becomes an important element to be taken into account in managing the relationship between decisions, and time may also place clear limits on efforts aimed at rationalising an organisation.[25] The overall consequence is that organisational rationality in this sense takes precedence over the rationality of single decisions and immediate goals, such as efficiency.

In terms of a more general, abstract sociological analysis, organisations can be viewed, in fact, as social systems composed of decisions. As such, their

18 Thompson (1967: 19).

19 Simon (1976: xxvii).

20 Simon (1976: xxviii ff.).

21 See, for example, the introductory essay in Warglien/Masuch (eds) (1996: 1–34).

22 See, for example, Clegg (1990: 116 ff.), Holton (1992) and Schultz (1995). Clegg warns against both 'over-socialised' and 'under-socialised' explanations in connection with the sociological use of the concept of culture.

23 Turner (ed) (1990: 1). Adams/Ingersoll (1990) warn against a misplacement of the concept of culture and its inappropriate use outside its discourse of origin (anthropology, sociology). According to these authors, the concept is properly used if it refers to the larger culture as an element across many organisations, but not to indicate an organisation's own culture as a unique, particular quality.

24 Luhmann (1991: 342 f.)

25 Luhmann (1991: 345 ff.).

purpose is not to realise certain goals, but rather to link and coordinate decisions.[26] Decisions are social events whose identity is based on the choice between several possibilities or alternatives. Since any alternative can be selected, a decision constitutes a contingent event whose assessment is closely linked to a particular context.[27]

Organisations emerge as social systems when decisions are adopted and systematised in the form of selective system/environment relationships in open choice situations. Such situations are determined by the search for preliminary decisions that will limit the organisation's decision margin. Thus, the organisation is encouraged to take the existence of decisions in its environment as its starting point, before it can proceed to clarify its goals. Stated in different terms: it is the particular form adopted by the communication process which constitutes an organisation, rather than the goals it pursues or the problems it purports to solve.[28] In this respect, organisations conceive of their relationship to their environment as a decision, provided they can find an interpretation according to which decisions occur in the environment and organisations in it are also capable, or it can be reasonably assumed that they are capable, of relating to the organisation in the form of decisions.[29]

Modern society depends on and fosters the emergence of organisations, as a result of three structural conditions:[30]

- —The existence of a differentiated economic system, based entirely on monetary values. Any economic transaction is viewed as a disposition over money, that is, as a decision. This condition was identified by sociologists as a pre-condition for bureaucratisation.
- —The legalisation of the maintenance and continuation of daily life. The organised mechanisms of the legal system and welfare bureaucracies can only work on the assumption that their clients decide too.
- —The decisional possibilities that derive from the educational and professional choices individuals are obliged to make.

Whereas these and other structural conditions foster the original creation of organisations, it is the secondary building of organisations which increasingly dominates in contemporary society. The existence of organisations is the indispensable pre-condition, and the main motive, for the creation of organisations, in other words, organisations establish other organisations.

> The network of inter-organisational relationships stimulates its own growth; whether this is for the sake of cooperation or conflict, is a second question. Associations and interest groups are established on the assumption of the existence of organisations in

[26] Luhmann (1991: 339 f.). This means that decisions are the basic, ultimate unit of organisations, ie, they cannot be broken down into simpler units, except for further decisions.

[27] Luhmann (1991: 337 f.).

[28] Luhmann (1991: 355, 359).

[29] Luhmann (1991: 359).

[30] Luhmann (1991: 360 f.).

their environment capable of deciding, which allow them to choose between cooperation and conflict.[31]

For our purposes here, three dimensions, levels, components, or orders of organisational action can be distinguished:[32]

—The *institutional component*: the goals and objectives pursued by the organisation.
—The *technological component*: the typical operations and the knowledge, methodologies, and technical instruments used to perform such operations.
—The *structural component*: the coordination and control of the tasks and persons that participate in the organisation.

Each dimension can be said to require its own form of rationality. However, as already stated, the central problem of an organisation—its overall rationality—lies in the links and coordinating mechanisms existing between its various dimensions. In particular, structural action (or organisational action, in a strict sense) is instrumental in linking institutional action and technology within the organisation, and in defining differences between organisations, such as the variability of structures and the autonomy, or dependence, of the organisation's goals from the institutional system of society at large.[33]

Coordination and control assume different forms in different organisations, depending on the institutional goals pursued by the organisation and the technologies employed by it. Coordination and control possess an intrinsic logic. Such logic must relate to the logic of technical and institutional action, in order to be able to create a coherent, valid structure. Thus, the interpretation of homologies and differences in organisational action across different social fields depends mostly on an analysis of the relationships between the logic of organisational action and the logic of institutional and technical action.[34]

What Kind of Organisations are Courts?

Courts can undoubtedly be characterised as organisations in the general sense described above. Nevertheless, they possess specific features that set them apart from other organisations. What specific type of organisations are courts?

A widely held view in the literature regards courts as 'professional(ised) organisations'.[35] This description is more specific and has the advantage of

[31] Luhmann (1991: 361) (translation by HFF).
[32] Maggi (1984: 289). See also Thompson (1967: 16 ff.).
[33] Maggi (1984: 290).
[34] Maggi (1984: 294).
[35] See, for example, Röhl (1993b: 13 ff.), Blankenburg/Wolff (1972) and Blankenburg (1982). Ackermann/Bastard (1993b: 32) speak of courts as 'professional bureaucracies.' See also Emsellem (1982: 23 ff.), Seron (1990: 456) and Saari (1982: 33 ff.).

permitting comparisons with other professional organisations, such as hospitals and universities. It indicates that judicial work is organised around professional competence and that professionals exercise ultimate control over the quality of the organisation's output.[36] However, it is problematic in that it does not explain why the function performed by judges has to assume the *form* of an organisation. And it seems to suggest that profession and organisation, while dependent on each other, represent different, perhaps incompatible forms of authority, a point which is of relevance for a discussion of the processes of professionalisation and bureaucratisation that can be observed in connection with the courts. Nevertheless, these criticisms do not render the concept useless. They simply call for further analysis and clarification.

Courts as Professional Organisations

To say that courts are professional organisations implies an internal hierarchy, a precedence in authority: the professionals—in this case, the judges—perform the central tasks for which the organisation exists by managing its core technology, ie, the treatment of cases according to the rules and methods of the law. The non-professional roles in the organisation—provided they can be clearly distinguished from the professional ones[37]—are supposed to act only in support of the core professional functions. Thus, 'organisation,' in a strict sense, would refer to the administrative structures and institutional processes that provide support and enable professional work to be performed within the courts.

Although this concept of courts as 'professional organisations' seems to suggest an opposition or contrast between profession and organisation, such a view would encounter difficulties in explaining why the judges' *professional* status is also an *organisational* status, with specific rights, obligations and accountability procedures (even adopting the form of a distinctive career, the judicial career, in civil-law countries),[38] and why the adequate performance of the judicial role is dependent on, and even *requires*, the existence of a formal organisation.[39] Instead, the judge's role has to be conceived of as an *organised, administrated* role, which is why the organisation cannot be said to exist merely as a subordinate or supporting element of judicial work proper. In modern society, adjudication is necessarily performed within the framework of a professional organisation, and professional and bureaucratic elements in the courts are closely interrelated.

Holding a different view is not only an academic misperception. Judges themselves are not always aware of the extent to which their professional role is

[36] Ackermann/Bastard (1993b: 32 f.).

[37] Emsellem (1982: 27) notes the difficulty of distinguishing and separating the work of professionals from the work of other personnel.

[38] Fix-Fierro (1997).

[39] Luhmann (1976: 36) defines formal organisation in terms of the particular expectations that members of the organisation must necessarily accept as a condition for belonging to the organisation.

affected by organisational variables, as if their duties were performed in a social vacuum or as if they only required a more or less explicit basis in the law. For instance, a survey conducted in 1990 on the first experiences with the new Uruguayan Code of Civil Procedure found that judges did not perceive the connection between 'court organisation' and the 'administration of justice,' or only insofar as the organisation contributed to delaying judicial work, as a result of which the organisation was associated with red tape, bureaucracy, incompetence, and the like. They felt very little involvement with administrative tasks, and, for example, very few of them pointed to deficiencies in the training of judicial personnel as an administrative issue.[40]

Why are courts organisations? Why is the professional status of judges embedded in a formal organisation? Niklas Luhmann's answer, for example, is that the formal role of a judge contributes to the closure of the legal system by helping enforce the prohibition of denial of justice. Only courts, as the center of the legal system, have the *legal* obligation to decide any issue submitted to their decision, and on becoming members of the judicial organisation, judges accept this obligation: 'Only through organisation is the universality of the power of having to decide all legal issues guaranteed'.[41] Moreover, in order to become members of the judicial organisation, judges must first have been admitted to the *legal profession*, whose standards they are also obliged to respect. Thus, not only the organisation but also the profession serve, both, as the central conditions for the autonomous, trustworthy operation of the courts as legal institutions in modern society. Both are, in Luhmann's terms, functionally equivalent means of ensuring a combination of independence, subordination to legal texts, and the prohibition of the denial of justice for the courts. For this reason, a wide range of organisational and professional modalities of courts are found across countries and regions.[42]

As organisations, courts also participate in political and economic processes. Courts are a part of the organised apparatus of the state. Their operation depends on the state's authority and power, but the state's functions are also dependent on the services provided by the courts. At the same time, court activities have major economic implications, not only in terms of the economic consequences of their decisions, but also to the extent that they are charged with the administration of scarce resources.[43] These three aspects—legal, political, and economic—can be matched with the three dimensions of organisational action mentioned earlier:

[40] Cisa (1991: 185 f.).

[41] Luhmann (1993: 320 f.) (translation by HFF). Luhmann also notes that in the literature, the purely organisational legitimisation of judge-made law is seldom employed, and he points to other useful contributions of organisation to judicial work (for example, relieving judges from the consequences of their decisions).

[42] Luhmann (1993: 328 ff., 330).

[43] Cf Hazard, Jr. (1965).

—The institutional component corresponds to the 'political' dimension of the courts.
—Judicial technology is determined and administered by the profession, as represented by the judges and other judicial officials.
—The structural component manages the resources necessary for the operation of the organisation *stricto sensu*, although it also provides the conditions for the successful application of judicial technology and the adequate development of the institutional dimension of the courts.

The Bureaucratisation and Professionalisation of Courts

So far, the discussion on the organisational nature of courts has remained at a very general level. In this section, I attempt to examine and clarify, in a more specific manner, the relationship between the professional and the structural (bureaucratic or administrative) dimensions of courts, since this relationship may have a significant impact on potential efficiency-enhancing strategies. An immediate reason for this discussion are the frequent claims (and complaints) that Anglo-American (mostly US) courts have been undergoing a process of 'bureaucratisation' which undermines the traditional values of adversarial adjudication.[44]

Bureaucratisation in this sense is mainly exemplified by the case-management techniques increasingly applied by Anglo-American judges in order to achieve a more expeditious disposition of cases, but it can be traced back to other structural developments in litigation.[45] In contrast to this trend, we consider a parallel process in civil-law countries that can be called 'professionalisation'. Although it develops at different levels, this may be a converging tendency between both legal traditions, and this should tell us something about the growing importance of administration and management for the operation of the courts.

With respect to these processes of bureaucratisation and professionalisation, it may be useful to clarify first the relationship between 'bureaucracy' and 'profession' as forms of authority. Svante Beckman has proposed a typology of authority based on a double distinction between institution/person-based and goal/status-based authority, according to Table 2:[46]

[44] See, for example, Fiss (1983), Resnik (1982) and Heydebrand/Seron (1990). This discussion can be easily framed in terms of the 'efficiency-vs.-justice' trade-off examined in ch 2.

[45] See generally Clark (1981) and Heydebrand/Seron (1990).

[46] Beckman (1990: 129). Beckman attempts to investigate the problem of professionalisation, ie, the increase in the relative importance of socially sanctioned expertise, according to two taxonomic tools that relate to the organisation of work and the role of expertise as giving rise to different forms of authority. The four types of work he examines, depending on the degree of formal training required and the relative autonomy in work, are: 'proletarian' work, 'skilled labor' work, 'vocational' work and 'professional' work. The latter is characterised by the requirement of substantial formal training and a high degree of autonomy in work.

Table 2
Typology of authority
(Beckman 1990)

<table>
<tr><th></th><th>Goal-based</th><th>Status-based</th></tr>
<tr><td rowspan="2">Institution-based</td><td>Bureaucratic authority</td><td rowspan="2">Rights-authority</td></tr>
<tr><td rowspan="2">Professional authority</td></tr>
<tr><td rowspan="2">Person-based</td><td rowspan="2">Community authority</td></tr>
<tr><td>Expert authority</td></tr>
</table>

According to this typology, there are four main forms of authority: bureaucratic authority, rights authority, expert authority, and community authority. 'Bureaucratic authority' refers to institutionally defined rules and roles relating to goals and contractual tasks. 'Rights authority' depends on accepted obligations linked to the rights attached to owners of institutionally ascribed status. 'Expert authority' is goal-based and derives from the presumed performance skills of persons, while 'community authority' attaches to person and status, and instructions from this source carry authority by force of a sense of community. These types of authority conflict with each other, with maximum conflict to be expected along two diagonals: between the expert and rights types of authority, and between the bureaucratic and community types of authority.[47]

Professional authority, which derives from socially sanctioned expertise, lies on the borderline between expert and bureaucratic authority, containing elements of both. It clearly belongs to the 'modern,' goal-based type of authority, but is ambiguous in the person/institution dimension. In such a middle position, professional groups are forced to conduct a battle for authority on two fronts: against the wholly institutionalised, role-bound authority of bureaucracy, and against the wholly person-based authority of 'free expertise', which 'is not institutionally boosted by credentials and authorisation'.[48] The middle position also

> allows professionals to alternate between stressing the merits of institutionally guarded authority, as against agents on the 'free market' of expertise, and the merits of personal quality and institutional independence as against bureaucratic structures

an ambiguous standing which is essential to professional authority.[49]

[47] Beckman (1990: 129 f.).
[48] Beckman (1990: 131).
[49] Beckman (1990: 132).

The typology helps explain why the two-fold processes of the 'bureaucratisation' of professional roles and the 'professionalisation' of bureaucratic roles may occur in contemporary society. However, from the point of view of *actual* social trends, it is the 'bureaucratisation' of professions which has attracted the most attention. 'Bureaucratisation' in this sense means the tendency of professions to lose formal legal autonomy in labour markets by becoming increasingly employed in public and private bureaucracies.[50]

This trend has been well documented with respect to the legal profession. In many countries, the number of self-employed or independent lawyers has been declining in relative terms, compared with the growing proportion of salaried lawyers who work in either private companies, law, accounting or consulting firms, or in government agencies, frequently under the instructions or supervision of non-lawyers.[51] In the United States, for example, between 1954 and 1970, the number of self-employed lawyers increased by 19 per cent, while the number of lawyers employed by the federal government rose by 108 per cent and those employed by state governments by 167 per cent. The number of lawyers employed in business increased almost fivefold between 1951 and 1980, while that of self-employed lawyers did not even double.[52]

In terms of social authority, however, it is not clear that professional authority has lost its relative importance. While the type and degree of authority exercised by groups of professionals is dependent on the type of functions they actually exercise in organisations, the exercise of expert authority itself is not directly dependent on enjoying formal autonomy.[53] In Beckman's typology, the question of professionalisation or, conversely, of bureaucratisation is, in his own words, not directly a matter of formal organisation, but rather of the 'changing relative social efficiency of different types of authority in the overall pattern of authorisation in society'.[54]

We shall try now to establish a connection between Beckman's typology and the discussion on the bureaucratisation of courts. We do not know, as yet, whether bureaucratisation, or professionalisation for that matter, have the same

[50] Beckman (1990: 133 ff.).

[51] Abel (1989b) and Szelényi/Martin (1989: 276 ff.).

[52] Abel (1989b: 103 f.). Szelényi/Martin (1989. 276 ff.) mention four categories of countries and forms of bureaucratisation:

- —'Latin' countries, where self-employment remains dominant (Italy, Spain, France and Germany).
- —Common-law countries, where solo practice has declined, but lawyers have mainly opted for employment by other lawyers in law firms (the United States).
- —Countries in which bureaucratisation occurred within government (Norway, where 44% of all lawyers were employed in the public sector); and
- —Countries where bureaucratisation occurred within business (such as Belgium).

[53] Beckman (1990: 134).

[54] Beckman (1990: 134). Davies (1983) challenges the representations of bureaucracy and profession as immanent structures and stresses the need to abandon notions of a professional-bureaucratic dichotomy.

meaning (ie, forms of authority and their relative social efficiency) when used in that new context. However, we may obtain additional help for approaching this issue from a more precise description of the bureaucratic and professional elements in courts and their relative importance in different legal traditions. Indeed, the common-law and civil-law models of the judicial process have been called 'professional' and 'bureaucratic', respectively, as they have existed for a long time.[55]

It is a well-known fact that one significant difference between the civil-law and common-law traditions lies in the selection process of judges, the social significance accorded to their professional role, and the ways in which judicial functions are performed. In this sense, the common-law tradition has been described as embodying a 'professional' model of justice on account of the following general traits:[56]

—Judges are selected from among distinguished members of the legal profession, usually after many years of practice; therefore, their role is not regarded as a separate branch but rather as a continuation of the legal profession.
—There is also no specific or obligatory training for becoming a judge.
—Judicial posts do not form a part of an organised and hierarchical career, where advancement is subject to administrative criteria, such as seniority.

For these reasons, among others, observers of the common-law world would hesitate, with good reason, to describe courts as bureaucratic organisations. Bureaucracy

> implies hierarchy, relatively clear agreement on organisational goals, the existence of efficacious means for securing compliance with these goals, and a substantial degree of organisational autonomy from the larger environment,[57]

and few of these conditions would seem applicable to the courts. A system of courts of different hierarchy does not necessarily imply a hierarchy in the bureaucratic sense, although it may serve as a device for the selective control of decisions made by lower authorities.[58]

What then do those who claim that the Anglo-American judicial process has become increasingly bureaucratised in recent times mean? Evidently, they do not mean the strengthening of hierarchical relations in court systems, or a reduction of the social value of the judicial profession as such. They refer instead to the organisational changes wrought in the courts as a response to growing caseloads. For some, this kind of bureaucratisation is a worrisome, insidious development, since it alters the distinctive nature of the judicial function in adversary

[55] Guarnieri (1994), Guarnieri/Pederzoli (1996: 66 ff.). This difference lies in the different model of state that supports it. See Damaška (1986: 71 ff.).
[56] Guarnieri (1994: 56 ff.) and Guarnieri/Pederzoli (1996: 66 ff.).
[57] Feeley (1979: 16).
[58] Cf Shapiro (1980).

procedures.[59] They claim, for example, that case management, which is one of such responses, has given rise to a new form of 'judicial activism,' whose benefits seem to have little empirical support, and whose problematic by-products may mean fewer procedural safeguards and less justice.[60]

A few empirical studies seem to confirm the notion that the change in the number, type and, above all, mode of disposition of cases in American courts is actually largely due to administrative and managerial developments. David S Clark has statistically documented such changes for the United States federal courts.[61] He has identified a trend 'from adjudication to administration', meaning that the main mode of dispute settlement changes primarily from adjudication to administrative techniques. In his opinion, a major driving force behind this development has undoubtedly been the political movement for judicial reform and its emphasis on efficient caseload management. But the increase in mass procedures that are mostly subject to routine treatment, as well as the rise in public law litigation requiring the involvement of the judge in complex social policy issues, have also made a significant contribution.[62] The result has been a process of bureaucratisation of the federal judiciary, furthered and reinforced by the creation of national and regional administrative structures linked to district courts and by the adoption of standardised rules that limit the professional autonomy of the judge. Given the constitutional functions of courts, this should not be deemed unproblematic.[63]

Another study on the US federal district courts, by Wolf Heydebrand and Carroll Seron, reaches a similar conclusion: that the organisation of judicial work and the predominant forms of case disposition in those courts have profoundly changed in recent decades.[64] Based on quantitative, qualitative and historical data, they attempt to establish an empirical relation between environmental forces (political economy and demography) and caseloads, court organisation, and judicial decision-making:[65]

> Under the double impact of increasing demand for services and limited fiscal and organisational resources, the administration of justice is rationalised. Courts are changing from professionally and collegially controlled, semifeudal domains of judges, to modern, businesslike, administrative agencies concerned with speed, efficiency, productivity, simplification, and cost-effectiveness in the delivery of judicial services. Adjudication, under the aegis of due process and adversary procedure, is moving toward case-management, plea bargaining, and informal negotiation within

59 See Resnik (1982) and Hoffman (1982).

60 Resnik (1982). That this is not a development that affects only American courts is shown by recent proposals of the Lord Chancellor in England to adopt case management as a reform strategy for the English courts. See some of the essays published in Zuckerman/Cranston (eds) (1995).

61 Clark (1981).

62 Clark (1981: 66).

63 Clark (1981: 76f., 150).

64 Heydebrand/Seron (1990).

65 Heydebrand/Seron (1990: 1).

> an organisationally integrated system based on technical-managerial expertise and computerised information technology.[66]

Heydebrand and Seron make an important point when they repeatedly emphasise that the transformations they are describing do not simply imply a change towards a traditional 'bureaucratic' model, in the sense of a bifurcation of bureaucratic and professional functions that translates into an expansion of administrative support services.[67] Instead, it is a movement towards new forms of technical and social rationalisation of the judicial system as a whole (which they call 'technocratic rationalisation'), in an attempt to increase its overall flexibility, responsiveness and crisis-management capacity. It is a mode of administration that is neither 'professional,' with 'autonomous or dominant judges upholding the adversary system and the rule of law,'[68] nor 'bureaucratic,' with 'hierarchical lines of authority, a strict division of labor and formal organisational procedures and rules.'[69] A further consequence is that the nature of the services provided by the courts has also changed, from a professional service to a kind of 'commodity production.'[70]

Not surprisingly, Heydebrand and Seron are highly critical of this development towards technocratic justice. They claim that it undermines an independent judiciary and contributes to its gradual decline.[71] And although they do not directly address the issue of the quality of justice that results from the changes they analyse, it is clearly suggested that the technocratic model does not satisfy their conception of justice, as they express a definite preference for a 'democratic model of justice'.[72]

The trend towards bureaucratisation, or technocratic rationalisation, as analysed by Clark, Heydebrand and Seron, and others, should be fairly evident for any observer. What is less evident is their largely negative interpretation of this phenomenon.[73] However, it is an issue that cannot be completely resolved. The concept of justice will always be subject to debate. The defenders of managerial methods will never renounce their claim that efficient judicial management creates more, rather than less, room for substantive justice, and for giving proper consideration to those cases that warrant it from a legal or social point

[66] Heydebrand/Seron (1990: 3).

[67] Heydebrand/Seron (1990: 210). The concept of the judicial role as an organised role says as much, insofar as the judicial function is itself subject to administration, not separated from it.

[68] Heydebrand/Seron (1990: 212) point out that it may contribute to a process of de-professionalisation.

[69] Heydebrand/Seron (1990: 14).

[70] Heydebrand/Seron (1990: 13 ff., 211 f.).

[71] Heydebrand/Seron (1990: 14, 213).

[72] At the end of their study, Heydebrand and Seron (1990: 206 ff.) examine the responses to a crisis in the rule of law and the administration of justice in terms of six possible models of justice: traditional, professional, bureaucratic, technocratic, economic, and democratic (described on 215 ff.). Despite their evident preference for the democratic model, they themselves admit that this model is 'largely Utopian' (216).

[73] See, for example, the critical review of Heydebrand and Seron's study by MacIntosh (1993) and their response in the same journal. Heydebrand/Seron (1993).

of view.[74] And there will be always some dispute as to the assumption of a golden age of adversarial adjudication which underlies some of these critical analyses.[75]

The 'bureaucratisation' of the courts in the common-law world should be seen in a broader historical perspective. It will then become apparent that case management is but one discernible manifestation of a much larger process of judicial rationalisation that has made the common-law tradition slowly converge, in certain respects, with the civilian legal systems, which began and completed their own rationalisation process somewhat earlier. One example of this was the abolition of the forms of action, and the establishment of a judicial hierarchy, more like the court organisation existing on the Continent, in nineteenth century England.[76] The United States judicial system, while more 'rationalised' at its inception than the English courts of the time, was still undergoing a vast process of unification and rationalisation of state court systems as late as the 1970s.[77]

For a long time, a common feature of both legal traditions was that the court system was administrated and staffed, and indeed still is to some extent, by the executive power, as a historical reminiscence of the jurisdictional powers of the king. In addition to this limited similarity regarding their origins, court organisations in civil-law countries possess certain features that distinguish them quite clearly from the 'professional' model just described and which approximate them to ordinary bureaucratic organisations. Thus, it is not completely unjustified to call them 'bureaucratic,' even for historical reasons.

In civil-law countries, the bureaucratic components of courts can be traced back to the Middle Ages. A few centuries later, the courts became increasingly consolidated in the wake of the French Revolution, which spurred a process of rationalisation and hierarchical arrangement of the rather chaotic patchwork of multiple, overlapping jurisdictions.[78] Other historical developments also contributed to the process of bureaucratic rationalisation of the judiciary. On the Continent, the doctrines of the separation of powers and of the general will as embodied by the legislator, had the effect of generating a conception of the judicial function as a mechanical application of legislation, without the judges having any possibility of making law or even of interpreting it.[79] The selection of judges and the administration of the court system remained firmly in the hands of the executive power, which permitted, preserved or promoted the consideration of judges as civil servants, subject to a status and to professional career lines similar to those of a normal bureaucratic career.[80]

[74] See, for example, Saari (1982: 14).
[75] See Friedman (1984: 168 f.).
[76] Jolowicz (dir.) (1992: 9 ff.) and Glenn (1995).
[77] See, for example, Scheb, II/Matheny (1988) and Flango (1994).
[78] Vincent *et al.* (1996: 4 f.).
[79] It should be remembered that the French Supreme Court, the *Cour de Cassation*, was initially a body close to the legislature charged with preventing the incorrect application of laws by the judges.
[80] Fix-Fierro (1997: 247 ff.).

The traditional traits of the 'bureaucratic' model of justice are as follows :[81]

—Judges form a separate branch of the legal profession. They are mainly selected through public examinations, open to candidates who have recently graduated from university.
—Training in judicial work is carried out within the judicial institution itself,[82] and judges are expected to be able to occupy any judicial post.
—The judicial organisation is hierarchical, in the sense that the advancement and promotion of judges from the lower positions depends on seniority and merit, as assessed in a more or less discretionary manner by their fellow judges in higher positions or by the Ministry of Justice.

Understandably, the professional element in this model, in the sense of the specific and creative contribution made by an expert authority to the solution of the problems submitted to it, is rather marginal. As one observer has eloquently put it:

> . . . it can be said that the professional activity of judges has traditionally been considered in a residual mode, as an interstitial space at the interior of prevalent behaviors, which are non-professional in nature.[83]

Judges adopt a rather low profile and are rarely identified as outstanding personalities in society.[84] They do not openly claim a political role or power for themselves outside the judicial institution. Internally, hierarchical relations circumscribe and check the independence of the individual judge.

Nevertheless, the traditional role of judges in civil-law countries has been undergoing a profound transformation in the last decades, towards a more prominent role and position, which approximates it to the judicial role in common-law countries.[85] This trend could be partly described as a process of

[81] Guarnieri (1994: 56) and Guarnieri/Pederzoli (1996: 66 ff.).

[82] Many countries have established specialised institutions for this purpose, known as 'judicial schools,' notably France and Spain. See Guarnieri/Pederzoli (1996: 41).

[83] Ferrarese (1984: 131). Chapter VI is significantly titled: 'I Magistrati, tra burocrazia e professione' ('Judges between bureaucracy and profession'). Ferrarese adds that the tendency to overlook the problem of the professional identity of judges has developed in two directions:

—Reducing the professional activity of judges to a mere reflection of their class position and their ideology;
—Reducing such activity to an effect of pressures which, in a broad sense, can be defined as bureaucratic in nature: position in the judicial hierarchy, criteria for career advancement, for recruitment and socialisation, etc. (131).

[84] As opposed to the prominent social position enjoyed by judges in common law countries. However, Abel (1989a: 172) points to the paradoxical position of the judiciary in the American legal profession: on the one hand, it enjoys extraordinary power and prestige because of its prominent law-making role. On the other, the process by which (most) judges are selected does not inspire respect. By contrast, in 'most civil law countries, the judiciary is a distinct branch of the civil service, which attracts many of the most talented law graduates and retains them throughout their careers, those who demonstrate the greatest ability being elevated to higher courts.'

[85] Some of the reasons that explain this have been examined in ch 1 as general reasons for the growing relevance of courts in the contemporary world.

'professionalisation', that is, as the re-evaluation of the specifically professional elements in the judicial process.

An initial aspect of professionalisation in this sense is the larger social role and the law-making powers that civilian judges have finally been acknowledged,[86] a hard-won recognition that is reinforced by increasing specialisation and which finds its most prominent expression in constitutional courts. This larger social role is a natural consequence of the larger role of legislation and administration in the welfare state, which calls for a greater degree of control that can only be provided by the courts, the most prominent example of which is, again, constitutional justice. As Mauro Cappelletti wrote: courts have to choose

> between . . . sticking within the traditional, typically nineteenth-century limits of the judicial function, and . . . rising to the level of the other branches, indeed becoming themselves the 'third giant' to control the mastodon legislator and the leviathan administrator.[87]

Another more central aspect, which goes hand in hand with the one just mentioned, is the distinctive, autonomous identity that the traditional judicial career has achieved. This has been accomplished in several countries, mainly through the establishment of a specialised body to which the administration of the organised role of judges and other judicial officials has been entrusted: the Council of the Judiciary.[88]

The Council of the Judiciary is a special public body first established in Spain and Italy at the beginning of the twentieth century. After the Second World War, it spread to many other civil law countries, in both Europe, including some former socialist countries, and Latin America.[89] It has the explicit goal of enhancing the independence and autonomy of judges and courts,[90] and therefore, their professional function and identity, from executive or bureaucratic agencies, through its intervention in the process of selection, appointment, advancement and discipline of judges and other judicial officials.[91]

It can be argued that the Council of the Judiciary contributes to the professionalisation and the 'de-bureaucratisation'[92] of the courts and the judge's role, at least in the following respects:[93]

[86] See, for example, Cappelletti (1989: 30 ff.).

[87] Cappelletti (1989: 19).

[88] The names given to this institution have some variants. It is called the Superior Council of the Magistracy (*Conseil Superieur de la Magistrature*, *Consiglio Superiore de la Magistratura*) in France and Italy, for example, whereas in Spain, it is the General Council of the Judicial Power (*Consejo General del Poder Judicial*). For a brief explanation of the origins and diffusion of this institution, see Fix-Zamudio/Fix-Fierro (1996).

[89] Fix-Zamudio/Fix-Fierro (1996).

[90] The French *Conseil Superieur de la Magistrature* is formally an auxiliary to the President of the Republic, who is the appointed guarantor of judicial independence, according to Article 64 of the 1958 Constitution, as amended.

[91] Fix-Zamudio/Fix-Fierro (1996) and Guarnieri/Pederzoli (1996: 74).

[92] 'Professionalisation' and 'de-bureaucratisation' are not strictly equivalent, but closely interrelated in this context.

[93] See Fix-Fierro (1995b). The Council of the Judiciary can be said to be the professional organisation of the professional organisations called courts.

—*Composition*: the Council is normally composed of a majority of judges from all levels and categories of the judiciary, so the natural hierarchical bias existing between those levels and categories is somehow attenuated by the voice that is also given to the lower ranks; and of a minority of other legal professionals, who are supposed to prevent the judicial institution from becoming too closed and inward-looking.

—*Control of judicial training institutions* (judicial schools) specifically established for the training and selection of candidates to judicial posts and for the continuing education of sitting judges; this gives the Council significant leverage over the professional ideology that pervades the judiciary.

—*Participation in the appointmentof judges*: the selection, appointment and advancement of judges are increasingly carried out through objective procedures (public examinations) that reduce the discretionary powers of the selecting or appointing organ.

—*Institutional role as a representative body of the judiciary*, capable of setting or influencing judicial policy, both inside and outside the judicial institution.

A final question that must be still addressed is the relationship between the processes of 'bureaucratisation' and 'professionalisation' as regards efficiency. Both processes can be seen as efficiency-enhancing trends, but their impact on the efficient operation of the judicial process is different. Bureaucratisation clearly aims to produce a more flexible, effective treatment of the courts' workload. Conversely, professionalisation is less significant for the efficient operation of courts, but more important as regards the institutional and social efficiency of adjudication.

The Unit of Analysis and the Inter-organisational Approach

Another question that must be dealt with in the context of this general organisational approach to the courts concerns the appropriate 'unit of analysis'. Four possible choices have been employed as a unit of analysis:

—The individual court.

—The court system, ie, the set of courts that form an interrelated unit or jurisdictional order.

—The courtroom workgroup.

—The individual court as it interacts with other organisations.

Organisational studies on the courts usually adopt either approach. We shall now briefly discuss the justification for each.

The most evident approach is to consider one or several *individual courts* as the unit of analysis. A court is a unit that can be easily identified by legal and organisational criteria. It is clearly differentiated from a specific environment, which allows one to study the particular contribution to its operation of the factors existing in the environment as they affect, for example, the number and type of cases to be processed.[94]

Secondly, the entire *court system* can be adopted as the unit of analysis. Again, it is possible to examine the relationships of the court system as a whole to other organisations in its environment, such as another branch of government, or to consider the internal relationships, for example, of a hierarchical or administrative nature, between the units that compose the court system. Due to its complexity, it is to be expected that such an approach will rarely be used, if at all, perhaps mostly in an implicit manner.[95]

A third perspective focuses on the *internal working of the courts*. Within a court, the courtroom workgroup can be identified as an organisation of its own, which is responsible for the speed and ways in which cases are processed. This approach has been especially employed for the analysis of the criminal process in the United States.[96] It seems to benefit from the common-law type of oral procedure, in which several actors establish identifiable interaction patterns, mostly in face-to-face exchanges. Such patterns affect specific case outcomes and can be compared across courts. However, this approach could also be used to analyse the working of courts in general, whenever certain actors establish identifiable interaction patterns that have an impact on court operation, such as crisis management.

However, members of the courtroom workgroup (judges, prosecutors, attorneys and social workers) also belong to *other organisations* (sometimes called 'sponsoring' or 'parent' organisations) meaning that they respond, to a greater or lesser degree, to the interests and strategies of these other organisations. This implies that interactions between these actors are not only marked by the specific structures and norms within the group,[97] but also by the norms and goals of the parent organisations. Thus, a dual allegiance of the courtroom workgroup members emerges, and the group must strive to reconcile or overcome competing orientations of its members, as well as sharing work orientations with other organisations.[98]

The fourth approach generalises the insight that various organisations contribute to the shaping of judicial outcomes, not only *the* court organisation, and focuses on the relationships established between the court and these other organisations. What is the position of courts vis-a-vis the latter? Several models are conceivable from a management perspective.[99]

A first model conceives of the court as a self-contained organisation, a large machine that must be maintained as a forum for dispute settlement 'when

[94] Heydebrand/Seron (1990: 9 ff.).

[95] See, for example, Posner (1996).

[96] See, for example, Eisenstein/Jacob (1977).

[97] Jacob (1976: 158): 'Their workload, working conditions, and their product result from their courtroom interactions rather than from directives of their parent organisation'.

[98] Jacob (1976: 158 f.).

[99] Martin/Maron (1991: 270 ff.). This means that other perspectives can reach different conclusions.

attorneys are ready'.[100] Another view holds the court to be the preeminent organisation, 'located amidst but also at the apex of a powerful network of organisations and interest groups'.[101] Finally, a third model views the court as an organisation within a multi-organisational system, in which the court 'does have special responsibilities for coordinating the system', but is not the preeminent organisation within it; the court 'becomes a facilitator of common direction even though organisations within the judicial network retain independent goals.'[102]

An *inter-organisational* approach[103] is indispensable if one wishes to understand the different rationalities and goals that cooperate or conflict with each other within the courts as well as the tensions between them that shape case outcomes. As Martin and Maron put it, there are three sources of tensions:

> First, within the judicial system there is a tension between expectations for a hierarchy among organisations and the need for extensive inter-organisational networking. Second, there is a tension between expectations that the court should be the preeminent, impartial, dispassionate, dispute-resolving organisations within the judicial system and at the same time that it also be the preeminent administrative body responsible for overseeing and regulating the entire system. Third, there is a tension between the need for an integrated administrative justice system and the need to maintain a separation of power between the judicial and executive branches of local government.[104]

The inter-organisational approach to the study of the courts is much more complex, but at the same time, it may prove to be a more powerful tool for explanation. The most important consequence of this perspective may be the insight that certain effects that are generally attributed to the courts, such as delay, should be attributed to the interaction of different organisations or to actors not directly controlled by the courts themselves, such as attorneys.[105]

The Influence of the Organisational Context

In this section we will describe several empirical studies that refer to certain aspects and dimensions of court organisation that have been briefly developed above. With regard to the problem of rational behaviour and efficiency, most of these studies offer, first, an explicit or implicit critique of the economic approach, and secondly, an alternative or complementary interpretation. Such

[100] Martin/Maron (1991: 271).
[101] Martin/Maron (1991: 274 ff.).
[102] Martin/Maron (1991: 278).
[103] On the present relevance of this approach see Calás/McGuire (1990).
[104] Martin/Maron (1991: 269 f.).
[105] See Welsh/Pontell (1991), who examine interorganisational changes in three California counties under court orders to reform local jails. They conclude that while courts orders resulted in tighter coupling of the subsystems and more proactive interagency responses, they initially led to increased interagency conflict.

an interpretation does not exclude the role of efficiency concerns in the judicial process, but places them in a qualified context.

Organisational studies of the judicial process, most visibly exemplified by studies of the pervasive phenomenon of plea-bargaining in American criminal courts, can be interpreted as a more or less explicit critique of the economic approach to litigation. Despite the basic and apparent compatibility of economic assumptions with behaviours that can be empirically observed in the courts, it can be also argued that these assumptions, and the models that derive from them, fail to take into account some elements—such as uncertainty—that can only be more appropriately described and interpreted in terms of organisational dimensions and constraints, for example, in terms of the technology employed by the organisation.[106] In other words: the organisation has to be assumed as the *context* of rational decisions and behaviours, however they may be defined or modeled, within the courts. Otherwise, *differences* in disposition patterns between and across jurisdictions cannot be completely or satisfactorily explained.[107]

The influence of the organisational context can be generalised, negatively, as a critique of any rationality model or theory that seeks to explain judicial *outcomes*[108] on their terms alone, including purely organisational approaches, and positively, as the possibility of integrating, synthesising and extending the explanatory power of such models and theories. Thus, for example, an empirical study on criminal sentencing outcomes in 73 counties in the state of Minnesota attempts to do precisely this with regard to three theoretical approaches to criminal sentencing: a formal legal theory, a substantive political theory, and an organisational maintenance theory.[109]

The formal legal theory states that sentencing is primarily determined by legal variables; the substantive political theory holds that sentencing is determined by legal and social status variables, while the organisational maintenance theory finds that sentencing is determined by legal and processing (operational) variables.[110] The study conducts a statistical analysis of a sample of 1,532 felony cases ending in conviction which were initiated during the first six months of 1983.[111] The dependent variable—sentencing—is measured according to the probability of receiving a prison-term sentence and to the length of the sentence received.[112] The independent variables—legal, social, and processing variables—are implemented through one or more measures.[113] A measure of

[106] This is the central thesis in Matheny (1980).

[107] Matheny (1980: 281) and Dixon (1995: 1164 ff.).

[108] It should be emphasised that, although we are referring to *outcomes* here, an implicit notion in the idea of *organisational* context is that the *process* is also of central importance, even when such outcomes are explained in terms of some substantive rationality (for example, of a political nature).

[109] Dixon (1995: 1157 f.).

[110] Dixon (1995: 1157 f., 1159 ff.).

[111] Dixon (1995: 1168).

[112] Dixon (1995: 1171).

[113] Dixon (1995: 1172 ff.).

bureaucratisation is introduced 'to test whether the level of bureaucratisation of judicial and prosecutorial administration where cases are processed conditions the effects of legal, processing, and social variables on sentencing'.[114]

The results of the study are revealing of what the 'organisational context' means for the multiple variables that influence sentencing outcomes. When the organisational context in which a case is processed is omitted, the organisational maintenance theory is better able to predict prison and sentence length.[115] If, on the other hand, the two dimensions of bureaucratisation are introduced, the relevance of the different theories and their variables is *modified*. In the author's own words:

> The findings from the analysis of both judicial and prosecutorial contexts reveal that the formal legal theory is supported under conditions of low bureaucratisation and the organisational maintenance theory is supported under conditions of high bureaucratisation, whether it be judicial or prosecutorial. This pattern persists for both the prison and the sentence length decisions, but is stronger for the sentence length decision.[116]

In conclusion: the study's findings 'point to the limitations of any sentencing theory that fails to address the organisational context of sentencing.'[117]

Courtroom Workgroups and Plea-bargaining in the Criminal Process

Plea-bargaining, ie, the admission by a defendant of a certain degree of guilt in exchange for a reduction in the charges or the sentence offered, is a widespread method in the American criminal justice system for disposing of criminal cases by bypassing the costly, time-consuming jury (and sometimes bench) trial.[118] Implicitly or explicitly, plea-bargaining is assumed to be an efficiency device in criminal procedure. This assumption stems mainly from two interrelated sources.

—For historical reasons, Anglo-American judicial procedure is based on the notion of trial by jury, and this notion determines some of judicial procedure's most salient features. This is true, for example, of the trial as a concentrated, oral exposition of adversary argument; the finality of the first instance decision; the limited possibility of appeal, etc.[119] As much as trial by jury is recognised as a right of the defendant, it is a right that can be, and

[114] Dixon (1995: 1176). Two components of the bureaucratic organisation of the judiciary are measured: complexity of division of judicial labor and decentralisation of judicial decision-making. Two measures of the bureaucratisation of the prosecutors' offices are likewise taken into account: prosecutorial complexity (number of divisions or departments) and decentralisation of decision-making (plea-bargaining) (at 1178 f.).

[115] Dixon (1995: 1181 f.).

[116] Dixon (1995: 1183).

[117] Dixon (1995: 1192 f.).

[118] Friedman (1984: 166 ff.).

[119] Damaška (1986: 57 ff.).

actually is, usually waived. Conversely, the prosecutor has the power to decide which cases to prosecute and which sentences to demand.[120]

—Trial by jury is cumbersome, costly, time-consuming, and most of all, a procedure of uncertain outcome for both prosecutors and defendants. In view of ever rising caseloads, it is further assumed that the criminal justice system would simply break down if all cases led to a trial by jury, and that plea-bargaining is a necessary evil that cannot be avoided, much less prohibited, as has sometimes been attempted.

Empirical studies on plea-bargaining in American courts have mainly tried to answer two questions: what are the factors that favor bargaining over jury trial, and, likewise, bench trial over jury trial? To what extent is 'case pressure', ie, the need for judges, prosecutors and attorneys to expeditiously process as many cases as possible, a factor that explains the prevalence of plea-bargaining? In other terms: is efficiency the overriding concern in the context of plea-bargaining? The empirical evidence gathered by those studies is inconclusive and may be subject to interpretation.

A study conducted in the 1970s on felony dispositions in three American cities sought to determine the factors responsible for the choice of guilty plea over trial and of bench trial over jury trial in view of increasing workloads.[121] The study examined the case of 1,500 defendants for each of three cities, Baltimore, Chicago, and Detroit. The study found that in addition to defendant or case characteristics, the different outcomes in the three cities, in both the preliminary hearings and the plea-bargaining process, depended on the structures and norms of the workgroup operating in the courtroom.

The courtroom workgroup has characteristics commonly found among other organised workgroups, such as relationships of authority and influence; common goals; specialised roles; a variety of tasks and work techniques; and varying degrees of stability and familiarity.[122] Among the organisational characteristics of workgroups and their environments, including sponsoring organisations and the larger context, two were closely related to the choices mentioned above (ie, guilty plea over trial, and bench trial over jury trial): *familiarity* between the members of the workgroup, and the *incentives* motivating their behaviour.[123] Familiarity produced pleas, because through familiarity, negotiations reduced uncertainty. This was the case of Chicago, described as a city of 'workgroup negotiation.' Production and financial incentives, as well as uncertainty reduction, produced bench trials, as in Baltimore, a 'city of trials.'

[120] By contrast, prosecutors in the Continental tradition are much more bound by legal rules, so that in principle they do not have the choice between prosecuting or not, if the legal conditions for doing so are met. However, this does not imply that negotiation with defendants does not occur, particularly if the evidence is not very clear. It simply means that negotiation is not a prominent, official method of dealing with cases, which is why it may manifest itself in other forms.

[121] Eisenstein/Jacob (1977).

[122] Eisenstein/Jacob (1977: 20 ff.). See also an empirical study by Lipetz (1980).

[123] Eisenstein/Jacob (1977: 62 ff., 251 f.).

When courtroom workgroup members were less familiar with each other and incentives for bench trials were missing, jury trials became more prevalent, as in Detroit, described as a city of 'bureaucratised plea bargaining.'[124]

A similar approach was adopted by another study that focuses on the 'courtroom elite,'[125] as it calls the courtroom workgroup composed of the judge, the prosecutor and the defense attorney. Members of a courtroom elite have a shared interest in processing cases expeditiously, which is reinforced by certain environmental constraints, such as due process expectations. This shared interest stems from the particular incentives each member of the courtroom elite faces,[126] and translates into high rates of guilty pleas. The empirical evidence analysed by this study showed that 56 per cent of all cases in a trial sample were guilty pleas, accounting for about 80 per cent of all convictions.[127] Only 12 per cent of defendants were sent to trial, and 60 per cent were convicted. Where the defendant appeared to resist efforts by the courtroom elite to maintain a cordial atmosphere and expeditiously process cases, he was sanctioned quite harshly, and sanctions were more severe when workloads were more pressing.[128] Thus, defendants were punished not so much for their actual crime, but for the 'crime' of disturbing the smooth working of the courtroom elite.

A study on the operation of the lower criminal courts in Connecticut specifically examined the caseload-pressure hypothesis.[129] For this purpose, it compared a high-volume, heavy-caseload court with a low-volume, lighter caseload court in a neighbouring community, in relation to several indicators of adversarial proceedings. The study found that there was a lack of trials in both courts, regardless of their respective caseloads. Similarly, the rate of motions by defense attorneys willing to take advantage of adversary proceedings failed to reveal substantial differences between both courts: around 90 per cent of the cases were resolved without filing motions.[130]

As for plea bargains, the percentage of total charge reductions was compared, rather than the rate of guilty pleas. Here, the percentage of guilty pleas involving a plea to a lesser charge was considerably higher in the heavier caseload

[124] Eisenstein/Jacob (1977: 65–171, 251 f.).

[125] Nardulli (1978).

[126] Nardulli (1978: 67 ff.), mentions, for example, the following:

- —Average fees of private counsel are low, which produces an interest in processing a large number of cases;
- —For judges, prosecutors and public defenders, the engine of their common interest is not caseload pressure, but the structure of workloads; presumption of guilt is another important factor that contributes to the routine nature of court work:
- —There are no professional or financial incentives to engage in formal, adversarial proceedings as a matter of course;
- —The power of courtroom elites derives from discretion, distributed among members in such a way that none can dominate criminal court operations.

[127] Nardulli (1978: 184).

[128] Nardulli (1978: 217, 219).

[129] Feeley (1979: 245 ff.).

[130] Feeley (1979: 251 f.).

court than in the low-volume court, suggesting that in the latter court there was 'less need or pressure to settle cases by reducing charges.'[131] The difference was much more significant if only felony charges that eventually led to misdemeanor convictions, were considered.[132] The profile of sentences failed to reveal any major differences between the two courts. Pretrial release of defendants on bail, which could be expected to be more restrictive in the high-volume court, also showed no dramatic differences.[133] Courtroom observation was unable to reveal significant differences in the rapid, perfunctory manner in which cases were handled by both courts, except for the actual length of time they were in session.[134] In short, among all possible indicators of adversary proceedings, caseload could only be strongly related to charge reduction.

A fourth study examined plea-bargaining as experienced by prosecutors, judges, and defense attorneys.[135] Specifically, the study explored the 'post-recruitment adaptation of new prosecutors, defense attorneys, and judges to the 'plea-bargaining court"; it tried to find out how newcomers adjusted to plea-bargaining and what the adaptation process and the substantive outcomes were.[136] As part of the study, the efficacy of the 'case-pressure hypothesis' was also tested. As in other studies, the relative lack of trials versus alternate modes of case disposition was again confirmed. Furthermore, statistical data going back to the final decades of the nineteenth century showed that this lack of trials was not a recent phenomenon and that plea-bargaining was as prevalent in low-volume as it was in high-volume courts.[137]

The rate of trials remained constant in the three busiest courts even when a change in jurisdiction was introduced that reduced case pressure without modifying personnel levels.[138] The author concludes:

> Rather than being simply an expedient dictated by unmanageably large case loads, plea-bargaining is integrally and inextricably bound to the 'trial' court . . . The decision to plea-bargain is not fundamentally a function of case pressure; other factors and incentives account for the decision to go to trial or to plea-bargain.[139]

A further statistical study on the emergence of implicit plea-bargaining—as opposed to explicit plea-bargaining—in the US federal district courts during the Progressive and Prohibition eras[140] examined three competing explanations for plea-bargaining, each of which received qualified support:

131 Feeley (1979: 253).
132 Feeley (1979: 254).
133 Feeley (1979: 256 f.).
134 Feeley (1979: 258 ff.).
135 Heumann (1978).
136 Heumann (1978: 1).
137 Heumann (1978: 28).
138 Heumann (1978: 30).
139 Heumann (1978: 32).
140 Padgett (1990).

—The *administrative capacity argument*: Prohibition was a massive, extremely discrete, moderately long-lasting shock to the court system. Massive caseload brought about an increase in plea-bargaining, but only in districts with high caseload pressure.

—The *substantive justice argument*: plea-bargaining is an effort to substitute flexible sentencing standards, which remain sensitive to the idiosyncratic background of the crime, for the rigid and often harsh provisions of the criminal code.[141]

—The *strength of the state's case argument*: plea-bargaining is a method whereby the prosecutor can secure at least some punishment for factually guilty defendants, whom the prosecutor is not sure he can convict.

Finally, two more studies seem to offer contradictory evidence. The first study examined the effects of a 1975 felony plea-bargaining ban in the Texas district courts in El Paso.[142] Relying on an interrupted time series analysis with data for the 1968–83 period, the study tested the hypothesis that the discontinuance of plea-bargaining affected court caseloads, specifically the proportion of cases going to jury trial and the disposition rate. The study found a considerable increase in the proportion of cases going to jury trial immediately after the implementation of the ban and a substantial but gradual decrease in the disposition rate, to which the jury trial contributed substantially. The study's findings suggested 'that the ban on explicit plea-bargaining did affect the district courts' ability to move the felony docket efficiently.'[143]

The second study, an analysis of the lower (municipal) courts of Philadelphia, tries to show that there are courts where a high proportion of dispositions and determinations of guilt can be attributed to genuine adversarial trials, and that 'mass processing and pleas of guilt need not dominate the courtroom scene'.[144] After allowing for the appropriate adjustments and qualifications (to inflated trial rates), the study found that contested trials (without a jury) still made up about 50 per cent of all dispositions by trial or guilty plea, a figure in sharp contrast to the equivalent figure of less than 10 per cent in other American cities.[145] The higher proportion of trials stemmed from a particular court organisation and culture that fostered specific professional attitudes and behaviour patterns.[146]

* * *

141 Cf Feeley (1979: 273 f.): 'The normative stance that facilitates this 'short circuiting' (ie, plea-bargaining) is a consensus by nearly everyone involved in almost every case that the defendant is in fact responsible for *some* wrongdoing connected with the charges'. By dispensing with the trappings of formal procedure, equitable, substantive justice can be provided in an efficient manner.

142 Holmes *et al.* (1992).

143 Holmes *et al.* (1992: 139).

144 Schulhofer (1985: 520).

145 Schulhofer (1985: 524).

146 Schulhofer (1985: 590).

The empirical studies just described hinge on the fundamental distinction between two different and apparently mutually exclusive modes of criminal case disposition: the adversary trial and plea-bargaining. However, the distinction is not always clear, since it is necessary to define what characterises the form and degree of 'adversariness' of a judicial proceeding.[147] And even if the indicators of an adversarial process can be identified and measured, trials and plea-bargaining may prove to be less mutually exclusive than generally assumed. Indeed, it is possible to conceptualise criminal case processing by American courts as a recursive process in which adversarial and non-adversarial phases alternate.[148]

In order to determine the place of efficiency devices in the judicial process, it is important to look for the point of reference and evaluation of the distinction. Such a point of reference is an 'adjudicative ideal,'[149] as defined precisely by the adversarial trial, however fictitious or unattainable it may be from a historical point of view, and the criteria of due process with which such trial must comply. Therefore, any alternate mode of disposition that departs from the ideal, and notwithstanding the powerful constraints to which it may respond, can be viewed (and disqualified) as providing less justice and as deriving from alien concerns, such as speed, self-interest, amicable work relations, avoidance of uncertainty, and the like.

What these studies show, instead, is a much more complex picture, in which the organisational context of the judicial process usually, but not always, structures the *general* incentives for *all* participants in a way that is more or less *consistent* with *social expectations* and with the *rational use of social resources*. In other words: although *one* instrument or device often apparently or most visibly responds to efficiency considerations—such as plea-bargaining—it is the complex interplay of internal and external variables and the articulation of the three dimensions of organisational action already discussed, that modify the operation of the adjudicative ideal and contribute to the real practices that deviate from it. Here, such variables include familiarity between participants; socialisation and work routines; organisational culture; caseload pressure; the participants' notion of substantive justice, uncertainty over outcomes, etc. It is interesting to note that the adjudicative ideal itself may cause such deviation, for example, by raising process costs, as in the lower criminal courts. Hence: 'the process is the punishment.'[150]

[147] Feeley (1979: 250 ff.). Feeley proposes to use formal motions by the defense and sentence practices as indicators of an adversarial process, in addition to trials. Plea-bargaining can also be understood in at least two ways: as the product of joint negotiation, or as a process that establishes the 'going rate' or 'price' for particular crimes (253). See also Schulhofer (1985: 527 f.), who proposes a notion of adversariness based on the defense's efforts to win acquittal and to forcefully contest the prosecutor's charges.

[148] See Emmelman (1996).

[149] See Feeley (1979: 278 ff.).

[150] Feeley (1979: 199 ff.).

Although these studies refer specifically to the American criminal process, a more general conclusion may be drawn regarding the problem of efficiency devices and strategies. Whatever is regarded as an efficiency device is variable and dependent on a particular legal, institutional, and organisational culture. Whatever does not belong to the core ideals and expectations of the legal process in a particular society or legal tradition, will probably be seen as responding to more or less unrelated concerns, such as efficiency. This may help explain, for example, why case and court management have varying degrees of relevance in different legal traditions.

The Internal Organisation of Courts

The empirical studies discussed above refer mainly to the routines and procedures developed within a 'courtroom workgroup' for the efficient disposition of cases. In this section, however, we shall describe another set of studies concerned with the internal organisation of the courts, ie, the structures for the admission, distribution and control of judicial work in a broad sense. These studies deal with the general, permanent organisation of judicial work in the courts rather than the specific arrangement developed by a workgroup for the disposition of individual cases. Some of these studies have been written from a managerial perspective, that is, with the aim of recommending changes in the courts' management structures and work routines. As one would expect, there will be a certain amount of overlapping with the managerial issues that will be discussed later.

One of the first organisational studies in this respect is a study on the Italian '*Corte di cassazione*', the Italian Supreme Court, published in 1969.[151] The study seeks to analyse the characteristics of the division of labour in the Court and the Attorney General's office ('*Procura generale*') regarding the main objectives of this jurisdiction, as well as the characteristics of the professional staff serving in the various organisational positions of both offices.[152] This analysis includes the examination of the organisation and flow of judicial work, as well as of some of the factors that cause delay in the decision of cases. One particular goal of the study was of a practical nature: to provide an empirical, documented foundation for the reform and modernisation of the administration of justice.[153]

The analysis of the judicial workflow included the following aspects:[154]

[151] Di Federico (1969). According to Di Federico, it is at least the first organisational study on the Italian administration of justice (20).

[152] Consequently, the study excluded any systematic analysis of the organisational units composed of auxiliary personnel. Equally absent is any systematic consideration of external or environmental factors, such as the lack of adequate facilities or the attorneys' professional attitudes, as well as of their impact on the judicial workflow. Di Federico (1969: 25).

[153] Di Federico (1969: 20). In the last section, the study examines the usefulness of different writing, printing and electronic devices for documentation purposes.

[154] Di Federico (1969: 290 ff.).

—The documentation services prior to the judicial work proper (mainly the '*ruolo*' and the '*massimario*').
—The activities for the organisation, coordination and preparation of judicial decisions, such as hearing calendars, establishment of panels, assignment of specific tasks.
—The preparation phase for the discussion of appeals, including the preparation of written and oral motions by the Attorney General's office.
—The conduct of public hearing, and participants in those hearings.
—The operation of the '*camera di consiglio*' ('panel chamber').
—The control of unity of doctrine by the '*Procura generale*'.
—The extension of judgments, the '*massimazione*' and the control of adherence to precedents.

In particular, the study found dysfunctional aspects and problems in relation to the following areas:

—The prevailing division of labour in the Court and the Attorney General's office.[155]
—The relationship between the uniformity of judicial doctrine as a goal and the prevailing division of labour in the sub-units of the Court.[156]
—The projected and actual number of professional personnel ('*personale togato*'), the age of this personnel, the problem of their residence outside the Court's location, and its rotation and turnover rate.[157]
—The privileged position of civilian sections in the distribution of organisational resources.[158]
—The increasing workloads and the pending business of the civil jurisdiction.
—The practice of granting '*provvedimenti di clemenza*' in criminal jurisdiction.

What are the factors that influence and determine existing patterns for the division of labor in a court? What are the effects of these patterns on the efficiency of judicial work? Regarding the first question, it appears that *court size* and *structure*, as well as the *scope of jurisdiction* (general or specialised), certain *personal traits* of the judges, and the *type of community* in which the court operates, play an important role in defining the modes and degrees of the internal division of labour. As regards the second question, there seems to be evidence that an *extreme internal division of labour*, especially if it dissociates judicial work proper from the activities that give support to it, generates coordination and articulation problems that a managerial approach would attempt to solve. We shall briefly describe a few studies here that help to contextualise these problems.

155 Di Federico (1969: 42 ff.).
156 Di Federico (1969: 50 ff.).
157 Di Federico (1969: 54 ff.).
158 Di Federico (1969: 90 ff.).

The first study concerns the working habits and strategies of American trial judges.[159] Although it mainly examines the judges' working patterns, the study also attempts to establish a link with certain structural factors influencing them. American trial judges normally work in courts of general jurisdiction composed of several judges.[160] In urban areas, the assignment and decision of cases depend on court size and specialisation by type of case, the existence of formal divisions within the court, but also, on the past experience and expertise of a judge, and his or her disposition rate and sentencing philosophy. In addition to these factors, there are specific case assignment systems, such as the individual or master calendar, and specific work cycles, such as weekly or monthly terms. Judges are rotated, and rotation follows time patterns also dependent on court size. Finally, court politics, including partisan politics, may also play a role. In rural areas, where there are normally no judges sitting permanently in the courthouses, 'circuit riding' is the form in which judicial work is organised, a form that also admits a variety of modalities.[161]

Since the early 1990s, the German Federal Ministry of Justice has commissioned a series of studies, mostly of an empirical nature, under the heading 'Structural Analysis of the Administration of Justice'.[162] Several of these studies, mainly undertaken by private consulting firms, have analysed the internal organisation of the courts and proposed a number of measures designed to improve and rationalise it.[163] Here, I shall attempt to briefly describe the situation diagnosed by some of them, leaving their managerial proposals for later.

The first study concerns the collegiate courts of first instance of the ordinary jurisdiction (civil and criminal) and the corresponding appeals process.[164] The study examined two sections: the judicial and the administrative sections.[165]

A diagnosis of the judicial section brought the following management aspects to light:[166]

[159] Ryan *et al.* (1980).

[160] Ryan *et al.* (1980: 47 ff.).

[161] Ryan *et al.* (1980: 53 ff.).

[162] '*Strukturelle Analyse der Rechtspflege*'. See the introduction by van Raden and Strempel in WIBERA (1991: 7 ff.) on the purposes and research lines of this series. The structural analysis of the administration of justice pursues two main goals: to show the possibilities of an urgent quantitative relief of the courts, which promise to be successful independently from the procedural and staffing measures that have been usual so far; and to show ways for a qualitative improvement in the administration of justice, particularly with an intention of making it more understandable and convincing for the citizen. The series comprises studies with three main research lines: the coordination of judicial and extra-judicial conflict settlement; the legal design of court procedures; and the organisation of the courts and internal processes, which is the one that interests us here.

[163] See for example, WIBERA (1991), Koetz *et al.* (1992;1993).

[164] Koetz *et al.* (1993).

[165] On average, 60% of the court personnel belonged to the judicial section and 40% to the administrative section. Koetz *et al.* (1993: 11).

[166] Koetz *et al.* (1993).

—The dominant form of the division of labour is the classic separation between business office (‘*Geschäftsstelle*’) and secretariat (‘*Kanzlei*’).[167]
—The high degree of division of labour leads to a high number of file transportation steps (27 out of the 62 tasks in an appeal involve file transportation).
—The basic distribution of tasks between the business office and the secretariat is often insufficient.
—The dominant form in which the writing service is organised is through a central office; the increase in writing homework increases coordination and communication problems.
—The increasing size of the courts leads to a corresponding increase in problems such as anonymity, lack of motivation and lack of service capabilities.

The administrative section displayed the following traits:

—The organisational structure is not always uniform and transparent; tasks and powers are not evenly distributed.
—Administrative offices are partly charged with tasks that are unrelated to the court’s functions.
—The existing structures of administrative offices are personally rather than functionally oriented.
—Functions that belong together, such as organisation and computers, are fragmented across different offices, which causes coordination and communication problems, redundancies and a waste of resources.
—Organisational structures have developed historically and are therefore characterised by a certain lack of flexibility, which affects the possibility of introducing new tasks and technological devices (computers).
—The court manager’s position lacks a clear organisational definition, which leads to problems of power and accountability.

A survey on the organisation of the courts in the new German states conducted in 1991, that is, the year after unification,[168] revealed similar problems: a strict division of labour between subordinated offices, such as the writing office, the business office and the secretariat. Thus, for example, the simplest writing task had to be performed by the central writing office. In addition to this, the spatial separation between the offices translated into frequent file transportation steps, although this was somehow attenuated by the direct delivery of the files. All this required immense efforts to achieve coordination and control. By contrast, there was a limited capacity to provide services, such as information, to citizens and attorneys. The existing division of labour had negative psychological consequences, particularly in the writing office: the fragmentation of the assigned

[167] In the business office, three principles of organisation combine: its own processing organisation, the professional organisation of judicial activities, and the service organisation for the court’s clients. Bauer *et al.* (1983: 14 f.).

[168] Koetz/Frühauf (1996).

tasks fostered a feeling of emptiness and monotony, a lack of motivation and self-initiative, and a diminished sense of responsibility, as well as selfishness.

Compared to their West German counterparts, the business office was usually smaller, as was the number of judges. There was no need for internal specialisation among the office's employees, which resulted in a series of positive effects: the work situation was more orderly; employees had a better overview of their work as well as an intrinsic motivation to carry it out; there was a heightened sense of responsibility and less need to transport files.

The former German Democratic Republic's jurisdiction had some interesting organisational features of its own.[169] These included the strict work schedules for judges and court staff,[170] as well as the much shorter periods for the disposition of cases. Legal advice was provided by both judges and clerks.[171] The system for classifying and keeping files was much simpler and easier to understand. The card system for controlling files was also simpler and allowed for decentralised handling. Each court had its own funds for certain expenses. Unfortunately, some of these positive features were being phased out or had already disappeared, as the Western legal system and its organisational technology were being transplanted in their entirety to the new states.[172]

In short: some of these studies show that the internal division of labor in the courts is basically a function of a court's size and of a traditional understanding of the separation between judicial and non-judicial tasks. Even judicial tasks in a broad sense can experience a fragmentation that leads to numerous coordination and articulation problems, as demonstrated by the existing separation of business office and secretariat in the German courts. Although the separation is not without problems of its own, it is the *relationship* established between both offices that yields negative results. For this reason, the existing relationship has been described as a 'disintegration model', based on the accumulation of diverse weaknesses existing in the courts. Some of the weaknesses, besides the separation of business office and secretariat, included the fragmentation of the secretariat into several writing units; the fragmentation of the tasks of the business office; the introduction of additional management levels and functions; the lack of spatial proximity between the offices; the sharp division of labor within each office; and the enormous need for file transportation. If the separation were retained, the cure for such weaknesses would be the partial (re)integration of some of the tasks concerned.[173]

[169] Koetz /Frühauf (1996: 172 ff.).

[170] Judges were available at least one day a week for an informal conversation.

[171] A judge's advice could have the effect of discouraging a filing with the court, while the clerk would normally give advice on the technical requirements for such a filing once the citizen had decided to bring suit.

[172] Koetz/Frühauf (1996: 190 f.) speak of a lost opportunity, insofar as the positive features of the former GDR's jurisdiction did not stand a chance against Western competition. See also Rennig/Strempel (eds) (1996).

[173] See Koetz *et al.* (1992: 26, 32 ff.).

The negative consequences of the fragmentation of tasks within the courts suggest that their internal organisation is in need of rationalisation, along the lines of any modern, service-oriented management. This is, in essence, the main justification for court management.

Adjudication, Administration, and Organisational Roles

So far, the internal operation of the courts, ie, the distribution of judicial and non-judicial work, has been examined from a purely organisational point of view. According to this perspective, there is no qualitative distinction between these two types of work. However, some of the studies described here show that, in practice, there is a clear distinction between adjudicative and administrative tasks in a broad sense. Depending on the particular traits of each jurisdiction, the relationship between both types of tasks ranges from complete separation to varying degrees of integration, as embodied in certain roles (for example, that of a presiding or chief judge).

We previously cited a Uruguayan study showing that judges failed to understand, and in fact were uninterested in, the impact of the organisational and administrative dimensions of the courts on their professional role. However, this does not mean that no relationship exists or that a complete separation is always possible.

A French study published in the early 1980s describes the various models of the relationship between adjudication as a professional task and the administrative support it requires, as well as what the author terms '*organisational roles*', ie, roles that are not simply restricted to either a purely professional or purely administrative task.[174] The study analysed the operation of five French courts of first instance ('*tribunaux de grande instance*') in the Parisian suburbs. Three of them were selected on the grounds of the process of administrative and institutional transformation they had recently undergone. Two others were chosen to investigate the activity of prosecutors (the '*parquet*') in criminal cases.[175]

The relationships between the professional and some of the administrative functions supporting it are first described in connection with the role of the clerk ('*greffier*'). Here, the study found three models of such a relationship in one of the courts analysed:[176]

—Administrative tasks were organised as an autonomous, pooled sector of activities, independent from the judges, who in the last resort had no intervention in it, even with respect to the execution of their own work. This was the case of the 'criminal chain', where the clerk's role was regarded as that of a '*gestionnaire*' ('manager').

[174] Emsellem (1982: 165 ff.).
[175] Emsellem (1982: 35).
[176] Emsellem (1982: 157).

—In the case of civil justice, the clerk's role was organised in a decentralised system that accompanied judicial work in the form of the classical assistance of a chamber or specialised clerk ('public official').

—On the other hand, in the juvenile offenders' court, professional and administrative activities were intimately linked, and adapted to each other's rhythms and difficulties, in the clerk's role as the 'judge's assistant.'

The three types of roles are located at points of increasing proximity to the purely professional activity.[177]

On the other hand, the judge's role operates in a context devoid of collective life in which professional and administrative tasks are generally separated. Moreover, the relative mobility required by the judge's advancement within the judicial career had the effect of reinforcing the attachment of professionals to their profession rather than the organisation. However, the judge's indifference towards, or his detachment from, the administrative aspects of judicial work did not always reflect a traditional attitude. It stemmed rather from organisational factors, such as the size of the court, its internal structure and division of labour, all of which conditioned the individual judge's opportunity to have a full knowledge of the court's operation and to become involved in administrative issues.[178]

In the court analysed, only professionals, ie, judges, performed organisational roles. This was the case of the chief judge, who occupies a statutory position that entrusts him or her with the responsibility of managing and coordinating different activities and offices. In addition to the responsibility of participating in and deciding on certain judicial proceedings, the chief judge ('*chef de juridiction*') had a *professional* responsibility for the operation of the court, which was different from the responsibility that involved, on the one hand, the organisation of judicial work, and on the other, the administration and management of the court itself.[179]

The chief judge's professional responsibility referred to the contents of the professional activities of the court's members. It covered the determination of specialisations, an advisory role towards the other judges, the definition of the overall orientations of judicial decision-making (such as the harmonisation of precedents), and the direction of training activities for future judges. The chief judge's more administrative tasks comprised the coordination of the judicial personnel's activities, the organisation of hearings, the assignment of judges, as well as the administration of the budget and file management (distribution of cases, monitoring of the proceedings, etc.).[180] As can be seen, the chief judge's organisational role included at least three different combinations of professional,

177 Emsellem (1992: 158).

178 Emsellem (1982: 161 ff.).

179 Emsellem (1982: 173). Such responsibilities are shared, in fact, by the other chief official in the court, the state attorney ('*procureur de la République*').

180 Emsellem (1982: 173).

administrative and managerial responsibilities, ie, these responsibilities were not either purely professional or administrative but a varying combination of both along a wide spectrum.

However, in the performance of an organisational role such as the chief judge's, neither the administrative dimension, which necessarily attaches to any leadership responsibility, nor the organisational dimension, which derives from the structural features of the organisation, such as its size, are subordinated to the professional dimension but rather informed by its particular rationality. Thus, whereas the professional dimension cannot be the sole object of the chief judge's direction powers, on account of the other judges' professional independence, this dimension expresses itself in the professional considerations on which organisational and administrative activities are based.[181]

Courts and Other Organisations

We have already referred to the possibility and advantages of an inter-organisational approach in an analysis of courts as organisations. The inter-organisational perspective posits, in essence, that the operation of courts is not only affected by its internal organisation, but also by other organisations that are linked to it. In fact, many actors in the judicial arena belong to various organisations or, at least, respond to other organised interests. The concepts of 'tight' and 'loose' coupling, used to analyse decisions within one organisation in terms of their predictable or indiscernible effect on each other, can also be applied to inter-organisational relations, to the extent that predictability and certainty constitute central problems in this respect. As shown by several of these studies, the interrelationship between organisations has a direct impact on the production and distribution of judicial services.

This insight is of fundamental importance for any change or reform project that seeks to alter the operation of the courts by modifying procedural rules or other internal aspects alone. In this section we shall present some studies that help illustrate the influence of these other organisations in relation to the courts.

The Judges' Sponsoring Organisations

Judges are usually seen as the central actors in the judicial arena, who, because of such centrality and by virtue of the dogma of judicial independence, are not subject to any authority or decision within the boundaries of their court. They themselves are used to being considered as 'autonomous decision makers', and as unquestioned rulers in their domain, and therefore expect everyone else

[181] Emsellem (1982: 179 ff.). Emsellem speaks of the subordination, to a large extent, of all the court's activities to its professional goal; her description of the dimensions that interact within an organisational role do not imply subordination to but rather the penetration of professional considerations.

around them to conform to this view.[182] We have already seen that judicial status itself is an organised, administrated role, and that this notion has significant consequences for the way such a role is conceived of and performed. But do judges belong and respond to organisations other than the court organisation? Is their professional authority constrained or affected by these other organisations? What is the broader organisational context of their professional work? Are there any other horizontal relationships between judges besides the hierarchical authority lines to which they belong?

A recent study on the judges' sponsoring organisation, ie, the bench, in a single large, urban court in the United States (Circuit Court of Cook County, Illinois) examines the degree of coupling between trial judges, in order to 'illuminate the ways in which they collaborate with one another or stand in another's way'.[183] Here, 'coupling' refers to the degree to which the actions of one participant have predictable consequences for another within an organisation.[184] 'Where there is tight coupling, decisions made in one unit or level of an organisation have predictable consequences in other levels or units';[185] conversely, activities are loosely coupled if the consequences of one person's actions are indiscernible or unpredictable.[186]

At the time, the court examined was composed of 400 judges and, as such, was the largest unified court in the United States. The judges' sponsoring organisation comprises a congregation of judges, which meets at different forums. The tightly and loosely coupled elements of the bench are regarded as stemming from different features of the court's structure.[187]

The most significant elements of tight and loose coupling involve the assignment of judges to particular tasks by the chief judge. The chief judge's assignment powers create a considerable degree of tight coupling in the bench. Assignments are of varying desirability (for example, high-volume courts are less desirable than low-volume courts). Thus, the chief judge is able to 'couple perceived performance with desirable or undesirable assignments'.[188]

However, the chief judge's powers are constrained by significant elements of loose coupling. The first one stems from the way in which circuit judges arrive at and remain on the bench (either through appointment or election), and the chief judge has little influence on it, but such influence is greater for the election of associate judges.[189] Another element of loose coupling concerns the internal operation of the court's divisions. There are no uniform policies governing the

182 Jacob (1997: 3).
183 Jacob (1997: 4).
184 Jacob (1997: 6).
185 Jacob (1997: 7).
186 Jacob (1997: 6). Jacob notes that 'tight' and 'loose' coupling are not equivalent to the centralised/decentralised distinction, since the latter distinction refers to the locus of authority when decisions are made, whereas coupling refers to the effects of decisions (at 7).
187 Jacob (1997: 8 f.).
188 Jacob (1997: 10 f.).
189 Jacob (1997: 13 f.).

assignment of judges within divisions, and internal procedures vary in each division.[190]

There are also other instances and sources of tight and loose coupling. However, it is important to note that tight and loose coupling are juxtaposed. Loose coupling of units within the court 'produces a chief whose role it is to link the units more tightly to one another'.[191] This is evident in the chief judge's efforts to manage the docket and thus satisfy the court's constituencies (attorneys, the business community, public officials such as the state's attorneys and the police, as well as other litigants and interest groups). Nevertheless, the degree to which such efforts are successful remains limited.[192]

In conclusion, there are 'both pockets of tight coupling and segments of loose coupling within the judges' sponsoring organisation'.[193] The consequences derived from the location of those pockets and the tensions between them occur in three areas: the locus and style of administrative innovation in the court; the responsiveness of the bench to its constituencies, and the allocation of resources and services.[194] Regarding the latter aspect, which is the one that interests us most here, the author observes:

> Responsiveness to clientele groups creates distinctive allocations of resources in the courts that have serious consequences for the delivery of justice to various segments of the population. These include the segregation of litigants, the allocation of judicial talent, the rationing of court time, and the mobilisation of political support for the judiciary.[195]

Litigants are segregated in significant ways by the division of labor between various segments of the court: for example, the separation between juvenile, adult felony, and civil cases, handled by separate divisions and assigned to different locations (juvenile and criminal courts buildings are located outside the central business sector of the city). The assignment of judges has a similar effect:

> The least-experienced and least-qualified judges work in high-volume courts that predominantly service the poor. These are clients represented by low-status attorneys who do not bring much clout to the table if they seek better judges, better facilities, or more thorough consideration.[196]

Indeed, it is the chief judge's need to maintain a certain level of political support for the court, and the tensions between loosely and tightly coupled elements of

[190] Jacob (1997: 14). Nevertheless, tight coupling is again produced within each division, since the presiding judges have the *de facto* authority to assign judges in their division to any of their courtrooms.

[191] Jacob (1997: 19).

[192] Jacob (1997: 20).

[193] Jacob (1997: 23).

[194] Jacob (1997: 24).

[195] Jacob (1997: 26).

[196] Jacob (1997: 26).

the bench, which affect the rationing of resources among the various sections of the court and particularly of court time.[197]

The study just summarised concerns the interactions between all the members of the bench in a certain jurisdiction. However, there are other sponsoring organisations of judges that can affect the efficient running of the entire court system. These are *selective* organisations, since they are not composed of all members of the bench but result from a selection process by its members. They can either have *governance functions* with respect to the judiciary *as a whole* or represent or coordinate the *group interests* of judges.

Examples of the judges' governance organisations are the Council of the Judiciary, which exists in many civil-law countries, or the Judicial Conference in the United States. Owing to the difficulties associated with a global perspective, there seem to be few organisational studies on the governance organisations of the judiciary. Nevertheless, the associative movement of judges and its impact on the court system seems to have received more attention from empirical research, particularly in countries such as Italy, France and Spain.[198]

Italy provides a fascinating example of the interaction between both types of sponsoring organisations.[199] Under the Italian Constitution of 1948, the governance of the judges' status and responsibilities has been conferred on the '*Consiglio Superiore de la Magistratura*', which means that the judges themselves, or rather, their representatives, determine their own institutional status (recruitment, assignments, transfers, advancement, and disciplinary measures), since they have a two-thirds majority in the Council. This basic arrangement, designed to sever most of the institutional links between the judiciary and the political system, has resulted in a further transformation of the judicial status and role due to the increasing influence of the Italian judges' association ('*Associazione Nazionale Magistrati Italiani*', ANMI) within the Council. Specifically, several amendments to the rules for the election of the judges' representatives have resulted in a reduction of the influence exerted by the highest posts in the judicial hierarchy and in a growing influence of the leaders of the various ideological factions that coexist within the Association.[200]

The judges' association has managed to produce a tight coupling between the group interests of the bench and the governance mechanisms administrated by the Council of the Judiciary. Indeed, Italian judges have succeeded in abolishing virtually all organisational constraints on the judicial career system and all hierarchical relations that derive from it. Consequently, seniority is acknowledged as the only criterion that governs the professional advancement of the individual judge, which no longer depends on actual examinations and evaluation mechanisms. Judges may even obtain the title and salary of higher positions in

[197] Jacob (1997: 27).

[198] See, for example, Lyon-Caen (1981), Deville (1992) and Bea Pérez *et al.* (1988).

[199] See Guarnieri/Pederzoli (1996: 54 ff.). See also Canosa/Federico (1974) and García Pascual (1997: 197 ff.).

[200] Guarneri/Pederzoli (1996: 56).

the judicial hierarchy without actually performing the corresponding functions.[201] It is easy to see why such a system is bound to foster low professional motivation, a diminishing sense of accountability, a lack of real career incentives and therefore, a search for recognition and opportunities outside the judicial institution.[202] It will also obviously have an impact, as shown in the study of the Chicago bench, on the form and conditions for the provision of judicial services, upon which we can only speculate.

Police and Prosecutors

Socio-legal research has long analysed the influence of police and prosecutorial behaviour on the number and types of cases that reach the criminal courts (selectivity), as well as the consequences of such selective behaviour for the outcome of these cases in the courts. Such a selection process has been conceived of as a series of successive, more or less isolated stages, in which the relevant actors behave within particular institutional or personal constraints that contribute to the progressive reduction and concentration of the number and categories of cases.

The inter-organisational perspective may place a different emphasis on the reasons that explain these phenomena. It may show that the process observed is the result of inter-organisational relations rather than of constraints to which more or less isolated actors are subject, and that the participating organisations frequently have diverging interests and goals that make cooperation difficult.

Thus, for example, it can be shown that the police do not have a great interest in making more arrests than necessary for the maintenance of order, or arrests that necessarily lead to a conviction: 'arrest not leading to conviction can serve a number of valued police functions'.[203] Furthermore, considerable effort is required to assure a conviction, so unless the violation is serious enough, the police may not see the need to undertake it, because they 'sometimes view the evidentiary requirements imposed by the courts as unworkable'.[204] On the other hand, it is somewhat ironic that good police work 'may contribute to weak cases for prosecutors'.[205] Although prosecutors 'are part of the same state apparatus as the police', they are 'influenced by very different goals, pressures, and expectations', which, in turn, are 'reinforced by differences in social background, education, and career aspirations';[206] they are not directly involved with order maintenance but with the formality of an autonomous legal system.[207]

[201] Guarnieri/Pederzoli (1996: 57).
[202] Guarnieri/Pederzoli (1996: 58).
[203] Feeley/Lazerson (1983: 225).
[204] Feeley/Lazerson (1983: 228).
[205] Feeley/Lazerson (1983: 228).
[206] Feeley/Lazerson (1983: 229).
[207] Feeley/Lazerson (1983: 232).

Differences between police and prosecutorial work represents 'a conflict of organisational standards and needs',[208] especially if the police have not been directly placed under the authority of prosecutors, as occurs in the United States at least. However, legal 'obligations and structural constraints require a minimum of cooperation even in the face of estrangement'.[209] In this respect, there are a number of ways in which institutions with divergent goals and interests can seek to attenuate conflict and pursue cooperation, such as the following, several of which are present in police-prosecutors relations:[210]

—The development of exchange relationships.
—The mutual acceptance of conflict-resolution institutions.
—The adoption of coordinating mechanisms.
—The emergence of informal boundary-spanning institutions.
—The integration into more powerful organisations.

In short, here we have another example of interaction between organisations which affects judicial work, but over which the courts have relatively little control. Police work is of central relevance for the disposition of criminal cases, and for this reason, among others, they are subject to the courts' directives. The courts may prescribe standards for making arrests, but ultimately, they 'are dependent upon the police to implement them'.[211]

Attorneys and the Bar

Attorneys, the organised bar, have both common and antagonistic interests with respect to the courts. Attorneys and judges apparently share a common concern for the effectiveness of the justice system and for the prestige and social influence of the legal profession. However, they also have divergent, sometimes contradictory concerns. To judges, effectiveness may mean rationalisation, speediness, and increased productivity in the disposition of cases, particularly at times of scarce resources. To attorneys, it means the efficient management of files and the control of procedure in their clients' interests. These concerns are not always compatible with each other. Therefore, their relationship may be expected to assume the form of either cooperation or conflict, including the dynamic transformation of one into the other in alternating cycles. In either case, the form assumed by the relationship between bench and bar is influenced or affected by organisation. This is borne out by a study on the relationships between two French courts of first instance ('*tribunaux de grande instance*') in two medium-sized judicial districts and the local bar.[212]

[208] Feeley/Lazerson (1983: 229).
[209] Feeley/Lazerson (1983: 233).
[210] Feeley/Lazerson (1983: 233).
[211] Feeley/Lazerson (1983: 232 f.).
[212] Ackermann/Bastard (1993a) and (1993b: 69–89).

In Bar A, distrust and hostility of the attorneys towards the judges prevailed. Attorneys were highly critical of the changes introduced in the administration of justice, since they felt that their interests and concerns were being neglected. The new president of the bar then decided to launch a cooperation effort, which soon succeeded in establishing a more relaxed climate. Both sides committed themselves to mutual adjustments and concessions. However, the positive results initially observed threatened to disappear. The strict rules the bar had agreed to impose on itself implied the need to rely on members' cooperation, which was not completely guaranteed, given the low degree of internal discipline and solidarity prevailing in the organisation.

In Bar B, the starting situation was the opposite, since the attorneys initially evaluated the court in positive terms. However, some reservations were expressed regarding the notion of judicial productivity, as reflected in judicial statistics. A cooperative system between bench and bar had been in place for some time, facilitating a climate of mutual understanding and dialogue. Suddenly, the court suspended the cooperation unilaterally, due to a pressing lack of resources and to the arrival of a new presiding judge, as a result of which the relationship entered a phase of conflict.

The Challenges of Change and Reform

No institution can afford to remain static and unchanged. Courts, too, are frequently subject to reform efforts. We have seen that costs and delay, which are usually seen as a function of court overload, are a major reason behind judicial reform. However, why is it that certain reform efforts succeed while others do not? This is a question of the utmost importance, because we are not only interested in studying the operation of the courts and the factors that affect court efficiency for their own sake, but also with the purpose of identifying efficiency-enhancing strategies which are likely to be successful. We suspect that the complex nature of courts and court systems as organisations provides part of the answer. In other words: any change introduced into the system is affected by complex organisational and inter-organisational structures. In this section, we shall explore some of the general reasons why change that is initiated from the outside, especially by way of amendments to procedural rules, encounters significant obstacles to its implementation within the court system, and how change is generated, spread and rationalised within the judicial institution.

Reform Impact

Two studies published in the late 1970s and the beginning of the 1980s, reflect, from a more or less explicit organisational perspective, on the reasons for the limited success or failure of criminal justice system reforms in the United

States.[213] To this end, they review several reform efforts and the relevant evaluation studies.[214] They basically conclude that change initiated and implemented from outside the judicial system has little likelihood of success if it fails to take into account the complex organisational and incentive structures in which such modifications are to be inserted.

The first study begins with the observation that, in criminal justice reform, 'a historic pattern of proposals, implementation, and ultimate failure is consistently reenacted'.[215] The repetition of failure can largely be attributed to recurring misperceptions about the nature of the judicial process and about how behavior within that process can be modified.[216] It should be recognised that formal rules do not define the essential character of the behavior of the actors involved in the judicial process. Instead, behavior is shaped by more immediate practical constraints in a context where discretion plays a significant role.[217]

Reform has been implemented in various ways such as legislation, appellate decisions and bureaucratic administration. They all make certain assumptions about how judicial behaviour can be modified and focus on different structures and resources.[218] Any such assumption must first ask why 'a participant in the judicial process (*should*) alter behavior in response to reform',[219] and never lose sight of the fact that

> current practice in the judicial process is neither random nor arbitrary. Rather, it reflects long-standing accomodations of various interests. Since this accomodation is likely to be regarded as desirable by practitioners, change will not occur spontaneously but must be induced by reform. That is, the reform must stimulate change by supplying adequate incentives or the impact will be negligible.[220]

A reform is an external variable that proceeds from

> a judgement that the current performance of the judicial process is deficient. Even if couched in such terms as due process or equal protection, this judgement is a statement of policy preference that *ex hypothesi* contradicts the operative priorities reflected in current practice.[221]

This will generate opposition or indifference to reform objectives. 'In most instances, not only is there no general desire to change, but there is a systemic tendency to retain the status quo'.[222] System impact, which can be defined as any

[213] Nimmer (1978) and Feeley (1983).
[214] As, for example, with the impact of speedy trial laws.
[215] Nimmer (1978: 1).
[216] Nimmer (1978: 2).
[217] Nimmer (1978: 28).
[218] Nimmer (1978: 19 ff.) refers to five limited premises for altering behavior: the technocratic premise; the resource premise; the rule-obedience premise; the pragmatist premise; the administrative law premise.
[219] Nimmer (1978: 26).
[220] Nimmer (1978: 26).
[221] Nimmer (1978: 175 f.).
[222] Nimmer (1978: 176 f.).

behaviour change within the organisation or system studied induced by a reform, occurs only if a reform supplies incentives *sufficient* to overcome existing motivation.[223]

The second study cited makes similar observations and reaches similar conclusions.[224] According to the author, criminal justice reform deals with three main problems: the incentive for initiating reform, the implementation process, and evaluation.

Regarding the *incentive for initiating reform*, the author notes that given a lack of incentives for system-wide changes within the courts, the impulse for innovation usually comes from the outside. Reforms often fail because reformers offer simple solutions for complex day-to-day problems, undercutting implementation on the way:[225] 'those that are in the best position to assess the needs of the courts have the least incentive to innovate, while those who have the incentive do not have the detailed knowledge'.[226]

Implementation becomes problematic partly because of several features of the courts that exacerbate the tendency to failure:[227]

—The fragmentation of the criminal justice system facilitates judgments of success even as reforms fail.
—Many reforms have sought to circumvent sluggish institutions by creating new programs, but these quickly become part of the problem.
—The success of reform programs has been often declared prematurely.

Finally, there are also the methodological problems of *evaluation*. A scientific evaluation is unavoidable because there is no other rigorous way to find out whether a reform has been successful or not. Here the author points to an inescapable paradox: the more rigorous an evaluation, the more likely it is to sound inconclusive.[228] This is hardly encouraging for policy-makers who expect rather clear-cut problem definitions and workable answers to them.[229]

The Internal Generation, Dissemination, and Rationalisation of Change

The problems raised by judicial reform are not reduced to the overall success or failure of externally induced change. There is always a crucial local dimension that cannot be overlooked. Changes are often generated and propagated by local initiatives, and even when changes are centrally ordained, they are always subject to local interpretations and adaptations. This is clearly shown by a

223 Nimmer (1978, 3, 177).
224 Feeley (1983).
225 Feeley (1983: 191 ff.).
226 Feeley (1983: 196).
227 Feeley (1983: 199).
228 Feeley (1983: 203).
229 It is sometimes easier to reach a consensus on the diagnosis of problems than on appropriate solutions and their eventual success.

French study on eight medium-sized courts of first instance (‘*tribunaux de grande instance*’), conducted from an organisational perspective by two sociologists. The study illustrates and explains how the imperatives of modernisation and effectiveness, to which the judicial institution must now respond, translate into management practices that arise from the local characteristics of the courts and the specific concerns of the judges and officials in charge of them.[230]

The general context for local change is characterised by an extremely limited margin for the management of court resources by the responsible officials.[231] The professional independence of judges prevents these officials from introducing changes into the organisation of judicial work—be they reforms promoted by the Ministry of Justice or changes sought in themselves—without engaging in negotiations with all the participants concerned or entering into more or less explicit agreements.

In particular, the study identified several court management styles in the eight courts related to the management of change:[232]

—*Voluntaristic management*: this type of management relies on an overall policy for a programme of change. It expresses itself in transformation projects designed both to enhance the effectiveness of court services as well as to attain a higher control of case flow and impact of decisions rendered. Here, the initiative lies with both chief officials of the court, the chief judge and the state attorney. They agree to a plan for common action and the implementation of change. However, the voluntaristic nature of the modifications of working habits becomes a source of internal tensions.

—*Management based on opportunity and alliances*: this management style is characterised by the absence of coordination and agreement between both chief officials and, therefore, by the introduction of single, discrete reforms. Either because only one of those officials is interested in really starting and carrying out change, or because both are so concerned with their respective spheres of action, changes have to be negotiated with the judges and alliances have to be worked out.

—‘*Reactive*’ *management*: the two court chief officials are on good terms with each other, but are skeptical of changes and unaware of the need or the value of investing in management and reform. They are mostly concerned with judicial work and its quality. However, their lack of interest in change does not prevent them from leaving the possibility of introducing innovations open to the judges and other court officials. Nevertheless, such innovations are more dependent than anywhere else on the permanence of the persons who introduced them in the first place.

Thus, despite the identical formal structures between these courts, and the fact that they are bound by similar constraints, there are considerable differences in

230 Ackermann/Bastard (1993b: 10).
231 Ackermann/Bastard (1993b: 16 f.).
232 Ackermann/Bastard (1993b: 37 ff.).

the implementation of changes and the management styles adopted by their chief officials. These differences depend less on the personality of those officials than on the nature of the relations they establish.[233]

The means by which innovations appear, are propagated, or disappear within the judicial institution are closely linked to the mobility of judges and their periodic transference to other jurisdictions.[234] Change is generated at different points in the judicial system, on the initiative of the judges themselves and for the purpose of solving the problems with which they are confronted, and is then transmitted to other jurisdictions, following specific, complex patterns. However, it is not uniformly propagated, because innovations are constantly displaced or reinterpreted according to local conditions, and may also eventually disappear.[235]

Such initiatives can be examined along two dimensions: the horizontal and the vertical dimensions.[236] The horizontal dimension refers to the movements of individual judges from one court to another and to the 'tool box' of solutions to organisational or procedural problems they carry with them. Passage from one court to another helps to enrich the 'tool box', by incorporating new experiences into it. However, the innovations left behind have to find a successor willing to adopt them again, if they are to survive. The vertical dimension of the propagation of changes is linked to the organisational features of each court, which determine the likelihood that the innovations proposed by the judges will be integrated into the set of solutions that the court has found in order to deal with its local problems.[237]

In conclusion: a consideration of the local ways in which change is generated and adapted is important for the image of any modernisation policy, particularly if it appears to be a technocratic response, uniformly imposed on all courts, for the sake of a more accurate evaluation of their activity and needs, as well as of the rationalisation of their functioning:[238]

> Modernisation appears rather as a result of solutions produced locally by the courts in an attempt to solve the contradiction between the limitation of available resources and the need to assure the quality of the services provided.[239]

Changes in court organisation and procedure—and this is best exemplified by the use of computers—show the ever-present tension between the trend towards uniformity and the diversity that is an outcome of the local mechanisms for the introduction and adaptation of new devices.[240] In fact, for such tension to be

[233] Ackermann/Bastard (1993b: 48).
[234] Ackermann/Bastard (1993b: 13–27; also 1996).
[235] Ackermann/Bastard (1993b: 15).
[236] Ackermann/Bastard (1993b: 18 ff.).
[237] Ackermann/Bastard (1993b: 18 f.).
[238] Ackermann/Bastard (1993b: 49.
[239] Ackermann/Bastard (1993b: 49) (translation by HFF).
[240] Ackermann/Bastard (1993b: 25–6).

productive and successful, it is necessary to find and implement an articulation between local initiatives and national modernisation programmes.[241]

* * *

Some of the studies summarised above prove the importance of personal and collective interaction as it contributes to the development of a specific legal and organisational culture unfolding on its own local dynamics. No matter how distant the origins of a legal institution or of reform impulses may be, they must always be redefined and renegotiated at the level of local practice. Thus, the problem of reform lies not in the effectiveness of central or of local impulses alone, but in a combination of both.

More generally, the usefulness of studying courts, judges, attorneys and other actors participating in the judicial arena as organised actors responding to internal and external impulses, has been clearly shown. In fact, it is suggested that, in order to be effective and successful, changes require the condensation of social action. This means the generation of pressure on actors to adopt an organised form which entails both opportunities and limitations. Thus, for example, in the case of the French attorneys in the cities of A and B: internal solidarity—an organisational variable—seemed to be a condition for the continuation of any cooperation effort between bench and bar. This helps counteract the impression that attorneys are not an organised actor at the interactional level, but, at best, a fairly powerful corporate interest that must be reckoned with.

PROCEDURE

Judicial procedure and the organisations we call courts are evidently dependent on each other. But how? What are the appropriate concepts for describing and explaining this relationship? To clarify this mutual dependence, it is necessary to understand first that procedure and organisation overlap to a certain extent, since both attempt to structure judicial work in view of the goal of producing legal decisions. However, it is also important to distinguish between procedure and organisation, if we are to assess the possibilities of manipulating them, whether separately or jointly, for the purpose of achieving a higher degree of court efficiency.

From a legal point of view, a procedure is a structured set of acts carried out by persons performing special roles (plaintiff, defendant, judge, and attorney) with the purpose of producing a binding decision that will dispose of a legal controversy. Procedural acts and roles are regulated by legal rules enacted either by legislatures or issued by a highest court or even defined locally by each court. Procedural rules presuppose the existence of an organisation, at least in the

[241] Ackermann/Bastard (1993b: 110).

sense that they do not usually regulate everything that is necessary to achieve the procedure's main goal. From this perspective, procedure is a necessary but insufficient condition for establishing an organisation around it, if we do not count the fact that courts as organisations handle a great number of procedures at the same time. Procedure nowadays means *mass business* for the courts. So it may perhaps be useful to distinguish between the *adjudicative process* as the institutional goal around which a court organisation is established, and the *individual procedures* (proceedings) of different types that are constantly reenacted by such organisation. Frequently, organisational studies on the courts view procedure (or rather the adjudicative process) as a by-product of court organisation, when, in fact, the opposite is true: the adjudicative process lies at the centre of judicial organisation. Hence, it is possible to show how the court apparatus has articulated itself as a function of adjudication rather than vice versa.[242]

A procedure is also a *social system*, a differentiated set of specific social communications.[243] As a social system, procedure is autonomous in time and space. Not only do parties have a different perception of time within a procedure, for example, depending on whether delay is an advantage or a disadvantage for them, but procedure creates its own particular social time and own rhythm. (For this reason, among others, procedures can never become speedy enough).[244] Furthermore, it possesses its own role structure. It is not just composed of an invariable ritual,[245] but requires decisions as premises for further decisions.[246] It has a specific goal, ie, the production of one, as yet uncertain, final decision that can be recognised by the legal system and incorporated into its structures.[247]

But is procedure a (formal or informal) organisation? Judging from the elements of organisational theory we have provided above and from the discussion of the organisational nature of courts, procedure(s) can undoubtedly be described as an organisation both different and independent from court organisation. This helps explain, for example, why the courtroom workgroup has been identified as an organisation of its own: it is a 'procedural organisation', so to speak.

If procedures are temporary organisations, then their relationship with the permanent organisation of the courts can be conceptualised in inter-organisational

[242] López Ayllón (1988: 1020). This view is consistent with Luhmann's assertion that organisation and profession (the judge's role) have the function of guaranteeing the closure of the legal system (1993) and Shapiro's suggestion that courts emerge when the intervention of a third party in a dispute makes it necessary to prevent the triadic relation from collapsing into a situation of 'two against one' (1981: 1 ff.).

[243] Luhmann (1983: 38 ff.).

[244] Luhmann (1983: 45). On the role of time and space in judicial procedure, see also Garapon (1985; 1997) and Cordero (1985: 310 ff.).

[245] Ritual, however, is important for judicial procedure. See Garapon (1985; 1997) and Cordero (1985: 430 ff.).

[246] Luhmann (1983: 38).

[247] The element of uncertainty is of central importance for a procedure to be started and to develop its legitimising effects. Luhmann (1983: 40, 51 f.).

terms, and more specifically, as an example of fairly tight coupling. In order to operate in a reliable way and produce decisions, the relationship between the procedural organisation and the court organisation must be both close and predictable. This is mainly accomplished through the partial identity of actors participating in both[248] and by the detailed legal regulation of their main structures and ways of operating, frequently within the same legal code.

We have seen how the 'organisational context' affects the production of judicial decisions. The procedural organisation may also influence court organisation. Its autonomy fosters and provides opportunity for conflict and cooperation.[249] It produces informal expectations and practices to which court organisation must adjust. The two-way influence is exemplified by 'local legal culture' as an explanatory factor for the pace of litigation.[250]

Hence, any modification to either organisation will affect the operation of the other. But this also has significant implications for judicial reform: it is not enough either to introduce changes into judicial procedure *or* into the operation of the court organisation. The incentives operating in *both* organised systems have to be altered if any reform effort is to be successful.

In this section, we shall examine the ways in which the processing capacity of the courts is affected, or can be enhanced, by procedural rules, structures and incentives. Such a strategy is based on the notion that procedure can and should be rationed, rather than (or in addition to) discouraging litigation.[251] Accordingly, judicial procedures should be made simpler, speedier and cheaper, so that they remain accessible for those who really need them, even at the expense of some reduction in the quality of judgments.[252]

Attempts have been made to accelerate procedures mainly by modifying procedure itself or the time periods required to complete various procedural stages. This strategy undoubtedly can and does actually achieve positive results, at least temporarily. However, empirical studies for the evaluation of this kind of modifications, such as those summarised below, sometimes yield inconclusive or contradictory results, which reinforces the hypothesis that procedural reforms engender an insufficient response if only *legal* structures are modified. For this reason, other alternatives have been explored, such as the use of financial incentives, the recourse to simpler or more summary procedures to obtain the same outcomes; the introduction of oral or written proceedings, etc. The other main strategy focuses on the administration of the court system as well as on court and case management.

[248] As, for example, in the case of the judge, although it sometimes is an institutional rather than a personal identity. Different judges may participate at different stages of the *same* procedure. By contrast, the parties' role is much more personal, to the extent that their absence or lack of willingness terminates the procedure.

[249] Luhmann (1983: 50).

[250] See, for example, Church, Jr. *et al.* (1978).

[251] See Zuckerman (1995).

[252] Zuckerman (1995: 158).

For reasons of space, the whole range of possibilities for increasing procedural efficiency cannot be considered here. Thus, for example, we have not examined the leading role the judge can assume as an engine of procedure, especially in the gathering of evidence. This is an important difference between the civil-law and the common-law traditions that has already been discussed in connection with the topic of procedural justice.[253] We shall encounter this problem again when examining the uses of case management. However, some of the solutions discussed below imply such a role (for example, the use of time limits). It is hoped, nevertheless, that this section will provide a sufficient number of examples so that the main issues and possibilities become reasonably clear.

The Acceleration of Criminal Proceedings

The speediness of criminal procedure is a matter of the utmost importance, especially when the accused person has been arrested and remains in prison for the duration of the proceedings.[254] In light of the presumption of innocence, it would be unfair to defendants to prolong their time in prison beyond a strictly necessary period, if there is a possibility that they will be acquitted at the end of the trial. However, speediness is not only in the interest of defendants, because public opinion and victims alike are interested in swift punishment, especially for the most serious offenses.[255] Since evidence decays with time, proceedings should be accelerated as much as possible, but without affecting the right to defense.

It would appear that criminal proceedings take too long everywhere.[256] The causes of delay are not difficult to name: the increased burden placed on the procedure in order to avoid judicial error; the increase in crime rates, combined with an inadequate level of resources available for the criminal justice system.[257] As a consequence, a whole set of measures and strategies have been applied to reduce such delay, which can be grouped into two main categories: the total or partial elimination of criminal proceedings, and procedural rearrangement.[258]

[253] See ch 2.

[254] See the general report by Pradel (1995), published in English, French and Spanish, on the celerity of criminal procedure in comparative law. See also the fourteen national reports and the other summary reports contained in the same issue of the *International Review of Penal Law/Revue Internationale de Droit Penal.*

[255] Pradel (1995: 343).

[256] Pradel (1995: 344) offers some figures: in the Netherlands, it takes twelve to thirteen months between the date of the offense and the decision of the lower court; in France, the average length of the preparatory investigations rose from 5.94 months in 1968 to 8.53 in 1977 and to 12.4 months in 1993.

[257] Pradel (1995: 344 f.).

[258] Pradel (1995: 346, 357) calls them: 'celerity by means of procedural exclusions,' and 'celerity by means of procedural rearrangement.'

The first category means that certain cases are kept away from the criminal justice system (by complete decriminalisation, transferral to administrative authorities, disposition by the public prosecutor, and the like) or that certain stages of the proceedings are eliminated or abridged.[259] The second strategy encompasses the introduction of time limits and the establishment of special procedures.[260] Indeed, many legal systems have introduced time limits by way of a general clause (for example: 'within a reasonable period of time') or by indicating specific time periods.[261] However, legal systems impose different sanctions when time limits are exceeded. Some of them authorise the suspension or staying of the proceedings, releasing the defendant from detention; others see no grounds for invalidating or staying the proceedings.[262] In Latin American countries, for example, the 'prisoner without a sentence' is a widespread phenomenon, since a large proportion of *all* accused persons in prison have not been tried within the time limits stipulated by the law.[263]

Here, we shall only refer to the empirical testing of time limits introduced in the so-called 'speedy trial laws' in the United States. Recognising that delay can sometimes be attributed to prosecutors' offices rather than to the courts, an innovative system of financial incentives was used in the city of New York in an attempt to speed up the prosecution of defendants. It should be noted that this latter strategy, although intended to *accelerate criminal proceedings*, did not actually introduce any changes into *procedure*, but instead modified organisational variables. It is included here, however, because of its intrinsic interest and in contrast with procedural time limits.

Time Limits

Since the 1960s, most states and the federal government of the United States have passed so-called 'speedy-trial laws'.[264] Such laws typically require courts to bring defendants to trial within a specified period of time, usually four to six months. Time limits contained in these laws vary in strictness. The laws may contain tolling provisions, which stop the clock for specified reasons, such as the defendant's failure to appear.[265] The consequences for exceeding time limits may also vary. The case is usually dismissed, unless the time limit is tolled,

[259] Pradel (1995: 346 ff.).

[260] Pradel (1995: 357 ff.).

[261] Thus, for example, the Mexican Constitution of 1917 states that defendants shall be tried within four months if the offense carries a maximum penalty of two years in prison or within one year if the maximum penalty exceeds that time, except when defendants request an extension of time for their defense (Article 20, section VIII).

[262] Pradel (1995: 358 ff.).

[263] See Pérez Perdomo (1991) and Cosacov *et al.* (1983: 61 ff.). The latter study found, through interviews, that 26% of defendants had been in prison longer than the constitutional time limits.

[264] Marvell/Luskin (1991: 343). See Appendix A, which lists the twenty-nine states that had speedy trial laws as of 1991 (at 356 f.).

[265] Marvell/Luskin (1991: 343).

although some laws provide for the defendant to be released from pretrial custody if the time limits are not met.[266]

Since the avowed purpose of speedy trial laws is to reduce delay, they are therefore evaluated with reference to this goal.[267] It seems, however, that empirical evaluation poses significant methodological difficulties, and it is likely that for this reason, among others, the respective studies yield mixed results. Some found at least partial evidence that speedy trial laws reduce delay, while others were unable to establish such a relationship.[268] Following is a brief description of a few studies on this issue.

A study on the implementation and impact on criminal litigation delay of the federal Speedy Trial Act of 1974, based on statistical data for the federal courts for the 1971–81 period, concluded that 'the federal justice system achieved relatively high levels of compliance with the Act's time limits during the past five years', ie, 1977 to 1981.[269] However, the amount of time that elapsed in processing most criminal cases changed little during the period:

> the median elapsed time from filing to disposition was relatively constant between 1977 and 1981, and a major decline in elapsed processing time occurred only among the slowest cases handled in federal courts,

which can perhaps be explained by an increased application of the Act's provisions for excluded processing time.[270] The dismissal sanction was only effective during the final year of the five-year period cited.[271]

A two-year study on the impact of a speedy trial statute in three Ohio courts, based on interviews, observations and a sample of 2,267 cases filed over a ten-year period, concluded that these rules were successful in reducing delay.[272] It found that processing times were substantially lower for cases filed in the year after the statute went into effect in two of the three courts.[273] However, a few years before the enactment of the speedy trial statute, another delay reduction program had been established, meaning that it was difficult to separate the impact of the statute from that of the earlier programme.[274]

[266] Marvell/Luskin (1991: 356) consider that the latter category of laws are not strict enough to be considered 'speedy trial laws'. The same applies to laws pertaining to misdemeanors, rather than felonies; that require that the defendant be brought to trial within a specific number of court terms; that give the trial judge discretion over whether the case is to be dismissed, or that pertain only to defendants incarcerated following conviction for another crime.

[267] Marvell/Luskin (1991: 343 f.).

[268] Marvell/Luskin (1991: 344 f.) point out that all studies finding no relationship have inadequate sample sizes, while the better-designed studies do find an impact.

[269] Bridges (1982: 71). Marvell/Luskin (1991: 344) consider the single time series of eleven years used by this study as insufficient for proper analysis.

[270] Bridges (1982: 71f.).

[271] Bridges (1982: 72). For a skeptical assessment of the Speedy Trial Act of 1974 and of speedy trial rules in general, see Feeley (1983: 156–88) and Nimmer (1978: 143–56).

[272] Grau/Sheskin (1982).

[273] Grau/Sheskin (1982: 109 f.).

[274] Marvell/Luskin (1991: 344).

Using a pooled time series-cross section design, another study evaluated the impact of speedy trial laws in the felony courts of the states of Connecticut and North Carolina.[275] On the one hand, the study found no sign that the Connecticut law had reduced delay. On the other, it found strong evidence that speedy trial laws had reduced delay in North Carolina.[276] As a control, the study conducted numerous replications with different measures of delay and produced consistent results for each state.[277] Regarding the impact of the North Carolina law, it could not be ascertained beyond doubt that it was the speedy trial law that had reduced delay. However, no other factor was found that might have accounted for the statewide occurrence that had actually acted to reduce delay, 'except for a general climate of delay reduction of which the speedy trial law was a key ingredient.'[278]

The general conclusion may be that, depending on their particular features and provisions, laws of this type may be helpful in reducing delay in criminal proceedings. However, there are also reasons to remain skeptical regarding their suitability as a general strategy for delay reduction. It may be argued that speedy trial laws only focus on one type of delay, so that even when they are effective, there is no guarantee that other problems of delay are ameliorated; and, in fact, they may be exacerbated.[279] It can also be said that protecting the right to a speedy trial and eliminating judicial delay are not identical or consistent undertakings: the right to a speedy trial concentrates on harm to the defendant, while judicial delay is considered a problem even if it benefits, and was sought by, the defense.[280]

Another line of criticism focuses on the possible impact of these laws on the quality of justice, as perceived by judges and attorneys, and on the way they may alter the meaning and modes of the judicial role.[281] Finally, a less-than-ideal endorsement of speedy trial laws for policy-makers may stem from the recognition that 'the current state of knowledge does not permit us to determine why particular reforms are or are not effective,'[282] although this does not preclude reasonably well-founded speculation.

In view of all these criticisms, but without overlooking the fact that these laws actually work to some degree, it may be advisable to undertake a preliminary assessment of what impact time limits would have on actual proceedings. Thus, in England, section 22 of the Prosecution of Offences Act 1985 empowered the Home Office Secretary to apply time limits, separately in custody and bail cases,

275 Marvell/Luskin (1991).
276 Marvell/Luskin (1991: 351).
277 Marvell/Luskin (1991: 348 f.).
278 Marvell/Luskin (1991: 351).
279 Feeley (1983: 185). 'Imposing time limits does little to tackle the various underlying causes of delay of all sorts, nor does it do anything substantial to affect the incentives of court officials, a step that appears to be indispensable to devising effective management improvements'.
280 Nimmer (1978: 147).
281 See Grau/Sheskin (1982: 117 ff.).
282 Marvell/Luskin (1991: 343, 352 f.).

to specified stages of criminal proceedings up to the start of trial, although this definition of statutory time limits was preceded by field trials in selected Crown Court and magistrates' courts.

> The trials were designed to examine the practical implications of limits for the parties and the courts and to assist in identifying *deadlines which were realistic yet tight enough to act as a discipline*, thereby minimising time spent awaiting trial.[283]

The Use of Financial Incentives

As already noted, delay in the disposition of criminal cases is not always solely the fault of the court, but may also be the responsibility of a different organisation: the prosecutor's office. Thus, an interesting alternative strategy for accelerating criminal proceedings may be to provide appropriate incentives for this organisation. Such a strategy was applied during the 1980s in the city of New York through a Speedy Disposition Program (SDP) that provided financial incentives for the city's six district attorneys' offices.[284]

The Program was born 'out of the horror engendered in city officials when a Federal judge ordered several hundred inmates awaiting trial to be released from overcrowded jail' and from 'a sense of powerlessness with respect to regulating or even coordinating the practices of the city's District Attorneys. . . .'[285] An analysis by New York's Office of Management and Budget concluded that even a marginal decrease in the number of 'long-term detainees' (defendants awaiting trial more than six months in jail) 'would produce a substantial easing of pressure on detention space.'[286] The Program's goal was to achieve a reduction in the number of long-term detainees 'in a context in which traditional regulatory or 'command and control' policy tools were clearly unavailable.'[287]

The SDP provided an initial amount of money to be distributed as 'seed money,' beginning in 1984, among the New York's DAs' offices. In order to receive their share, the district attorneys agreed to try to reduce both the number of long-term detainees and the number of older pending felony cases in their borough. By agreeing to participate in the SDP, the district attorneys placed their offices in a two-year competition

> in which those showing the greatest success in reducing the number of old pending cases, and long-term jail cases, would be allocated the greatest share of an additional . . . incentive pool.[288]

The specific delay-reduction programs to be established by each office and the use of the money provided by the Program were entirely in the hands of individual district attorneys.

[283] Morgan/Vennard (1989: 1) (emphasis added).
[284] See Heumann/Church (1990) and Church/Heumann (1992).
[285] Heumann/Church (1990: 83).
[286] Heumann/Church (1990: 83).
[287] Heumann/Church (1990: 83).
[288] Heumann/Church (1990: 83).

By traditional standards and indicators, the SDP was much more of a failure than a success. City-wide results showed that during the first year of the programme, there was a modest decrease in the number of long-term detainees (roughly 10 per cent), while the number of cases involving defendants detained for six to nine months remained approximately the same, resulting in a net decrease in total cases involving six-month or longer detention of 3.8 per cent.[289]

During the second year, the number of long-term detainees rose sharply, by more than 28 per cent for cases over nine months old, and by 16.6 per cent for cases over six months old.[290] Results were scarcely more encouraging for the number of old cases before New York's Supreme Court: a fairly substantial decrease (of 23.7 per cent) in the number of 11-month-old cases was achieved at the end of the first year, followed by a 12.9 per cent increase during the second year. The net improvement was therefore slightly less than 14 per cent. A net increase in the number of cases pending between 6 and 11 months 'resulted in a dampening of the reduction in the aggregate number of 6-month-and-older cases to 4.5 percent'.[291]

However, there were significant inter-borough variations. In one borough (Manhattan), there were substantial reductions in the number of old pending cases and long-term detainee cases for both years of the programme. In another borough (Bronx County), the first year witnessed the most significant reductions of any county in either year. Two other major district attorneys' offices (Brooklyn and Queens) failed to achieve net reductions in either year of the programme.[292] These variations call for some explanation.

Brooklyn and Queens, the two boroughs that failed to achieve net reductions after two years, established reduction programmes that relied on cooperation with the courts—a cooperation that was not always guaranteed—and they redirected resources to deal with the older cases, thus placing an additional strain on other parts of the office. Another possible reason for their failure is that they established what amounted to 'crash programs' designed as a temporary response to a systemic problem.[293] Bronx County achieved the greatest reductions of any office the first year. However, it seems that the major impetus for this substantial decrease came from the court, with cooperation and help from the district attorney, so 'it does not appear that the district attorney's made any *systematic* changes in response to SDP.'[294] Manhattan, the most successful office, placed no reliance on the courts and instituted no special 'old cases' unit; on the contrary, without any major changes in basic office structure and case-handling procedures, 'the office set up a number of seemingly minor alterations designed as a shift in internal office priorities.'[295]

289 Heumann/Church (1990: 85).
290 Heumann/Church (1990: 85).
291 Heumann/Church (1990: 85, 87).
292 Heumann/Church (1990: 87).
293 Heumann/Church (1990: 87 ff., 91 f.).
294 Heumann/Church (1990: 93).
295 Heumann/Church (1990: 89).

In aggregate numbers, as explained earlier, SDP was clearly a failure: at the end of the two-year programme, jail overcrowding remained a critical problem in New York.[296] However, the programme demonstrated that it is possible to alter established norms and bring about changes in the priorities of 'entrenched criminal justice bureaucracies' through financial inducements,[297] especially when some degree of competition is involved.

The Acceleration of Civil Proceedings

Public interest in the expeditiousness of civil proceedings appears to be less acute than in the case of criminal proceedings. Traditionally, it has been considered that only 'private' interests are involved in civil disputes and, therefore, the pace of litigation has been predominantly under the control of the parties. The resolution of private disputes through adjudication, however, also generates public costs, and as a result of growing concern over court efficiency, the celerity of civil proceedings has also become an important issue.[298] For this purpose, a variety of measures and strategies have been proposed or tried.[299] They range from a general structural alteration that takes away from the parties some of the control they exert over the proceedings and gives it to the judge or to other court officials, to the use of time limits, as in criminal proceedings.[300] These possibilities have been considered either as alternatives or in addition to more traditional strategies, which seek the simplification and acceleration of procedures, for example, by reducing waiting periods or through the increased use of oral or written proceedings. Another strategy considers the use of special abbreviated procedures and various procedural tracks.

Simplification

In 1976, the German Code of Civil Procedure ('ZPO') was amended by a 'Law for the Simplification and Acceleration of Judicial Proceedings'.[301] Among other

296 Heumann/Church (1990: 95).

297 Heumann/Church (1990: 96).

298 For example, see Levon-Guérin/Chadelat (1998) in relation to France, where 'the excessive sluggishness of procedures' is said to border on 'judicial paralysis' (at 177).

299 See again Levon-Guérin/Chadelat (1998) for an overview of the reforms introduced in France since the early decades of the 20th century and the measures now under consideration and intended to accelerate case processing.

300 See, for example, Longan (1993). There are usually certain time limits on civil proceedings: opportunities for filing motions and briefs, or producing evidence. When these time limits are not respected, the respective right is lost.

301 Rottleuthner-Lutter/Rottleuthner (1989: 31). According to one observer, this amendment was a response to the success of the so-called 'Stuttgart model' of civil procedure, to be discussed later, as it sought to provide a legal basis for a number of the fundamental ideas of this model. Unfortunately, according to the same source, the legislature failed to include a number of the prerequisites that had contributed to the success of the Stuttgart model: the written preliminary procedure was not designed as a formalised procedure with firmly established deadlines which could be

significant modifications, the amending law was designed to accelerate proceedings through a 'concentration' of various procedural stages. This goal was achieved through the elimination of as many hearings as possible. Under certain conditions, written proceedings made the complete elimination of hearings possible. Moreover, waiting periods between procedural steps were reduced and the possibility of requesting continuances was also limited.

Several years later, a study to evaluate the impact of this legislation on the duration of judicial proceedings was carried out.[302] The study comprised all civil cases (about 5.4 million) filed in the lower courts ('*Amtsgerichte*') and the regional courts of first instance ('*Landgerichte*') during a six-year period, beginning a year and a half before the entry into force of the amendments (January 1975 to December 1980; the law went into effect on 1 July, 1977). On the basis of these data, time series were constructed for their statistical analysis in the form of an 'interrupted time-series quasi-experiment'. The idea of this methodology was to determine whether the normal development of a time series was 'interrupted' by some external intervention and what the effect of such intervention was over time.[303] Additionally, two samples were taken with the purpose of evaluating changes at the individual case level.[304]

Statistical analysis for the lower courts showed that the amendments had led to a reduction of 7.8 days in the duration of proceedings, considering an average processing time of 110 days (level of significance: 5 per cent). The greatest reduction was observed, in both absolute and relative terms, in those proceedings ending with settlement, with attorneys assisting both parties, and in contentious proceedings, where evidence had been gathered and examined.[305] Interestingly enough, the reduction did not lead to a higher number of dispositions, in either total numbers or per judge. This apparent paradox can be explained by considering that it is possible to reduce the average duration of a proceeding by lowering the waiting time between hearings but without altering the average processing time per case. The authors see this as confirmation that the reduction in processing time was achieved precisely by observing the concentration principle established by the legislature.[306]

As regards the courts of first instance, statistical evaluation proved to be far more difficult, due to the organic reform that was passed at the same time (involving the establishment of specialised courts for family matters), which

independently monitored by the office of the clerk; the time and energy of the judge would be absorbed by fairly routine matters. Moreover, the amendment failed to ensure that disputes of 'higher complexity' be heard and decided by a judicial panel rather than by a single judge. See Bender (1979: 460 f.).

[302] See Rottleuthner-Lutter/Rottleuthner (1989), Rottleuthner/Rottleuthner-Lutter (1990) and Böhm (1992).

[303] Rottleuthner-Lutter/Rottleuthner (1989: 30).

[304] Rottleuthner-Lutter/Rottleuthner (1989: 30 f.).

[305] Rottleuthner-Lutter/Rottleuthner (1989: 41 f.). In the first case, there was a reduction of 16.2 days, although the average duration of proceedings was 148 days; in the second, there was a reduction of 15.2 days, with an average duration of 193 days.

[306] Rottleuthner-Lutter/Rottleuthner (1989: 44).

altered the jurisdiction of the other courts. Family cases filed both before and after the legislative intervention were thereby excluded from statistical analysis. However, the organic reform entailed changes in organisation and personnel in those court chambers that had also heard family matters before the amending law went into force. To take this situation into account, a distinction was made between 'mixed' chambers, ie, those that heard family matters before the reform, and 'pure' chambers, those that did not.[307]

When both types of chambers were considered, the average reduction effect was 9.7 days. The reduction was greater regarding contentious proceedings ending with judgment and proceedings ending with settlement. This effect was more evident in the 'pure' than in the 'mixed' chambers. In the group of proceedings with the longest processing times (disposition through contentious judgment, with gathering and examination of evidence), no significant reduction for both types of chambers could be identified for the post-intervention phase. Finally, five groups of matters before the 'pure' chambers experienced first a reduction and then an increase in processing time, which means that the effect of the legislative amendments was temporary rather than permanent.[308]

Simplification in the sense of a less formal procedure, however, may not be beneficial for all types of procedure. This is shown by a German statistical study on the *potential* advantages for the rationalisation and efficiency of civil justice through the use of a simplified procedure for small claims.[309] The study was intended as an evaluation of a legislative proposal, recently under discussion, for the reinstatement of an informal or free procedure, as opposed to the normal procedure, for the handling of claims under a certain amount (1,000 DM) in the lower courts ('*Amtsgerichte*').[310]

On the basis of judicial statistics and the analysis of previous surveys, the study concludes that the potential for rationalisation and efficiency-enhancement through an informal procedure is extremely low and, therefore, not justified. This is primarily due to the low amount at stake and the simple structure of small claims.[311] A threshold of one thousand DM would cover 43 per cent of all cases and 37 per cent of the total work capacity of the lower civil courts, meaning that no more than 15 per cent of the judges' working time, or an equivalent of five hours a week, can be simplified or rationalised. In other words: judicial practice and procedural principles in the lower courts would have to be completely altered if such a time reduction were to be achieved.[312] On the other hand, a much higher threshold, above 1,500 DM, would have the unwelcome consequence of including more than 50 per cent of all cases, thus making the informal procedure the rule rather than the exception.[313]

[307] Rottleuthner-Lutter/Rottleuthner (1989: 44 f.).
[308] Rottleuthner-Lutter/Rottleuthner (1989: 46 ff.).
[309] Wollschläger (1991a and b).
[310] Wollschläger (1991a: 15).
[311] Wollschläger (1991a: 95).
[312] Wollschläger (1991a: 83).
[313] Wollschläger (1991a: 89).

Oral or Written Proceedings?

An important difference between the legal traditions of the common- and the civil-law, which is rooted in their historical origins, lies in the varying degrees to which they have relied on written or oral proceedings. Oral proceedings have predominated in common-law systems as a consequence of the need to present all the relevant evidence to a group of lay persons (the jury) in sessions that are as short and concentrated as possible. By contrast, the predominance of written proceedings can be found in civil-law systems as a result of the influence of medieval canon law and the fairly central role played by the judge in directing the proceedings. In the contemporary world, however, judicial proceedings in most countries are the result of a combination of written and oral stages of procedure. Nevertheless, the need to modernise the administration of justice and to reduce delay has led reformers to consider the possibility of altering the existing balance between the oral and written stages, as the case may be, to shorten the proceedings and reduce processing times.

The use of one or more oral hearings may be an efficient way of handling a case, but it usually creates a significant management problem, in terms of how to schedule hearings requiring the personal appearance of the parties, witnesses, and so on. One possibility of solving this problem is for the court to assume a higher degree of control over the scheduling process and, consequently, over the parties themselves. Another is, precisely, to substitute written documents for as many personal appearances of the parties as possible. Thus, the Lord Chancellor's 1995 'Access to Justice' report—an interim report on the civil justice system in England and Wales[314]—examined the possibility of introducing written briefs and motions to replace oral hearings, for the purpose of effectively abbreviating procedures.

In many civil-law systems, the problem has been the opposite: how to replace a procedure that relies excessively on written documents and generates 'idle time,' during which 'nothing happens,' for the parties and the courts. Continental European countries have been attempting to modernise judicial proceedings since the beginning of the twentieth century by incorporating a higher degree of orality into them and by striking a balance between the written and oral stages of proceedings. A good example of this is the so-called 'Stuttgart model', as implemented in German civil courts after 1967.[315]

The history of German civil procedure could be described as the constant interchange between the principles of orality and writing and by the failure of either principle to demonstrate its absolute validity. The same could be said of the various hybrid arrangements developed unsystematically in practice.[316]

314 See Zuckerman/Cranston (eds) (1995).
315 See Bender (1979).
316 Bender (1979: 437).

> The Stuttgart model is an attempt at joining these two principles in such a way that each principle is employed in precisely that segment of the proceedings where, as a consequence, an optimal result can be expected, so that when one of the principles is employed, then it is used with a minimum of dilution.[317]

Proceedings according to the Stuttgart model are characterised by a written preliminary procedure and an oral trial or main hearing ('*Hauptverhandlung*'),

> a term taken from German criminal procedure with the intention of signifying that the decision of a case should be based (solely) on the outcome of a (preferably single) oral hearing,

that is, during this hearing the entire body of the dispute should be subject to a comprehensive examination.[318]

The Stuttgart model was the subject of various empirical tests.[319] Most surveys made a positive evaluation of the model in all respects, such as case processing time; number of required hearings; compliance with deadlines; higher settlement rate; fewer appeals and less reversals on appeal; lower costs as regards attorney time; higher degree of satisfaction among attorneys and judges, etc. One survey formulated and proved the following hypotheses:[320]

—The duration of proceedings can be shortened if the oral hearing is prepared more intensively and is conducted in a more concentrated, thorough manner.
—Of all preparatory measures, the most effective is requiring the personal appearance of the parties.
—The presence of the parties at the hearing increases the likelihood that the case will be settled and reduces the number of appeals.
—The active cooperation of the parties at the hearing leads to judgments of better quality.
—The number of procedural steps is reduced.

Many Latin American countries are still trying to modernise their judicial systems and their procedural codes through the introduction of the principle of orality into their excessively written judicial proceedings, as attested by the papers presented at an international conference on the subject.[321] Unfortunately, not all of them clearly define the reforms introduced or their impact,[322] as assessed by empirical means, so we shall now summarise some of the findings in two countries where the introduction of a new code of procedure appears to have achieved

[317] Bender (1979: 437).
[318] Bender (1979: 437). For a fuller description of the model, see pages 438 ff.
[319] Bender (1979: 462 ff.).
[320] Conducted by Bender himself (1979: 464 ff.).
[321] See Varios (1993).
[322] Regarding Chile, we are told that in Santiago the average duration of an ordinary procedure, including both instances, is five hundred days. Prior to the entry into force of Law no. 18.705 it was 973 days, but we do not learn more specific details about this law nor are we told whether the reduction is due to the principle of orality. See Tavolari Oliveros (1993: 231 ff.).

significant reductions in processing times, one by way of a higher degree of orality (Uruguay) and the other by the provisional acceleration of written proceedings, prior to the establishment of a truly oral trial (Costa Rica).

In *Uruguay*, a new Code of Civil Procedure, which introduced trial by oral hearing, came partially into force in 1989 and has been fully implemented since January 1992.[323] Just over two years after the introduction of the procedural reform, it was noted that case processing time had dropped and that with few exceptions, there was no significant backlog that prevented an efficient scheduling of hearings. According to data covering nine months of 1992, in Montevideo, the capital, courts were conducting two to five hearings each day, scheduled for dates close to the conclusion of the initial written stage of the proceedings. On average, a preliminary hearing could be scheduled no more than four (and usually no more than two) months after suit had been filed, with the exception of labour proceedings, where a hearing was scheduled an average of six months after the filing of suit.[324] It should be noted that procedural reform was accompanied by other significant organisational changes, such as the introduction of a computerised system for the random assignment of cases to the courts in Montevideo and the creation of a significant number of new judicial posts.[325]

In *Costa Rica*, a new Code of Civil Procedure went into force in May 1990. In this new code, the principle of orality was introduced for the examination of evidence, but it was not implemented at the outset because of the cost of increasing the number of courts. For this reason, the new procedure initially consisted of simple, speedy written proceedings. According to an opinion poll conducted among attorneys and judges of four judicial offices, a majority of judges (57.1 per cent) and attorneys (81.25 per cent) felt that the new procedure was more expeditious than the previous one.[326]

Procedural Alternatives and Tracks

This section examines a series of efficiency-enhancing strategies designed mainly to replace, in whole or in part, ordinary judicial proceedings with different adjudicative procedures or with non-adjudicative procedures, such as ADR. Both cases involve alternative procedures which can largely be chosen by the parties or the judges themselves, the main idea behind them being to adapt procedure to the nature and scope of claims and litigants, in order to achieve the best possible outcome. Cases brought before the courts may often follow different 'tracks', depending on their characteristics, the litigants' choice and the

323 Torello (1993).

324 Torello (1993: 127). Average processing time is reduced by cases that are disposed of in a very short time, either because only one party appears or because of the conciliatory activity performed by the judge during the preliminary hearing.

325 Torello (1993: 122, 126).

326 Arguedas Salazar (1993: 158 ff.).

judges' decision. Such tracks also offer alternative adjudicative procedures that may replace normal or ordinary judicial proceedings either partly or wholly. As one observer puts it:

> Rather than seeking the impossible, which is to design a unitary system that can cater to (all interests), we should seek to isolate broad categories of interests and design a system of alternatives which can accommodate them.[327]

Alternative Dispute Resolution (ADR)

A substantial body of literature is concerned with so-called 'alternative dispute resolution' (ADR), ie, dispute settlement which does not rely on authoritative or binding resolution by a third party (as is the case with conciliation and mediation) or does so in a more informal manner (as is the case with arbitration). ADR can be used as an alternative procedure either outside the courts or after suit has been filed.[328] ADR proceedings within the courts are intended to be more expeditious, as well as more satisfactory to participants, than normal adjudication would be, which has been often demonstrated by empirical research.

Nevertheless, the most difficult question is to determine what the impact of these alternative procedures is on the *overall* efficiency of the courts within which they are conducted as well as on the litigation rate, considering that adjudication and ADR coexist within the same court and share its resources. It is a well-known fact that, for a variety of reasons, a large proportion of cases are not terminated by judgment, so that if mediation and conciliation were to be actively pursued, a higher settlement rate might arguably help speed up adjudication. However, an economic analysis of ADR may show that this is not always the case. *Ex post* ADR proceedings will not always be cheaper or quicker, and, above all, they may cause higher litigation rates, as the filing of a suit may be the only way to have access to ADR, or else when an unsuccessful ADR proceeding still results in full litigation.[329] A few empirical studies on the so-called court-annexed arbitration in the United States have demonstrated precisely this.

Court-annexed arbitration programmes divert certain classes of cases to a relatively informal hearing before one or more experienced attorneys who provide a decision on the dispute. The parties to the case may then either accept the award or reject it and demand trial *de novo*.[330] The need to evaluate such programs both in themselves and as regards their impact on the overall court functioning, has produced a large body of empirical literature.[331] This type of

[327] Armstrong (1995: 112).
[328] This corresponds to Shavell's (1995a) distinction between *ex ante* and *ex post* ADR.
[329] See Shavell (1995a).
[330] McCoun *et al.* (1988: v).
[331] See for example an overview in Hensler (1990).

evaluation is fraught with difficulties, because, at the very least, it is necessary to establish a comparison between the period before and after the inception of a program, as well as between cases diverted to arbitration and non-arbitrated cases. The main results of two such studies, which offer interesting data on the operation of alternative informal procedures within a court, are summarised below.

The first study refers to the mandatory arbitration of automobile injury lawsuits which the state of New Jersey initially introduced as an experimental procedure in two counties in 1983 and which was adopted statewide in 1985.[332] Evaluation research was based on a random sample of 1,000 automobile negligence cases filed in eight New Jersey courts in the second half of 1983, before the programme's inception, and in the second half of 1985. The latter included cases assigned to arbitration as well as cases that were not. Data were obtained from court records and from a survey of attorneys.[333]

The study reached the following main conclusions:[334]

—The programme captured a significant fraction of auto negligence cases, although relatively few of them were disposed of by an arbitration judgment: in the sample, 68 per cent of cases were assigned to the programme, but many settled before they reached an arbitration hearing, About 55 per cent of assigned cases were actually arbitrated and about 40 per cent of those were terminated by arbitration judgment.

—More than half the arbitrated cases were appealed, but *de novo* trials were rare (about 10 per cent of arbitrated cases), which suggests that appeal was used primarily as a bargaining tactic, as over 80 per cent of appealed cases settled before a trial took place.

—The study was unable to detect a significant effect on the trial rate, which was initially quite low (5 per cent), so a larger sample would have been needed to detect a significant reduction.

—Cases assigned to the programme were more likely to be adjudicated: before the programme was introduced, most answered cases were settled or dismissed without an adjudicatory hearing (trial). Arbitration was more likely to divert many more cases from settlement than from trial,[335] since it provided disputants with an alternative adjudicatory option.

—Assigned cases terminated at a slower rate; delay being apparently linked to the scheduling of arbitration hearings, although twelve months after the initial filing the pace accelerated.

—The programme appears to have slightly increased case activity by attorneys and court staff: including a new set of litigation activities brought about by introduction of arbitration; scheduling, preparing for, and participating in an arbitration hearing.

[332] McCoun *et al.* (1988: v) and McCoun (1991).

[333] McCoun *et al.* (1988: vi).

[334] McCoun *et al.* (1988: vi–ix).

[335] See percentages in McCoun (1991: 238).

—The programme did not have a measurable effect on attorney hours and fees.
—Disputants were generally fairly positive in their evaluation of arbitration: the majority of litigants and attorneys rated arbitration as a more efficient procedure than either trial by jury or trial by judge.

The second study concerned the arbitration of high-stakes cases in a federal district court.[336] The study resorted to a experimental design in which cases were removed from the arbitration process at random and placed in a 'control group' subject to non-arbitration pretrial procedures. This provided a standard against which to measure the arbitration-eligible 'experimental group'.[337] Data were collected on 350 cases filed between 1 January 1985 and 31 December 1987. Information was gathered from attorneys participating in these cases; litigants in arbitration-eligible and control group cases were interviewed.[338]

The main findings were as follows:[339]

—The arbitration programme increased the likelihood that cases would be pursued to the point of being answered: approximately 64 per cent of contract cases and 84 per cent of tort cases in the experimental group were answered, whereas in the control group, only 43 per cent of contract cases and 79 per cent of tort cases were answered.
—The arbitration programme also increased the likelihood that a case would receive some form of adjudicative hearing: approximately 33 per cent of experimental group cases, but only 15 per cent of control group cases, had some form of adjudication.
—The arbitration programme appears to have resulted in lower private costs.
—No definitive information was obtained on whether arbitration reduced the public cost of litigation, due to the relatively small sample of cases. It was estimated that arbitration cases cost the court an average of 1,209 dollars, whereas the control cases cost 1,240 dollars, a difference that was not statistically significant.[340]
—Case duration was not greatly affected by the arbitration programme: the experimental group cases took an average of 285 days to close; while control group cases took an average of 282 days.
—Both individual and corporate litigants reacted favorably to the arbitration programme.
—Attorneys generally responded favourably to the programme.

The findings of both studies seem to be consistent and suggest the conclusion that an arbitration programme does not necessarily translate into visible

[336] Lind (1990).
[337] Lind (1990: xii).
[338] Lind (1990: xiii).
[339] Lind (1990: xiv f.).
[340] Lind (1990: xv): 'The arbitration program has its own administrative costs, and the data were insufficient to determine whether these expenditures are offset by other savings from the court.'

efficiency gains for the overall operation of the courts.[341] If ADR succeeds in diverting a significant number of cases from trial, 'then it is likely to reduce public and private litigation costs as well as court congestion and delay.'[342] However, in a situation where delay and the costs of adjudication encourage litigants to settle privately, 'a program that offers an informal alternative might induce many of them to change their minds and wait for a hearing.'[343] In other words: court-annexed arbitration undoubtedly operated as an alternative, but as an alternative to bilateral settlement rather than to trial. This conclusion is significant not only for court-annexed arbitration, but also for any less formal alternative procedure that will coexist in court with ordinary judicial procedure.

Provisional Determinations and Summary Proceedings

Modern legal systems often establish *summary judicial proceedings* for the provisional determination or protection of a legal right, in cases where urgent intervention is called for or where there is a clear presumption of the existence of such a right (a notable example of this is the collection of money debts on the basis of an enforceable title). However, such proceedings typically fail to resolve the merits of the dispute, so that an ordinary or main judicial procedure is needed to produce a final decision. An interesting development in this area seems to be the displacement or substitution, under certain conditions, of the main procedure by a provisional determination.

A comparative legal study on the German '*einstweilige Verfügung*' ('provisional determination') and the French '*ordonnance de referé*'[344] points out that the provisional decisions produced by these proceedings tend to displace the main procedure and to make it dispensable.[345] This is usually the case when such proceedings concern a clear legal situation and there are no doubts about the outcome of a future main proceeding. Through the likely avoidance of main proceedings courts would be effectively relieved of lengthy, costly procedures.

The study does not offer an empirical evaluation of the '*ordonnance de referé*', although it does reproduce the transcript of an interesting interview between the first president of the *Cour de Cassation* and the study's author, in which the former explains and reflects on the actual functions accomplished by

[341] For a more positive account of a court-annexed arbitration program, see Gatowski *et al.* (1996). This study concerns the evaluation of court-annexed arbitration in Clark County, Nevada, introduced in 1992.The study concludes that this programme was successful in increasing the pace of litigation, reducing costs associated with litigation, maintaining the satisfaction of participants and generally improving the quality of civil justice. Arbitrated cases were compared with 'trial track' cases filed two years earlier (1990). Since arbitration was mandatory for all civil cases under a threshold amount, with few exceptions, what is being evaluated here is the substitution of one procedure for another. The study does not say whether arbitrated cases were diverted from settlements, or what the overall impact of the programme was on *all* litigated cases.

[342] McCoun (1991: 242).

[343] McCoun (1991: 242).

[344] Weber (1993).

[345] Weber (1993: 119 ff.).

this summary proceeding and the '*juge de referés*' in France.[346] The president notices that because of the central importance of time in a judicial proceeding, the *referé* has been able to displace main procedures under certain conditions, for example, where the parties are no longer willing to litigate for several years, as a result of which the main trial becomes of secondary importance. In urgent cases and those where a clear legal situation prevails, the possibility of a provisional determination makes the main trial superfluous. For this reason, he proposes recognising an '*ordonnance de referé*' as final where no party initiates a main procedure within a certain period of time. In this context, the '*juge de referés*' is a judge who is permanently available in circumstances where an urgent decision is required to eliminate an illegal situation. Thus, people are not encouraged to behave illegally, knowing that it might take several months to correct such illegal behaviour.

The president also pointed out that there were no statistical data on the percentage of cases where the '*ordonnance de referé*' effectively terminated the dispute without having recourse to the main procedure. In his experience, however, there had been no cases where a main trial had produced an outcome significantly different from that of the *referé*.[347]

There are indications that in other countries, such as Japan and the Netherlands, summary proceedings of this type have broadened their function, partially assuming the role of the main trial.[348] Thus, for example, the *Kort Geding* in the Netherlands has become increasingly important as a genuine, publicly accepted alternative to normal procedure.[349] It is used in urgent cases where a decision is in the immediate interest of the parties, as for example, in relation to the occupation of buildings, asylum matters, labour disputes and unfair trading practices. Despite the lack of reliable statistical data, there are indications that in a majority of cases, a main proceeding was not initiated, despite the fact that the provisional decision did not stand in the way of a future proceeding. Thus, it was reported that in about 95 per cent of cases, the parties were satisfied with the *Kort Geding* decision of first instance. However, field research raised doubts about the widespread notion that the *Kort Geding* provided a final solution to disputes: in Amsterdam, 8 per cent of *Kort Geding* decisions were appealed, and according to a survey of attorneys, in 40 per cent of cases, further proceedings connected with the dispute were initiated, although they usually encompassed other claims. Only a small proportion of *Kort Geding* proceedings, mainly related to debt collection, could be seen as an equivalent to a main proceeding.[350]

The wider issue at stake here is whether and under what conditions summary proceedings develop with the aim of producing provisional determinations of

[346] Weber (1993: 122 ff.).
[347] Weber (1993: 127).
[348] Blankenburg/Leipold (1991: 109).
[349] Blankenburg/Leipold (1991: 114).
[350] Blankenburg/Leipold (1991: 115).

this type as an alternative to ordinary judicial proceedings. According to two German scholars, besides the factual situation, where excessive delay may lead to the exclusive use of summary provisional proceedings, certain elements of legal design contribute to this possibility, such as the following:[351]

—There must be a broad availability of summary proceedings coupled with broad discretion for the judge to determine whether the summary procedure is appropriate for a particular case.
—It is necessary to entrust decisions concerning this type of proceedings to judges who enjoy special authority and recognition (such as presiding judges).
—An oral hearing must be conducted within a short period of time.
—The proceedings must have the ability to determine the existence of a clear, not easily disputable material and legal situation, which must be translated into a decision that does not limit the legal consequences, as well as the power to enforce such a decision.
—An appeal must be available, even to the highest body of the judicial hierarchy.

Single-judge vs Panel Proceedings

An empirical study conducted in Germany examined the quality of proceedings carried out under the authority of a single judge as compared to panel proceedings.[352] Under certain conditions, the German Code of Civil Procedure[353] enables cases that would normally be heard by a panel of judges or chamber, to be transferred to one of its members. The comparison between the two types of proceedings is made possible and facilitated by the fact that, in principle, both single-judge and panel proceedings handle the same type of case.

The study first found that the courts made extremely variable use of this possibility, ranging from 0 per cent to 80 per cent in the various courts. It therefore attempted to explain the reasons for this divergence, the criteria for the transfer, and the possible differences in quality between single-judge and panel decisions, or between panels showing different transference rates.[354]

As regards the quality of both types of proceedings, the study obtained the following results:[355]

—*Number of dispositions*: 'zero chambers',[356] both large and small, showed the lowest figures, while the chambers with a transference rate

[351] Blankenburg/Leipold (1991: 119 f.).
[352] Rottleuthner (1991), Rottleuthner *et al.* (1992).
[353] See the German '*Ziviliprozessordnung*' (ZPO), § 348.
[354] Rottleuthner *et al.* (1992: 11). The study used a wide range of survey instruments: file sample (5,010 files from 113 chambers); interviews with judges; analysis of control cards, and questionnaires.
[355] Rottleuthner *et al.* (1992: 14 ff., comparison table at p 16).
[356] These are the chambers with a transference rate of 1.5% or less. Rottleuthner *et al.* (1992: 12).

between 20 per cent and 30 per cent had the highest numbers. A similar result was obtained from a comparison of the relationship between the number of dispositions and the number of pending cases, but here the difference between the larger chambers was more significant than between the smaller ones.

—*Speed*: chambers dispose of non-transferred cases more rapidly than single judges on their own: within six months, the chamber will have completed 70 per cent of its cases, and the judge only 54 per cent. Chambers with a transference rate of over 50 per cent are the most expeditious. The chambers' greater speed is due to the fact that the more time-consuming and work-intensive types of cases (ending with settlement or contested judgment) are transferred to single judges. The number of hearings is an important factor as regards speed, because chambers dispose rapidly of cases that do not require a hearing. If a hearing is conducted, the speed of chambers is similar to that of single judges; conversely, single judges are quicker if the number of hearings increases.

—*Settlement rate*: the single judge's settlement rate is significantly higher than the chambers' rate. The higher rate can be explained by the fact that cases where both parties appear are more frequently handled by single judges, together with the fact that such cases show an above-average settlement rate. Chambers with the highest transference rates are also those that dispose of a higher number of cases through settlement.

—*Appeal rate*: according to official statistics, the appeal rate for chambers is nearly 25 per cent higher than that for single judges, although sharp divergences in the appeal rates may be due to mistakes in the control cards used for generating these data. Conversely, the file sample revealed a slightly higher appeal rate for chambers (48.6 per cent vs 45 per cent for single judges), which can be explained by the higher amounts at stake before the chambers. As for the success rate of appeals, the proportion of appeals that are either remanded for a new decision or invalidated and decided by the appellate court itself, is the same for both chambers and single judges.

All in all, there seems to be no significant difference in quality between both types of procedures. Judges find both advantages (speed, procedural control) and disadvantages (less quality, lack of organisational control, inconsistent decisions) in single-judge proceedings. Attorneys seem to be fairly satisfied with single-judge proceedings and do not find any significant quality differences.[357]

ADMINISTRATION

One important aspect of court efficiency is undoubtedly related to the organisation and administration of the *court system*: the selectivity, operation and

[357] Rottleuthner *et al.* (1992: 17).

performance of the individual court is dependent on structural and institutional factors that affect it as a part of a larger system. This section provides a brief inventory and a general analysis of such factors. They range from what one could call the institutional design of the court system and its articulation with the other branches of government, to the appropriate number of the courts and their territorial distribution, and they certainly include the administration, in a broad sense, of the court system. As one would expect, given the complexity of this subject, few studies have attempted to provide an integral analysis of an entire court system.[358]

'Administration' and 'management' are often used interchangeably in the literature on organisations. However, as used in this chapter, a distinction between both concepts might be drawn in the following terms: 'management' would refer to the control of behavior *within* organisations, and

> includes matters such as motivation, personnel management and development, leadership, and job design and enrichment—the objective of management being to get people to perform in ways that enhance organisational efficiency and effectiveness.[359]

On the other hand, the concept of 'administration' concerns the behaviour *of* organisations and focuses on

> matters of organisational design, intra- and inter-organisational relations, program design and implementation, and the development of governing rules, procedures, and processes.[360]

In the context of our topic, 'judicial administration' is understood as a broader concept than 'court management', since it entails 'the fundamentals of judicial system design that extend well into the realms of forthright values choice'; as, for example, in the scheme for selecting judges or the appropriate size and scope of territorial jurisdictions.[361]

Organisation and Administration of the Court System

Here, *organisation of a court system* refers to the basic structure and powers of such a system as they may affect its performance. Such a structure creates specific problems of articulation, cooperation and administration between the courts as units of a court system, and between the court system and other institutions.

First, a distinction must be drawn between unified, bifurcated and segmented court systems. *Unified court systems* consist of a single hierarchy of courts. This model admits of two variants: one in which all courts belong to only one formal

[358] The example is again Posner (1996).
[359] Boyum/Hudzik (1991: 551).
[360] Boyum/Hudzik (1991: 551 f.).
[361] Boyum/Hudzik (1991: 550).

organisation, and another in which specialised courts have been established outside the ordinary court system, but whose decisions are subject to review by the ordinary courts. This is the case, for example, in the United States. An example of a *bifurcated court system* is the double hierarchy of ordinary and administrative courts in France, each headed by its own highest judicial body, the *Cour de Cassation* and the *Conseil d'Etat*, respectively. This model has been followed by several countries in Europe and Latin America. Germany, on the other hand, provides an example of what may be termed a *segmented court system*, composed of five independent judicial branches. To complicate matters further, both bifurcated and segmented court systems also allow the existence of specialised courts outside them.

Countries with a federal system of government generally have both federal and local courts,[362] which creates a problem of defining whether or not both systems will encompass a full hierarchy of courts, the allocation of jurisdiction between the two systems, and the responsibilities of federal and local governments for the establishment and maintenance of the courts. The United States judicial system is characterised by the coexistence of two full, independent judicial hierarchies: the federal and the state courts.[363] This model has largely been followed in Latin America by other federal countries, such as Argentina, Brazil and Mexico.

One important problem to be solved by this federal model is the extent to which decisions by local courts may be appealed before a federal court, since there is always a certain amount of pressure to appeal to ever higher judicial authorities. Thus, if this pressure is not resisted to a certain extent, federal courts may end up being swamped by local matters, and local courts further debilitated and deprived of their autonomy. Here, we find the contrasting experiences of the United States, on the one hand, and Mexico and Argentina, on the other. In the United States, up to 95 per cent of all judicial proceedings start and finish before the state judiciaries. Relatively few state cases are brought to a federal court, partly because of the discretionary powers of both the state and the federal supreme courts in the review of lower court decisions. In Argentina and Mexico, on the contrary, federal courts have responded to social pressure by opening more and more the door to the appeal of state or provincial court decisions.[364]

[362] An exception is Venezuela, a federal country which 'nationalised' its court system in 1945, establishing a single, national hierarchy of courts.

[363] See Carp/Stidham (1993: 19 ff.).

[364] In Argentina, the so-called 'extraordinary remedy' ('*recurso extraordinario*') that can be used whenever a 'federal question' is raised in a proceeding before a provincial court, has become more and more an 'ordinary' remedy, because the federal courts have used the concept of 'arbitrary decision' ('*sentencia arbitraria*') to cover more and more grounds for appeal. See Sagüés (1989: 313). In the case of Mexico, during the second half of the 19th century the Supreme Court of Justice yielded to litigant pressure, fueled by distrust of the local courts, that sought a broad possibility of appealing local judicial decisions before the federal courts. On the basis of a constitutional provision, the incorrect application of an ordinary statute was regarded as a violation of a constitutional right that made a federal remedy available. This created a *de facto* unified judicial hierarchy, to the extent that a large number of state judicial decisions were being challenged before the federal courts. See Fix-Fierro (1998).

In other federal systems, such as those of Canada and Germany, the federal courts are only the courts of last resort, that is, these countries do not possess a complete hierarchy of federal courts. This model has the advantage of avoiding some of the thorny jurisdictional problems that plague other federal systems.

The second central aspect of the court system's organisation is the relationship of the courts to other branches of government. Despite the increasing levels of autonomy enjoyed by court systems in many parts of the world, they are still dependent on other institutions for their operation, for example, as regards resources, appointments, administration and governance, enforcement of judgments, procedural rules, etc.

As mentioned earlier, the complexity of the internal and external relationships of court systems generates, raises a series of interesting problems of articulation, coordination, judicial policy-making and implementation, as well as other issues regarding the advantages and costs of such a complex arrangement. Thus, for example, the proliferation of specialised courts outside the ordinary court system raises the issue of whether a single, integrated judicial organisation should also exist for the sake of efficiency.

Although court efficiency has become a relevant topic in today's discussion on judicial reform, most studies seem to focus solely on the *existing* court system's structure, and few empirical studies, if any, seem to deal with the thorny issue of whether such a structure should be modified or kept at all. While it is always possible to increase court efficiency *within* the existing structure of the court system, such potential gains are dependent on, and limited by, the *organisational starting point*.[365] In other words: the institutional design itself should be analysed, so as to consider such potential gains from a global perspective, even if, from a practical point of view, a radical reform is unlikely to take place.

The *administration of the court system*, which is different from the management of individual courts and cases, includes the following main aspects:

—The governance of the court system, ie, the definition of the general guidelines and policies of the organisation.
—The administration of the professional status of judges and other judicial officials.
—The general organisation of judicial work proper.
—The administration of judicial resources, including the decision to establish new courts or to rationalise existing ones.

The administration and governance of the court system has become more and more *autonomous* and *specialised*, in the sense that there has been a growing tendency to place it in the hands of the judicial institution itself. In other words, it has been increasingly claimed as a legitimate part of judicial tasks and powers and as a necessary outflow of judicial independence.

[365] Cf Calabresi (1990).

Nowadays, the administration and governance of court systems are based on three models, which we shall call the *judicial*, the *executive* and the *mixed* model. The *judicial model* implies that the administration and governance of the court system has been entrusted, as far as possible, to the judicial institution itself, which possesses its own specialised bodies to this effect. I say 'as far as possible', because the court system may still be dependent on the legislature and the executive for the appointment of judges or certain members of the judicial administrative body. Thus, for example, the federal courts in the United States are administered by the Administrative Office of the United States Courts (USCAO).

The USCAO was established in 1938 to exercise the administrative functions that had hitherto been performed by the Department of Justice.[366] The Judicial Conference of the United States, composed of the chief judge of each of the circuits, one district judge from each of the twelve regional circuits, and the chief judge of the Court of International Trade, and presided by the chief justice of the Supreme Court, is the (non-permanent) body responsible for setting judicial policy.[367] A similar situation prevails in Latin American countries (such as Colombia and Mexico) which have established a permanent Council of the Judiciary with very broad powers, encompassing not only the more traditional areas of judicial career and discipline, but also the whole range of administrative functions required by the court system.[368]

The *executive model* means that a department of the executive branch of government, usually called the Ministry of Justice, is charged with all the relevant governance and administrative functions of the court system. This is the case, for example, in England, where the Lord Chancellor's Department is responsible for all governance and administrative functions related to the courts, including the selection of judges.[369]

Given the trend towards greater autonomy of the judicial branch, however, the executive model seems to be increasingly replaced by the *mixed model*, where the governance and administrative functions of the courts are shared, to varying degrees, by the Ministry of Justice and the judiciary itself. Thus, for example, the Council of the Judiciary in several European countries (France, Spain, Italy, and Portugal) participates, to a greater or lesser extent, in the selection, appointment and advancement of judges, as well as in judicial discipline. Some of these Councils also have other limited powers of an administrative

366 Carp/Stidham (1993: 69 ff.). The Administrative Office is an agency of the Judicial Conference, although its director is appointed by the Chief Justice.

367 The Conference deals with topics such as establishing policy on the temporary assignment of judges within circuits, recommending new judgeships, increasing judicial salaries, developing budgets for court operation, promulgating and revising the various rules of federal civil and criminal procedure, and making recommendations that may take the form of proposed legislation to be ultimately approved by Congress. Carp/Stidham (1993: 69).

368 Fix-Zamudio/Fix-Fierro (1996).

369 See Rozenberg (1995: 7 ff., 52 f.). In 1993 the government announced that the court service in England and Wales would become an executive agency from April 1995, with more delegated authority in operational matters.

nature in a broad sense (regarding the assignment of judges, for example, or the opening hours of the courts), while the bulk of the administration proper of the court system and its resources is still the responsibility of the Ministry of Justice.

No general assessment can be made as to the efficiency of any of these arrangements, since they depend on the particular political and institutional factors prevailing in each country. Nevertheless, it is fairly clear that nowadays the administration of a court system has become a specialised field in the hands of professionals, a large proportion of whom are drawn from the ranks of the judiciary itself.[370] This is regarded as a means of making such specialised administration compatible with the largest possible degree of autonomy and independence of the judiciary.

With respect to this problem of compatibility, it may be argued, as a Spanish lawyer does in a study significantly entitled 'The independence of the judge and judicial disorganisation,'[371] that judicial independence has become such a powerful value, that the executive and legislative branches, even society itself, have been put *sub iudice*, so to speak. The expectation that the judge will control political power has resulted in a paradox: the same organ has to obey and disobey political decisions (the laws) at the same time.[372] In the final analysis, this runs counter to the hierarchy, coordination and predictability in the application of the laws that the *organised* administration of justice requires in order to be effective. A solution to this problem may require a greater separation between the political function of controlling power and the administrative function of adjudicating disputes.[373]

Whether both diagnosis and remedy are correct or not,[374] they make us aware that an independent judiciary and an autonomous administration of the courts also entail costs that society should be willing to pay if it is true that independence and autonomy are values held in such high esteem.

Establishment and Territorial Distribution of the Courts

Establishment or Rationalisation?

A fundamental problem that the administration of a court system must deal with is the appropriate growth rate of the judicial apparatus. It is evident that

[370] In countries where these responsibilities have been entrusted to the Ministry of Justice, many of its officials have been recruited from among judicial officials. The Italian law on the Superior Council of the Judiciary establishes rules for the commissioning of judges to the Ministry (Article 15, in Fix-Zamudio/Fix-Fierro 1996: 148).

[371] Hernández Martín (1991: 191 ff.).

[372] Hernández Martín (1991: 197).

[373] Hernández Martín (1991: 199).

[374] The paradox to which Hernández Martín points (1991) is of a much more fundamental nature. According to Niklas Luhmann (1993: 309 f.) courts are the center of the legal system because they manage and cover the system's fundamental paradox: that the attribution of the values 'legal' and 'illegal' can be *legally* decided over.

growing litigation rates require the establishment of new courts and the appointment of new judges, in order to cope with the increased demand for judicial services, as well as to promote a more or less uniform distribution of litigation across the courts. There is no easy answer to this problem, however, since it becomes necessary to define rigorous criteria according to which new judicial resources should be put into action.

A primary indicator in this respect is *caseloads*. Excessive caseloads certainly justify the establishment of new courts and judgeships. But when can caseloads be considered excessive? How many cases can a judge be reasonably expected to examine and decide in a year? No clear-cut, general answer is possible. There are a number of factors that must be taken into account if a comparison across courts is to be at all meaningful. These include the existence or otherwise of specialised courts, ie, whether the courts have to deal with different types of cases (civil, criminal), the type and degree of complexity of the case (for example, the number of hearings required and the stage at which those cases are normally disposed of), etc.

Thus, *specific, weighted measures* should be determined for each court system and each type of court, measures that indicate *comparable workloads*, rather than caseloads, since a case is a unit that is difficult to define and compare. For example, the Federal Judicial Center in the United States has used time series to determine the average amount of judge time required for disposing of the different types of cases and to construct a weighted caseload per district judge that can be used to determine if and when more judges should be authorised for a certain district.[375] In his study on the US federal courts, Richard Posner constructs an 'effort index' to identify the subject-matter areas 'in which federal courts encounter disproportionately great or disproportionately little difficulty, as proxied by the way in which the case is disposed of'.[376] Thus, for example, the average difficulty of a case in the district court is proxied by the ratio of the percentage of trials in a subject matter-area to the percentage of cases filed in that area: criminal cases have a weight of 3.2. because they are 3.2 times more likely to be tried than the average case.[377]

Another difficult question to answer is what is the *maximum workload* that a judge should handle in a year?[378] On the basis of previous workload standards, minimum, medium and maximum statistical averages, as well as comments made by interested parties, a recent report on the state of the administration of justice in Spain suggests maximum workload figures, ie, those beyond which a judicial organ cannot be expected to perform adequately, for different types of courts. Suggested rates include 850 contentious cases per year for single civil

[375] Posner (1996: 227).

[376] Posner (1996: 228 ff., tables 7.4. and 7.5).

[377] Posner (1996: 230 f.).

[378] Posner (1996: 227) points out that such determination is critical to deciding whether more judges are actually needed, 'yet, in the present state of the science of judicial administration, it is almost purely subjective.'

courts; 850 cases per year for family courts; 650 cases per year for criminal courts; and 350 to 400 cases per judge per year for chambers of collegiate courts.[379]

There are other secondary criteria for determining the need for establishing new courts or judgeships. Such criteria require, for example, that the judiciary be present in the entire territory of a country, especially in faraway places, or that courts be established in localities that are important from a political or social point of view (capital cities or trading centers). This may come, however, at the cost of creating regional disparities in court caseloads or even of having under-worked judges and underutilised capacities.[380]

But even if strict limits to judicial workloads are defined, it will not always be easy to establish new courts or create new judgeships whenever a maximum workload measure is surpassed. Scarce resources are an important constraint to take into account, especially in times of fiscal austerity, but unlimited growth may also involve inconvenience and costs, such as the need to appoint under-trained judges or having to provide for the unification of a greater number of inconsistent decisions. Therefore, *rationalisation* of the existing courts may be sometimes a more viable strategy for obtaining greater processing capacity.

Rationalisation may translate into different measures and changes: a redefinition of the jurisdictional boundaries between different courts; the specialisation of judges and courts; the unification and consolidation of existing courts; and the internal restructuring of the courts, including a different use of existing resources, as well as the introduction of managerial concepts and techniques.

Courts of General or Specialised Jurisdiction

Another important aspect of the organisation of a court system is the decision to establish courts of general (mixed) or specialised jurisdiction. Given the general trend in society towards a greater division of labour and specialisation, it can be confidently said that this fact alone would also mandate a corresponding development in the administration of justice. And indeed, courts and court systems are becoming increasingly specialised, since specialisation is generally acknowledged to have the potential to enhance efficiency, among other possible advantages.[381] Thus, at present, courts are not only specialised in the more traditional fields of the law, such as civil, criminal or labour law, but have also been established in legal areas that are much more reduced and which require considerable legal and technical expertise, such as intellectual property or international trade.

It is important to take into account that significant differences exist in this respect between the two main Western legal traditions. As a rule, European

[379] Consejo General del Poder Judicial (1997: 92 ff.).

[380] Posner (1996: 231) shows, for example, that the District of Columbia Circuit is 'underworked by contemporary standards'.

[381] See Legomsky (1990: 17).

judiciaries are much more specialised than their American (or English) counterparts. For Richard Posner, the main explanation may lie in the degree of responsibility placed on judges relative to lawyers. European judges perform tasks that in common-law systems are performed by specialised lawyers, so they need to be specialists. Furthermore, the existence of career judiciaries places European legal systems in a better position to impart specialised training to judges.[382] We might also add that perhaps the higher degree of rationalisation and codification of substantive and procedural law in Continental legal systems are also more amenable to judicial specialisation.

Court specialisation has the potential to enhance efficiency in the following respects:[383]

—It can be a device for deflecting cases from the general courts at a time when the latter are overburdened.
—It means less time spent by litigators educating the adjudicators on basic aspects of the specialised area and a greater opportunity for focusing on the problems specific to the case.
—It decreases the occasions on which two or more adjudicators will have to deal with the same, or a closely related issue; consequently, the possibility of having inconsistent decisions is also reduced.
—It enables procedure to be tailored to the subject matter.[384]
—It allows steps to be eliminated by replacing both the courts of general jurisdiction and one or more administrative tribunals.
—It can avoid venue disputes as happens in the general courts.

However, specialisation may not only have positive effects on efficiency:[385]

—Jurisdictional disputes with general courts are always possible when a specialised court is assigned exclusive jurisdiction.
—A legal generalist might sometimes be aware of an easy solution in an analogous area of the law.
—It may require long-distance travel for litigators or members of the court.
—Fluctuations in the volume of cases can produce indefinite periods in which the unit is either too busy or too idle.

The general advantages and disadvantages of specialisation, however, do not yet determine when and how the establishment of a specialised court is justified.

382 Posner (1996: 246).

383 Legomsky (1990: 17 f.). See also the case for specialised federal courts of appeals in the United States in Posner (1996: 244 ff.).

384 'When a tribunal must employ a common procedure for differing types of disputes, there is a risk of over-judicialisation in some categories of cases, and too little formality in others.' Legomsky (1990: 17).

385 Legomsky (1990: 18). See also an analysis of other similar objections to specialisation in Posner (1996: 254 ff.). For example: that specialised courts will more readily identify with the goals of a government program, providing less 'insulation' between the coercive powers of the state and their application to the individual citizen; judicial specialisation would reduce 'cross-pollination' of legal ideas; specialisation may generate a mismatch between supply and demand, etc.

There are some general and specific criteria that may help analyse this decision in a concrete situation. As a rule, specialisation is justified if benefits outweigh costs for certain types of cases and stages of decision.[386] More specifically, the following criteria, proposed by Stephen Legomsky, favor specialisation:[387]

—*Mix of law, fact, and discretion*: a predominance of discretionary decisions and fact questions at the initial hearing stage usually favors specialisation.
—*Technical complexity.*
—*Degree of isolation*, characterised by 'discreteness,' ie, legal issues in one area can ordinarily be resolved without reference to the resolution of legal issues in other areas, and 'uniqueness,' that is, analogies to issues outside that area are relatively infrequent.
—*Cohesiveness*: high degree of interrelationship within a single subject-area.
—*Degree of repetition*: high number of similar cases and need for consistency in their resolution.
—*Degree of controversy.*
—*'Clannishness'*: the existence of a closed group of private lawyers, government officials, expert witnesses, etc.[388]
—*Peculiar importance of consistency*, both in terms of equality and law-and-policy issues.
—*Dynamism*: rapidly changing subject matter.
—*Logistics*: volume, time per case, and geographic distribution.
—*Special need for prompt resolution.*
—*Unique procedural needs.*

Of course, there are different ways, and degrees, of introducing specialisation into the administration of justice, which do not necessarily require the creation of a *specialised organisation*. The most obvious form of specialisation is the *functional* specialisation of judges, ie, the full-time performance of adjudicative functions by persons who have been trained as lawyers.[389] The second step toward specialisation is the *subject-matter* specialisation of judges,[390] in other words, the training and concentration in an identifiable area of the law or a specific stage of judicial proceedings,[391] which is usually coupled with the creation of specialised sections, divisions or chambers within a court. Another final step may be the establishment of a specialised court as an independent organisational unit.

386 Legomsky (1990: 20).

387 Legomsky (1990: 22 ff.).

388 We may also add potential parties (plaintiffs and defendants).

389 Posner (1996: 248). It should be recalled that despite the continuing trend towards judicial specialisation, in many parts of the world, a considerable number of judges, usually in the lower courts, are lay persons performing a part-time occupation (for example, magistrates in England).

390 Posner (1996: 248).

391 Some countries have judges who are specialised in certain stages of criminal proceedings, as for example, the stage of investigation or the execution of sentences.

An interesting and, in Germany at least, unusual example of specialisation is provided by the 'international' division of the Hamburg district court, first established in 1971 and now comprising three chambers.[392] It appears the special division was established to counter complaints that judges were not qualified to deal with international cases.[393] The Hamburg international division hears cases where one party is not German or is a company not domiciled in Germany, or cases where foreign or unified international law may apply.[394] In comparison with ordinary domestic matters heard by other chambers of the court, the average amount of claims is higher in the international division while the average duration of cases and number of hearings, with and without taking of evidence, are also slightly higher.[395] This is to be expected, since international cases will presumably be more complex and time-consuming.

If the international cases[396] handled by the Hamburg international division are compared with those heard by ordinary court chambers, one would expect specialisation to demonstrate its advantages. The study's results, however, do not appear to confirm this hypothesis. The mean duration of international cases was 220 days in the international division and 208 in ordinary chambers. The assumption that this was due to a more thorough consideration of cases in the international division (for example, through a higher number of hearings, more taking of evidence, frequency of judgments and settlements, etc.) was not clearly supported by the data.[397] There were, nevertheless, twice as many pleadings requesting the application of foreign law, and less pleadings based on unified law (commercial disputes are sent to the commercial chambers). Whereas 16 per cent of judgments in the international section were based on foreign law, this was true of only 6 per cent of judgments rendered by ordinary chambers. The reverse situation was observed as regards judgments based on unified law.[398]

The study concludes that 80 per cent of international cases were handled as if they were ordinary cases. The remaining 20 per cent were dealt with more thoroughly,

> taking foreign law more seriously, encouraging attorneys not to grasp the first opportunity of a choice of (German) law, and even—in very exceptional cases—taking evidence in a foreign country.[399]

Nonetheless, 'the additional effort of judges is not too impressive: in international matters they only had to write eight judgments based on foreign or unified law in 1988'.[400]

[392] Gessner (1996b: 150 f., 181–5).
[393] Gessner (1996b: 181 f.).
[394] Gessner (1996b: 182).
[395] Gessner (1996b: 183).
[396] The definition of an international case is narrower here, comprising only those cases where one of the parties does not reside in Germany.
[397] Gessner (1996b: 183).
[398] Gessner (1996b: 184).
[399] Gessner (1996b: 185).
[400] Gessner (1996b: 185).

Territorial Distribution

The territorial distribution of courts has several interesting aspects. The sociological dimension refers to the social factors that condition a particular judicial map. The political dimension inquires about the connections between the courts and the state apparatus and authority.[401] However, it has also an efficiency component, which concerns the uniform distribution of levels of litigation in a certain territory and the costs of access of the population to the courts generated by geographical distance. In other words: an efficient territorial distribution of the courts seeks to minimise the costs resulting from uneven levels of litigation in a certain jurisdiction and from the physical distance that litigants have to cover in order to have access to them.[402]

Is it possible to determine an efficient territorial distribution of courts and, if so, with what methodology? A study on this particular issue was carried out in Chile as part of a larger project for the modernisation of the courts.[403] In the seventies, a new territorial division was established in Chile, and, as a result, the Executive and the Judiciary created a committee responsible for evaluating the changes the court system had to undergo to adjust to the new territorial organisation. Among other proposals, the committee produced a report recommending the establishment of 57 new courts and suggesting that, as far as possible, the territorial jurisdiction of the courts should coincide with the existing territorial divisions for the purposes of internal governance and administration. However, the goal of determining the number and territories of the courts according to objective criteria was not fully accomplished.[404] This was the purpose of the study summarised here.

The study first notes that between 1980 and 1989, changes in the spatial distribution of ordinary courts proceeded very slowly, and were not based on any guiding criteria or explicit policy. In fact, courts were preferably established in locations where one or several courts already existed, with the result that in 1989, one or more courts were already located in 36 per cent of municipalities.[405] The methodology proposed for assessing the efficiency of the territorial distribution of courts is objective, in so far as it operates purely on the basis of quantitative data. This allows one to measure the extent to which the principles of equity and efficiency have been respected. The end result indicates the degree to which the processing capacity of the court concerned is being used, as well as the distance at which the least favoured inhabitant is to be found.[406] Where the constraints imposed by this methodology for the establishment of courts are

[401] See, for example, Commaille (1990; 1999).
[402] All these dimensions have a justice component: access, and therefore, representativeness of issues handled and resolved.
[403] Vrsalovic Mihoevic (1991).
[404] Vrsalovic Mihoevic (1991: 181).
[405] Vrsalovic Mihoevic (1991: 188, 190).
[406] Vrsalovic Mihoevic (1991: 202).

not respected, it is possible to measure the extent to which it deviates from the efficiency and equity criteria defined by the model.[407]

The model works with some fairly simple data. It calculates the average number of cases handled by the courts over several years ('service rate'). It then produces a 'base population unit,' defined as the number of persons who generate a number of cases that can be efficiently handled by a court.[408] To calculate this unit, the service rate is divided by the average per capita and per year number of cases filed before the courts during a certain period. As a base territorial unit, the study includes the possibility of grouping together municipalities from the same region.[409]

This methodology was then applied to a single region.[410] The calculations indicated the proposed number of courts for each group of municipalities and the percentage of utilised capacity for each court. In comparison with the existing situation, the results obtained recommended an increase of six courts and a new arrangement of their territorial jurisdiction on the basis of groups of municipalities.

The Recruitment of Judges

The recruitment of judges is a topic of central importance for any theoretical examination of the role played by courts in contemporary society. It is assumed that the method of selection and appointment, as well as the previous professional experience or the specialised training of a candidate to a judicial post, largely guarantee that the judiciary will also behave independently from the other branches of government and social forces, and in loyalty towards the letter and the spirit of the law.

Both legal traditions—ie, civil and common law—have developed fairly elaborate mechanisms and procedures for ensuring, as far as possible, that these two goals are accomplished. Nevertheless, these mechanisms and procedures are somewhat paradoxical. On the one hand, they purport to select the most appropriate candidates from the point of view of their professional expertise and capacity, ie, to act free from political influences. On the other hand, a certain degree of political control is introduced or tolerated within the selection or appointment process, to the extent that courts exercise real power and social influence which needs to be checked somehow. Political elements are usually more visible in the selection and appointment of judges in the Anglo-American legal tradition, but they also exist in countries that have instituted a professional judicial career. It should be remembered that even where this selection and

[407] Vrsalovic Mihoevic (1991: 203).
[408] Vrsalovic Mihoevic (1991: 205).
[409] Vrsalovic Mihoevic (1991: 207).
[410] Vrsalovic Mihoevic (1991: 209 ff.): the area chosen is Region V, Valparaíso, the third most populated in the country.

appointment process is in the hands of an autonomous body, like the Council of the Judiciary, the composition of this organisation itself is partly the product of political interests and negotiations.[411]

From the point of view of efficiency, the recruitment process of judges is interesting in two interrelated respects. First, to the extent that professionally qualified judges are better able to produce socially efficient outcomes in their decisions than non-qualified judges, which is a hypothesis subject to some theoretical dispute but more or less unquestioned in practice. Secondly, to the extent that the process itself is costly and may be more or less adequate from the perspective of the incentives it provides for selecting the best candidates.

There are many interesting studies on the selection and appointment process of judges, particularly from a political point of view. However, there appear to be far fewer studies that examine this problem from the point of view of *organisational efficiency*. An outstanding example of this latter perspective is a study on the recruitment process of Italian judges, published in the late 1960s.[412] Although the selection process of Italian judges seems to have changed greatly since then, we shall nevertheless summarise the most important conclusions of this study, on account of the intrinsic interest of some of the central aspects it describes.

The author of the study noted that, at the time, the Italian administration of justice did not regard the recruitment process as an efficiency problem, ie, it did not consider it from the perspective of the ratio between the resources employed and the units produced. It did not, and actually could not, pose questions such as the following: what is the overall cost of all recruitment operations? What is the cost of selecting each judge that enters office? In what way would it be possible to achieve the same results at a lower cost, by restructuring the selection process?[413]

The study examines the delay between the time when the need to occupy a judgeship arises, and the point when the new judges effectively begin to perform their functions. This time is divided into two periods: the first period, of varying duration, lasts from the moment that a vacancy is produced to the appointment of new judges through an examination ('*concorso*', or contest) of the candidates; the second period lasts from the moment of appointment to the actual assumption of official duties, as the law required a minimum period of practice prior to the actual performance of judicial duties. The first period alone could last between *two* and *three years*![414]

The organisations responsible for the administration of justice had identified several causes for the lack of effectiveness of the recruitment process. After

[411] For a fascinating case study, on Japan and the United States, which links judicial independence to political elections, and specifically, to the long-term expectations of the governing party, and less to appointment procedures and performance evaluations, see Ramseyer (1994).

[412] Di Federico (1968).

[413] Di Federico (1968: 100 f.).

[414] Di Federico (1968: 102).

1950, fourteen of the nineteen examinations carried out had failed to select a sufficient number of candidates to occupy the outstanding vacancies. The bodies responsible for carrying out the examination considered that the legal training of the candidates, including the winners themselves, was not adequate and failed to meet the expectations and needs of the courts. The official diagnosis attributed this, as well as the decreasing participation in the examinations, to the diminishing attractiveness of the initial salary and of the judicial career as a whole; to the diminishing number of law graduates and the increase in more attractive positions in the labour market, and the delay between the examination and earning the first salary.[415] Therefore, certain steps were taken to shorten the time required by the recruitment process, for example, by admitting candidates just after finishing law school or by postponing the consideration of the candidates' personal and professional background after the written tests.[416] Likewise, it was proposed that new judges be given a much higher salary and more attractive career incentives.[417]

The study analyses some of these conclusions and faults them for their lack of empirical foundation. It does not find that the number of law students had been diminishing or that the judicial institution had to select its new members from second-rate graduates.[418] On the contrary, the administration of justice was still able to recruit its new members from among students who had finished law school with the highest grades. A different problem altogether was that law school did not provide the necessary training for also obtaining the highest grades in an examination.[419] For this reason, after finishing law school, candidates to an examination had to prepare for the written tests for several months.

The study concluded that the quantitative and qualitative deficiencies of the recruitment process were due to the fact that supply by the labour market was not sufficiently qualified to satisfy the minimum knowledge requirements that the administration of justice considered necessary for participating in the practical training stage prior to becoming a judge. Therefore, the solution was to lower admission standards and to provide appropriate courses for adjusting the knowledge and abilities possessed by the young recruits to the needs of the recruiting institution.[420]

415 Di Federico (1968: 104 ff.).

416 Di Federico (1968: 120 ff.).

417 Di Federico (1968: 124).

418 Di Federico (1968: 107 ff.).

419 In this respect, the correspondence between law school grades and examination grades is inverted: a large percentage of participants obtain the highest university degrees and the lowest grades in the examination. Di Federico (1968: 117).

420 Di Federico (1968: 122 f.).

MANAGEMENT

This section briefly examines the management perspective as it applies to the courts as organisations. As already stated, management concerns the control of behaviour within organisations. In the realm of the courts, management comprises the whole range of organisational tasks and activities designed to enhance quantity and quality in the provision of services by the courts. A managerial perspective in the study of the courts also has the advantage of allowing comparisons with management problems faced by other public and private organisations.[421]

A distinction will be made between court management and case management. Generally speaking, case management can be seen as a part of court management. However, the distinction is useful not only because both concepts may concern different problems and solutions, but also because they display a varying degree of relevance in the different legal traditions.

Reference will be made to studies and experiences that do not merely attempt to explain the operation of the courts from a general organisational point of view, as shown above, but which explicitly consider the need, and the possibility, of introducing an active managerial perspective for solving some of the problems that affect court operation.

Court Management

'Court management' can be said to have two interrelated meanings: on the one hand, and according to the concept proposed above, it generally refers to the control of behaviour within the organisations called courts, or, in somewhat different terms, it refers to a decentralised form of administration of the court system, since each individual court must perform internal organisational and administrative tasks that cannot be left entirely up to a centralised body to decide. Hence, a central problem of court management lies in the appropriate balance that must be found between a centralised administration and the decentralised organisational and administrative autonomy that an individual court must enjoy in order to operate satisfactorily, as well as in the appropriate coordination that should exist between both organisational levels.[422]

A second, more restricted meaning of 'court management' is connected to the concepts of efficiency and effectiveness in the context of judicial reform and modernisation policies, which in turn are conditioned by a more demanding,

[421] Saari (1982: 4): court management is interdisciplinary, 'a fact not too different from business-management or other government-management fields.'

[422] This point is explicitly emphasised by Ackermann/Bastard (1993b) with respect to the problem of innovations in the courts.

uncertain social environment.[423] From this point of view, the management of court organisations is subjected to a redefinition which comprises a multiplicity of changes: the renewal of human and material resources; the enhancement of service structures and working methods; the implementation of new judicial procedures and the introduction of management and evaluation tools.[424] Thus, management modalities become more conscious, more goal-oriented and more explicit.[425] In other words: when the need for rationalisation and modernisation of the courts becomes a publicly perceived problem and a motivation for explicit judicial policies, then court management can be seen as a distinctive reform movement and, consequently, as a reason for judicial studies and research.

Nowhere is the latter aspect more visible than in the United States, where court management has generated a distinctive movement, with its own scholars, institutions, conferences and professionals.[426] Although court management in this sense is a relatively recent phenomenon, concern with 'judicial administration' dates back at least to the beginning of the twentieth century, as attested by Roscoe Pound's famous 1906 speech on 'The Causes of Popular Dissatisfaction with the Administration of Justice.' Reformers like Pound and Taft advocated higher degrees of efficiency, integration, unification, and coordination in the federal judicial system through changes in the organisation of the courts and the development of auxiliary agencies within the judicial branch.[427] Their efforts bore important fruit in the 1920s and 1930s.[428]

In 1967, court management and administration received a further boost with the creation of the Federal Judicial Center, a judicial agency which, among other tasks, is charged with making recommendations to improve the administration and management of US federal courts.[429] Nowadays, professional court managers are a common feature of American courts. Quite aside from the occasional debate on whether or not they actually constitute a profession, as well as the extent to which they are needed,[430] they certainly perform a variety of roles in managing the operational functions of courts in caseflow, personnel, finance, organisation, and records.[431] In order to be successful in this endeavor, a series of issues have to be sorted out first, such as the appropriate training for court managers, their role as court leaders and their relationship to the judges, etc.[432]

[423] Cf Saari (1982: 13)

[424] Ackermann/Bastard (1993b: 9).

[425] Ackermann/Bastard (1993b: 111).

[426] See, for example, Friesen/Gallas/Gallas (1971), Saari (1982), Boyum/Hudzik (1991) and the papers in this special issue of the *Justice System Journal* on court management. From a Continental perspective, Röhl (1993b).

[427] Carp/Stidham (1993: 67).

[428] Carp/Stidham (1993: 68).

[429] Carp/Stidham (1993: 71 f.).

[430] Saari (1982: 17): for example, courts 'are relatively unaware of human factors of management unless a court manager is contributing toward increased sensitivity of such factors to enhance organisational climate.'

[431] Saari (1982: chap. 4).

[432] *Justice System Journal* (1991), special issue on court management.

In civil-law countries, the managerial perspective is beginning to take hold, as demonstrated by a few studies that have adopted this orientation.[433] On the other hand, it is also true that the court management movement may not have the same profile here as in common-law countries. Differences in organisation and procedure give court administration and management in common-law jurisdictions a wider margin for development. Many aspects of organisation and procedure that can be determined by the individual court in common-law jurisdictions are usually incorporated into procedural codes and the organic laws of the courts in civil-law jurisdictions.[434] Despite this important difference, court management becomes a significant operational tool and a useful intellectual perspective for the successful tackling of similar problems faced by courts across countries and legal traditions.

Courts as Service Organisations

From a managerial perspective (and from a broad economic point of view), courts are *service providers*. The main service is conflict resolution under known standards for resolution,[435] with management being a tool for the rational application of resources that a service orientation requires. The service perspective has certain implications. It focuses on aspects such as the nature of demand, the cost of the service relative to equivalent services, the conditions under which it is delivered, quality as it relates to price, the needs and expectations of clients, and so on. Such a service is also assumed to be provided in a constantly improved manner.

For this reason, courts and other organisations concerned with judicial policy have begun to develop quality standards and benchmarks for evaluating the performance of courts. Thus, for example, the Centre for Court Policy and Administration of the University of Wollongong, Australia, following similar efforts and experiences in the United States and other countries, developed a project on 'client services in the local courts,' on behalf of the New South Wales Local Courts and in cooperation with them.[436]

The evaluation was carried out on the basis of five principles, each of which was developed through several standards, which in turn gave rise to a number of benchmarks to indicate conformity with each standard.[437] The five principles were:[438]

433 For example: Ackermann/Bastard (1993b) and the German studies on the 'Structural Analysis of the Administration of Justice'. For a much earlier statement, see Zwiesele/Bender (1972).

434 Röhl (1993b: 16).

435 Saari (1982: 4).

436 Condie *et al.* (1996a and b) and Mohr *et al.* (1997).

437 Mohr *et al.* (1997: 167) point out that the research team was encouraged by its court-based partners to prefer practical performance measures over elaborate or technical measures. 'This approach will help to promote the adoption of standards by the courts as a useful working tool.'

438 First listed in this form by the US National Center for State Courts in 1990. Mohr *et al.* (1997: 162).

—Access to justice.
—Expedition and timeliness.
—Equality, fairness and integrity.
—Independence and accountability.
—Public trust and confidence.

The second principle, for instance ('expedition and timeliness') is further defined by the following standards:[439]

—*Caseflow management*: the court complies with the established guidelines for timely case processing while, at the same time, keeping up with the incoming caseload.
—*Scheduling*: the court's procedures and processes ensure that client attendance at court involves minimal inconvenience.
—*Registry client service*: the Registry responds to telephone and personal attendance promptly, and responds to requests for information and other services within a reasonable period of time which assures their effective use.

The standard related to scheduling generates, in turn, the following benchmarks:[440]

—Clients are required to attend no more than three hearings in order to finalise their matter.
—Clients are not required to wait more than two hours after their scheduled appointment before they are actually attended to by the court.
—Waiting times are equitable, so that unrepresented parties are not disadvantaged by reason of the lack of representation.

It may be argued that most of these standards and benchmarks fail to address the substance or the quality of dispute resolution itself,[441] as if the service provided were just the package rather than the contents. However, such criticism misses the mark, because, first, it is not their purpose, and secondly, the substance and quality of dispute resolution are guaranteed by other means. Nevertheless, it should be remembered that efficiency is a component of justice.

Conflict resolution is not only a service, but also a *public service*, provided by public institutions under quasi-monopolistic conditions with the aim of satisfying a need of general interest.[442] This requires that the provision of such a service follow certain principles and respect certain standards, such as the principles of 'equality', 'free provision', 'judicial neutrality', and 'continuity of service'.[443] *Equality* means the possibility for any citizen to have access to the

[439] Condie *et al.* (1996a: 10 f.).
[440] Condie *et al.* (1996a: 10 f.).
[441] For a *discussion on the quality of dispute resolution, see the special issue of the Denver University Law Review*, vol 66, no 3 (1989), especially the paper by Bush (1989).
[442] Cf Vincent *et al.* (1996: 128) and Ministère de la Justice (1989).
[443] Vincent *et al.* (1996: 128 ff.).

same courts for the resolution of their disputes under the same substantive and procedural rules.[444] The principle of *free provision* is not always formally guaranteed by all legal systems, but dispute resolution by the courts is usually heavily subsidised by the state, in the sense that citizens have to pay very low or symbolic fees for obtaining access to the courts (other expenses, such as attorney's fees, are usually not subsidised). *Judicial neutrality* supplements the principle of equality in a particular case, since the judge must resolve any dispute from a position of fairness and impartiality that must not be to the disadvantage of any of the parties. Finally, *continuity of service* means that, with a few, limited exceptions, this public service is available at all times.

The notion that justice is a service that can be bought and sold like any other commodity[445] may be evident and even unavoidable if we consider that any organised apparatus demands scarce resources to operate and that such resources always have alternative uses that have to be justified in terms of efficiency.[446] However, this is still not universally accepted. It is resisted, for example, by those who believe that adjudication is a necessary evil at best, not an everyday type of service, perhaps because such a view may encourage litigation by making it as morally acceptable as any other normal economic transaction.[447] Nor is it wholly accepted by those who consider a service perspective, together with its economic consequences, as 'technocratic' and 'undemocratic.'[448] Finally, it does not seem to be the prevailing mentality among those charged with providing such service, nor among those supposedly benefited by it, as shown by certain studies on the German courts, significantly carried out by private consulting firms.[449]

Thus, for example, a comparative organisational investigation of the German administrative and fiscal courts points out that the citizen has a reduced sense of the court as a modern service-providing enterprise and that 'human resources' is an alien word for the justice administration itself.[450] In addition to other problems related to the organisation of judicial work, it found that material infrastructure, for example, was not adequate for motivating the personnel and for presenting the courts as important institutions to the public seeking justice.[451] Similarly, another study on the organisation of the German collegiate courts of first instance noted the deficient 'service readiness' of these courts due to the lack of features such as adequate service at the entrance, user-friendly opening hours, hearing rooms in good condition, and a cafeteria or snack bar.[452]

[444] Vincent *et al.* (1996: 130).
[445] Cf Landes/Posner (1979).
[446] See Hazard, Jr. (1965) and Fix-Fierro (1995a: 69 ff.).
[447] See, for example, Carrington (1979).
[448] See Heydebrand/Seron (1990).
[449] See, for example, WIBERA (1991) and Koetz *et al.* (1992; 1993).
[450] WIBERA (1991: 13).
[451] WIBERA (1991: 14).
[452] Koetz *et al.* (1993).

Management Strategies and Styles

Court management strategies and styles vary widely across courts, depending on many factors, such as the practical constraints that affect judicial work locally; the acceptance of conscious management; the personality of chief officials and the work relationship they establish with their subordinates and other organisations. The assumptions or the organisational model underlying the particular management options adopted are also relevant.[453]

Thus, the division of labour within the court may require changes not only for the purpose of achieving greater effectiveness in the disposition of cases, but also to create more favorable conditions for the reproduction of judicial work, such as, for example, a reduction in the costs of coordination; the introduction of motivational incentives for judicial personnel; or by enhancing a court's capacity for confronting and solving 'crises.'

Several organisational studies on the courts deal with issues similar to those mentioned above. This is true, for example, of the 'disintegration' model that characterises the division of labour in German courts, and the recommendation to turn it into more of a 'partial integration' model. This model, while maintaining the existing separation between business office and secretariat, would introduce simple organisational measures for increasing the integration of tasks and ensuring a better judicial workflow: spatial concentration; no further specialisation in the separation between both offices; transportation of files by employees themselves, etc.[454]

Another study, published in the early 1980s, sought to contribute to the 'humanisation' of court work, and for this purpose, it assessed the experimental introduction of a 'group business office' ('*Gruppengeschäftsstelle*') at a lower court in the northern German city of Hamburg.[455] Instead of a high degree of centralisation and specialisation of labour, which confers on the 'processing' organisation a predominance over other expectations, such as those of judges and clients, the business office is to be organised around the concept of decentralised, mixed, independent, and self-coordinating workgroups. Such an organ-

[453] See, for example, Dahlin (1986: 1 ff.), who compares two models of court management: a traditional model, based on the concept of a hierarchical and centrally directed system, and an alternative model. The traditional model would respond to organisational and managerial assumptions generally consistent with the classical, machine or closed models of general organisation theory. The alternative model, developed by the Institute for Court Management, established in 1970, is the consequence of several considerations: judicial administration is based on more than functional requirements, the special normative role of courts in American history, the ambiguity in judicial goals, and the need for judicial independence. Therefore, it can be concluded that courts require a strong internal administrative capacity, but not a hierarchical one. Instead, a decentralised mode of organisation and a consultative, collegial model of management is to be preferred. In an ambiguous world, solutions to problems are likely to be partial and dated. Therefore, organisational design and management techniques should be more oriented towards requirements for learning and evolution, than certainty and control, and diversification and experimentation, rather than standardised practices, may often be needed at local levels (42 f.).

[454] Koetz *et al.* (1993: 37 ff.).

[455] Bauer *et al.* (1983).

isational principle also requires more time and participation from all persons involved in the formulation and acceptance of coordinating rules. A similar demand is placed on the judges, who must not only fit in with the processing organisation of the business office, but also with the demands of their colleagues.[456]

Both the project team and an external research group evaluated the experimental design.[457] The project team found that participants positively evaluated aspects such as 'increased performance,'[458] 'enhancement of working conditions' and 'enhancement of collaboration.' As regards the aspect of efficiency, not only was court performance enhanced in objective terms (by a reduction in processing time, for example), but the subjective perception of this change by participants also translated into a higher degree of personal satisfaction together with a general improvement in the quality of judicial work.[459]

The external research group, whose task it was to evaluate the extent to which the original goals of the project had been accomplished rather than carrying out research of their own, agreed with the project team that there had been more rationalisation, enhanced service provision, and work had been humanised in comparison with the previous organisation. However, the original aims of the project had not been achieved in several respects.[460] The research group indicated a series of difficulties and consequences associated with the experimental introduction of a group business office.

The first difficulty arose from the need to recruit participants for the experiment on a more or less voluntary basis. Although there was a general consensus on the deficiencies of the existing organisation, willingness to participate decreased to the extent that existing routines and power positions were called into question.[461] This made it necessary to 'negotiate' with potential participants and to make 'concessions' as to their future position and tasks, at the price of weakening the experimental model considerably.[462] Interestingly, bargaining and criticism of the proposed model ceased with the introduction of office technology. Technology created a new reality and introduced new constraints to which participants had to adapt.[463] The research group concluded that the experiment had demonstrated the compatibility of decentralisation and de-specialisation with the introduction of advanced office technology.[464]

[456] Bauer *et al.* (1983: 15).

[457] Bauer *et al.* (1983: 170 ff., 191 ff.).

[458] Bauer *et al.* (1983: 219) mention, for example, that processing time for workgroups in the civil section was measurably and drastically reduced, with a reduction of between four and six weeks. This means a reduction of about 40% for cases with a disposition time of less than three months, accounting for approximately 65% of all proceedings.

[459] Bauer *et al.* (1983: 187 ff.).

[460] Bauer *et al.* (1983: 191).

[461] Bauer *et al.* (1983: 192 ff.).

[462] Bauer *et al.* (1983: 197 ff.).

[463] Bauer *et al.* (1983: 200 f.).

[464] Bauer *et al.* (1983: 203 f.).

These two studies suggest that an unhealthy work atmosphere and the excessive fragmentation of tasks generate costs that will not be alleviated through further specialisation, but through a different means of integrating and coordinating tasks. In other words: a new type of management and coordination of a more horizontal nature is called for, and its introduction is not necessarily easy or lacking costs of its own (for example, higher salaries). Likewise, two other studies show the need for courts to exercise a firm but flexible degree of internal and external control in order to solve, or effectively prevent, the workload crises that invariably arise.

The first study, a French study on the organisation of eight '*tribunaux de grande instance*' to which we referred earlier,[465] compares the functioning of two courts from the point of view of their effectiveness.[466] Both courts operate on the basis of autonomous working units or 'cells' with a low level of interaction between them. One of the courts appears to perform better and to be more effective. This court is described as a 'well-oiled machine,' in which officials are extremely concerned with the efficient running of their units and exercise a considerable level of control. The other court is far less concerned with effectiveness and control. The authors believe that this slight but significant difference may affect the courts' ability to handle changes, such as the replacement of their responsible officials or the introduction of new conceps of work organisation. The 'more effective' court may experience more adaptation problems and display a greater potential for conflict, as its members may be unable to see the need to change when everything is running so well. Conversely, the other court may be better able to adjust at the human level through agreement and compromise,[467] while the 'more effective' court will probably be less able to cope with sudden workload crises, since it is already operating at full capacity.

The second study, from England, analyses the 'organisational culture' in magistrates' courts in relation to the scheduling of court appearances.[468] Such appearances pose problems since most hearings do not proceed as expected. Consequently, courts are seldom able to adhere to a set timetable and trials frequently collapse.[469] The aim of the study was therefore to identify aspects of good scheduling practice and factors that might account for variations in performance. Although the various scheduling techniques employed by the courts were certainly of interest in this respect, the study focuses on the less tangible aspects of organisational culture, on the assumption that they might prove to be a more significant element.[470]

[465] Ackermann/Bastard (1993b).
[466] Ackermann/Bastard (1993b: 51–68).
[467] Ackermann/Bastard (1993b: 68).
[468] Raine/Willson (1993).
[469] Raine/Willson (1993: 237).
[470] Raine/Willson (1993: 239).

Eight magistrates' court areas were selected and their organisational cultures evaluated on the basis of interviews. The framework for comparing the culture of the selected courts was defined by two dimensions:[471]

—The extent to which the court took the lead and controlled the work that passed through it (control).
—The extent to which the court actively invested in strategy, both internally and externally (strategy).

These two dimensions yielded four possible combinations:

—*Higher control/higher investment in strategy*: these were low-delay courts, where the individual victim, witness and defendant took precedence over the comfort of professionals; the administration of the court is visible, monitored and accountable (*accountability culture*).
—*Lower control/higher investment in strategy*: these courts worked smoothly and efficiently; all practitioners accommodated each other (*negotiating culture*).
—*Lower control/lower investment in strategy*: the court does not hold the other parties accountable; negotiation is not an effective course of action, since there appears little that the court can offer or deny the other parties (*coping culture*).
—*Higher control/lower investment in strategy*: no court operated on the basis of such a culture, which could be called *whimsical dictatorship*.

The study concluded that courts

> which place emphasis on strategic negotiation with professional users appear to be more efficient in their use of court time and hear more trials in full and dispose of more trial cases on the day they are listed: but unless this is backed by high 'control' they may well have worse delay.[472]

On the other hand, courts that take control and demand that professional users be accountable to the court and to the community 'will usually have a lower delay but are likely to suffer at least a medium level of trial collapses. . .'[473]

Case Management

Why Case Management?

Case management may be defined as the conscious intervention of court officials in the treatment of *individual cases*, through various techniques, with the purpose of disposing of them in a more speedy, just, and inexpensive manner. As an

[471] Raine/Willson (1993: 245 ff.).
[472] Raine/Willson (1993: 250).
[473] Raine/Willson (1993: 250).

American *Litigation Management Manual* puts it: 'Case management must be directed at tailoring dispute resolution procedures and techniques to the available resources and the needs of the case.'[474] Thus, it is assumed that, because cases are different, they will require different degrees and forms of managerial intervention: (management) choices will be

> influenced by such factors as the case's magnitude, complexity, and novelty and the ability, tactics, and attitudes of the attorneys, and they will be guided by local rules, orders and practice, the district's expense and delay reduction plan, circuit law, and the judge's informed discretion.[475]

In this respect, case management has developed in, and is a distinctive feature of, common-law, especially American jurisdictions.[476] Case management responds to the need to dispose efficiently of rising caseloads, incorporating procedural innovations and articulating new rights and remedies.[477] The central idea behind case management is that efficiency is promoted less by changes in jurisdiction and procedural reforms than by court monitoring and control measures on the behaviour of all participants.[478] Consequently, case management has brought about a change in the classic role of the common-law judge, from that of a detached participant to playing a critical role in shaping litigation and influencing results, both before and after trial. Trial judges have thus become mediators, negotiators and planners, a shift that has prompted a great deal of criticism.[479]

One implication of the increased level of court control over litigation is a decrease in the level of control exercised by the litigants and their attorneys. Adversary litigation is not eliminated, but subjected to control and even discouraged if it entails more costs than benefits.[480] By contrast, in civil-law jurisdictions there seems to be less need, and therefore potential, for case management. Even in private law litigation, the civilian judge has traditionally exercised a greater degree of control, especially over the gathering of evidence. On the other hand, as mentioned earlier, the civilian judge enjoys much less discretion in shaping procedure on the basis of local needs. Of course, this does

[474] Federal Judicial Center (1992: 2).

[475] Federal Judicial Center (1992: 3).

[476] On the origins and development of case management in the United States see Scott (1995) and Marcus (1995). A central recommendation in the Lord Chancellor's 1995 report (*Access to Justice*) on civil justice in England and Wales is the adoption of case management, ie, a transfer of responsibility for the management of civil litigation from litigants and their advisers to the courts. Marcus (1995: 235) argues that case management might be frustrated in England because of differences between the English and American legal systems.

[477] Resnik (1982: 391).

[478] Scott (1995: 4 f.), Resnik (1982: 395).

[479] Resnik (1982: 377, 379).

[480] Federal Judicial Center (1992: 3): 'Taking management seriously as a judicial responsibility does not mean taking the case away from the attorneys. What it means is giving direction to the litigating activity of attorneys, fixing bounds, and applying means of control as necessary.'

not mean that certain case management techniques cannot be introduced into civil-law jurisdictions, such as for the scheduling of hearings.[481]

The scope of case management techniques is extremely broad. It includes the selection of the appropriate calendar[482] and scheduling systems,[483] as well as techniques for encouraging settlement; the introduction of computer-based management programmes; the employment of auxiliary court officials such as 'special masters' and 'magistrate judges,' charged with preparing and overseeing certain procedural stages and with deciding certain minor issues; the use of procedural devices such as the pre-trial conferences, and the disposition of cases through 'mini-trials', summary judgments and ADR. Each and every one of the various procedural stages a case goes through has its own appropriate techniques, as do certain special types of matters.[484]

Two main types of criticisms have been levelled at case management. The first is of a more philosophical and systemic nature, ie, that case management is a threat to the judge's impartiality, thereby promoting the erosion of traditional due process safeguards, and that by enhancing the power of judges, it tends to undermine traditional constraints on the use of that power.[485]

> Seduced by controlled calendars, disposition statistics, and other trappings of the efficiency era and the high-tech age, managerial judges are changing the nature of their work . . . Judges alone are supposed to rule without concern for the interests of particular constituencies. Judges alone are required to act with deliberation—a steady, slow, unhurried task.[486]

481 For an example of the differences in court output patterns that distinctive local rules can produce, see Miller *et al.* (1971), who compared the consequences of local rules governing pretrial procedures, schedules of operation, setting methods, jury and non-jury interaction, use of visiting judges, and docketing techniques in four Texan courts.

482 For example, a master vs. an individual calendar. A master calendar means that case assignment is centrally controlled and that cases may be assigned to different judges at different procedural stages. An individual calendar means that one judge is responsible for an individual case during its entire life in court. The relative efficiency of both systems was frequently discussed in the late 1960s and early 1970s. For an evaluation of both calendar systems, see Luskin (1988–9).

483 For an exploration of the insights and techniques that management science can offer for the optimal use of time and the scheduling of procedural stages, see Nagel (1986) and Nagel *et al.* (1978). For example, *optimum sequencing* means that delay can be reduced by the order in which cases are heard, even if there is no reduction in arrivals, no acceleration in the servicing time per case, and no increase in judge time. Optimum sequencing, however, requires statistical prediction analysis for the different set of cases as to time consumed. Another type of sequencing is the sequencing of stages within cases, rather than the sequencing of cases. Nagel *et al.* (1978: 132). Obviously, techniques recommended by management science may not always be implemented if they collide with procedural and justice requirements. As Ryan (1978: 144 ff.) rightly points out: optimum sequencing 'requires a preference, or value judgment, that cases should not necessarily be heard in the order in which they enter the system.' Cases requiring longer trial times are penalised and while this 'may be desirable practice from a utilitarian philosophy', it may not be 'from other political or philosophical perspectives' (146).

484 See Federal Judicial Center (1992).

485 Resnik (1982: 424 ff.).

486 Resnik (1982: 445).

The other line of criticism raises doubts about the effectiveness of case management in achieving its avowed purposes. While it is recognised that case management has won support among the judiciary, as well as from attorneys and academics,[487] and while some of its successes are readily acknowledged,[488] it is still claimed that there is no unequivocal and compelling empirical evidence that case management reduces cost litigation and delay or that it is sufficient to prevent and reduce delay.[489]

Managing to Reduce Delay

Several studies have attempted to answer the question of whether, and under what conditions, case management contributes to delay reduction.

A study sponsored by the National Center for State Courts and the National Conference of Metropolitan Courts in the United States in the late 1970s,[490] tested various types of case management in eight courts to determine which techniques were successful, if at all. The participating jurisdictions yielded mixed results. It was thought that the reasons for the varying levels of achievement might be related to the various case management techniques implemented,[491] although environmental, organisational and attitudinal differences among the sites were also involved.[492] Thus, the study attempted to identify the factors, other than specific management techniques, that seemed to influence and define limitations on the success of a delay reduction programme. The following were identified as prerequisites for successful change:[493]

—Commitment to and organisation of support for change.
—The acceptance of the court's responsibility for the pace of litigation;
—Sufficient time for implementation.
—Informed judges and bar involvement.

Another study also sought to identify the factors that had contributed, to varying degrees, to the successful introduction of delay reduction programmes in criminal cases in four courts. Such factors were the following:[494]

487 Marcus (1995: 232 f.).

488 Resnik (1982: 415 ff.) concedes that case management may have contributed to delay reduction in the courts and also praises other secondary successes, such as the wealth of new information about the federal courts it has produced, since managerial judging depends on information about case processing, and the increase in attorney accountability, since attorneys now have a need to prepare and manage clients' cases more rapidly and efficiently. See also Marcus (1995: 233).

489 Marcus (1995: 233 f.) and Resnik (1982: 380, 417 ff.). See also Steelman (1997).

490 Sipes *et al.* (1980).

491 Sipes *et al.* (1980: 41 ff.). The reports of experiments and techniques in judicial management in individual courts are given in the appendices.

492 Sipes *et al.* (1980: 25).

493 Sipes *et al.* (1980: 25 ff.).

494 Ryan *et al.* (1981: 70 ff.).

—Lack of opposition.
—Nucleus of supportive local actors.
—Incremental changes.
—Coercion/persuasion from higher courts.
—Improved communication among 'sponsoring organisations'.
—Additional resources.
—Compatibility with local socio-legal culture.
—Incentives for the participants.

A study which analysed the causes of delay in the Los Angeles Superior Court—one of the largest trial courts and one with the most delays—and evaluated the effectiveness and cost of various strategies for reducing delay, proposed a series of recommendations aimed at strengthening case management, on the basis of available empirical evidence, an assessment of the court's particular situation and previous reform efforts.[495] The recommended options, which give an idea of the wide range of managerial measures that can be implemented, were as follows:

—Continue experimentation with and implementation of active judicial management of civil cases.
—Experiment with a judge-team calendar system of civil cases.
—Adopt and enforce realistic time standards for civil case disposition and the completion of various stages in the life of a case.
—Strengthen enforcement of the court's policy of no continuance without good cause.
—Evaluate recently enacted limitations on the volume of and time spent on discovery.
—Retain the arbitration programme and monitor and enforce early time limits on initiating and completing the arbitration process.
—Hold a settlement conference conducted by a neutral lawyer soon after each civil case is at issue; then hold no more than one judicial settlement conference per case, within a month of the actual trial date.
—Experiment with strong judicial management of civil trials to reduce the average trial length.
—Experiment with different time standards tailored to the type of civil case. These should include time for both the disposition and completion of the various events in the life of a case; and
—Give priority in scheduling trials to cases with shorter estimated trial lengths.

[495] Kakalik *et al.* (1990: 81–108). See also Selvin/Ebener (1984) on the history of civil delay in this court. According to the latter study, the Los Angeles Superior Court had had a chronic problem of increasing delay since the 1920s, even during periods of declining litigation rates, and cyclical efforts to reduce delay had yielded some results, but only for fairly limited periods of time.

Finally, a study on a large metropolitan court of general jurisdiction which had a serious congestion problem with over 70,000 backlogged cases showed that it was possible to achieve a significant reduction in delay through a combination of case management techniques.[496] The court in question implemented three programs: a joint status report project, which required all currently pending cases to file a status report under threat of dismissal; the requirement of a case scheduling order at the time of case filing; and an individual calendar system, where 60 per cent of civil/domestic cases were randomly assigned to the civil/domestic bench six months before trial.[497] Clear goals, early court control over the scheduling of case events, and ongoing monitoring reports were the main concepts recognised as contributing to success in the delay-reduction programme.[498]

[496] Michels (1992: 1995).

[497] Michels (1995: 73). The court had previously implemented various incremental programmes, such as ADR and lower trial-setting rations, although none had significantly alleviated the worsening situation.

[498] Michels (1995: 82 f.).

Epilogue

A RECAPITULATION

If the reader has been patient enough to follow us so far through the maze of concepts and empirical studies related to court efficiency, he or she may have been left with the impression that no answer has been given to some of the questions posed at the beginning of the introductory chapter, and that apparently no clear thesis has emerged yet as a sort of connecting bridge between the different chapters of this study. And perhaps this impression might be at the same time unjustified and justified. Therefore, it is quite convenient to recapitulate the two main, simple ideas that can be extracted from what has been said up to now.

The first idea can be stated as follows: economic rationality—ie efficiency—has penetrated the legal and judicial systems at all levels and dimensions, from the level of society as a whole to the day-to-day operation of the judicial process, from the institutional role performed by adjudication in society to the organisational context of judicial decisions.[1] This is clearly demonstrated by the discourse and expectations of all actors involved in the legal process: judges and attorneys, politicians and public officials, scholars and ordinary citizens. Some of them may not be completely aware of it, or they may even reject the very notion that efficiency is a central goal for adjudication. However, like the famous character in Molière's play, it is an undeniable fact that all of them speak the language of economic rationality. In other words: far from being an alien value with respect to the legal and judicial process, efficiency has simply become an inseparable part of the structure of expectations we address to the legal system.

The second idea is just as simple: economic rationality is not, and should not necessarily be, the prevalent value or the overriding concern in the context of legal decision-making. On the contrary, economic rationality is subject to all kinds of constraints deriving from the legal tradition, the political environment, even the social climate. Its influence is less the result of its supposed intrinsic dominance and more an outcome of local conditions and concrete negotiations with other values and interests. Therefore, its place and relevance will vary greatly across legal contexts.

Let us now recapitulate, as an illustration of these two conclusions, a few short propositions on the varying place and relevance of economic rationality in law and adjudication. They have been extracted and reformulated from the preceding chapters:

[1] Cf the distinction between 'institutional efficiency' and 'organisational efficiency' proposed by North (1990).

—The minimisation of the sum of error and direct costs in adjudication is not equivalent to the unilateral maximisation of efficiency over justice.
—Court efficiency cannot be determined if not by comparison with the performance of the market and legislature, ie, court efficiency is always relative to the efficiency of other institutions.
—The economic model of litigation does not fully predict disputant decisions, nor is it capable of determining the specific social factors that help explain them.
—The process for reaching legal decisions has a value of its own for participants that is independent from the value (efficiency) of the outcome for such participants. If litigation is not fair, citizens will have little incentive to use the courts, regardless of how efficient the outcome may be. And if they are willing to sacrifice efficiency, the higher social costs thus generated may be more than compensated by lower social conflictivity and higher legitimacy and acceptance of institutional decisions.
—'Justice' and 'efficiency' can be defined in terms of each other when considered in the course of time. Only in this limited sense can efficiency be viewed as a new ideal of justice for the legal system.
—Economic rationality is but one of several rationalities that may collide within the legal system. The legal system will not be overrun by their claim to universal dominance as long as it is able to deconstruct and reconstruct them as legal rationality, ie, subject to equal and unequal treatment in view of past and present legal practices.
—Justice is not a market, but there is a (restricted) market for justice. Therefore, demand will hardly, if ever, reach a state of equilibrium with respect to the supply of judicial services. Therefore, gains in court efficiency will always be temporary.
—Selectivity is a function of the technical interpretation of legal rules and the size of available resources relative to the institutional role played by the courts in a given political system.
—ADR is not necessarily cheaper and speedier than ordinary adjudication; it may both reduce and increase costs. However, it has a crucial role to play in helping regulate the demand for, and the supply of, judicial services.
—'Legal rationalisation' and 'systemic stabilisation' are the (efficient) institutional response to the phenomenon of mass litigation.
—Economic rationality in organisations, such as the courts, is altered by the organisational need to link and coordinate internal and external decisions with each other.
—The place and relevance of efficiency devices in adjudication, such as plea bargaining in the American criminal process, depends on an 'adjudicative ideal' defined by legal history and tradition. Efficiency may be seen as a (problematic) response to interests and values that deviate from the adjudicative idea.
—Procedures can never become speedy enough because, as autonomous social systems, they create their own particular social time and rhythm.

—Courts are social institutions that use scarce social resources. They produce a service called 'adjudication'. For these reasons alone, economic rationality is relevant for the assessment of their operation.

In the end, it may well be that the never-ending pursuit of efficiency turns out to be, socially speaking, less grandiose and appealing than the never-ending quest for justice, but it will be just as unavoidable. No more and no less.

Bibliography

ABEL, Richard L (1973): 'A Comparative Theory of Dispute Institutions in Society', *Law and Society Review*, vol 8, no 2, Winter, 217–343.

—— (ed) (1982a): *The Politics of Informal Justice; vol 1: The American Experience; vol 2: Comparative Studies* (New York-London-Toronto-Sydney-San Francisco, Academic Press).

—— (1989a): *American Lawyers* (New York-Oxford, Oxford University Press).

—— (1989b): 'Comparative Sociology of Legal Professions', in ABEL/LEWIS (eds), 80–153.

ABEL, Richard L and LEWIS Philip SC (eds) (1989): *Lawyers in Society. III: Comparative Theories* (Berkeley-Los Angeles-London, University of California Press).

ABEL, Rolf D (1991): 'Organisation der Verwaltungsgerichte und Finanzgerichte. Konzeption und Ergebnisse aus einem Forschungsprojekt im Rahmen der Strukturanalyse der Rechtspflege (SAR) des Bundesministeriums der Justiz', *Zeitschrift für Rechtssoziologie*, Jhg. 12, Heft 2, 210–16.

ABRAHAM, Henry J (1998): *The Judicial Process. An Introductory Analysis of the Courts of the United States, England and France*, 7th edn (New York-Oxford, Oxford University Press).

ACKERMANN, Werner and BASTARD Benoit (1992): 'Les jeux organisationnels dans l'activité de justice', in François OST and Michel VAN DE KERCHOVE (eds), *Le jeu: un paradigme pour le droit* (Paris, LGDJ) 66–77 (Collection Droit et Societé, 2)

—— (1993a): 'Une coopération conflictuelle: les relations entre les barreaux et les tribunaux de grande instance', *Droit et Societé*, nos 23–24, 59–77.

—— (1993b): *Innovation et gestion dans l'institution judiciaire* (Paris, LGDJ) (Collection Droit et Societé, 6).

—— (1996): 'The Diffusion of Innovation in the Judicial System', in WARGLIEN/MASUCH, 73–88.

ADAMS, Michael (1981): *Ökonomische Analyse des Zivilprozesses*, mit einem Geleitwort von CC VON WEIZSÄCKER (Königstein/Ts, Athenäum Verlag) (Justiz und Gesellschaft, Bd. 15).

ADAMS, Guy B and INGERSOLL Virginia Hill (1990): 'Painting Over Old Works: The Culture of Organization in an Age of Technical Rationality', in TURNER (ed), 15–31.

AMADEO MURGA, Antonio J (1993): 'La justicia apelativa en Puerto Rico: una crisis crónica', *Revista del Colegio de Abogados de Puerto Rico*, vol 54, no 2, abril–junio, 1–86.

APPELBAUM, Richard P, FELSTINER William LF and GESSNER Volkmar (eds) (2001): *Rules and Networks. The Legal Culture of Global Business Transactions* (Oxford, Hart Publishing).

ARGUEDAS SALAZAR, Olman (1993): 'La reforma procesal en Costa Rica', in VARIOS, 133–81.

ARMSTRONG, Nick (1995): 'Making Tracks', in ZUCKERMAN/CRANSTON (eds), 97–118.

ARNAUD, André-Jean and FARIÑAS DULCE María José (1996): *Sistemas jurídicos: elementos para un análisis sociológico* (Madrid, Universidad Carlos III-BOE).

ARTS, Wil and VAN DER VEEN Romke (1992): 'Sociological Approaches to Distributive and Procedural Justice', in Klaus R SCHERER (ed), *Justice. Interdisciplinary Perspectives* (Cambridge, Cambridge University Press) 143–176.

ASHENFELTER, Orley, EISENBERG Theodore and SCHWAB Stewart J (1995): 'Politics and the Judiciary: The Influence of Judicial Background on Case Outcomes', *Journal of Legal Studies*, vol XXIV, June, 257–281.

ATKINS, Burton M (1990): 'Communication of Appellate Decisions: A Multivariate Model for Understanding the Selection of Cases for Publication', *Law and Society Review*, vol 24, no 5, 1170–1196.

AUMÜLLER, Thomas and STREMPEL Dieter (eds) (1996): *Strukturelle Veränderungen in der Justiz. Bericht der Arbeitsgruppe der Landesjustizverwaltungen*, Köln, Bundesanzeiger (Beiträge zur Strukturanalyse der Rechtspflege).

BALLÉ, Catherine (1979): 'Le Tribunal de Grande Instance. Une approche organisationnelle', in CNRS (ed), *Connaissance et fonctionnement de la justice pénale: perspectives sociologiques et criminologiques* (Paris, CNRS) 126–143.

——BASTARD Benoit, EMSELLEM Denise and GARIOUD Georges (1981): *Le changement dans l'institution judiciaire. Les nouvelles juridictions de la péripherie parisienne* (Paris, La Documentation Française).

BANCO INTERAMERICANO DE DESARROLLO (ed) (1993): *Justicia y desarrollo en América Latina y el Caribe* (Washington, DC, BID).

BARCLAY, Scott (1997): 'Posner's Economic Model and the Decision to Appeal', *Justice System Journal*, vol 19, no 1, 77–99.

BARZEL, Yoram (1989): *Economic Analysis of Property Rights* (Cambridge, Cambridge University Press).

BAUER, Volker, BLANKENBURG Erhard and TREIBER Hubert (Red.) (1983): *Arbeitsplatz Gericht. Modellversuch zur Humanisierung der Gerichtsorganisation* (Frankfurt-New York, Campus Verlag).

BAYLES, Michael D (1990): *Procedural Justice. Allocating to Individuals*, (Dordrecht-Boston-London, Kluwer Academic Publishers) (Law and Philosophy Library).

BEA PÉREZ, Emilia, LOPEZ TERRADA Carmen, DE LUCAS MARTIN Francisco Javier and VIDAL GIL Ernesto Jaime (1988): 'El asociacionismo judicial en España, hoy: Notas para un trabajo de sociología de los jueces', *Sociologia del diritto*, vol XV, no 2, 89–103.

BECKER, Gary (1986): 'The Economic Approach to Human Behavior', in Jon ELSTER (ed), *Rational Choice*, (NY, New York University Press), 108–122 (Readings in Social and Political Theory; first published in BECKER, Gary (1976): *The Economic Approach to Human Behavior* (Chicago, Chicago University Press).

BECKMAN, Svante (1990): 'Professionalization: Borderline Authority and Autonomy in Work', in Michael BURRAGE and Rolf TORSTENDAHL (eds), *Professions in Theory and History. Rethinking the Study of Professions* (London-Newbury Park-New Delhi, Sage Publications) 114–138.

BENDER, Rolf (ed) (1972): *Tatsachenforschung in der Justiz. Einführung in die Methoden*; (Tübingen, JCB Mohr) (Paul Siebeck).

——(1979): 'The Stuttgart Model', in Mauro CAPPELLETTI (gen ed), *Access to Justice* (Milano-Aalphenaandenrijn, Giuffrè-Sijthoff and Noordhoff. vol II, book 2) 431–475.

——and WAX Peter (1972): 'Organisation und Verfahrensweise der 19 Oberlandesgerichte. Leitstudie zum Versuch einer Quantifizierung von Leistungskriterien und zur vergleichenden Analyse von Gerichten', in BENDER (ed), 179–195.

——and SCHUMACHER Rolf (1980): *Erfolgsbarrieren vor Gericht. Eine empirische Studie zur Chancengleichheit im Zivilprozeß des Instituts für Rechtstatsachenforschung Stuttgart e.V.*, (Tübingen, JCB Mohr) (Paul Siebeck).

Benson, Bruce L (1990): *The Enterprise of Law. Justice Without the State*, San Francisco, Pacific Research Institute for Public Policy.

Bergoglio, María Inés (2001): *Litigar en Córdoba. Investigaciones sociológicas sobre la litigación*, (Córdoba, Triunfar).

Berman, Harold J (1983): *Law and Revolution. The Formation of the Western Legal Tradition*, (Cambridge, Mass., Harvard University Press).

Bernard, Claude (1996): *La justice*, Paris, (Le Monde-Éditions-Marabout).

Binder, Alberto M (1993): 'Crisis y transformación de la justicia penal en Latinoamérica', in Varios, 67–95.

Black, Donald (1973): 'The Mobilization of Law', *Journal of Legal Studies*, vol II, 125–149.

—— (1989): *Sociological Justice*; (New York-Oxford, Oxford University Press).

Blankenburg, Erhard (1980): 'Mobilisierung von Recht. Über die Wahrscheinlichkeit des Gangs zum Gericht, die Chance des Erfolgs und die daraus folgenden Funktionen der Justiz', *Zeitschrift für Rechtssoziologie*, Jhg. 1, Heft 1, 33–64.

—— (1981–82): 'Legal Insurance, Litigant Decisions, and the Rising Caseloads of Courts: A West German Study', *Law and Society Review*, vol 16, no 4, 601–624.

—— (1982): 'Die Justiz als Arbeitsorganisation', *Zeitschrift für Rechtssoziologie*, Jhg. 3, Heft 1, 158–162.

—— (ed) (1989a): *Prozeßflut? Studien zur Prozesstätigkeit europäischer Gerichte in historischen Zeitreihen und im Rechtsvergleich*, (Köln, Bundesanzeiger).

—— (1989b): 'Prozeßflut und Prozeßebbe—Über die Fähigkeit der Gerichte, mit Rechtsstreitigkeiten fertig zu werden', in Blankenburg (ed) (1989a), 9–20.

—— (1992): 'Legal Cultures and Litigation Flows Before European Courts in Historical and Comparative Perspective', *Justice System Journal*, vol 16, no 1, 101–110.

—— (1994a): 'La mobilisation du droit. Les conditions du recours et du non-recours a la justice', *Droit et Societé*, no 28, 691–703.

—— (1994b): 'The Infrastructure for Avoiding Civil Litigation: Comparing Cultures of Legal Behavior in The Netherlands and West Germany', *Law and Society Review*, vol 28, no 4, 789–808.

—— (1998): 'Unsinn und Sinn des Annahmeverfahrens bei Verfassungsbeschwerden', *Zeitschrift für Rechtssoziologie*, Jhg. 19, Heft 1, 37–60.

—— and Wolff Heimfrid (1972): 'Das Gericht als professionalisierte Organisation', in Bender (ed), 223–230.

——, Gottwald Walther and Strempel Dieter (eds) (1982): *Alternativen in der Ziviljustiz. Berichte, Analysen, Perspektiven*; (Köln, Bundesanzeiger) (Rechtstatsachenforschung, hrsg. vom Bundeministerium der Justiz)

—— and Voigt Rüdiger (eds) (1987a): *Implementation von Gerichtsentscheidungen*, Opladen, Westdeutscher Verlag (Jahrbuch für Rechtstheorie und Rechtssoziologie, 11).

—— (1987b): 'Implementation von Gerichtsentscheidungen', in Blankenburg/Voigt (eds), 10–22.

——, Leipold Dieter and Wollschläger Christian (eds) (1991): *Neue Methoden im Zivilverfahren. Summarischer Rechtsschutz und Bagatellverfahren*, (Köln, Bundesanzeiger) (Beiträge zur Strukturanalyse der Rechtspflege).

—— and Leipold Dieter (1991): 'Summarischer Rechtsschutz als Alternative zum Normalverfahren?', in Blankenburg/Leipold/Wollschläger (eds), 109–123.

Böhm, Ellen (1992): 'Evaluation des Gesetzes zur Beschleunigung und Vereinfachung gerichtlicher Verfahren mit der Survival Analyse', *Zeitschrift für Rechtssoziologie*, Jhg. 13, Heft 1, 131–140.

BORUCKA-ARCTOWA, M (1989): 'Causes et origines des problemes actuels de surcharge: aperçu sociologique', in WEDEKIND (ed), 45–66.

BOYUM, Keith O and MATHER Lynn (eds) (1983): *Empirical Theories About Courts* (New York-London, Longman).

—— and HUDZIK John K (1991): 'Overview from the Editors of the Special Issue', *Justice System Journal*, vol 15, no 2, 550–562 (special issue on 'Court Management').

BOZA, María Eugenia and PÉREZ PERDOMO Rogelio (eds) (1996): *Seguridad jurídica y competitividad* (Caracas, IESA).

BRIDGES, George S (1982): 'The Speedy Trial Act of 1974: Effects on Delay in Federal Criminal Litigation', *Journal of Criminal Law and Criminology*, vol 73, no 1, Spring, 50–73.

BRIGHAM, John (1993): 'Order Without Lawyers: Ellickson on How Neighbors Settle Disputes', *Law and Society Review*, vol 27, no 3, 609–617.

BUDAK, Ali Cem (1998): 'Cross-border Debt Collection: Examples of Turkey and Germany', in GESSNER/BUDAK (eds), 17–53.

BUMILLER, Kristin (1980–81): 'Choice of Forum in Diversity Cases: Analysis of a Survey and Implications for Reform', *Law and Society Review*, vol 15, nos 3–4, 749–774.

BURGOS, José Germán (1992): 'La justicia colombiana: en la hora del ajuste', in *El otro derecho*, Bogotá, vol 4, núm 2, julio, 61–89.

BUSCAGLIA, Edgardo and DAKOLIAS Maria (1996): *Judicial Reform in Latin American Courts: The Experience in Argentina and Ecuador* (Washington DC, The World Bank) (World Bank Technical Paper 350).

—— (1999): *Comparative International Study of Court Performance Indicators. A Descriptive and Analytical Account* (Washington, DC, The World Bank).

BUSH, Robert A Baruch (1989): 'Defining Quality in Dispute Resolution: Taxonomies and Anti-Taxonomies of Quality Arguments', *Denver University Law Review*, vol 66, no 3, 335–380 (Quality of Dispute Resolution Symposium Issue)

BUSSMANN, Kai-D and LÜDEMANN Christian (1995): *Klassenjustiz oder Verfahrensökonomie? Aushandlungsprozesse in Wirtschafts- und allgemeinen Strafverfahren* (Pfaffenweiler, Centaurus-Verlagsgesellschaft).

CALABRESI, Guido (1980): 'About Law and Economics: A Letter to Ronald Dworkin', *Hofstra Law Review*, vol 8, 553–562.

—— (1990): 'Il futuro dell'analisi economica del diritto', in POCAR/VELICOGNA (eds), 46–54.

—— (1991): 'The Pointlessness of Pareto: Carrying Coase Further', *Yale Law Journal*, vol 100, 1211–1237.

CALAS, Marta B and MCGUIRE Jean B (1990): 'Organizations as Networks of Power and Symbolism', in TURNER (ed), 95–113.

CALSAMIGLIA, Albert (1988): 'Justicia, eficiencia y derecho', *Revista del Centro de Estudios Constitucionales*, Madrid, núm. 1, septiembre–diciembre, 305–335.

—— (1993): 'Justicia, eficiencia y optimización de la legislación', in *Racionalidad y eficiencia del derecho*, (México, Fontamara), 27–72 (Biblioteca de Ética, Filosofía del Derecho y Política, 24)

CANON, Bradley C and JOHNSON Charles A (1999): *Judicial Policies. Implementation and Impact*, 2nd ed. (Washington DC, CQ Press).

CANOSA, Romano and FEDERICO Pietro (1974): *La magistratura in Italia del 1945 a oggi* (Bologna, Il Mulino).

CAPPELLER, Wanda de Lemos (1991): 'Entre o ceticismo e a utopia: a sociologia juridica latino-americana frente ao debate europeu', in CORREAS (ed), 75–90.

CAPPELLETTI, Mauro (1989): *The Judicial Process in Comparative Perspective* (Oxford, Clarendon Press).

—— (1993): *Dimensiones de la justicia en el mundo contemporáneo. (Cuatro estudios de derecho comparado)*, (México, Porrúa).

CARP, Robert A and STIDHAM Ronald (1993): *Judicial Process in America* (Washington DC, CQ Press).

CARRINGTON, Paul D (1979): 'Adjudication as a Private Good: A Comment', *Journal of Legal Studies*, vol VIII, no 2, March, 303–317.

CASTELLANO, Cesare, PACE Carlo, PALOMBA Giuseppe and RASPINI Gioacchino (1970): *La efficienza della giustizia italiana e i suoi effetti economico-sociali*, seconda edizione riveduti e ampliata, prefazione di Giovanni DEMARIA (Bari, Editori Laterza).

CELLA, Gian Primo (1990): 'Comportamento economico e razionalita sociale', *Sociologia del diritto*, vol XVII, nos 1–2, 77–87.

CHIASSONI, Pierluigi (1992): *Law and Economics. L'analisi economica del diritto negli Stati Uniti* (Torino, G Giappichelli Editore).

CHUNG, Wai-Keung and HAMILTON Gary G (2001): 'Social Logic as Business Logic: *Guanxi*, Trustworthiness, and the Embeddedness of Chinese Business Practices', in APPELBAUM/FELSTINER/GESSNER (eds), 325–346.

CHURCH, JR., Thomas W (1981): 'Who Sets the Pace of Litigation in Urban Trial Courts', *Judicature*, vol 65, no 2, August, 76–85.

—— (1985): 'Examining Local Legal Culture', *American Bar Foundation Research Journal*, no 3, Summer, 449–518.

—— *et al.* (1978): *Justice Delayed. The Pace of Litigation in Urban Trial Courts* (Williamsburg, Va., National Center for State Courts).

—— and HEUMANN Milton (1992): *Speedy Disposition. Monetary Incentives and Policy Reform in Criminal Courts* (NY, State University of New York Press).

CIDAC (1994): *A la puerta de la ley. El Estado de derecho en México* (México, CIDAC-Cal y arena).

CISA, Agustín (1991): 'El cambio en organizaciones complejas: el caso de la modificación del proceso civil uruguayo', *Revista de la Facultad de Derecho y Ciencias Sociales*, Montevideo, año XXXII, nos 1–2, enero–junio, 183–194.

CLARK, David S (1981): 'Adjudication to Administration: A Statistical Analysis of Federal District Courts in the Twentieth Century', *Southern California Law Review*, vol 55, no 1, November, 65–152.

—— (1990):'Civil Litigation Trends in Europe and Latin America since 1945: The Advantage of Intracountry Comparisons', *Law and Society Review*, vol 24, no 2, 549–569.

CLEGG, Stewart R (1990): *Modern Organizations. Organization Studies in the Postmodern World* (London-Newbury Park-New Delhi, Sage Publications).

COASE, Ronald H (1978): 'Economics and Contiguous Disciplines', *Journal of Legal Studies*, vol VII, 201–211.

—— (1988): *The Firm, the Market and the Law* (Chicago-London, University of Chicago Press).

COLEMAN, Jules L (1980): 'Efficiency, Utility, and Wealth Maximization', *Hofstra Law Review*, vol 8, 509–551.

COMMAILLE, Jacques (1990): 'Territoire judiciaire, territoire social: pour une théorie sociologique de la justice', in André-Jean ARNAUD (ed), *Sociology of Law. Splashes and Sparks*; (Oñati, IISL), 91–100 (Oñati Proceedings, 2)

COMMAILLE, Jacques (1999): 'La déstabilisation des territoires de justice', *Droit et Societé*, nos 42–43, 239–264.

——and PERRIN Jean-François (1985): 'Le modèle de Janus de la sociologie du droit', *Droit et Societé*, no 1, août, 95–110.

CONDIE, Brendan, GAMBLE Helen, MOHR Richard and WRIGHT Ted (1996a): *Client Services in Local Courts. Standards and Benchmarks* (Wollongong, Centre for Court Policy and Administration).

——(1996b): *Client Services in the Local Courts. The Review Process*, (Wollongong, Centre for Court Policy and Administration).

CONSEJO GENERAL DEL PODER JUDICIAL (1997): *Libro blanco de la justicia* (Madrid, CGPJ).

COOK, Beverly B (1994): 'A Critique of the Supreme Court's 1982 Agenda: Alternatives to the NYU Legal Model', *Justice System Journal*, vol 17, no 2, 135–151.

COOTER, Robert D (1989): 'The Coase Theorem', in John EATWELL, Murray MILGATE and Peter NEWMAN (eds), *Allocation, Information, and Markets* (NY-London, WW Norton) 64–70 (The New Palgrave, 1987).

——(1995): 'Law and Unified Social Theory', *Journal of Law and Society*, vol 22, no 1, March, 50–67.

——and ULEN Thomas (1988): *Law and Economics* (New York, Harper Collins).

——and RUBINFELD Daniel L (1990): 'Trial Courts: An Economic Perspective', *Law and Society Review*, vol 24, no 2, 533–546.

CORDERO, Franco (1985): *Riti e sapienza del diritto* (Roma, Laterza).

CORREA SUTIL, Jorge (ed) (1993): *Situación y políticas judiciales en América Latina*; Santiago de Chile, Universidad Diego Portales (Cuadernos de análisis jurídico—serie Publicaciones especiales)

CORREAS, Oscar (ed) (1991): *Sociología jurídica en América Latina* (Oñati, IISL) (Oñati Proceedings, 6).

COSACOV BELAUS, Gustavo, GORENC Klaus-Dieter and NADELSTICHER MITRANI Abraham (1983): *Duración del proceso penal en México*, (México, INACIPE) (Cuadernos del Instituto Nacional de Ciencias Penales, 12).

COSSIO DIAZ, José Ramón (1996): *Jurisdicción federal y carrera judicial en México*, (México, UNAM). (Cuadernos para la Reforma de la Justicia, 4).

——(1997): *Derecho y análisis económico* (México, ITAM-FCE).

COTTERRELL, Roger (1995): *Law's Community. Legal Theory in Sociological Perspective* (Oxford Socio-Legal Studies) (Oxford, Clarendon Press).

CROZIER, Michel (1985): *Le phénomene bureaucratique. Essai sur les tendances bureaucratiques des systèmes d'organisation modernes et sur leur relations en France avec le système social et culturel* (1963) (Paris, Editions du Seuil).

CURRIE, David P (1990): *Federal Jurisdiction in a Nutshell*, 3rd ed (St. Paul, Minn., West Publishing Co).

DAHLIN, Donald C (1986): *Models of Court Management* (Millwood, NY.-London, Associated Faculty Press).

DAKOLIAS, Maria (1996): *The Judicial Sector in Latin America and the Caribbean. Elements of Reform* (World Bank Technical Paper, 319) (Washington, DC, The World Bank).

——(1999): *Court Performance around the World. A Comparative Perspective* (World Bank Technical Paper, 430) (Washington, DC, The World Bank).

DAMAŠKA, Mirjan R (1973): 'Evidentiary Barriers to Conviction and Two Models of Criminal Procedure: A Comparative Study', *University of Pennsylvania Law Review*, vol 121, 506–589.

——(1986): *The Faces of Justice and State Authority. A Comparative Approach to the Legal Process* (New Haven-London, Yale University Press).

DAVIES, Celia (1983): 'Professionals in Bureaucracies: The Conflict Thesis Revisited', in Robert DINGWALL and Philip LEWIS (eds), *The Sociology of Professions. Lawyers, Doctors and Others* (Basingstoke-London, The MacMillan Press (reprint 1992)) 177–194.

DEAKIN, Simon (1996): 'Law and Economics', in THOMAS, Philip A (ed), *Legal Frontiers* (Aldershot, Dartmouth) 66–105.

DE GEEST, Gerrit (1995): 'Toward an Integration of Economic and Sociological Approaches', *European Journal of Law and Economics*, vol 2, no 4, December, 301–308.

DENTI, Vittorio (1986): 'Riflessioni sulla crisi della giustizia civile', *Sociologia del diritto*, vol XIII, nos 2–3, 59–79.

DEVILLE, Anne (1992): 'L'entrée du Syndicat de la Magistrature dans le champ juridique en 1968', *Droit et Societé*, no 22, 639–671.

DI FEDERICO, Giuseppe (1968): *La giustizia come organizzazione: Il reclutamento di magistrati*, prefazione di Gino MARTINOLI (Bari, Laterza) (Biblioteca di cultura moderna, 641).

——(1969): *La giustizia come organizzazione: La Corte di Cassazione*, prefazione di Gino MARTINOLI, contributi di Giorgio FREDDI e Renato BORRUSO (Bari, Laterza) (Biblioteca di cultura moderna, 674).

DIXON, Jo (1995): 'The Organizational Context of Criminal Sentencing', *American Journal of Sociology*, vol 100, no 5, March, 1157–1198.

DOMINGO VILLEGAS, Pilar (1995): *Rule of Law and Judicial Systems in the Context of Democratisation and Economic Liberalisation: A Framework for Comparison and Analysis in Latin America* (Mexico, CIDE) (Centro de Investigación y Docencia Económicas, División de Estudios Políticos, Working Paper 25).

DONOHUE III, John J (1988): 'Law and Economics: The Road Not Taken', *Law and Society Review*, vol 22, no 5, 903–926.

DOUGLAS, Roger (1994): 'Social Class and Court Outcomes: Making Sense of the Empirical Literature', *Law in Context*, Melbourne, vol 12, no 1, 97–128.

DUNGWORTH, Terence and PACE Nicholas (1990): *Statistical Overview of Civil Litigation in the Federal Courts* (Santa Monica, RAND) (The Institute for Civil Justice) (R-3885-ICJ).

DWORKIN, Ronald M (1980a): 'Is Wealth a Value?', *Journal of Legal Studies*, vol VIII, 191–226.

——(1980b): 'Why Efficiency? A Response to Professors Calabresi and Posner', *Hofstra Law Review*, vol 8, 563–590.

EDELMAN, Lauren B and CAHILL Mia (1998): 'How Law Matters in Disputing and Dispute Processing (Or, the Contingency of Legal Matter in Informal Dispute Processes)', in Bryant GARTH and Austin SARAT (eds), *How Does Law Matter?* (Evanston, Northwestern University Press-ABF) 15–44 (Fundamental Issues in Law and Society Research, 3)

EDER, Klaus (1986): 'Prozedurale Rationalität. Moderne Rechtsentwicklung jenseits von formaler Rationalisierung', *Zeitschrift für Rechtssoziologie*, Jhg. 7, Heft 1, 1–30.

EGGERTSSON, Thráinn (1990): *Economic Behavior and Institutions* (Cambridge, Cambridge University Press).

EISENBERG, Theodore (1990): 'Testing the Selection Effect: A New Theoretical Framework with Empirical Tests', *Journal of Legal Studies*, vol XIX, no 2, Part 1, June, 337–358.

EISENSTEIN, James and JACOB Herbert (1977): *Felony Justice. An Organizational Analysis of Criminal Courts* (Boston-Toronto, Little, Brown and Company).

ELDER, Harold W (1989): 'Trials and Settlements in the Criminal Courts: An Empirical Analysis of Dispositions and Sentencing', *Journal of Legal Studies*, vol XVIII, no 1, January, 191–208.

ELLICKSON, Robert C (1991): *Order Without Law. How Neighbors Settle Disputes* (Cambridge, Mass. Harvard University Press).

EMMELMAN, Debra S (1996): 'Trial by Plea Bargain: Case Settlement as a Product of Recursive Decisionmaking', *Law and Society Review*, vol 30, no 2, 335–360.

EMSELLEM, Denise (1982): *Pratique et organisation dans l'institution judiciaire* (Paris, La Documentation Française).

ESTREICHER, Samuel and SEXTON John (1986): *Redefining the Supreme Court's Role. A Theory of Managing the Federal Judicial Process* (New Haven-London, Yale University Press).

FALKE, Josef and GESSNER Volkmar (1982): 'Konfliktnähe als Maßstab für gerichtliche und außergerichtliche Streitbehandlung', in BLANKENBURG/GOTTWALD/STREMPEL (eds), 289–315.

FARBER, Henry S and WHITE Michelle J (1994): 'A Comparison of Formal and Informal Dispute Resolution in Medical Malpractice', *Journal of Legal Studies*, vol XXIII, no 2, June, 777–805.

FARIA, José Eduardo (1992): *Justiça e conflito. Os juízes em façe dos novos movimentos sociais*, 2nd edn. (São Paulo, Editora Revista dos Tribunais).

—— (1996): 'A crise do Poder Judiciário no Brasil', *Justiça e democracia. Revista semestral de informação e debates*, São Paulo, no 1, 18–64.

FAUGERON, Claude (1981): 'Justice et opinion publique. L'ere du soupçon', *Pouvoirs*, no. 16, 89–96 (La justice)

FEDERAL JUDICIAL CENTER (1992): *Manual for Litigation Management and Cost and Delay Reduction* (Washington, DC, Federal Judicial Center).

FEELEY, Malcolm M (1973): 'Two Models of the Criminal Justice System: An Organizational Perspective', *Law and Society Review*, vol 7, no 3, Spring, 407–425.

—— (1979): *The Process is the Punishment. Handling Cases in a Lower Criminal Court* (New York, Russell Sage Foundation).

—— (1983): *Court Reform on Trial. Why Simple Solutions Fail* (NY, Basic Books).

—— and LAZERSON Mark H (1983): 'Police Prosecutor Relationships: An Interorganizational Perspective', in BOYUM/MATHER (eds), 216–243.

—— and RUBIN Edward L (2000): *Judicial Policy Making and the Modern State. How the Courts Reformed America's Prisons* (Cambridge, Cambridge University Press).

FELSTINER, William LF, ABEL Richard L and SARAT Austin (1980–81): 'The Emergence and Transformation of Disputes: Naming, Blaiming, Claiming . . .', *Law and Society Review*, vol 15, nos 3–4, 631–654.

FERRARESE, Maria Rosaria (1984): *L'istituzione difficile. La Magistratura tra professione e sistema politico* (Napoli, Edizione Scientifiche Italiane).

—— (1988–89): 'Civil Justice and the Judicial Role in Italy', *Justice System Journal*, vol 13/2.

—— (1995): 'Istituzioni normative ed evoluzione economica: D.C. North sociologo del diritto?', *Sociologia del diritto*, vol XXII, no 3, 19–40.

FERRARI, Vincenzo (1990a): *Developing Sociology of Law. A World-Wide Documentary Enquiry* (Milano, Giuffré).

——(1990b): 'Introduction' to FERRARI (ed) (1990a), xv–li.

——(ed) (1991): *Laws and Rights. Proceedings of the International Congress of Sociology of Law for the Ninth Centenary of the University of Bologna (May 30–June 3, 1988). Panels and sessions* (Milano, Giuffré).

FIELD, Stewart and THOMAS Philip (eds) (1994): *Justice and Efficiency? The Royal Commission on Criminal Justice* (Oxford, Blackwell) (published simultaneously as vol 21, no 1 of the *Journal of Law and Society*)

FISS, Owen M (1984): 'Against Settlement', *Yale Law Journal*, vol 93, 1073–1090.

FIX-FIERRO, Héctor (1995a): *La eficiencia de la justicia (Una aproximación y una propuesta)* (México, UNAM) (Cuadernos para la Reforma de la Justicia, 1).

——(1995b): 'Los Consejos de la Judicatura entre profesión y organización', *Coloquio internacional sobre el Consejo de la Judicatura* (México, Consejo de la Judicatura Federal-UNAM) 71–89.

——(1997): 'La carrera judicial como forma de administración y organización del estatuto profesional de los jueces', in *Memorias del Quinto Aniversario del XXII Circuito del Poder Judicial de la Federación* (México, CJF) 245–262.

——(1998): 'Judicial Reform and the Supreme Court of Mexico: The Trajectory of Three Years', *United States-Mexico Law Journal*, vol 6, Spring, 1–21.

——and LOPEZ AYLLON Sergio (1997): 'The Impact of Globalization on the Reform of the State and the Law in Latin America', *Houston Journal of International Law*, vol 19, no 3, Spring, 785–805.

FIX-ZAMUDIO, Héctor and FIX-FIERRO Héctor (1996): *El Consejo de la Judicatura*, (México, UNAM) (Cuadernos para la Reforma de la Justicia, 3).

FLANDERS, Steven (1980): 'Modeling Court Delay', *Law and Policy Quarterly*, vol 2, no 3, July, 305–320.

FLANGO, Victor E (1994): 'Court Unification and Quality of State Courts', *Justice System Journal*, vol 16, no 3, 33–55.

——and ROTTMAN David B (1992): 'Measuring Trial Court Consolidation', *Justice System Journal*, vol 16, no 1, 65–74.

FLEMMING, Roy B (1990): 'The Political Styles and Organizational Strategies of American Prosecutors: Examples from Nine Courthouse Communities', *Law and Policy*, vol 12, no 1, January, 25–50.

——NARDULLI Peter F and EISENSTEIN James (1987): 'The Timing of Justice in Felony Trial Courts', *Law and Policy*, vol 9, no 2, April, 179–206.

——(1992): *The Craft of Justice. Politics and Work in Criminal Court Communities* (Philadelphia, University of Pennsylvania Press).

FORTE, Francesco and BONDONIO Pier Vincenzo (1970): *Costi e benefici della giustizia italiana. Analisi economica della spessa pubblica per la giustizia* (Bari, Laterza) (Biblioteca di cultura moderna, 694).

FRANK, Jürgen (1986): 'Die "Rationalität" einer ökonomischen Analyse des Rechts', *Zeitschrift für Rechtssoziologie*, Jhg. 7, Heft 2, 191–211.

FREYHOLD, Hanno von (1996): 'Cross-Border Legal Interactions in New York Courts', in GESSNER (ed), 43–148.

——, GESSNER Volkmar and OLGIATI Vittorio (1996): 'The Role of Courts in Global Legal Interaction', in GESSNER (ed), 269–281.

FRIED, Jonathan T (1995): 'Improving the Administration of Justice in the Americas. Protection and Guarantees for Judges and Lawyers in the Exercise of Their Functions', *Revista IIDH*, San José, Costa Rica, no 22, julio–diciembre, 65–171.

FRIEDMAN, Lawrence M (1975): *The Legal System. A Social Science Perspective* (New York, Russell Sage Foundation).

——(1984): *American Law. An Introduction* (New York-London, WW Norton and Company).

——(1985): *Total Justice* (New York, Russell Sage Foundation).

——(1990): 'Opening the Time Capsule: A Progress Report on Studies of Courts Over Time', *Law and Society Review*, vol 24, no 2, 229–240.

——and PÉREZ PERDOMO Rogelio (eds) (2003): *Legal Cultures in the Age of Globalization: Latin Europe and Latin America* (Stanford, Stanford University Press).

FRIESEN, JR., Ernest C, GALLAS Edward C and GALLAS Nesta M (1971): *Managing the Courts* (Indianapolis-NY, Bobbs-Merrill).

GALANTER, Marc (1974): 'Why the "Haves" Come Out Ahead: Speculations on the Limits of Legal Change', *Law and Society Review*, vol 9, no 1, Fall, 95–160.

——(1980): 'Legality and its Discontents: A Preliminary Assessment of Current Theories of Legalization and Delegalization', in Erhard BLANKENBURG, Ekkehard KLAUSA and Hubert ROTTLEUTHNER (eds) (1980): *Alternative Rechtsformen und Alternativen zum Recht* (Opladen, Westdeutscher Verlag) 11–27 (Jahrbuch für Rechtstheorie und Rechtssoziologie, 6).

——(1983a): 'Reading the Landscape of Disputes: What We Know and Don't Know (and Think We Know) About Our Allegedly Contentious and Litigious Society', *UCLA Law Review*, vol 31, no 1, October, 4–71.

——(1983b): 'The Radiating Effects of Courts', in BOYUM/MATHER (eds), 117–142.

——(1988): 'The Life and Times of the Big Six: Or, the Federal Courts since the Good Old Days', *Wisconsin Law Review*, vol 6, 921–954.

——(1990): 'Case Congregations and their Careers', *Law and Society Review*, vol 24, no 2, 371–395.

GARANT, Patrice (1994): 'La crise de la justice: Épidermique ou profonde', *Windsor Yearbook of Access to Justice*, vol 14, 255–268.

GARAPON, Antoine (1985): *L'ane portant des reliques. Essai sur le rituel judiciaire*, préface de Jean CARBONNIER (Paris, Le Centurion).

——(1996): *Le gardien des promesses. Justice et démocratie*, préface de Paul RICOEUR (Paris, Éditions Odile Jacob).

——(1997): *Bien juger. Essai sur le rituel judiciaire*, préface de Jean CARBONNIER (Paris, Éditions Odile Jacob).

GARCIA COTARELO, Ramón (1986): *Del Estado del bienestar al estado del malestar (La crisis del Estado Social y el problema de la legitimidad)* (Madrid, Centro de Estudios Constitucionales).

GARCIA PASCUAL, Cristina (1997): *Legitimidad democrática y Poder Judicial* (Valencia, Edicions Alfons El Magnanim-Generalitat Valenciana) (Estudios universitarios, 66).

GARCIA PELAYO, Manuel (1991): *Burocracia, tecnocracia y otros escritos*, in *Obras completas* (Madrid, Centro de Estudios Constitucionales) vol II, 1385–1546.

GATOWSKI, Sophia I, DOBBIN Shirley A *et al.* (1996): 'Court-annexed Arbitration in Clark County, Nevada: An Evaluation of Its Impact on the Pace, Cost, and Quality of Civil Justice', *Justice System Journal*, vol 18, no 3, 287–304.

GENN, Hazel, with NATIONAL CENTRE FOR SOCIAL RESEARCH (1999): *Paths to Justice. What People Do and Think About Going to Law* (Oxford Hart Publishing).

GEPHART, Werner (1995): 'Gesellschaftstheorie und ökonomische Analyse des Rechts', *Zeitschrift für Rechtssoziologie*, Jhg. 16, Heft 1, 156–169.

GESSNER, Volkmar (1976): *Recht und Konflikt. Eine soziologische Untersuchung privatrechticher Konflikte in Mexiko* (Tübingen, JCB Mohr) (Paul Siebeck).

——(1994): 'Global Legal Interaction and Legal Cultures', *Ratio Iuris*, vol 7, no 2, July, 132–145.

——(ed) (1996a): *Foreign Courts. Civil Litigation in Foreign Legal Cultures* (Aldershot, Dartmouth) (Oñati International Series in Law and Society)

——(1996b): 'International Cases in German First Instance Courts', in GESSNER (ed), 149–207.

——and BUDAK Ali Cem (eds) (1998): *Emerging Legal Certainty: Empirical Studies on the Globalization of the Law* (Aldershot, Dartmouth) (Oñati International Series in Law and Society).

——and THOMAS John (eds) (1988): Socio-Legal Research and Policy Studies, special issue of *Law and Policy*, vol 10, nos 2–3, April–July.

GIBSON, James L, CALDEIRA Gregory A and BAIRD Vanessa A (1998): 'On the Legitimacy of National High Courts', *American Political Science Review*, vol 92, no 2, June, 343–358.

GILLES, Peter (1992): *Ziviljustiz und Rechtsmittelproblematik. Vorstudie zur Analyse und Reform der Rechtsmittel in der Zivilgerichtsbarkeit* (Köln, Bundesanzeiger) (Beiträge zur Strukturanalyse der Rechtspflege).

GILLESPIE, Robert W (1976): 'The Production of Court Services: An Analysis of Scale Effects and Other Factors', *Journal of Legal Studies*, vol V, no 2, June, 243–265.

GLENN, H Patrick (1995): 'The Common Law in Canada', *Canadian Bar Review*, vol 74, June, 261–292.

GOODMAN, Carl F (2001): 'The Somewhat Less Reluctant Litigant: Japan's Changing View Towards Civil Litigation', *Law and Policy in International Business*, vol 32, no 4, 769–810.

GOTTWALD, Walther (1990): 'Die Zivilrechts(alltags)praxis—ein Findelkind der Implementationsforschung?', in RAISER/VOIGT (eds), 66–85.

GRAU, Charles W and SHESKIN Arlene (1982): 'Ruling Out Delay: The Impact of Ohio's Rules of Superintendence', *Judicature*, vol 66, nos 3–4, September–October, 108–121.

GRAVELLE, Hugh (1995): 'Regulating the Market for Civil Justice', in ZUCKERMAN/CRANSTON (eds), 279–303.

GRIFFITHS, John (1983): 'The General Theory of Litigation—A First Step', *Zeitschrift für Rechtssoziologie*, Jhg. 4, Heft 2, Dezember, 145–201.

GROSS, Samuel R (1987): 'The American Advantage: The Value of Inefficient Litigation', *Michigan Law Review*, vol 85, 734–757.

——and SYVERUD Kent D (1991): 'Getting to a No: A Study of Settlement Negotiations and the Selection of Cases for Trial', *Michigan Law Review*, vol 90, no 2, November, 319–393.

GUARNIERI, Carlo (1994): 'Justice et politique: le cadre institutionnel', *Cahiers français*, Paris, no 268 (*Les régimes politiques européens en perspective*), octobre–décembre, 53–71.

——and PEDERZOLI Patrizia (1996): *La puissance de juger. Pouvoir judiciaire et démocratie*, préface de Antoine GARAPON (Paris, Éditions Michalon).

HAMMERGREN, Linn (1998): *The Politics of Justice and Justice Reform in Latin America. The Peruvian Case in Comparative Perspective* (Boulder, Westview Press).

HANSSEN, F Andrew (1999): 'The Effect of Judicial Institutions on Uncertainty and the Rate of Litigation: The Election versus Appointment of Judges, *Journal of Legal Studies*, vol XXVIII, January, 205–232.

HARTLEY, TC (1994): *The Foundations of European Community Law. An Introduction to the Constitutional and Administrative Law of the European Community*, 3rd edn (Oxford, Clarendon Press).

HAYDEN, Robert M and ANDERSON Jill K (1979): 'On the Evaluation of Procedural Systems in Laboratory Experiments. A Critique of Thibaut and Walker', *Law and Human Behavior*, vol 3, nos 1–2, 21–38.

HAZARD, JR., Geoffrey (1965): 'Rationing Justice', *Journal of Law and Economics*, Chicago, vol VIII, October, 1–10.

HENCKEL, Hans-Joachim (1991): *Zivilprozeß und Justizalternativen in Brasilien. Recht, Rechtspraxis, Rechtstatsachen—Versuch einer Beschreibung* (Frankfurt a.M.-Bern-New York-Paris, Peter Lang) (Schriften der Deutsch-Brasilianischen Juristenvereinigung, Band 14).

HENSLER, Deborah R (1990): 'Court-Ordered Arbitration: An Alternative View', *The University of Chicago Legal Forum*, 399–420 (reprinted as RAND/RP-103)

HERNANDEZ MARTIN, Valeriano (1991): *Independencia del juez y desorganización judicial* (Madrid, Civitas-Ministerio de Justicia).

HERRERO, Carmen (1993): 'Racionalidad individual-irracionalidad social: el conflicto justicia-eficiencia', *Doxa*, Alicante, núm 13, 49–67.

HEUMANN, Milton (1978): *Plea Bargaining. The Experiences of Prosecutors, Judges, and Defense Attorneys* (Chicago, The University of Chicago Press).

—— and CHURCH Thomas W (1990): 'Criminal Justice Reform, Monetary Incentives, and Policy Evaluation', *Law and Policy*, vol 12, no 1, January, 81–102.

HEYDEBRAND, Wolf (1977): 'The Context of Public Bureaucracies: An Organizational Analysis of Federal District Courts', *Law and Society Review*, vol 11, no 5, 749 ff.

—— and SERON Carroll (1990): *Rationalizing Justice. The Political Economy of Federal District Courts* (Albany, State University of New York Press).

—— (1993): 'Rationalizing the Social Organization of Justice: Response to McIntosh', *Law and Social Inquiry*, vol 18, no 4, Fall, 707–710.

HIRSCH, Werner Z (1988): *Law and Economics. An Introductory Analysis*, 2nd edn (Boston, Academic Press).

HOFFMAN, Richard B (1982): 'The Bureaucratic Spectre: Newest Challenge to the Courts', *Judicature*, vol 66, no 2, August, 60–72.

HOLMES, Malcolm, DAUDISTEL Howard C and TAGGART William A (1992): 'Plea Bargaining Policy and State District Court Caseloads: An Interrupted Time Series Analysis', *Law and Society Review*, vol 26, no 1, 139–159.

HOLTON, Robert J (1992): *Economy and Society* (London-New York, Routledge).

HOLZSCHECK, Knut, HÖRMANN Günter and DAVITER Jürgen (1982): *Praxis des Konsumentenkredits. Eine empirische Untersuchung zur Rechtssoziologie und Ökonomie des Konsumentenkredits* (Köln, Bundesanzeiger((Rechtstatsachenforschung, hrsg. vom Bundesministerium der Justiz).

HÖRMANN, Günter (1987): 'Gerichtliche Schuldbeitreibung und ihre Umwelt. Zur Entwicklung der gerichtlichen und außergerichtlichen Durchsetzung von Geldforderungen in der Bundesrepublik Deutschland', in BLANKENBURG/VOIGT (eds), 72–94.

Howard, Robert M, Chard Richard E, Kaji Joel T and Davis Jeffrey (2000): 'Pre-Trial Bargaining and Litigation: The Search for Fairness and Efficiency', *Law and Society Review*, vol 34, no 2, 431–456.

Hurst, James Willard (1980–81): 'The Functions of Courts in the United States: 1950–1980', *Law and Society Review*, vol 15, nos 3–4, 401–471.

Hylton, Keith N (1993): 'Asymmetric Information and the Selection of Disputes for Litigation', *Journal of Legal Studies*, vol XXII, no 1, January, 187–210.

Ietswaart, Heleen FP (1984): 'Some Notes on the Relations Between Empirical Research and Theory', in Konstanze Plett and Klaus Ziegert (eds), *Empirische Rechtsforschung zwischen Wissenschaft und Politik. Zur Problemlage rechtssoziologischer Auftragsforschung (Kolloquium im Max-Planck-Institut für ausländisches und Privatrecht, Hamburg, 30. und 31. März 1982)* (Tübingen, JCB Mohr) (Paul Siebeck), 210–220.

——(1989): 'Die Entwicklung des Geschäftsanfalls bei Amtsgerichten in Frankreich', in Blankenburg (ed), 159–230.

Ilanud-Fiu (eds) (1987): *La administración de justicia en Honduras. Descripción y análisis del sector*, (Tegucigalpa, ILANUD-FIU).

Ishikawa, Akira (1998): 'The 'Small Judiciary' Policy in Japan', *Verfassung und Recht in Übersee/Law and Politics in Africa, Asia and Latin America*, 31. Jhg., 2. Quartal, 151–159.

Jacob, Herbert (1976): 'Criminal Courts as Organizational Phenomena', in Lawrence Friedman and Manfred Rehbinder (eds), *Zur Soziologie des Gerichtsverfahrens (Sociology of the Judicial Process)* (Opladen, Westdeutscher Verlag) 155–172 (Jahrbuch für Rechtstheorie und Rechtssoziologie, 4).

——(1983): 'Courts as Organizations', in Boyum/Mather (eds), 192–215.

——(1997): 'The Governance of Trial Judges', *Law and Society Review*, vol 31, no 1, 3–30.

——, Blankenburg Erhard, Kritzer Herbert M, Provine Doris Marie, and Sanders Joseph (1996): *Courts, Law, and Politics in Comparative Perspective* (New Haven-London, Yale University Press).

Jarquin, Edmundo and Carrillo Fernando (eds) (1997): *La economía política de la reforma judicial* (Washington DC, BID).

Johnston, Jason Scott (1990): 'Law, Economics, and Post-Realist Explanation', *Law and Society Review*, vol 24, no 5, 1217–1254.

Jolowicz, JA (1989): 'Managing Overload in Appellate Courts: "Western" Countries', in Wedekind (ed), 71–94.

——(dir.) (1992): *Droit anglais*, 2nd edn. (Paris, Dalloz).

Kagan, Robert A: (1984): 'The Routinization of Debt Collection. An Essay on Social Change and Conflict in the Courts', *Law and Society Review*, vol 18, no 3, 323–371.

——(1991): 'Adversarial Legalism and American Government', *Journal of Policy Analysis and Management*, vol 10, no 3, Summer, 369–406.

Kakalik, James S, Selvin Molly and Pace Nicholas M (1990): *Averting Gridlock. Strategies for Reducing Delay in the Los Angeles Superior Court* (Santa Monica, RAND) (The Institute for Civil Justice) [R-3762-ICJ].

Kaplow, Louis (1994): 'The Value of Accuracy in Adjudication: An Economic Analysis', *Journal of Legal Studies*, vol XXIII, 307–355.

Kaufman, Irving R (1990): 'Reform for a System in Crisis: Alternative Dispute Resolution in the Federal Courts', *Fordham Law Review*, vol LIX, no 1, October, 1–38.

KEMPIN, JR., Frederick (1990): *Historical Introduction to Anglo-American Law* (St. Paul, Minn., West).

KESSLER, Daniel, MEITES Thomas and MILLER Geoffrey (1996): 'Explaining Deviations from the Fifty-Percent Rule: A Multimodal Approach to the Selection of Cases for Litigation', *Journal of Legal Studies*, vol XXV, no 1, January, 233–259.

KING, Michael and SCHÜTZ Anton (1994): 'The Ambitious Modesty of Niklas Luhmann', *Journal of Law and Society*, vol 21, no 3, September, 261–287.

KLEIN, Jürgen M (1987): 'Die Vollstreckung von Geldforderungen durch den Gerichtsvollzieher (aus rechtstatsächlicher Sicht)', in BLANKENBURG/VOIGT (eds), 49–71.

KNIEPER, Rolf (1991): *Nationale Souveranität. Versuch über Ende und Anfang einer Weltordnung* (Frankfurt a.M., Fischer Taschenbuch Verlag).

KNIFFKA, Rolf (1981): 'Das Ansehen der Justiz in der Öffentlichkeit', *Zeitschrift für Rechtssoziologie*, Jhg. 2, Heft 2, 225–240.

KOETZ, Axel G (1991): 'Strukturanalyse der Rechtspflege: Organisation der Amtsgerichte', *Zeitschrift für Rechtssoziologie*, Jhg. 12, Heft 2, 197–209.

——FRÜHAUF Ludwig and KIENBAUM Unternehmensberatung GmbH (1992): *Organisation der Amtsgerichte* (Köln, Bundesanzeiger) (Beiträge zur Strukturanalyse der Rechtspflege).

——WERNER Marcus, HAGENER Dirk, LÖW Hartmut and KIENBAUM Unternehmensberatung GmbH (1993): *Organisation der Kollegialgerichte und des Instanzenzuges der ordentlichen Gerichtsbarkeit* (Köln, Bundesanzeiger) (Beiträge zur Strukturanalyse der Rechtspflege).

——and FRÜHAUF Ludwig (1996): 'Gerichtsorganisation in den fünf neuen Bundesländern', in RENNIG/STREMPEL (eds), 139–189.

KOMESAR, Neil K (1994): *Imperfect Alternatives. Choosing Institutions in Law, Economics, and Public Policy* (Chicago, The University of Chicago Press).

KORNHAUSER, Lewis (1986): 'Economic Analysis of Law', *Materiali per una storia della cultura giuridica*, vol XVI, no 1, giugno, 233–247.

KRAFKA, Carol, CECIL Joe S and LOMBARD Patricia (1996): 'Stalking the Increase in the Rate of Federal Civil Appeals', *Justice System Journal*, vol 18, no 3, 233–247.

KRITZER, Herbert M and PICKERILL J Mitchell (1997): *Contingent Fee: Lawyers as Gatekeepers in the American Civil Justice System* (Institute for Legal Studies) (Dispute Processing Research Program Working Paper DPRP 12–13)

LANDES, William M (1971): 'An Economic Analysis of the Courts', *Journal of Law and Economics*, vol XIV, no 1, April, 61–107.

——and POSNER Richard A (1979): 'Adjudication as a Private Good', *Journal of Legal Studies*, vol VIII, no 2, March, 235–284.

——(1994): 'The Economics of Anticipatory Adjudication', *Journal of Legal Studies*, vol XXIII, no 2, June, 683–719.

LANGBEIN, John H (1985): 'The German Advantage in Civil Procedure', *University of Chicago Law Review*, vol 52, no 4, Fall, 823–866.

LEGOMSKY, Stephen H (1990): *Specialized Justice. Courts, Administrative Tribunals, and a Cross-National Theory of Specialization* (Oxford, Clarendon Press).

LEMENNICIER, Bertrand (1991): *Économie du droit* (Paris, Éditions Cujas).

LEVON-GUÉRIN, Francine and CHADELAT Catherine (1998): 'The Length of Civil First Instance and Appeal Procedures in France: Endemic Delay and the Need for Reform, *Liverpool Law Review*, vol XX, no 2, 177–199.

LIEBERMAN, Jethro K (1981): *The Litigious Society* (New York, Basic Books).

LIND, E Allan (1990): *Arbitrating High-Stakes Cases. An Evaluation of Court-Annexed Arbitration in a United States District Court*, (Santa Monica, RAND) (The Institute for Civil Justice) (R-3809-ICJ).

——(1994): 'Procedural Justice and Culture: Evidence for Ubiquitous Process Concerns', *Zeitschrift für Rechtssoziologie*, Jhg. 15, Heft 1, 24–36.

——*et al.* (1990): 'In the Eye of the Beholder: Tort Litigants' Evaluations of their Experiences in the Civil Justice System', *Law and Society Review*, vol 24, no 4, 953–956.

——and TYLER Tom R (1988): *The Social Psychology of Procedural Justice* (New York-London, Plenum Press).

LIPETZ, Marcia (1980): 'Routine and Deviations: The Strength of the Courtroom Workgroup in a Misdemeanor Court', *International Journal of the Sociology of Law*, vol 8, 47–60.

LYON-CAEN, Pierre (1981): 'L'experience du Syndicat de la Magistrature. Témoignage', *Pouvoirs*, no 16 (La justice), 55–78.

LONGAN, Patrick E (1993): 'The Shot Clock Comes to Trial: Time Limits for Federal Civil Trials', *Arizona Law Review*, vol 35, no 3, Fall, 663–718.

LOPEZ AYLLON, Sergio (1988): 'El proceso como espacio de encuentro entre lo social y lo jurídico. Una aproximación de sociología del derecho', in *Estudios en homenaje a Jorge Barrera Graf* (México, UNAM) t. II, 1015–1038.

——(1997a): 'The Impact of International Trade Agreements in the Legal Systems of the American Continent', *Houston Journal of International Law*, vol 19, no 3, Spring, 761–772.

——(1997b): *Las transformaciones del sistema jurídico y los significados sociales del derecho en México. La encrucijada entre tradición y modernidad* (México, UNAM).

——and FIX-FIERRO Héctor (1999): 'Communication Between Legal Cultures: The Case of NAFTA's Chapter 19 Binational Panels', in Louis PERRET, *The Evolution of Free Trade in the Americas/L'évolution du libre-échange dans les Amériques* (Montréal, Wilson & Lafleur) 3–48.

LUHMANN, Niklas (1976): *Funktionen und Folgen formaler Organisation* (1964), 3rd edn (Berlin, Duncker und Humblot).

——(1983): *Legitimation durch Verfahren* (1975) (Frankfurt a.M., Suhrkamp).

——(1984): *Soziale Systeme. Grundriß einer allgemeinen Theorie* (Frankfurt a.M., Suhrkamp).

——(1985): *A Sociological Theory of Law*, transl. by Elizabeth KING-UTZ and Martin ALBROW (London, Routledge and Kegan Paul).

——(1986): 'Die Weltgesellschaft' (1971), in *Soziologische Aufklärung 2* (Opladen, Westdeutscher Verlag) 51–71.

——(1988a): *Die Wirtschaft der Gesellschaft* (Frankfurt a.M., Suhrkamp).

——(1988b): 'The Sociological Observation of the Theory and Practice of the Law', *European Yearbook of the Sociology of Law*, 23–42.

——(1989): 'Law as a Social System', *Northwestern University Law Review*, vol 83, nos 1–2, 355–369.

——(1990): *Die Wissenschaft der Gesellschaft* (Frankfurt a.M., Suhrkamp).

——(1991): 'Organisation und Entscheidung', in *Soziologische Aufklärung 3* (Opladen, Westdeutscher Verlag) 335–389.

——(1993): *Das Recht der Gesellschaft* (Frankfurt a.M., Suhrkamp).

LUSKIN, Mary Lee (1978): 'Building a Theory of Case Processing Time', *Judicature*, vol 62, no 3, September, 115–127.

——(1988–89): 'Making Sense of Calendaring Systems: A Reconsideration of Concept and Measurement', *Justice System Journal*, vol 13, no 3, 240–250.

MACCORMICK, Peter (1994): 'Who Wins and Who Loses in the Provincial Courts of Appeal? A Statistical Analysis 1920–1990', *Canadian Journal of Law and Society*, vol 9, no 2, Fall, 21–40.

MACLEAN, Mavis (1993): 'Sociology of Law and Legal Policy in Great Britain', in Jean VAN HOUTTE and Francis VAN LOON (eds), *Sociology of Law, Social Problems and Legal Policy in Europe* (Leuven-Amersfoort, Acco) 39–47.

MAGGI, Bruno (1984): 'Teoria dell'organizzazione e sociologia del diritto', in Uberto SCARPELLI and Vincenzo TOMEO (eds), *Societa, norme e valori. Studi in onore di Renato Treves* (Milano, Giuffré) 285–307.

MARCUS, Richard L (1995): '"Déja Vu All Over Again?" An American Reaction to the Woolf Report', in ZUCKERMAN/CRANSTON (eds), 219–243.

MARGOLIS, Stephen E (1987): 'Two Definitions of Efficiency in Law and Economics', *Journal of Legal Studies*, vol XVI, no 2, June, 471–482.

MARTIN, John A and MARON Nancy C (1991): 'Courts, Delay, and Interorganizational Networks: Managing An Essential Tension', *Justice System Journal*, vols 14/3 and 15/1, 268–288.

MARVELL, Thomas B and LUSKIN Mary Lee (1991): 'The Impact of Speedy Trial Laws in Connecticut and North Carolina', *Justice System Journal*, vols 14/3 and 15/1, 343–357.

MATHENY, Albert R (1980): 'Negotiation and Plea Bargaining Models. An Organizational Perspective', *Law and Policy Quarterly*, vol 2, no 3, July, 267–284.

MCADAMS, A James (ed) (1997): *Transitional Justice and the Rule of Law in New Democracies* (Notre Dame-London, University of Notre Dame Press).

MCCOUN, Robert J (1991): 'Unintended Consequences of Court Arbitration: A Cautionary Tale from New Jersey', *Justice System Journal*, vol 14, no 2, 229–243, 251–256.

——LIND E Allan, HENSLER Deborah R, BRYANT David L and EBENER Patricia A (1988): *Alternative Adjudication. An Evaluation of the New Jersey Automobile Arbitration Program* (Santa Monica, RAND) (The Institute for Civil Justice) (R-3676-ICJ).

MCEWEN, Craig A and MAIMAN Richard J (1984): 'Mediation in Small Claims Court: Achieving Compliance Through Consent', *Law and Society Review*, vol 18. no 1, 11–48.

MCGREW, Anthony G (1998): 'Global Legal Interaction and Present-day Patterns of Globalization', in GESSNER/BUDAK (eds), 325–345.

MCINTOSH, Wayne (1993): 'Rationalizing the Quest for Justice in the US District Courts', *Law and Social Inquiry*, vol 18, no 4, Fall, 689–705.

MERCADO PACHECO, Pedro (1994): *El análisis económico del derecho. Una reconstrucción teórica* (Madrid, Centro de Estudios Constitucionales) (col. El derecho y la justicia, 38).

MERCURO, Nicholas and MEDEMA Steven G (1996): *Economics and the Law. From Posner to Post-Modernism* (Princeton, Princeton University Press).

MERRYMAN, John Henry, CLARK David S, and FRIEDMAN Lawrence (1979): *Law and Social Change in Mediterranean Europe and Latin America. A Handbook of Legal and Social Indicators for Comparative Study* (Stanford, Stanford Law School) (Stanford Studies in Law and Development, SLADE).

MICELI, Thomas J (1991): 'Optimal Criminal Procedure: Fairness and Deterrence', *International Review of Law and Economics*, vol 11, no 1, May, 3–10.

MICHALIK, Paul (1999): 'Justice in Crisis: England and Wales', in ZUCKERMAN (ed), 117–165.

MICHELS, M Janice (1992): 'Transition to Court Management of Cases from Filing to Disposition', *Justice System Journal*, vol 16, no 1, 89–99.

—— (1995): 'Case Management Techniques Work', *Justice System Journal*, vol 18, no 1, 79–89.

MILLER, Ralph I, RIDER Brian C and SHOOP G Paul (1971): 'Local Procedure and Judicial Efficiency: A Comparative Empirical Study of Metropolitan District Courts', *Texas Law Review*, vol 49, no 1, April, 677–746.

MILLER, Richard E and SARAT Austin (1980–81): 'Grievances, Claims, and Disputes: Assessing the Adversary Culture', *Law and Society Review*, vol 15, nos 3–4, 525–566.

MINISTERE DE LA JUSTICE (1989): *Le 'service public de la justice', un concept nouveau*, Paris (mimeo).

MNOOKIN, Robert and KORNHAUSER Lewis (1979): 'Bargaining in the Shadow of the Law: The Case of Divorce', *Yale Law Journal*, vol 88, 950–997.

MOHR, Lawrence B (1976): 'Organizations, Decisions, and Courts', *Law and Society Review*, vol 10, no 4, Summer, 621–642.

MOHR, Richard, GAMBLE Helen, WRIGHT Ted and CONDIE Brendan (1997): 'Performance Measurement for Australian Courts', *Journal of Judicial Administration*, Melbourne, vol 6, no 3, February, 156–169.

MORGAN, Gareth (1986): *Images of Organization* (London-New Delhi, Sage Publications).

MORGAN, Patricia and VENNARD Julie (1989): *Pre-Trial Delay: the Implications of Time Limits* (London, HMSO) (Home Office Research Study no. 110).

NAGEL, Stuart S (1986): *Law, Policy, and Optimizing Analysis* (NY-Westport-London, Quorum Books).

—— NEEF Marian and MUNSHAW Marian (1978): 'Bringing Management Science to the Courts to Reduce Delay', *Judicature*, vol 62, no 3, September, 128–143.

NARDULLI, Peter F (1978): *The Courtroom Elite: An Organizational Perspective on Criminal Justice* (Cambridge, Mass., Ballinger Publishing Company).

NATIONAL CENTER FOR STATE COURTS (ed) (1978): *The Public Image of Courts* (Williamsburg, Va., NCSC) (reprinted from *State Courts: A Blueprint for the Future*).

—— (1999): *How the Public Views the State Courts. A 1999 National Survey* (Williamsburg, Va., NCSC-The Hearst Corporation).

NELKEN, David (ed) (1997): *Comparing Legal Cultures* (Aldershot, Dartmouth).

NEMOGA SOTO, Gabriel Ricardo (dir.) (1996): *Justicia sin rostro. Estudio sobre la justicia regional* (Santafé de Bogotá, Universidad Nacional de Colombia).

NEUBAUER, David and MEINHOLD Stephen S (1994): 'Too Quick to Sue? Public Perceptions of the Litigation Explosion', *Justice System Journal*, vol 16, no 3, 1–14.

NIMMER, Raymond T (1978): *The Nature of System Change. Reform Impact in the Criminal Courts* (Chicago, American Bar Foundation).

NORTH, Douglass C (1990): *Institutions, Institutional Change and Economic Performance* (Cambridge, Cambridge University Press).

OGUS, Anthony, JONES-LEE Michael, COLE William and MCCARTHY Peter (1990): 'Evaluating Alternative Dispute Resolution: Measuring the Impact of Family Conciliation on Costs', *Modern Law Review*, vol 53, no 1, January, 57–74.

OLGIATI, Vittorio (1996): 'Cross-Border Litigotiation in Italy', in GESSNER (ed), 209–247.

OLSON, Walter K (1991): *The Litigation Explosion. What Happened When America Unleashed the Lawsuit* (New York, Truman Talley Books-Dutton).

PACE, Carlo (1970): 'La bonta dei giudizi', in CASTELLANO/PACE/PALOMBA/RASPINI, 159–196.

PADGETT, John F (1990): 'Plea Bargaining and Prohibition in the Federal Courts, 1908–1934', *Law and Society Review*, vol 24, no 2, 413–450.

PANTHER, Stephan M (1995): 'The Economics of Crime and Criminal Law: An Antithesis to Sociological Theories?', *European Journal of Law and Economics*, vol 2, no 4, December, 365–378.

PARDOLESI, Roberto (1990): 'Un moderno Minotauro: Law and Economics', in POCAR/VELICOGNA (eds), 225–243.

PASTOR, Santos (1989): *Sistema jurídico y economía. Una introducción al análisis económico del derecho* (Madrid, Tecnos).

PASTOR PRIETO, Santos (1993): *¡Ah de la justicia! Política judicial y economía* (Madrid, Centro de Publicaciones del Ministerio de Justicia-Civitas).

PATERNOSTER, Raymond, BRAME Robert, BACHMAN Ronet and SHERMAN Lawrence W (1997): 'Do Fair Procedures Matter? The Effect of Procedural Justice on Spouse Assault', *Law and Society Review*, vol 31, no 1, 163–204.

PELLEGRINI, Stefania (1992): 'Studi longitudinali sulla litigiositá', *Sociologia del diritto*, vol XIX, no 2, 115–132.

PEÑA GONZALEZ, Carlos (1991): 'Los abogados y la administración de justicia: resultados de una encuesta sobre funcionamiento del poder judicial', in Eugenio VALENZUELA S (coord.), *Proposiciones para la reforma judicial* (Santiago de Chile, Centro de Estudios Públicos) 367–395.

—— (1993): 'Informe sobre Chile', in CORREA SUTIL (ed), 285–423.

PÉREZ PERDOMO, Rogelio (1985): 'La administración de justicia en Venezuela: evaluación y alternativas', *Revista de Derecho Privado*, Caracas, núms 2–4, 49–79.

—— (1991): 'La duración de los juicios penales como problema de investigación socio-jurídica en América Latina', in FERRARI (ed) (1991), 401–445.

—— (1993): 'La justicia en tiempos de globalización: demandas y perspectivas de cambio', in BANCO INTERAMERICANO DE DESARROLLO (ed), 137–151.

—— (1996): 'De la justicia y otros demonios', in BOZA/PÉREZ PERDOMO (eds), 117–173.

POCAR, V and VELICOGNA N (1990): *Ragioni del diritto e ragioni dell'economia* (Milano, Franco Angeli) (also as *Sociologia del diritto*, no 19).

POLINSKY, A Mitchell (1989): *An Introduction to Law and Economics*, 2nd edn. (Boston-Toronto, Little, Brown and Company).

POSNER, Richard A (1973): 'An Economic Approach to Procedure and Judicial Administration', *Journal of Legal Studies*, vol II, 1973, 399–451.

—— (1979): 'Utilitarianism, Economics and Legal Theory', *Journal of Legal Studies*, vol VIII, 103–140.

—— (1990): *The Problems of Jurisprudence* (Cambridge, Mass. Harvard University Press).

—— (1995): 'The Sociology of the Sociology of Law: A View from Economics', *European Journal of Law and Economics*, vol 2, no 4, December, 265–284.

—— (1996): *The Federal Courts. Challenge and Reform*, 2nd edn. (Cambridge, Mass. Harvard University Press).

PRADEL, Jean (1995): 'The Celerity of Criminal Procedure in Comparative Law', *Revue Internationale de droit pénal/International Review of Penal Law*, 66e année, nouvelle série, 3e et 4e trimestres, 353–363.

PRESIDENT'S COUNCIL ON COMPETITIVENESS (1991): *Agenda for Civil Justice Reform in America (A Report from the)* (Washington, DC, Department of Justice) August.

PRIEST, George L and KLEIN Benjamin (1984): 'The Selection of Disputes for Litigation', *Journal of Legal Studies*, vol XIII, no 1, January, 1–55.

PRILLAMAN, William C (2000): *The Judiciary and Democratic Decay in Latin America. Declining Confidence in the Rule of Law* (Westport, Conn., Praeger).

RAINE, JW and WILLSON MJ (1993): 'Organizational Culture and the Scheduling of Court Appearences', *Journal of Law and Society*, vol 20, no 2, Summer, 237–252.

RAISER, Thomas and Rüdiger VOIGT (eds) (1990): *Durchsetzung und Wirkung von Rechtsentscheidungen. Die Bedeutung von der Implementations- und der Wirkungsforschung für die Rechtswissenschaft*, (Baden-Baden, Nomos Verlagsgesellschaft) (Schriftenreihe der Vereinigung für Rechtssoziologie, 15)

RAITERI, Monica (1988): 'Giustizia distributiva e funzione giudiziaria: Qualche osservazione nella prospettiva della analisi economica del diritto', *Materiali per una storia della cultura giuridica*, vol XVIII, no 1, 209–228.

——(1991): 'La cultura economica del giudice', in FERRARI (ed) (1991), 1071–1081.

——(1992): 'La funzione giurisdizionale tra redistribuzione economica e tutela dei diritti', *Materiali per una storia della cultura giuridica*, vol XXII, no 2, dicembre, 475–518.

RAMSEYER, J Mark (1994): 'The Puzzling (In)Dependence of Courts: A Comparative Approach', *Journal of Legal Studies*, vol XXIII, June, 721–747.

RAWLS, John (1973): *A Theory of Justice*, 5th printing (Cambridge, Mass., The Belknap Press of Harvard University Press).

REED, John H (1973): *The Application of Operations Research to Court Delay* (NY, Praeger Publishers).

REICH, Norbert (1992): 'Competition Between Legal Orders: A New Paradigm of EC Law?', *Common Market Law Review*, Leiden, vol 29, no 5, October, 861–896.

REMICHE, Benoit (1985): 'Le role de l'économie dans le mode juridictionnel de réglement des conflits', *Revue interdisciplinaire d'etudes juridiques*, Bruxelles, no 15, 171–208.

RENNIG, Christoph and STREMPEL Dieter (eds) (1996): *Justiz im Umbruch. Rechtstatsächliche Studien zum Aufbau der Rechtspflege in den neuen Bundesländern*, (Köln, Bundesanzeiger).

RESCIGNO, Mario (1985): 'L'istituzione giudiziaria e l'economia', *Rivista del diritto commerciale e del diritto generale dell obligazioni*, anno LXXXIII, gennaio–aprile, 1–14.

RESNIK, Judith (1982): 'Managerial Judges', *Harvard Law Review*, vol 96, no 2, December, 376–448.

RHODES, William M (1976): 'The Economics of Criminal Courts: A Theoretical and Empirical Investigation', *Journal of Legal Studies*, vol V, no 2, June, 311–340.

RICO, José Ma., SALAS Luis, GUTIÉRREZ Enrique and CRUZ Carlos (1988): *La justicia penal en Costa Rica* (San José, C.R., EDUCA).

RÖHL, Klaus F (1982): 'Rechtspolitische und ideologische Hintergründe der Diskussion über Alternativen zur Justiz', in BLANKENBURG/GOTTWALD/STREMPEL (eds), 15–27.

——(1987): 'Gründe und Ursprünge aktueller Geschäftsüberlastung der Gerichte aus soziologischer Sicht', in Peter GILLES, (ed) (1987): *Effiziente Rechtsverfolgung. Deutsche Landesberichte zur VIII. Weltkonferenz für Prozeßrecht in Utrecht*

1987/Efficiency in the Pursuit of Justice. German National Reports for the VIII. World Conference on Procedural Law in Utrecht 1987 (Heidelberg, CF Müller) 33–63.

RÖHL, Klaus F (1991): 'Court-Management in den USA', *Zeitschrift für Rechtssoziologie*, Jhg. 12, Heft 2, 217–231.

——(1993a): 'Verfahrensgerechtigkeit (Procedural Justice). Einführung in den Themenbereich und Überblick', *Zeitschrift für Rechtssoziologie*, Jhg.14, Heft 1, 1–34.

——(1993b): *Gerichtsverwaltung und Court-Management in den USA-Vom Effizienzmanagement zum Qualitätsmanagement* (Köln, Bundesanzeiger) (Beiträge zur Strukturanalyse der Rechtspflege).

——(with MAGEN Stefan) (1996): 'Die Rolle des Rechts im Prozeß der Globalisierung', *Zeitschrift für Rechtssoziologie*, Jhg. 17, Heft 1, 1–57.

——(1997): 'Procedural Justice: Introduction and Overview', in Klaus RÖHL and Stefan MACHURA (eds), *Procedural Justice* (Aldershot, Dartmouth) 1–35 (Oñati International Series in Law and Society).

ROSANVALLON, Pierre (1981): *La crise de l'État-providence*, (Paris, Éditions du Seuil).

ROSS, H Laurence (1980): *Settled Out of Court. The Social Process of Insurance Claims Adjustment*, rev edn (1970) (New York, Aldine Publishing Company).

ROTTLEUTHNER, Hubert (1987): *Einführung in die Rechtssoziologie* (Darmstadt, Wissenschaftliche Buchgesellschaft).

——(1991): 'Einzelrichter und Kammer: Eine rechtstatsächliche Untersuchung zum Einsatz des Einzelrichters: Paragraph 348 ZPO', *Zeitschrift für Rechtssoziologie*, Jhg. 12, Heft 2, 232–247.

——and ROTTLEUTHNER-LUTTER Margret (1990): *Die Dauer von Gerichtsverfahren. Evaluation der ZPO Vereinfachungsnovelle* (Baden-Baden, Nomos Verlagsgesellschaft) (Schriften der Vereinigung für Rechtssoziologie, Band 16).

——BÖHM Ellen and GASTERSTÄDT Daniel (1992): *Rechtstatsächliche Untersuchung zum Einsatz des Einzelrichters* (Köln, Bundesanzeiger) (Beiträge zur Strukturanalyse der Rechtspflege).

ROTTLEUTHNER-LUTTER, Margret and ROTTLEUTHNER Hubert (1989): 'Evaluation der ZPO-Vereinfachungsnovelle', *Zeitschrift für Rechtssoziologie*, Jhg. 10, Heft 1, 28–49.

ROZENBERG, Joshua (1995): *The Search for Justice. An Anatomy of the Law*, 2nd edn. (London, Sceptre).

RUBIN, Paul H and BAILEY Martin J (1994): 'The Role of Lawyers in Changing the Law', *Journal of Legal Studies*, vol XXIII, no 2, June, 807 ff.

RUBIO, Mauricio (1997): 'Normas, justicia y economía en Colombia', in JARQUIN/CARRILLO (eds), 339–385.

RUIZ HARRELL, Rafael (1996): 'El saldo de la impunidad', *Revista mexicana de procuración de justicia*, vol I, no 2, 15–30.

RYAN, John Paul (1978): 'Management Science in the Real World of Courts. The Orange County Court's Experience with Optimum Sequencing', *Judicature*, vol 62, no 3, September, 144–146.

——ASHMAN Allan, SALES Bruce D and SHANE-DUBOW Sandra (1980): *American Trial Judges. Their Work Styles and Performance* (New York, The Free Press).

——LIPETZ Marcia J, LUSKIN Mary Lee and NEUBAUER David W (1981): 'Analyzing Court Delay-Reduction Programs: Why Do Some Succeed?', *Judicature*, vol 65, no 2, August, 58–75.

SAARI, David J (1982): *American Court Management. Theories and Practices* (Westport-London, Quorum Books).

SADEK, Maria Tereza (1997): 'La crisis del Poder Judicial', in JARQUIN/CARRILLO (eds), 391–404.

SAGÜÉS, Néstor Pedro (1989): *Derecho procesal constitucional. Recurso extraordinario*, 2nd edn. (Buenos Aires, Astrea) vol 1.

SALAS, Luis and RICO José Ma (1989a): *La justicia penal en Honduras* (San José, C.R., EDUCA-UIF).

—— (1989b): *La justicia penal en Guatemala* (San José, C.R., EDUCA-UIF).

SANTOS, Boaventura de Sousa (1999): 'The Gatt of Law and Democracy: (Mis)Trusting the Global Reform of Courts', in Johannes FEEST (ed), *Globalization and Legal Cultures. Oñati Summer Course 1997* (Oñati, IISL) 49–86 (Oñati Papers, 7).

—— MARQUES Maria Manuel Leitao, PEDROSO Joao and FERREIRA Pedro Lopes (1996): *Os tribunais nas sociedades contemporâneas. O caso português* (Porto, Edições Afrontamento).

SARRE, Miguel and LOPEZ UGALDE Antonio (2002): *Administración de justicia en México. Indicadores en materia mercantil e hipotecaria* (México, ITAM-Gaxiola Moraila y Asociados, S.C.) (published as a special annex to *Este País*, 138, August).

SAVONA, Ernesto Ugo (1990): 'Un settore trascurato: l'analisi economica della criminalità', *Sociologia del diritto*, vol XVII, nos 1/2, 254–277.

SCHÄFER, Rudolf (1987): 'Städtebaupolitik vor dem Verwaltungsgericht. Am Beispiel der Rechtsprechung zur Gültigkeit von Bebauungsplänen', in BLANKENBURG/VOIGT (eds), 281–307.

SCHEB, II, John M and MATHENY Albert R (1988): 'Judicial Reform and Rationaliztion: The Diffusion of Court Reform Policies Among the American States', *Law and Policy*, vol 10, no 1, January, 25–42.

SCHEUERMAN, William E (1999): 'Globalization and the Fate of Law', in David DYZENHAUS (ed), *Recrafting the Rule of Law: The Limits of Legal Order* (Oxford, Hart Publishing) 243–266.

SCHULHOFER, Stephen (1985): 'No Job Too Small: Justice Without Bargaining in the Lower Criminal Courts', *American Bar Foundation Research Journal*, 519–591.

SCHULTZ, Majken (1995): *On Studying Organizational Cultures. Diagnosis and Understanding* (Berlin-New York, Walter de Gruyter).

SCOTT, IR (1995): 'Caseflow Management in the Trial Court', in ZUCKERMAN/CRANSTON (eds), 1–30.

SEAGLE, William (1952): *Law: The Science of Inefficiency* (New York, The MacMillan Company).

SELVIN, Molly and EBENER Patricia (1984): *Managing the Unmanageable. A History of Civil Delay in the Los Angeles Superior Court* (Santa Monica, RAND Corporation) (The Institute for Civil Justice) (R-3165-ICJ)

SERON, Carroll (1990): 'The Impact of Court Organization on Litigation', *Law and Society Review*, vol 24, no 2, 451–465.

SERVERIN, Évelyne (1993): 'Juridiction et jurisprudence: deux aspects des activités de justice', *Droit et Societé*, no 25, 339–349.

SHAPIRO, Martin (1980): 'Appeal', *Law and Society Review*, vol 14, no 3, Spring, 629–661.

—— (1981): *Courts. A Comparative and Political Analysis* (Chicago, The University of Chicago Press).

—— (1993): 'The Globalization of Law', *Indiana Journal of Global Legal Studies*, vol 1, issue 1, Fall, 37–64.

SHAVELL, Steven (1995a): 'Alternative Dispute Resolution: An Economic Analysis', *Journal of Legal Studies*, vol XXIV, no 1, January, 1–28.

——(1995b): 'The Appeals Process as a Means of Error Correction', *Journal of Legal Studies*, vol XXIV, no 2, June, 379–426.

SIEGELMAN, Peter and DONOHUE III John J (1990): 'Studying the Iceberg from the Tip: A Comparison of Published and Unpublished Employment Discrimination Cases', *Law and Society Review*, vol 24, no 5, 1133–1170.

——(1995): 'The Selection of Employment Discrimination Disputes for Litigation: Using Business Cycle Effects to Test the Priest-Klein Hypothesis', *Journal of Legal Studies*, vol XXIV, no 2, June, 427–462.

SIEGELMAN, Peter and WALDFOGEL Joel (1999): 'Toward a Taxonomy of Disputes: New Evidence Through the Prism of the Priest/Klein Model', *Journal of Legal Studies*, vol XVIII, January, 101–130.

SIMON, Herbert A (1976): *Administrative Behavior. A Study of Decision-Making Processes in Administrative Organization*, 3rd edn, with new Introduction (New York, The Free Press).

SIMSA, Christiane Elisabeth (1995): *Die gerichtliche und außergerichtliche Regulierung von Verkehrsunfällen in Deutschland und den Niederlanden* (Köln, Bundesanzeiger) (Beiträge zur Strukturanalyse der Rechtspflege).

SIPES, Larry L, CARLSON Alan M, TAN Teresa, AIKMAN Alexander B and PAGE JR. Robert W, (1980): *Managing to Reduce Delay* (Williamsburg, Va., National Center for State Courts).

SMITH, Christopher E (1995): *Judicial Self-Interest. Federal Judges and Court Administration* (Westport, Conn.-London, Praeger).

STAMMEL, Christine (1998): 'Back to the Courtroom? Developments in the London Reinsurance Market', in GESSNER/BUDAK (eds), 61–91.

STANLEY, Linda R and COURSEY Don L (1990): 'Empirical Evidence on the Selection Hypothesis and the Decision to Litigate or Settle', *Journal of Legal Studies*, vol XIX, no 1, January, 145–172.

STEELE, Eric H (1981): 'The Historical Context of Small Claims Courts', *American Bar Foundation Research Journal*, no 2, Spring, 293–376.

STEELMAN, David C (1997): 'What Have We Learned About Court Delay, "Local Legal Culture", and Caseflow Management Since the Late 1970s?', *Justice System Journal*, vol 19, no 2, 145–166.

STOCK, Johannes (1995): 'Der Geschäftsanfall der Zivilgerichte und die Filterwirkung außergerichtlicher Konfliktbearbeitung', in Walther GOTTWALD and Dieter STREMPEL (eds), *Streitschlichtung. Rechtsvergleichende Beiträge zur außergerichtlichen Streitbeilegung* (Köln, Bundesanzeiger) (Rechtstatsachenforschung).

——THÜNTE Petra-Ida, WOLFF Heimfried *et al.* (1995): *Schnittstellen von außer- und innergerichtlicher Konfliktbearbeitung im Zivilrecht. Bestandsaufnahme und Probleme in den neuen Bundesländern verglichen mit den Erfahrungen in den alten Bundesländern* (Köln, Bundesanzeiger) (Beiträge zur Strukturanalyse der Rechtspflege).

SUMMERS, Robert S (1974): 'Evaluating and Improving Legal Process—A Plea for 'Process Values'', *Cornell Law Review*, vol 60, no 1, November, 1–52.

SZELÉNYI, Ivan and MARTIN Bill (1989): 'The Legal Profession and the Rise and Fall of the New Class', in ABEL/LEWIS (eds), 256–288.

TANFORD, J Alexander (1991): 'Law Reform by Courts, Legislatures, and Commissions Following Empirical Research on Jury Instructions', *Law and Society Review*, vol 25, no 1, 155–175.

TATE, C Neal (1995): 'Why the Expansion of Judicial Power?', in TATE/VALLINDER (eds), 27–37.

——and VALLINDER Torbjörn (eds) (1995): *The Global Expansion of Judicial Power* (NY-London, New York University Press).

TAVOLARI OLIVEROS, Raúl (1993): 'El proceso civil chileno: una lectura desde el debido proceso y la eficacia de la jurisdicción de cara a la reforma', en VARIOS, 221–248.

TAYLOR, Michael C (1997): 'Why No Rule of Law in Mexico? Explaining the Weakness of Mexico's Judicial Branch', *New Mexico Law Review*, vol 27, Winter, 141–166.

TEUBNER, Gunther (1989): 'How the Law Thinks: Toward a Constructivist Epistemology of Law', *Law and Society Review*, vol 23, no 5, 727–757.

——(1992): 'Autopoiesis and Steering: How Politics Profit from the Normative Surplus of Capital', in Roeland J. In 'T VELD, Linze SCHAAP, Catrien JAM TERMEER and Mark JW van TWIST (eds), *Autopoiesis and Configuration Theory: New Approaches to Societal Steering* (Dordrecht-Boston-London, Kluwer Academic Publishers) 127–141.

——(1997a): 'Altera Pars Audiatur. Law in the Collision of Discourses', in Richard RAWLINGS (ed), *Law, Society and Economy. Centenary Essays for the London School of Economics and Political Science 1895–1995* (Oxford, Clarendon Press) 149–176.

——(1997b): 'Altera pars audiatur: le droit dans la collision de discours', *Droit et Societé*, no 35, 99–123.

THIBAUT, John and WALKER Laurens (1978): 'A Theory of Procedure', *California Law Review*, vol 66, 541–566.

THOMAS, Robert E (1995): 'The Trial Selection Hypothesis Without the 50 Per Cent Rule: Some Experimental Evidence', *Journal of Legal Studies*, vol XXIV, no 1, January, 209–228.

THOME, Joseph R (2000): 'Heading South but Looking North: Globalization and Law Reform in Latin America', *Wisconsin Law Review*, 691–712.

THOMPSON, James D (1967): *Organizations in Action. Social Science Bases of Administrative Theory* (New York, McGraw-Hill).

TIJERAS, Ramón (1994): *La revolución de los jueces. De Falcone a Barbero: una cruzada contra la corrupción política, el crimen internacional y la razón de Estado* (Madrid, Ediciones Temas de Hoy).

TOHARIA, José Juan (1987): *'¡Pleitos tengas! . . .' Introducción a la cultura legal española* (Madrid, CIS-Siglo XXI de España Editores).

——(2001): *Opinión pública y justicia. La imagen de la justicia en la sociedad española* (Madrid, Consejo General del Poder Judicial).

TORELLO, Luis (1993): 'Lineamientos generales de la reforma procesal civil y el caso concreto de la reforma en Uruguay', en VARIOS, 97–132.

TOURAINE, Alain (1992): *Critique de la modernité* (Paris, Fayard).

TRUBEK, David M (1980–81): 'Studying Courts in Context', *Law and Society Review*, vol 15, no 3–4, 485–501.

——GROSSMAN Joel B, FELSTINER William LF, KRITZER Herbert M, SARAT Herbert and Austin (1983): *Civil Litigation Research Project. Final Report* (Madison, Wis., Institute for Legal Studies) Parts A and B [vol. I: 'Studying the Civil Litigation Process: The CLRP Experience'; vol. II: 'Civil Litigation as the Investment of Lawyer Time'; vol. III: 'Other Studies of Litigation and Dispute Processing'].

TURNER, Barry A (ed) (1990): *Organizational Symbolism* (Berlin-New York, Walter de Gruyter).

TYLER, Tom R (1988): 'What is Procedural Justice? Criteria Used by Citizens to Assess the Fairness of Legal Procedures', *Law and Society Review*, vol 22, no 1, 103–135.

—— (1990): *Why People Obey the Law* (New Haven-London, Yale University Press).

VALLINDER, Torbjörn (ed) (1994): 'The Judicialization of Politics', *International Political Science Review*, vol 15, no 2, April.

—— (1995): 'When the Courts Go Marching In', in TATE/VALLINDER (eds), 13–26.

VANCE, Neil R and STUPAK Ronald J (1997): 'Organizational Culture and the Placement of Pretrial Agencies in the Criminal Justice System', *Justice System Journal*, vol 19, no 1, 51–76.

VAN LOON, Francis and LANGERWERF Etienne (1989): 'Prozeßhäufigkeiten und Prozeßmuster in Belgien', in BLANKENBURG (ed), 231–255.

—— DELRUE Stephane and VAN WAMBEKE Wim (1995): 'Sociological Research on Litigation: Perspectives and Examples', *European Journal of Law and Economics*, vol 2, no 4, December, 379–385.

VARIOS (1993): *Reformas procesales en América Latina: la oralidad en los procesos* (Santiago de Chile, Corporación de Promoción Universitaria) (Proyecto de Capacitación, Gestión y Política Judicial).

VELJANOVSKI, Cento (1990): *The Economics of Law. An Introductory Text* (London, The Institute of Economic Affairs) (Hobart Paper, 114).

VIDMAR, Neil (1984): 'The Small Claims Court: A Reconceptualization of Disputes and an Empirical Investigation', *Law and Society Review*, vol 18, no 4, 515–550.

—— (1987): 'Assessing the Effects of Case Characteristics and Settlement Forum on Dispute Outcomes and Compliance', *Law and Society Review*, vol 21, no 1, 155–164.

—— (1993): 'Verfahrensgerechtigkeit und alternative Konfliktbewältigung', *Zeitschrift für Rechtssoziologie*, Jhg. 14, Heft 1, 35–46.

VIDONI GUIDONI, Odillo (1997): 'Quale giustizia per il giudice di pace? Un'indagine esplorativa', *Sociologia del diritto*, vol XXIV, no 2, 93–137.

VINCENT, Jean, GUINCHARD Serge, MONTAGNIER Gabriel and VARINARD André (1996): *La justice et ses institutions* (Paris, Dalloz).

VRSALOVIC MIHOEVIC, Juan (1991): 'Una metodología para la distribución espacial de los tribunales', in CORPORACION DE PROMOCION UNIVERSITARIA (ed), *Proyecto de capacitación, formación, perfeccionamiento y política judicial. Administración de tribunales* (Santiago, CPU) t. II, 163–224.

WALCH, Matthew W (1994): 'Palmieri v. Estefan: Economic Inefficiency and Jurisdiction Over Foreign Affiliates in New York', *Law and Policy in International Business*, vol 25, no 3, Spring, 1059–1077.

WARGLIEN, Massimo and MASUCH Michael (1996): *The Logic of Organizational Disorder* (Berlin-New York, Walter de Gruyter).

WASILEWSKI, Rainer (1990): *Streitverhütung durch Rechstanwälte. Empirische Untersuchung von Umfang, Struktur und Bedingungen außergerichtlicher Beilegung zivilrechtlicher Streitigkeiten durch Rechtsanwälte*, Köln-Essen, Bundesanzeiger-Deutscher Anwaltverein (Anwaltsforschung, hg. vom Bundesministerium der Justiz und von der Bundesrechtsanwaltskammer).

WEBER, Gordon (1993): *Die Verdrängung des Hauptsacheverfahrens durch den einstweiligen Rechtsschutz in Deutschland und Frankreich. Eine rechtsvergleichende*

Untersuchung zur Stellung des einstweiligen Rechtsschutzes im Zivilprozeß beider Länder (Köln, Bundesanzeiger) (Rechtstatsachenforschung, hg. vom Bundesministerium der Justiz).

WEBER, Max (1984): *Economía y sociedad. Esbozo de sociología comprensiva*; 7th. printing of the 2nd Spanish edn, several translators (México, FCE).

WEDEKIND, W (ed) (1989): *Justice and Efficiency. General Reports and Discussions for the Eighth World Conference on Procedural Law (Utrecht, 1987)* (Deventer-Antwerp-Boston, Kluwer Law and Taxation Publishers).

WELLER, Steven, RUHNKA John C and MARTIN, John A, (1990): 'American Small Claims Courts', in WHELAN (ed), 5–23.

WELSH, Wayne N and PONTELL Henry N (1991): 'Counties in Court: Interorganizational Adaptations to Jail Litigation in California', *Law and Society Review*, vol 25, no 1, 73–101.

WHELAN, Christopher (ed) (1990): *Small Claims Courts. A Comparative Study* (Oxford, Clarendon Press).

WIBERA (1991): *Vergleichende Organisationsuntersuchung Verwaltungs/Finanzgerichte* (Köln, Bundesanzeiger) (Beiträge zur Strukturanalyse der Rechtspflege).

WOLLSCHLÄGER, Christian (1989): 'Die Arbeit der europäischen Zivilgerichte im historischen und internationalen Vergleich. Zeitreihen der europäischen Zivilprozeßstatistik seit dem 19. Jahrhundert', in BLANKENBURG (ed), 21–114.

—— (1991a): 'Bagatelljustiz? Eine rechtshistorische, rechtsvergleichende und empirische Untersuchung zur Einführung des vereinfachten Verfahrens am Amtsgericht', in BLANKENBURG/LEIPOLD/WOLLSCHLÄGER (eds), 13–108.

—— (1991b): 'Mehr Rechtsschutz ohne Zivilprozessrecht? Eine Prognose zum vereinfachten Verfahren in geringwertigen Streitigkeiten', *Zeitschrift für Rechtssoziologie*, Jhg. 12, Heft 2, 248–273.

—— (1997): 'Historical Trends of Civil Litigation in Japan, Arizona, Sweden, and Germany: Japanese Legal Culture in the Light of Judicial Statistics', in Harald BAUM (ed), *Japan: Economic Success and Legal System* (Berlin-New York, Walter de Gruyter) 89–142.

YALE LAW JOURNAL (1983): 'The Inefficient Common Law', *Yale Law Journal*, vol 92, no 5, April, 862–887.

YARNOLD, Barbara M (1995): 'Do Courts Respond to the Political Clout of Groups or to Their Superior Litigation Resources/"Repeat Player" Status?', *Justice System Journal*, vol 18, no 1, 29–42.

YNGVESSON, Barbara and HENNESSEY Patricia (1975): 'Small Claims, Complex Disputes: A Review of the Small Claims Literature', *Law and Society Review*, vol 2, no 2, Winter, 219–274.

ZAMORA, Stephen (1993): 'The Americanization of Mexican Law: Non-Trade Issues in the North American Free Trade Agreement', *Law and Policy in International Business*, vol 24, no 2, Winter, 391–459.

ZEMANS, Frances Kahn (1982): 'Framework for Analysis of Legal Mobilization: A Decision-Making Model', *American Bar Foundation Research Journal*, no 4, Fall, 989–1071.

—— (1991): 'In the Eye of the Beholder: The Relationship Between the Public and the Courts', *Justice System Journal*, vol 15, no 2, 723–740.

ZEPEDA LECUONA, Guillermo Raúl (1997): 'Análisis económico de los costos de acceso a la justicia en los ámbitos federal y local (Estado de Jalisco)', in AMDE (ed), *Justicia con eficiencia. Memoria del Primer Congreso Anual de la Asociación Mexicana de Derecho y Economía. Abril de 1996* (México, AMDE) 41–76.

ZUCKERMAN, AAS (1995): 'A Reform of Civil Procedure—Rationing Procedure Rather than Access to Justice', *Journal of Law and Society*, vol 22, no 2, June, 155–188.

——(1999): 'Justice in Crisis: Comparative Dimensions of Civil Procedure', in AAS ZUCKERMAN (ed), *Civil Justice in Crisis. Comparative Perspectives of Civil Procedure* (Oxford, Oxford University Press) 3–52.

——and CRANSTON Ross (eds) (1995): *Reform of Civil Procedure. Essays on 'Access to Justice'* (Oxford, Clarendon Press).

ZWIESELE, Rainer/BENDER, Rolf (1972): 'Betriebswirtschaftliche Methoden und Vorschläge zur Verbesserung der Justizorganisation', in BENDER (ed), 197–222.

Index

www.ingramcontent.com/pod-product-compliance
Ingram Content Group UK Ltd.
Pitfield, Milton Keynes, MK11 3LW, UK
UKHW020832290926
15470UKWH00009B/1854/J

9 781841 133829